Green Marketing Management

Green Marketing Management

Robert Dahlstrom
University of Kentucky

✦ SOUTH-WESTERN
CENGAGE Learning™

Australia • Brazil • Japan • Korea • Mexico • Singapore • Spain • United Kingdom • United States

SOUTH-WESTERN
CENGAGE Learning™

Green Marketing Management
Robert Dahlstrom

Vice President of Editorial, Business:
Jack W. Calhoun

Editor-in-Chief: Melissa Acuña

Acquisitions Editor: Mike Roche

Developmental Editor: Daniel Noguera

Editorial Assistant: Kayti Purkiss

Senior Marketing and Sales Manager:
Bill Hendee

Marketing Coordinator: Sarah Greber

Content Project Management:
PreMediaGlobal

Media Editor: John Rich

Production Technology Analyst: Starratt
Scheetz

Manufacturing Coordinator: Miranda
Klapper

Production Service: PreMediaGlobal

Copyeditor: Kim Husband

Senior Art Director: Stacy Jenkins Shirley

Cover Designer: Craig Ramsdell

Cover Image: ©Getty Images/Digital
Vision

For product information and technology assistance, contact us at
Cengage Learning Customer & Sales Support, 1-800-354-9706.

For permission to use material from this text or product, submit all requests online at **www.cengage.com/permissions.**

Further permissions questions can be emailed to
permissionrequest@cengage.com.

Library of Congress Control Number: 2010927469

Student Edition ISBN 13: 978-0-324-78914-0

Student Edition ISBN 10: 0-324-78914-9

South-Western Cengage Learning
5191 Natorp Boulevard
Mason, OH 45040
USA

Cengage Learning products are represented in Canada by Nelson Education, Ltd.

For your course and learning solutions, visit **school.cengage.com.**

Printed in the United States of America
1 2 3 4 5 6 7 14 13 12 11 10

To Susan, Meredith, and Patrick

Brief Contents

Contents

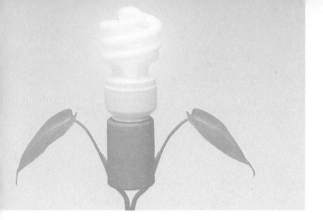

Preface

Welcome to the first edition of *Green Marketing Management*. I hope that this essay is the first of many editions of a text offering a new perspective on the relationship between the environment and commerce.

My interest in writing this book emerged during my 2005 sabbatical in Oslo. When I attended a meeting of Norwegian Fulbright fellows in Trondheim, I heard some compelling arguments about the utility of wind power and other alternative energy sources. This experience prompted me to begin investigating influences of commerce on greenhouse gas emissions, natural resource conservation, and biodiversity. I began searching for a comprehensive approach to marketing and sustainability that addressed these issues. Although I read intriguing work in strategy and economics, these studies did not capture the sets of sustainability issues most germane to marketing management. As my interest grew, I began to develop ideas related to a number of divergent aspects of marketing management and their interactions with the environment.

Over time, I began to recognize that markets operate within ecosystems. Although this observation seems obvious, it has historically not been incorporated into many managerial decisions. For many years, marketers—those involved in buying, selling, and consuming—have been able to take the environment as a given. Increasingly, however, the scarcity of resources demands consideration of the environmental antecedents and consequences of marketing action. Thus, the marketer must consider how consumption influences greenhouse gas production; energy consumption; water, land, and air quality; and biodiversity.

Philosophy

My goal in developing this text has been to develop a theoretically based and managerially relevant perspective on green marketing management. Given the strong need to couch consumption within the ecosystem, the text investigates a number of theoretical approaches not typically incorporated into marketing textbooks. The treatment of the commerce–environment interface, for example, relies heavily on environmental perspectives accumulated by the United Nations. The UN serves as a central clearinghouse of research in this vein, and it provides an opportunity to bring together logic developed within the natural sciences, social sciences, and industrial practice. I hope that this perspective is interesting and enlightening to the reader.

In order to make this book meaningful to current and future marketing managers, I have simultaneously striven to incorporate state-of-the-art examples of business practice. In each chapter, I have sought scenarios and examples of environmental issues that managers face today. Each chapter begins with a short vignette designed to illustrate current efforts to interact successfully with the environment. Nothing works quite as well as a good theory, and the application of theory provides great insight to managers. The examples are designed to illuminate theory and pique the reader's interest in the topic.

Structure of the text

In developing this book, I tried to organize these ideas in a manner that was consistent with other marketing management books. The book has five sections. In the first section, I define the subject matter of green marketing, and I illustrate how green marketing can be incorporated into strategic planning. The second section of the book addresses the interplay between the environment and consumption. Chapter 3 examines effects of consumption on the environment, whereas Chapter 4 examines efforts to constrain influences of consumption on the environment.

Section III examines the firm's efforts to offer superior value to consumers via sustainably oriented marketing practices. Chapter 5 addresses the discovery of value via target marketing and segmentation, and Chapter 6 addresses communicating value via promotional strategies. Chapter 7 examines new product strategies that provide value to consumers. In Chapters 8 and 9, I examine the delivery of value in supply chains and retailing. Chapter 10 discusses the declaration of value associated with sustainable pricing strategies. These chapters can be used in a stand-alone green marketing course, and they can augment other marketing management classes examining the marketing mix.

Section IV of this book is a departure from most marketing texts. Since four sectors of the economy are associated with more than 95% of greenhouse gas emissions, it is germane to consider issues endemic to each of these macroeconomic sectors. Thus, the chapters provide background on consumption in the household, services, transportation, and industrial sectors of the economy. The presentation of these chapters after the discussion of discrete sustainably oriented marketing practices facilitates student understanding of the interrelationship among elements of the marketing mix.

The final section of the book addresses the firm's efforts to report on sustainability. I present the essential tenets of sustainability reporting and reference reporting initiatives used across sectors of the global economy. This chapter underscores the relationship between marketing action and accounting. In addition, an understanding of these reporting procedures provides insight to financial markets.

I have incorporated a number of elements to enhance pedagogy. In addition to the vignettes presented at the beginning of each chapter, I provide numerous examples designed to illustrate the relevance of the subject to business practice. Key terms are provided at the end of each chapter, and these terms are highlighted in the accompanying text. Each chapter also offers a brief synopsis designed to complement the outline of the chapter. In addition, I have provided 10 questions at the end of each chapter. These questions can be used to stimulate understanding of the course subject matter within and beyond the classroom.

Acknowledgements

I would like to thank several people that had an influence on the development of this book. First, I would like to thank people in my home life that helped me to gain a broader understanding of the role sustainability. I thank Susan, my wife, Meredith, my daughter, and Patrick, my son, for helping me realize how we can incorporate sustainability into our daily lives.

I greatly appreciate the encouragement of my colleagues at the University of Kentucky. I am most grateful to Douglas J. Von Allmen for the generous endowment that enabled me to establish the Von Allmen Center for Green Marketing. Within Gatton College of Business and Economics, I am particularly indebted to Jim Donnelly and Steve Skinner for their guidance and advice throughout the development of this project. I also appreciate Glen Blomquist's advice concerning the role of environmental economics as it relates to green marketing. Beyond the business school, I recognize the advice of UK Faculty of the Environment. I particularly wish to thank Ernest Yanarella, Richard Levine, and Paul Bertsch for sharing their perspectives on sustainability and sustainable business practices.

I would also like to thank my colleagues at BI-The Norwegian School of Management for their advice throughout the development of this work. Arne Nygaard, my co-author for more than 20 years, has offered tremendous insight into sustainability issues in retailing.

The editorial, production, and marketing staff at Cengage deserve tremendous praise for all the work they did to make this book a possibility. I would particularly like to thank Mike Roche, my editor at Cengage, for his guidance. In addition, I recognize and greatly appreciate Daniel Noguera's efforts to manage the development process for this book.

Finally, I wish to thank the readers of this book. When I began writing this book, a friend suggested that it was meaningless to put these ideas to paper because they would be obsolete by the time the ink dried! *Green Marketing Management* strives to be a comprehensive approach to sustainability in marketing. I recognize, however, that we are in a nascent stage with respect to knowledge in this field. A book on this subject should strive to identify where we are and how we are progressing toward more sustainably oriented practices. As we develop this field, we will become aware of issues that complement the topics addressed in this first edition. I welcome the reader to help me make this book more insightful via the inclusion of additional theoretical and managerial perspectives. Please send this information to:

Robert Dahlstrom
425L B&E Building
Gatton College of Business and Economics
University of Kentucky
Lexington, KY 40506-0034 U.S.A.
Bob.Dahlstrom@uky.edu

About the Author

Robert Dahlstrom is the Bloomfield Professor of Marketing in the Gatton College of Business and Economics at the University of Kentucky. He is also the founding Director of the Von Allmen Center for Green Marketing in Gatton College of Business and Economics at the University of Kentucky. The Center seeks to develop green marketing curriculum, conduct environmentally oriented marketing research, and foster sustainability efforts in the community.

Prior to earning a PhD in marketing at the University of Cincinnati, Dr. Dahlstrom worked in sales, marketing, and system analysis in the computer industry. This experience and his interest in behavioral dimensions of interfirm relationships provide the background for a stream of research that examines interrelationships between distribution channels and the environment. He has published articles in the *Journal of Marketing Research*, the *Journal of Marketing*, the *Journal of Retailing*, the *Journal of the Academy of Marketing Science*, and elsewhere.

Over the course of his career, Dr. Dahlstrom has worked extensively with colleagues in Norway. He has earned a Norwegian Marshall Fund Fellowship and two Fulbright-Hays research fellowships for his Nordic research. He has also worked for BI-The Norwegian School of Management, where he has been active in research conducted with master's and graduate students. Collaboration with scholars in Scandinavia fueled a continuing interest in the relationship between the firm and the environment.

A passion for the classroom complements his interest in research. In a career that spans more than 20 years of instruction, he has taught business-to-business marketing, sales management, personal selling, international marketing, marketing management, marketing strategy, and green marketing management. In addition to his work in Lexington, Kentucky, he has also taught in Austria, Norway, and Greece. Recognition of the need for programs of instruction in sustainability prompted him to develop courses in green marketing management at the undergraduate and master's levels.

Green Marketing Management

Introduction

1

An Overview of Green Marketing

A. Introduction to Green Marketing

EnXco

Our journey into green marketing begins in Lakefield, Minnesota, where negotiations have been finalized between EnXco and 140 Minnesota landowners.[1] The project has great potential to be successful on multiple fronts. The new jobs will bring new *revenue* to the economy. EnXco indicates that the wind farm will deliver 200 construction jobs and add eight to 12 full-time jobs to the local economy.

The project will also demand long-term working *relationships* between EnXco and the landowners in Minnesota. The actual energy production will consist of 134 turbines, and these devices will be leased on the landowners' property. These turbines will rest on half-acre to 1-acre plots of land that will be leased for 30 years. Provisions have also been set up to recycle the turbines at the end of the lease period.

The area will also benefit from the production of 201 megawatts of *renewable energy*, which will replace the use of fossil fuels such as coal, oil, and natural gas. Interestingly, the energy will be produced in Minnesota but it will be transmitted to Indiana.

Energy needs are increasingly being met through wind power, and it is one of the fastest growing sources of energy around the world.[2] It provides many communities with a clean, local source of electricity so residents don't have to rely upon imported fossil fuels. The United States recently passed Germany as the country producing the most wind power. The U.S. Department of Energy estimates that renewable-generated electricity will account for 15.8% of total U.S. electricity generation in 2030, and wind power will be an important part of this dynamo.[3]

Despite the potential for wind power, it now accounts for only 1% of U.S. electricity use. One problem with wind is the reality that it does not blow all the time. Consequently, there must be backup power plants ready to turn on instantly if the wind slackens. Another issue is that the wind occasionally blows the hardest in remote plains that are far from cities that need the energy. The leading states for wind power are Texas, Iowa, and California. In Texas, the wind is strongest on the mesas and high plains of West Texas, hundreds of miles from Dallas and Houston. The logistical cost of installing turbines is significant, and the cost of transmission lines to these cities is appreciable.[4]

FIG. 1-1 EnXco Turbine farm in Solano County, California

Source: *iStockphoto.com/Terrance Emerson*

In addition to the development of land-based sites for turbines, offshore wind farms are also gaining momentum. Turbine installations in the water are expensive, but the wind blows much harder off the coasts. Unlike winds on continents, which blow strongest at night, offshore breezes can be strong in the afternoon and match the time when people are using the most electricity.

The company that is bringing wind power to Lakefield, Minnesota, is EnXco. Established in 1987, EnXco is an industry leader in wind project development and a premier provider of operation and maintenance services of wind power projects throughout North America. The mission of the firm is "turning innovative ideas and long-term relationships into ethical high-value sustainable business."[5] The company's focus on renewable energy has enabled it to build an organization of renewable energy experts. The experience and expertise of these specialists enables them to generate value and deliver results to energy supply-chain partners and developers.

The story of EnXco developing renewable energy is one example of green marketing. In today's economy, each of us has the opportunity to engage in green marketing. When we recycle aluminum cans, we are engaging in one form of green marketing. Similarly, when we buy a hybrid automobile, we are acting with a green approach to marketing. When General Electric invests in wind power, it is engaging in green marketing. When General Motors invests in researching environmentally friendly technologies for the Chinese market, it is also engaged in green marketing.

Each of these examples illustrates conditions under which people or institutions have chosen to act in a manner that is environmentally friendly. Nevertheless, we can each think of situations in which people do not engage in green marketing. Many of us have been litterbugs, and most of us have on occasion failed to purchase environmentally sound products despite their availability. Similarly, we are aware of situations in which energy companies did not act in the best interests of the environment.

It is because the challenge to green marketing is so great that it is important to study this subject. Indeed, the purpose of this book is to help individuals make informed decisions about choices that influence the environment. As we progress, however, we will find that many green decisions are more complicated than they appear. Furthermore, the decision to use an environmentally friendly approach at one stage in a supply chain has environmental implications for another level of the supply chain. For example, compact fluorescent light bulbs use 25% of the energy and last 10 times longer than conventional bulbs, but the mercury in these bulbs complicates their disposal.[6]

In order for us to understand green marketing, it is first important to have an appreciation of marketing. The American Marketing Association defines **marketing** as "the activity, set of institutions, and processes for creating, communicating, delivering, and exchanging offerings that have value for customers, clients, partners, and society at large."[7] This definition recognizes that marketing is an organizational function and set of activities undertaken to bring about exchanges of goods, services, or ideas between people. The definition recognizes that marketing is a philosophical orientation to the practice of doing business. This philosophical orientation emphasizes the satisfaction and value that customers, clients, partners, and society realize due to marketing action.

As marketing has evolved, individuals operating in various parts of the field have adopted alternative definitions of green marketing. Consumer researchers addressing green marketing have focused on the conditions that increase the potential for consumers to act in an ecologically responsible manner,[8] and they recognize marked variety among consumer interpretations of this responsibility.

Retailers and developers of green products emphasize product offerings that are environmentally friendly.[9] Thus, products such as organic vegetables, recycled paper, and phosphate-free detergents are referred to as green products. This definition of green marketing emphasizes product offerings that are not harmful to the environment, but it does not address the production processes employed to prepare the products.

Social marketing adopts a different vantage point and defines **green marketing** as the development and marketing of products designed to minimize negative effects on the physical environment. In contrast to the retailing perspective, the social orientation recognizes the pre- and postconsumption costs to the environment. Thus, automobile manufacturers attempt to raise production efficiency while simultaneously decreasing costs associated with disassembly and reuse after consumption.[10]

If we are to address the breadth of issues associated with an environmentally based approach to marketing, then it is essential to offer a definition that incorporates the logic of each of the orientations to green marketing.

We therefore define green marketing as the study of all efforts to consume, produce, distribute, promote, package, and reclaim products in a manner that is sensitive or responsive to ecological concerns. The inclusion of "all efforts to consume" recognizes that many entities are involved in green marketing. Green marketing is not limited to government or nongovernment organizations, nor is it solely an activity undertaken by consumers. Manufacturers, wholesalers, retailers, and services firms each has opportunities to contribute to green marketing. This definition also recognizes the need to consider the production, distribution, and reclamation of products as integrated components of the marketing effort. Efficiency at one stage of this process (e.g., distribution) may offer advantages in the channel, but the goal of green efforts is to limit the total ecological influence associated with consumption. Finally, green marketing must consider the promotional efforts employed to gain consumer support of ecologically friendly products.

We define **green marketing management** as the process of planning and executing the marketing mix to facilitate consumption, production, distribution, promotion, packaging, and product reclamation in a manner that is sensitive or responsive to ecological concerns. The management of green marketing activity continues to evolve as companies incorporate new thinking about climate change throughout their organizations. Initial green marketing efforts focused on the recycling of products such as aluminum cans and photocopier toner cartridges. Over time, firms have begun to consider ways to *modify inputs* to production that limit the influence of the products on the environment. For example, Staples reduced store operating overhead through centralized controls for lighting, heating, and cooling at its 1,500 stores. Staples saved $6 million over two years by controlling this production input into its value chain.[11] As this example illustrates, development is at the core of a green marketing approach. The study of green marketing reflects an interest in becoming more aware of ecological and sustainability issues and consistently working to achieve higher levels of sustainability.

Increasingly, firms are recognizing that outputs from the production process should be viewed under scrutiny of climate change as well. Savvy management recognizes that everything coming out of a production facility is a *product, by-product,* or *waste.*[12] Green products are recognized nationally or internationally through certification and eco-labeling. For example, the United States Environmental Protection Agency provides *Energy Star* labels for electronics and appliances that are environmentally friendly. In the United States, personal computers account for 2% of annual electricity consumption. The EPA's new Energy Star labels require computers possessing the label to be 65% more efficient than conventional products. Adoption of these new personal computers will enable industry to save $1.2 billion over the life of the products.[13]

Firms also are viewing by-products of production in novel ways. Shell Oil is pumping carbon dioxide, a refinery by-product, into 500 Dutch greenhouses. This action reduces emissions by 325,000 tons per year and saves greenhouses from having to burn millions of cubic meters of gas needed to produce carbon dioxide.[14]

The pursuit of waste reduction is a third aspect of the production process undergoing a green transformation. Companies recognize that efforts to constrain waste influence profitability. For example, Fetzer Vineyards took an aggressive approach when it set a goal of zero waste.[15] Fetzer has a companywide waste reduction program that involves recycling of bottles, cardboard, plastic, aluminum, paper, antifreeze, waste oil, fluorescent tubes, and glass. The firm has reduced the amount of waste it sends to landfills by 96% since 1990.

Each of these aforementioned activities represents a form of green marketing employed at various points in the supply chain. Increasingly, however, organizations recognize the interdependencies operating throughout an economy. Efforts to control costs and enhance productivity at one stage cannot occur at the expense of other stages.

The United Nations is an organization that has led the way in this recognition of the multiple interdependencies among nature, economy, and society. In December

1983, the United Nations commissioned research on development and the environment. The 1987 report summarizing this research defined **sustainability** as development that "meets the needs of the present without compromising the ability of future generations to meet their own needs."[16] Importantly, this edict recognizes that there are at any time limits on the ability of the biosphere to absorb human activity. There are also limits imposed by the state of technology and social organizations, but both of these factors can be managed and improved to foster economic growth.

Since the publication of this report by the United Nations, industry practice has embraced the notion that sustainability derives from focusing on the **triple bottom line**.[17] Figure 1-2 outlines the pursuit of sustainability. The sustainable organization must generate acceptable levels of economic performance, or it will not survive. It must also nurture social performance in its interaction with customers, suppliers, consumers, and other interest groups. Survival is also contingent on the firm's ability to achieve acceptable levels of environmental performance throughout the supply cycle from raw material procurement to postconsumption disposal. Figure 1-2 illustrates that these alternative bottom lines are not always compatible. For example, the firm can raise its short-term financial performance by ignoring the costs of waste produced in its manufacturing facilities. The sustainable organization, however, simultaneously works toward achieving heightened performance in the economic, social, and environmental realms.

EnXco and its operations in Minnesota illustrate a developing effort to achieve sustainability through triple bottom line performance. EnXco and the landowners benefit financially from the wind farm, and they must develop and maintain working relationships to ensure financial performance. As they nurture these financially rewarding relationships, they are also contributing markedly to the environment by using renewable sources of energy.

Sustainability initiatives are being developed to address a host of situations in which efforts are focused on current development without repercussions for future generations. The agricultural, manufacturing, and retailing sectors offer different examples of sustainability. In the agricultural sector, Costa Rica is making progress

FIG. 1-2
Sustainability
and the Triple
Bottom Line

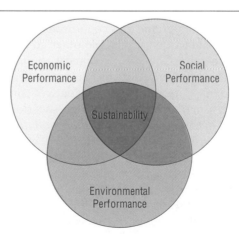

Source: *Craig R. Carter and Dale S. Rogers, "A Framework of Sustainable Supply Chain Management: Moving Toward New Theory,"* International Journal of Physical Distribution & Logistics Management 38 (5, 2008): 360–387. *Copyright 2008 by EMERALD GROUP PUBLISHING LIMITED. Reproduced with permission of EMERALD GROUP PUBLISHING LIMITED in the format Textbook via Copyright Clearance Center.*

toward production of sustainable bananas. Small-scale producers grow bananas without heavy agrochemical inputs. These locally controlled agricultural systems are supportive of local people, economies, and cultures.[18] In the manufacturing sector, the U.S. Department of Energy's Office of Industrial Technologies and the Aluminum Association have formed a partnership to improve technology competitiveness through collaborative planning and research. This private–public partnership seeks to make the industry profitable and ecologically sustainable. In the retail sector, Wal-mart has publicly committed to reducing packaging in its global supply chain by 5% by 2013.[19] As part of its effort to gain logistical sustainability, the firm developed a packaging scorecard to monitor supplier performance.

Together, these examples from a broad range of industries underscore the common interest in establishing green marketing initiatives. Firms may be hesitant to recognize the long-term merits of green marketing, but they cannot deny the short-run financial incentives established by regulators, trading partners, and consumers.

B. Why study Green Marketing?

Green marketing has positive influences on multiple participants in the economy. The *environment*, *developing economies*, *consumers*, *corporate strategy*, *the product*, *production processes*, and *supply chain* benefit from green marketing. Consider first the environmental benefits from green marketing.

Environmental Benefits   The obvious benefactor of green marketing is the environment. Chapter 3 of this book characterizes current conditions and trends in climate change, air, water, and soil conservation. Green marketing can have an influence on climate change in several substantial ways. Fossil fuel consumption is a major source of greenhouse gases associated with climate change. Two leading sources of climate change are the burning of coal for electricity and the burning of gasoline for automobile transportation. Green marketing initiatives focused on product development strategies reduce the need to rely on these forms of energy. For example, new appliances are designed with fuel efficiencies that markedly reduce energy consumption.

It is important to recognize that the consumer must incorporate concern for the environment with multiple other considerations. For example, potential consumers of the new Chevrolet Volt must reconcile the zero-fossil fuel consumption with the price differential for this car versus less expensive cars that produce more carbon dioxide. Green marketing initiatives contribute to the environment by incorporating green marketing strategies into superior value propositions for consumers.

Green marketing reduces *air pollution* in multiple ways. For example, New York Mayor Bloomberg has called for the complete replacement of taxis with hybrid cars by 2012. These hybrids will reduce New York City carbon dioxide emissions by 215,000 tons while doubling cab gas mileage. This efficiency means fewer emissions and lower air pollution. Similarly, agricultural run-off of fertilizer is a significant source of *water pollution*, but farming methods that eliminate inorganic fertilization reduce the amount of excess nutrients contaminating groundwater.[20] Soil pollution is a rising concern due in part to contaminants discarded in personal technological components. The need for remediation of pollution without removing soil is an increasingly important issue in industry.[21]

A related consequence of environmental change is the number of *endangered species*. Today there are more than 16,000 animal and plant species on endangered lists.[22] Their numbers increase every year due to deforestation, development, and climate change. Efforts to develop and consume environmentally friendly products, however, offer the potential to reduce the number of species on the endangered list.

Developing Economies The term *developing economies* refers to nations that have a relatively low gross domestic product (GDP) per capita. The low income, underdeveloped assets, and economic vulnerability endemic to these economies results in high dependence on the agricultural sector. Inhabitants in these markets, however, face increased exposure to drought, intense storms, floods, and environmental stress that limits the ability to enhance quality of life. Research performed by the United Nations indicates that inhabitants of these countries are much more likely to be affected by natural disasters than inhabitants in high-income countries.[23] Climate change limits agricultural productivity, increases water stress, raises sea levels, negatively transforms ecosystems, and thwarts human health. These factors do not operate in isolation; interactively, they contribute to hunger and poverty in developing markets. Green marketing and production stand to reduce climate change and consequently limit hunger and poverty.

As these developing economies progress, there will be increasing pressure on urban areas. More than half of world's population currently lives in urban areas, and the number is expected to increase over the next few decades. For example, current estimates forecast that nearly 300 million people will migrate to Chinese cities over the next 20 years.[24] Since the consumption of resources is a global issue, the extent to which consumers and industries adopt green marketing practices influences the global environment. Marketing of green technologies enables firms operating in these countries to leapfrog antiquated operations with efficient and environmentally friendly designs. For example, Cuba is upgrading analog telecommunications products with wireless phone systems and fiber-optic technologies.[25] New green technologies enable such economies to bypass antiquated technologies previously employed in mature-market economies.

Consumer Benefits Consumers benefit in several important ways through green marketing. These benefits often influence consumer decision making, and consumers will vary in the extent to which they value these benefits. Initially, consumers benefit from the knowledge that they are doing their part to reduce climate change. These consumers are likely to favor corporate efforts to reduce pollution over efforts to raise corporate profitability.[26] A nascent industry is developing that enables consumers to offset adverse effects of their action. For example, Terrapass enables consumers to purchase carbon offsets for their auto, air, or home emissions.[27]

Consumers also value the opportunity to be associated with environmentally friendly products and organizations.[28] For instance, the Body Shop's retail ambience prompts customers to associate their consumption with an environmentally friendly organization.[29]

Although green product initiatives may independently convince some consumers to buy, evidence suggests that ecologically based products alone will not be substantial drivers of sales. Consumers want ecologically friendly products without sacrificing other valuable features. Current marketing efforts, however, enable some firms to offer green products that provide initial product savings, lower energy costs, and access to new technologies.[30] For example, the LCD monitors marketed by Dell offer substantial savings over the CRT monitors currently being phased out of the product line. These new monitors are less expensive and employ the more recent computer display technology. The LCD monitors are also more energy efficient over time. Although green products in every industry will not enjoy the technological benefits similar to those for PC monitors, ecological benefits of products will augment or complement other product features valued by consumers.

Strategic Benefits Managers of corporate strategy realize multiple benefits from a green approach to marketing. Companies that incorporate ecological consciousness into their mission statements and strategy enhance their images among consumers, employees, investors, insurers, and the general public. As previously outlined, some *consumers* have strong affinities toward green products, and approaching the market with an ecological focus enhances image of the brand among these consumers.

Corporate initiatives that emphasize a green orientation to markets have several implications for the *workforce*.[31] First, potential employees may decide whether to interview with a firm based on the company's environmental image. When British Petroleum (BP) launched a new campaign labeled Beyond Petroleum, the company initially received substantial criticism based on the small percentage of revenues derived from industries other than gas and oil. Over time, however, BP was highly successful in establishing its position as an environmentally conscious firm. One notable outcome of this positioning is BP's recognition that attracting potential engineers to the firm is no longer a problem for the company.

The image further influences employee action after hiring. General Electric, for instance, engages employees to come up with novel solutions for the environment. The solutions include energy-efficient appliances, compact fluorescent lighting, and wind turbine power. Genzyme, a biotechnology firm, recently moved into a state-of-the-art green building complete with all-glass facades, 18 gardens, and conversational seating areas. After the firm moved into the facility, employees reported higher levels of job satisfaction. Moreover, employees reported that their increased sense of pride about Genzyme's commitment to the environment was their number one reason behind the new sense of productivity. Thus, enhanced corporate image augments recruiting, employee engagement in the firm's activities, and productivity.

Green marketing also has implications for *financial markets*. As fuel costs rise and greenhouse gas emissions escalate, investors are flocking to companies that can help alleviate these problems.[32] Investors are attracted to specialized green funds that feature portfolios of stocks from environmentally conscious firms. Alternatively, some market participants are investing in firms engaged in the development of alternative forms of energy.

Green marketing strategies enable firms to chart continued improvement in environmental performance. *Fortune* magazine is partnering with London-based AccountAbility and CSR Network to rank the 100 largest global corporations by the quality of their commitment to social and environmental goals.[33] Firm scores are based on the number of controversies involving the company, progress toward limiting carbon outputs, and stakeholder involvement. Firms that take an aggressive approach toward green marketing and follow-up on this effort can illustrate continuous improvement in environmental performance.

Corporate efforts to chart environmental performance enable companies to gain understanding of how the firm affects the environment as well as how the environment affects the firm.[34] Risk associated with finance, strategy, and operations are all affected by the firm's efforts to constrain its influence on the environment. Copious tracking of ecological performance provides the opportunity to manage the business risk stemming from environmental problems.

Although firms are generally not required to report assessment of green marketing activity, public reporting of these efforts offers three advantages.[35] First, these reports make companies more disciplined about reporting, which thereby reduces environmental risk. Second, this reporting puts all business practices under scrutiny and therefore helps identify cost savings and new business opportunities. Finally, public reporting of green marketing efforts clarifies corporate activity so that stakeholders begin to view the firm as a partner on the road to sustainable development. Consumers, employees, stockholders, insurers, and the general public become better informed about the environmental efforts of the firm when the firm reports green marketing efforts.

Green marketing also provides a strategic avenue that enables firms to develop alliances with interest groups outside the organization. Green marketing firms establish alliances with government, local communities, nongovernment organizations (NGOs), industry experts, and competitors.[36] DuPont has established an alliance with the Canadian government under which the firm agrees to collaborate with stakeholders, build sustainable communities, eliminate waste, and develop cleaner technologies.[37] The Canadian government is taking measures to recognize companies that demonstrate high levels of performance and adherence to compliance requirements. In addition, the government provides incentives to advance corporate social responsibility and seeks to streamline legislative requirements for innovations. Similarly, Swedish-based Lundin Mining is working with local communities in the Congo to increase local capacity and improve living conditions for the communities.[38] The drilling of 10 new freshwater wells is one aspect of Lundin's commitment to local communities. The actions taken at the federal level by DuPont and the local level by Lundin provide the opportunity for both firms to develop sustainable manufacturing in the markets they serve.

NGOs are self-governing and private not-for-profit organizations designed to improve the quality of life for disadvantaged people.[39] Although business firms' interactions with these entities have historically been contentious, recent activity with NGOs indicates opportunities to forge strong working relationships. The action of McDonald's illustrates how corporations can work with NGOs. McDonald's collaborated with the Environmental Defense Fund to phase out clamshell boxes because the manufacturing process used ozone-destroying chlorofluorocarbons (CFCs).[40] Importantly, these efforts frame perceptions of a firm's action and enable firms to establish ongoing commitments to the environment. The McDonalds–Environmental Defense Fund alliance resulted in the restaurateur purchasing more than $1 billion in recycled materials between 1990 and 1995—five years before schedule.

The McDonald's case underscores two additional strategic benefits of green marketing. Efforts to engage in environmentally conscious activity enable firms to improve their competitive positions and redefine markets. The competitive position changes in the market due to consumer observation and recognition of green marketing activity such as the recycling efforts of McDonald's. In addition, some segments of the investment community avoid investing in corporations associated with environmental damage.[41] Thus, reputations in consumer and financial markets benefit from green marketing activity.

Green marketing also enables companies to redefine markets. General Electric has committed to the need for cleaner, more efficient sources of energy, reduced emissions, and abundant sources of clean water. This commitment resonates throughout GE's product line and enables channel partners to refine markets. Boeing, a purchaser of GE's GEnx jet engines, markets its commercial aircraft as being quieter and more fuel-efficient and producing fewer emissions than its chief competitor, Airbus.[42]

Product Benefits In this section, we distinguish product from process benefits. Product benefits refer to components introduced into production outputs or services designed to benefit the consumer, whereas process benefits refer to tools, devices, and knowledge in throughput technology designed to facilitate manufacturing and logistics.[43] For example, a hybrid engine is a product innovation, whereas a just-in-time inventory system is a process innovation.

It is critical to recognize that the incorporation of product benefits must reflect genuine value for the relevant consuming public.[44] Thus, green products must improve environmental quality and customer satisfaction, as few markets will solely value enhancements to product quality. For example, Westinghouse developed an energy-efficient refrigerator in 1994 that was 30% more efficient than U.S. Department of Energy standards. Despite receiving a $30 million government award for consumer rebates, the elimination of CFC in the coolant system did not offset the $100–$150 premium associated with the new product.[45]

Green products have greater likelihood of succeeding, however, when environmental benefits augment consumer value assessments. Most value assessments—regardless of whether the product is green—center on price, quality, and performance. Green attributes rarely stand on their own and must complement other benefits to increase consumer value and ultimately consumption.[46] Rechargeable batteries offer convenience benefits that make them more attractive than their single-use counterparts. The reduced landfill benefit augments the convenience benefit to consumers. Although the initial price of rechargeable batteries exceeds the cost of the disposable units, many consumers understand the complete value offered by the multiple-use batteries.

The battery example underscores another benefit to green marketing, and that benefit lies in considering the value of the product throughout its life rather than the absolute initial cost. Auto purchasers that consider the relative lifetime operating costs of a hybrid versus internal combustion engine note marked disparities across brands. To the average driver that logs 15,000 miles per year and spends $2.87 per gallon of gas, it takes more than nine years to break even with the Honda Accord Hybrid compared with a similar gasoline-powered Accord. By contrast, driving the same mileage and assuming gasoline costs $4 a gallon, the Lexus GS450h four-door sedan hybrid breaks even immediately with the similar gasoline-powered Lexus GS430.[47] Increased fuel prices, longer driving distances, and reduced cost disparities with models using conventional engines are likely taken into consideration when the buyer evaluates the lifetime cost of the hybrid auto.

Greener products in many instances enable manufacturers to differentiate their products while also enabling consumers to take advantage of the latest technological developments. The Mini Cooper D, for instance, is distinguished from other products in its class by the amazing fuel efficiency of 60 mpg.[48] The fuel performance of this auto complements the styling and performance features that attract consumers to the Cooper.

In addition, green marketing prompts manufacturers to reassess the product packaging. Packaging protects products during shipping, enhances product desirability, and offers convenience in product handling. Marketers are pursuing ways to achieve these goals with less use of plastics and other petrochemical products. Procter & Gamble, for example, has removed the outside carton for its Sure and Secret deodorants. Elimination of this packaging decreases the amount of solid waste produced by consumers.[49] An important factor related to packaging is the cost of disposal of the product after consumption. In the personal computer market, Dell has developed a program that enables customers to recycle any PC through Dell. The company collects the item at no cost to the consumer and then reuses it through its charity partners such as Goodwill Industries, Inc., or recycles it through its network of electronics recyclers.[50]

Production Process Benefits Production processes focus on organizational efforts to produce the highest-quality products at the lowest possible cost. Process benefits accrue for handling of products, by-products, and waste. The materials costs associated with sustainable manufacturing techniques can be reduced in a number of ways. Mercer Color, for example, began using vegetable-based inks in 1990. Over time, the firm experienced a 25% reduction in ink costs as well as a more than 50% reduction in press washing costs.[51] Material costs can also be reduced via just-in-time (JIT) inventory procedures.[52] JIT enables companies to carry optimal levels of inventory that save space and energy.

By-product considerations also serve as incentives to engage in green production. The coal industry has developed procedures that modify the output of steam from power plants. This by-product is then is sent to a colocated ethanol plant. The result of this by-product modification is reduced greenhouse gas emissions along with decreases in mercury and nitrous oxide emissions. Fuel costs are lowered, and the plant earns revenue from hydrochloric acid sales and from sales of low-pressure steam to the ethanol plant.[53]

Advancements in the pharmaceutical industry illustrate efforts to limit waste. Chemists at Brock University have designed waste modification strategies that enable companies to process formerly hazardous waste into benign chemicals that can be disposed of in sewer systems.[54] This team has also transformed pharmaceutical by-products into analgesics, anesthetics, and antitumor drugs that treat cancer, infection, and diabetes.

Supply-chain Benefits Green marketing influences relationships among the firms that make up the channel from raw material mining to consumption. Green strategies that seek to eliminate waste in the supply chain result in firms analyzing truck loading and route planning in the delivery process.[55] Routing that seeks to eliminate fuel costs can maximize truck capacity utilization and improve customer service.

Increasingly, partners in the supply chain seek the ability to trace products throughout the supply chain. European Union law refers to traceability as "the ability to trace and follow food feed, or food-producing animal or substance intended to be or expected to be incorporated into food or feed, through all stages of production, processing and distribution."[56] Companies that adopt sustainable or green strategies for the production and distribution of food products provide a level of insurance of product quality. The ability to trace components throughout the distribution process is not limited to food, as the automotive and computing industries have also adopted forms of traceability.

C. Groups That Need to Understand Green Marketing

Green marketing is increasingly an important issue for most entities involved in marketing whether they are buyers, sellers, or regulators of an industry.[57] Consider how the following market participants can benefit from understanding green markets:

Consumers. Consumers that understand green marketing have the opportunity to reduce their personal influences on the environment. A growing number of consumers are particularly interested in ways to eliminate their negative influence on the environment, and green marketing efforts are focused on this activity. Furthermore, consumers often reap ancillary financial benefits from product offerings that are designed to be environmentally friendly. For example, the consumer that purchases a hybrid automobile has a heightened confidence that her means of transportation offers a smaller influence on the environment relative to alternative vehicles. Also, hybrid engines are twice as efficient as their conventional counterparts and get 30% to 60% better gas mileage.[58]

Governments. Federal, state, and local governments benefit in a number of ways due to green marketing. Just as consumers sometimes can lower expenditure costs and limit influences on the environment, governments similarly benefit from green procurement programs. For example, the city of Amsterdam uses cold lake water to air condition homes for more than 700,000 inhabitants. The program saves nearly $300,000 a year in electricity costs and uses just one-tenth of the power of a conventional cooling system.[59] In addition, governments that understand the market potential and limits of green marketing initiatives are in better positions to develop regulation strategies that serve the needs of society and industry.

Companies with established environmental reputations. Companies that have been singled out as standard bearers for green marketing expect significant scrutiny and publicity from environmentally questionable activity. For example, the Body Shop has a stellar record as a green-oriented firm, but it can anticipate substantial criticism if it fails to keep this orientation in all markets it serves. By contrast, companies such as Exxon that have been singled out for nefarious acts against the environment must address green marketing issues if they seek to change their reputations.

Companies highly dependent on scarce human capital. *Services* refers to intangible activities that organizations provide to consumers. In the United States, services account for more than 84% of the employment in the economy.[60] The intangible services are provided through human capital, and firms that operate in this sector of the economy must increasingly incorporate green marketing into their product offerings. In Las Vegas, for example, dentists are providing services to hotel and casino employees via mobile vans situated near the entertainment district.[61] The proximity of these facilities reduces fuel emissions by eliminating the need for employees to travel to the dentist. Consumer dental hygiene and worker productivity benefit from this eco-conscious service design.

Companies with high brand exposure. In their annual reports on the best 100 global brands, *Business Week* and Interbrands provide annual estimate of the earnings attributable to the brand.[62] As brands increase in appeal, they simultaneously increase the amount of scrutiny they incur. In contrast to reports of brands that have little brand equity, stories that indicate the activity of brands with high brand equity are likely to be viewed as more newsworthy. For example, newspaper articles critical of the processing of chickens will be of greater interest to the public when they refer to KFC rather than to any other brand in this industry. Firms with strong brand equity must address green marketing to limit the scrutiny they experience.

Companies with low market power. Companies that rely on other firms for substantial amounts of output must attend to the green marketing constraints leveled by the supplier. General Mills, one of the largest companies in the packaged grocery business, recently modified the shape of Hamburger Helper on the request of Wal-mart.[63] The retailer pointed out that the once-curly noodles in Hamburger Helper should be straight. This ecologically driven product modification reduced thousands of pounds of packaging and lowered the product's price. As buyers become more attuned to sustainability, suppliers reliant on these buyers must also increase their understanding of green marketing.

Companies operating in highly regulated industries. Government implements regulations to control the manner in which an industry operates. Industries that employ hazardous materials (e.g., the chemical industry) are subject to substantial regulations, and the increasing interest in green marketing fuels the need for industrial standards. Similarly, utilities, automobile producers, and airlines must address multiple stringent regulations. The electronics industries face increased scrutiny in the European Union due to "takeback laws" that require manufacturers to handle product disposal after consumer usage. In each of these industries, firms that take a proactive stance toward environmental regulation can implement regulations before adherence is required.[64]

Companies dependent on natural resources. Industries that are highly reliant on natural resources recognize the absolute limits in the availability of natural resources. These industries include oil, fish, and forestry. Natural production limits demand that firms understand eco-marketing activity that can conserve scarce resources.

Summary

Introduction to Green Marketing

The purpose of this chapter has been to introduce the study of green marketing. We defined green marketing as the study of all efforts to consume, produce, distribute, promote, package, and reclaim products in a manner that is sensitive or responsive to ecological concerns. We described an incremental process by firms that evolve in their efforts to pursue green marketing, and we subsequently defined sustainability as development that meets the needs of the present without compromising the ability of future generations to meet their own needs. Firms pursue sustainability via a triple bottom line perspective focused on achieving economic, relational, and ecological outcomes.

Why Study Green Marketing?

Beyond the environmental benefits that can accrue from green marketing, several sectors of the global economy benefit from green marketing. Emerging economies have potential to curb hunger and poverty by engaging in green marketing. Consumer welfare can benefit, and, similarly, corporate strategy can be enhanced by incorporating green marketing practices. Product development, production, and the supply chain all have potential to achieve higher levels of triple bottom line performance via green marketing.

Groups That Need to Understand Green Marketing

In addition to the need for consumers and government to understand green marketing, we characterized multiple types of firms that need to understand it. Companies with established environmental reputations and brand exposure need to understand the topic to retain their reputations and brand identities. Firms that are highly dependent on scarce human capital and those dependent on natural resources follow green marketing issues to ensure the productive use of these assets. Companies with low market power can develop competitive advantages, whereas companies in highly regulated industries that are proactive in green marketing initiatives can implement regulations and standards before they are required to do so.

Keywords

green marketing, 5

green marketing management, 6

marketing, 5

sustainability, 7

triple bottom line, 7

Questions

1. Is green marketing something done solely by corporations, or can anyone engage in green marketing?

2. Think about a local grocery store operating in your community. To what extent does it consume, produce, distribute, promote, package, and reclaim products in a manner that is sensitive or responsive to ecological concerns?

3. An entrepreneur claims not to focus on sustainability because attention to such matters results in poorer financial performance. How might one address such a statement?

4. Provide some examples of how consumers might act in a sustainable manner that meets the needs of the present without compromising the ability of future generations to meet their needs. How does this perspective influence how people shop, consume, and dispose of the things they buy?

5. Provide examples of companies that have acted in a sustainable manner whereby they meet the needs of the present without compromising the ability of future generations?

6. How might individuals and companies based in emerging economies benefit from the study of green marketing?

7. How does the study of corporate strategy benefit from incorporating a green marketing perspective?

8. If green marketing draws attention to the way things are consumed, then how is the study of green marketing relevant to production and supply chains?

9. Why would a company like McDonald's be concerned about green marketing?

10. Some companies have well-established reputations about their concerns for the environment. Why would such companies be concerned about green marketing issues?

Endnotes

[1] Ryan Brinks, "Lakefield Wind Project Detailed," http://www.lakefieldstandard.com/Stories/Story.cfm?SID=22843 (accessed April 28, 2010).

[2] *The New York Times*, "Wind Power," http://topics.nytimes.com/top/news/business/energy-environment/wind-power/index.html.

[3] U.S. Energy Information Administration, "How Much Renewable Energy Do We Use?" http://tonto.eia.doe.gov/energy_in_brief/renewable_energy.cfm (accessed April 28, 2010).

[4] Kate Galbraith, "Slow, Costly and Often Dangerous Road to Wind Power," *New York Times*, July 23, 2009, 18.

5 enXco, "About enXco," http://www.enxco.com/company_profile.php (accessed April 28, 2010).

6 Jim Carlton and others, "Nine Cities, Nine Ideas," *Wall Street Journal*, R1, R4.

7 American Marketing Association, "Dictionary," http://www.marketingpower.com/_layouts/Dictionary.aspx?dLetter=M (accessed April 28, 2010).

8 Johanna Moisander, "Motivational Complexity of Green Consumerism," *International Journal of Consumer Studies* 31, no. 4 (2007): 404–409.

9 Tim Craig, "Green is the New Black," *Retailing Today* 46, no. 1 (2007): 8.

10 M. R. Johnson and M. H. Wang, "Economical Evaluation of Disassembly Operations for Recycling, Remanufacturing and Reuse," *International Journal of Production Research* 36, no. 12 (1998): 3227–3252.

11 Nicholas Varachaver, "How to Kick the Oil Habit," *Fortune*, August 23, 2004, 100–114.

12 Daniel C. Esty and Andrew S. Winston, *Green to Gold* (New Haven, CT. Yale University Press, 2006); Robert A. Frosch, "Toward the End of Waste: Reflections on a New Ecology of Industry," *Daedalus* 125, no. 3 (1996): 199–212.

13 Colleen Taylor, "EPA Revises Energy Star," *Electronic News* 52, no. 44 (2006): 21.

14 Stafford, Ned, "Gas for the Greenhouse," *Nature* 442, no. 7102 (2006): 499.

15 Chrissy Kadleck, "Calif. Vineyard Cuts Environmental Impact," *Waste News*, August 6, 2007, 12.

16 Gro Brundtland, *Our Common Future: The World Commission on Environment and Development* (New York, NY. Oxford University Press, 1987), 24.

17 Sandra A. Waddock, Charles Bodwell, and Samuel B. Graves, "The New Business Imperative," *Academy of Management Executive* 16, no. 2 (2002): 132–148.

18 Carrie McCracken, "Sustainable Banana Project," September 1, 2009, www.awish.net/NA/banana_project.htm.

19 Mary Ann Falkman, "Sustainability: The Wal-mart Way," *Packaging Digest* 44, no. 20 (2007): 12.

20 Abigail A. Maynard, "Reducing Fertilizer Requirements in Cut Flower Production," *BioCycle* 44, no. 3 (2003): 43.

21 Mark Vigneri, Ron Adams, and Ron Scrudato, "Remediation for Those Hard-to-Reach Places," *Pollution Engineering* 39, no.6 (2007): 36–40.

22 Saheli Datta and Todd Woody, "8 Technologies for a Green Future," *Business 2.0* 8, no. 1 (2007): 81–88.

23 Kevin Watkins, "Human Development Report 2007/2008," *United Nations Development Programme*, Geneva, Switzerland, 31.

24 Stuart L. Hart and Mark B. Milstein, "Global Sustainability and the Creative Destruction of Industries," *Sloan Management Review* 41, no. 1 (1999): 23–33.

25 Timothy Ashby, "Silicon Island Cuba's Digital Revolution," *Harvard International Review* 23, no. 3 (2001): 14–18.

26 Clare D'Souza, Mehdi Taghian, and Rajiv Khosla, "Examination of Environmental Beliefs and Its Impact on the Influence of Price, Quality and Demographic Characteristics with Respect to Green Purchase Intention," *Journal of Targeting, Measurement and Analysis for Marketing* 15, no. 2 (2007): 69–78.

27 James Salzman and David Hunter, "Negligence in the Air: The Duty of Care in Climate Change Litigation" (Working paper, series no. 95, Duke University Law School, 2007).

28 Gert Cornelissen and others, "Positive Cueing: Promoting Sustainable Consumer Behavior by Cueing Common Environmental Behaviors as Environmental," *International Journal of Research in Marketing* 25, no. 1 (2008): 46–55.

29 Tony Kent and Dominic Stone, "The Body Shop and the Role of Design in Retail Branding," *International Journal of Retail and Distribution Management* 35, no. 7 (2007): 531–543.

30 The Editors of Consumer, *Reports Consumer Reports Buying Guide 2008*. 360.

31 Adrienne Fox, "Corporate Social Responsibility Pays Off," *HR Magazine*, August 2007, 2.

32 Jeffrey R. Kosnett, "GREEN is the Next Big Thing," *Kiplinger's Personal Finance*, October 2007, 32–34.

33 Telis Demos, "Accounting for Accountability," *Fortune*, November 1, 2007, 52–56.

34 See Note 12 above.

35 Ans Kolk, "Green Reporting," *Harvard Business Review* (January–February, 2000): 15–16.

36 See Note 12 above.

37 Chad Holliday, "Sustainable Growth, the DuPont Way," *Harvard Business Review* 79, no. 8 (2001): 129–132.

38 Lundin for Africa, "Pact Congo: Community Water Wells," http://www.lundinforafrica.org/s/Community_Water_Wells_DRC.asp (accessed April 28, 2010).

39 Anna C. Vakli, "Confronting the Classification Problem: Toward a Taxonomy of NGO's," *World Development* 25, no. 12 (1997): 2057–2070.

40 Edwin R. Stafford and Cathy L. Hartman, "Green Alliances: Strategic Relations Between Businesses and Environmental Groups," *Business Horizons* 2 (March–April, 1996): 50–59.

41 Barry H. Spicer, "Investors, Social Corporate Performance and Information Disclosure: An Empirical Study," *The Accounting Review* 55, no. 1 (1978): 94–111.

42 Carol Matlack, "Cleaning up with Next-Gen Jets," *Business Week*, June 25, 2007, http://www.businessweek.com/globalbiz/content/jun2007/gb20070622_950776.htm.

43 S. Gopalakrishnan and F. Damanpour, "A Review of Innovation Research in Economics, Sociology, and Technology Management," *Omega* 25, no. 1 (February, 1997): 15–28.

44 Jacquelyn Ottman, Edwin R. Stafford, and Cathy L. Hartman, "Avoiding Green Marketing Myopia," *Environment* 48, no. 5 (2006): 22–36.

45 Allen D. Lee and R. Conger, "Market Transformation: Does It Work? The Super Energy Efficient Refrigerator Program," *Proceedings of the 1996 ACEEE Summer Study*, (1996): 3.69–3.80.

46 See Note 12 above.

47 Andrea Coombes, "Deals Speed Up Hybrid Savings," *Wall Street Journal*, May 2, 2007.

48 Richard Truett, "Mini Cooper D(iesel) Delivers, But Not Here Yet," *Automotive News*, August 18, 2008.

[49] Jennifer Lawrence and others, "Toiletries to Strip Excess Packaging," *Advertising Age* 62, no. 20 (May 13, 1991): 3, 50.

[50] Joe Truini, "Dell Takes 'A Big Step Forward' with Free E-recycling," *Waste News*, December 4, 2006, 13.

[51] Lisa Cross, "How Print Got Green," *Graphic Arts Online*, March, 2007, 10–14.

[52] Food Logistics, "Technology Fuels Green Efforts," June 2007b, 38.

[53] Bob McIlvaine, "Byproducts can Make Coal Plants Green," *Power Engineering*, July, 2007, 38–42.

[54] Kaylynn Chiarello, "Industry Takes Steps toward Greener API Manufacturing," *Pharmaceutical Technology* 29, no. 11 (2005): 44–51.

[55] See Note 54 above.

[56] The European Parliament and the Council of the European Union, "EC Regulation No. 178/2002," *Official Journal of European Communities* L 31/1, (2002), http://eur-lex.europa.eu/LexUriServ/LexUriServ.do?uri=OJ:L:2002:031:0001:0001:EN:PDF (accessed April 28, 2010).

[57] See Note 12 above.

[58] Norma Carr-Rufino and John Acheson, "The Hybrid Phenomenon," *The Futurist*, July–August 2007, 16–25.

[59] Jim Carlton, "Nine Cities, Nine Ideas," *Wall Street Journal*, February 11, 2008, R1.

[60] Monthly Labor Review, "Industry Employment," *Occupational Outlook Quarterly Online* 53, no. 4 (winter 2009-10), http://www.bls.gov/opub/ooq/2009/winter/art04.pdf (accessed April 2010).

[61] James Flanigan, "Parking-Lot Dentistry Is Finding Its Niche," *New York Times*, August 17, 2006, 1.

[62] *Business Week*, "The Top 100 Brands," August 6, 2007, 59–64.

[63] Jack Neff, "Eco Wal-Mart Costs Marketers Green," *Advertising Age* 78, no. 39 (2007): 3, 42.

[64] Michael W. Toffel, "The Growing Strategic Importance of End-of-Life Product Management," *California Management Review* 45, no. 3 (2003): 102–129.

An Overview of Strategic Green Planning

A. Green Marketing Planning

TIMBERLAND INC.

In the fall of 2009, Timberland began incorporating recycled rubber into the outsoles of its Mountain Athletics and Earthkeepers lines of footwear.[1] The company plans to make more than 200,000 pairs of shoes using recycled rubber. Although most shoes are still made from virgin rubber, competitively priced recycled materials are making significant inroads into the market. Timberland hopes to increase the market share of these green materials via the introduction of recycled rubber into its footwear.

The decision to incorporate recycled materials into the product line is part of Timberland's longstanding commitment to the environment. The corporate strategy is based on a sustainability perspective that permeates everything it does. On a corporate level, the company has a commitment to corporate social responsibility that focuses on four themes. First, the company seeks to become carbon neutral in 2010. The firm approaches this goal by purchasing renewable energy where possible and generating its own renewable energy where clean energy is not available.

The second sustainability theme of the firm is to design recyclable products. Recognizing that the half-life of a shoe is rather short, the firm is striving to create low-cost products that are not only less harmful to the environment but also can become revenue-generating products after the productive life of the shoe. Three years ago, Timberland began labeling the overall amount of energy and the amount of energy from renewable sources associated with production and the supply cycle. In addition, each product is accompanied by a Nutrition Label indicating the climate impact, chemical usage, and resource consumption for the product.[2] The products also feature Green Index cards that provide an easy way to compare the footprints of footwear products.[3]

The third sustainability theme that permeates the organization concerns the environment and surroundings of the communities and workplaces in which the company operates. Timberland sponsors service events in which it works to strengthen communities by improving green spaces and access to the outdoors. Furthermore, it encourages employees to engage in community service in their communities.

The final theme of Timberland's sustainability mission concerns the workplace. Since the company realizes that the finished Timberland product is the result of efforts throughout the supply cycle, it monitors the entire supply chain

FIG. 2-1 Timberland
ad for Mountain
Athletics Footwear

Source: *Image courtesy of The Advertising Archives*

for human rights issues and sustainable business practices. When the company began assessing the energy content of its footwear, it was surprised to find that more than half of the energy used in making a pair of shoes comes from processing and producing the raw materials.[4] The second biggest energy drain is at the retail level, followed by factory operations. Transportation, the factor the company believed was the biggest producer of greenhouse gases in the supply cycle, turned out to be the lowest contributor to energy usage and carbon emissions.

The Timberland example illustrates how a firm can take a sustainability strategy and incorporate it throughout its marketing strategy. To make this transition from the plan to its implementation, every organization needs a roadmap outlining the direction the firm is pursuing. As organizations grow, each employee should have an understanding of the markets the firm serves, the customers within each market, and the product offerings designed to meet these consumers' needs. Strategic market planning is the process that outlines the manner in which a business unit competes in the markets it serves.[5] Strategic market decisions are based on assessments of product markets and provide the basis for competitive advantage in the market. The plan developed through this process provides a blueprint for the development of the skills and resources of a business unit and specifies the results to be expected.

The planning process involves anticipating future conditions and establishing strategies to achieve objectives. Interestingly, the planning process necessarily involves relating the marketing objectives of the firm to the environment.[6] Although strategists have long recognized the interaction between the firm and its environment, much of the research and planning process focuses on the influence of the environment on corporate decision making. Firms that incorporate sustainability concerns into strategic planning recognize that the activities and programs developed by the firm simultaneously influence the environment. For example, Toyota recognizes that gasoline prices represent a facet of the environment that influences consumer purchase decisions. In addition, Toyota also considers the influences of automobile production and operations on the environment.

A green planning process must explicitly examine the interaction of the environment with the corporate strategy. We therefore define **green marketing planning** as the process of creating and maintaining a fit between the environment and objectives and resources of the firm. *Fit* refers to the effort to understand how the environment both influences *and is influenced* by marketers. In Chapter 3, we will examine the interaction of firms, consumers, and individuals with the environment. The planning process begins with an in-depth analysis of the internal and external environment of the firm. Based on this situational analysis, the firm establishes its mission, objectives, strategy, implementation, and evaluation. As outlined in Figure 2-2, the planning process is a dynamic process that relies heavily on interaction with the environment.

Strategic marketing planning should accompany planning throughout all functional areas of the firm such as financial planning, production, and research and development.[7] The output of the planning process is a **marketing plan** that provides an analysis of the current marketing situation, opportunities and threats analysis, marketing objectives, marketing strategy, action programs, and projected income

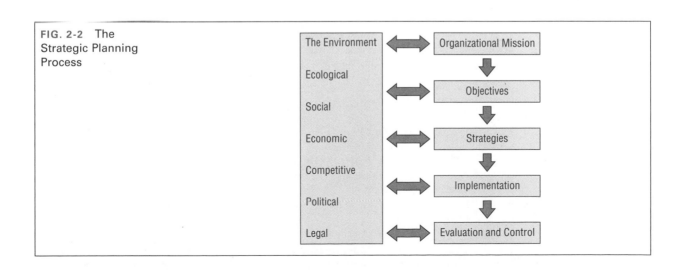

FIG. 2-2 The Strategic Planning Process

The Environment
Ecological
Social
Economic
Competitive
Political
Legal

Organizational Mission → Objectives → Strategies → Implementation → Evaluation and Control

statements.[8] This plan serves as the blueprint outlining how the organization will achieve its objectives. In addition, the plan informs employees regarding their functions and roles in the implementation of the plan. The plan also provides insight into the allocation of resources and the specification of tasks and responsibilities and the timing of marketing action.[9]

The mission statement should be formulated and articulated by upper management within the firm. The process of developing this statement and strategy demands buy-in by top management. In addition, articulation of the plan by senior executives signals to employees, customers, and stakeholders that the planning process is of central importance to the activity of the firm.

B. Incorporating a Green Perspective into the Mission Statement

The **mission statement** describes a firm's fundamental, unique purpose, indicating what the organization intends to accomplish, the markets in which it operates, and the philosophical premises that guide its actions.[10] The mission statement is an inspirational tool that provides motivation, direction, and insight into the company's character. For example, Figure 2-3 provides the mission statement and values of Duke Energy.

Importantly, the mission of the firm must consider the organization's history, its distinctive competencies, and its environment.[11] Energy firms such as Duke have been the target of litigation from the U.S. Environmental Protection Agency.[12] The explicit inclusion of sustainability in the mission, however, suggests that the firm seeks to separate itself from this history. In addition, the treatment of sustainability underscores the firm's recognition of the intense interaction between the company's operations with the environment. Finally, the mission statement indicates the distinctive competencies of the company that include diverse talents, passion, and open dialogue with their stakeholders.

FIG. 2-3 Duke Energy Mission and Values

Our Mission
At Duke Energy, we make people's lives better by providing gas and electric services in a sustainable way. This requires us to constantly look for ways to improve, to grow, and to reduce our impact on the environment.

Our Values

Caring — We look out for each other. We strive to make the environment and communities around us better places to live.

Integrity — We do the right thing. We honor our commitments. We admit when we're wrong.

Openness — We're open to change and to new ideas from our coworkers, customers and other stakeholders. We explore ways to grow our business and make it better.

Passion — We're passionate about what we do. We strive for excellence. We take personal accountability for our actions.

Respect — We value diverse talents, perspectives, and experiences. We treat others the way we want to be treated.

Safety — We put safety first in all we do.

The Duke Energy passage encompasses many traits associated with effective mission statements.[13] The mission is clearly articulated, relevant, and enduring. In establishing the mission, senior management provides a sense of direction to the organization. Employees and business partners are inspired to pursue specific action because the action is consistent with the message outlined in the mission. Note that the contrary is also true—constituents are unlikely to pursue activities that do not reflect the values expressed in the mission statement.

If the firm is to have a strategy that meaningfully incorporates green marketing and sustainability, then the mission statement must incorporate green marketing and sustainability. For example, P&G (Procter and Gamble) incorporates an external focus into its core principles for operations.[14] The firm recognizes that this external orientation requires the company to incorporate sustainability into its products, operations, and packaging. The company follows through with this commitment in several ways. First, P&G has adopted a sustainability perspective focused on improving lives for years to come. Second, the firm has a product safety initiative designed to enhance the environmental quality of products, packaging, and operations across the globe. Third, P&G has implemented a commitment to the environment. Since detergents and other products that the firm manufactures can have a significant influence on water and water treatment plants, P&G requires all ingredients to pass an environmental risk assessment before they can be integrated into products. These commitments to the environment flow from a corporate mission that emphasizes environmentalism and sustainability.

Although the mission statement should underscore the firm's commitment to sustainability, it is critical for this statement to be consistent with the level of sustainability currently pursued by the firm. For example, in 2000 BP developed a new symbol along with a media message that claimed the firm was moving "beyond petroleum."[15] The firm outlined a strategy that identified efforts to pursue energy from sources other than fossil fuels, but oil and gas accounted for approximately 98% of the firm's revenue. **Greenwashing** refers to situations in which there is a significant gap between the expressed and genuine commitments to sustainability. Environmentalists accuse oil firms of greenwashing when their investments in renewable energy are small compared with the money that goes into their oil and gas divisions.[16]

In the current business and regulatory climate, firms should also recognize that public statements about efforts to become sustainable subject the firm to greater scrutiny. In a global enterprise, these statements open up the firm to criticism from consumers and government organizations. For example, Coke and Pepsi are two global consumer products companies that each developed commitments to sustainability.[17] These firms and their affiliated bottlers necessarily have to account for the manner in which water is treated in the production process. Each firm's expressed commitment to sustainability has been accompanied by critiques in some markets about water filtration and handling.

Sustainability should be incorporated into the mission statement of the firm, but this focus should augment other driving forces within the firm. For example, Adidas explicitly recognizes that the company is a consumer-focused, innovative firm that manages a portfolio of brands that consistently deliver outstanding financial results.[18] The firm also affirms its desire to be a socially and environmentally responsible global organization. The Adidas values reflect the mounting evidence of the role of green marketing within the firm. Green marketing augments the other values of the firm and its product offerings, but it is rarely the primary motivation for consumption. The firm needs to incorporate its development of a green strategy as a facet of the value proposition.[19]

C. Integrating a Green Mission into Objectives, Strategy, and Marketing Tactics

If the mission statement incorporates discussion of sustainability, then there is a much greater likelihood that the objectives and strategy will be poised to consider the interaction of the firm with its environment. Figure 2-4 uses Timberland Apparel to illustrate the planning process. The firm's mission is to equip people to make a difference in their world.[20] Timberland pursues this mission by creating outstanding products and by trying to make a difference in the communities where employees live and work. Importantly, the firm views volunteering in communities and designing ecologically friendly products as ways to reduce the company's influence on the environment.

Organizational objectives are desired or needed results to be achieved by a specific time[21] and emerge from the development of the mission statement. For Timberland, one objective is environmental stewardship whereby the company is committed to becoming a carbon-neutral enterprise by 2010. This goal embodies three essential elements of objectives.[22] First, the objective precisely specifies the goals of the organization. If the objective is not precise and clear, employees will be less likely to achieve the desired outcome. Second, the objective is measurable and in this case leads to exact mechanisms for assessing pursuit of this objective. Objectives must be measurable if the firm is to assess the level of success in a meaningful way.

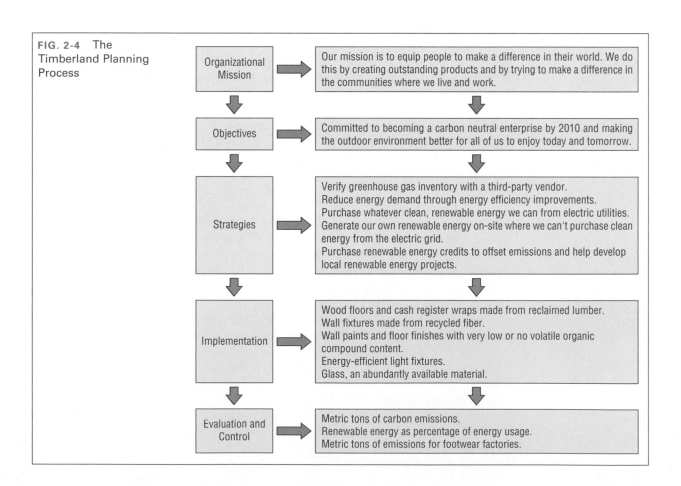

FIG. 2-4 The Timberland Planning Process

Organizational Mission → Our mission is to equip people to make a difference in their world. We do this by creating outstanding products and by trying to make a difference in the communities where we live and work.

Objectives → Committed to becoming a carbon neutral enterprise by 2010 and making the outdoor environment better for all of us to enjoy today and tomorrow.

Strategies → Verify greenhouse gas inventory with a third-party vendor. Reduce energy demand through energy efficiency improvements. Purchase whatever clean, renewable energy we can from electric utilities. Generate our own renewable energy on-site where we can't purchase clean energy from the electric grid. Purchase renewable energy credits to offset emissions and help develop local renewable energy projects.

Implementation → Wood floors and cash register wraps made from reclaimed lumber. Wall fixtures made from recycled fiber. Wall paints and floor finishes with very low or no volatile organic compound content. Energy-efficient light fixtures. Glass, an abundantly available material.

Evaluation and Control → Metric tons of carbon emissions. Renewable energy as percentage of energy usage. Metric tons of emissions for footwear factories.

Third, the objective must entail action commitments specifying the behaviors associated with achieving the objective. If the relevant action is understood, management can covert the objective into specific action associated in the marketing plan and strategy.

Corporate strategy outlines the direction the firm will pursue within its chosen environment and guides the allocation of resources and effort.[23] For Timberland, the strategy emphasizes third-party verification of energy use, efficient operations, use of clean renewable energy, and the purchase of energy credits to offset emissions.

Clearly articulated strategies based on measurable objectives enable management to develop specific implementation plans. The implementation process refers to the stage at which the firm directs specific effort to the realization of objectives. Although senior management establishes objectives and strategy, it is rarely involved in the implementation process. Thus, it is essential that management relay a message of sustainability throughout the strategic planning process.

Implementation includes determination of action plans and related tactics designed to enable the firm to realize objectives.[24] The action plans provide schedules and milestones, whereas the tactics refer to the specific activities that the firm will engage in to ensure that objectives are realized. For Timberland, some of these tactics include the types of fixtures installed at retail locations.

The final stage of the strategic planning process is the evaluation and control phase. At this point, management takes stock of the degree to which the firm has realized objectives. Importantly, the criteria that emerge from the plan are the factors incorporated into evaluation. These evaluative criteria should logically complement the mission and objectives. Again, if the mission and objectives do not incorporate sustainability, then the evaluation and control systems will not address these concerns. The commitment to sustainability must therefore accompany every phase of the strategic planning process.

D. The Interaction Between Strategy and the Environment

The presentation of strategic planning as a static step-by-step process facilitates presentation of the model. Nevertheless, the step-by-step process does not capture the manner by which planning occurs in many organizations. The multiple phases of this process are going on simultaneously. Senior management is reevaluating the tactical plans while employees are implementing specific facets of the plan.

A primary need for constant reassessment of strategic planning is the interaction with the environment. As we will elaborate in Chapter 3, entities in the firm ranging from CEO to field sales representative monitor changes in the environment and modify their behavior to accommodate this action. For example, as energy prices escalate, senior management must consider costs of reimbursement to sales representatives while sales representatives likely re-assess their sales call schedules and routes. Because the environment is subject to change that has a significant influence on marketing activity, it is essential for the marketing organization to monitor the environment. Thus, marketers evaluate the ecological, competitive, economic, social, political, and legal environments.

An increasing awareness in society is the recognition that marketing influences the environment. Marketers are increasingly monitoring their influences on the environment. For example, McDonald's historically used a polystyrene container known as a clamshell to package hamburgers and other sandwiches.[25] These clamshells created a difficult form of solid waste, were economically unattractive for recycling, and produced chloroflourocarbons (CFCs) that were harmful to the ozone.[26] In 1989, McDonald's began collaborating with the Environmental Defense Fund (EDF) to address waste management. At the time, McDonald's employed 500,000 people in 11,000 stores serving 22 million customers per day. The alliance prompted McDonald's in 1990 to replace the polystyrene with quilted paper made from polyethylene and paper. The new wrapper was less bulky, cheaper, required less energy to produce, and discharged less pollution.

The EDF–McDonald's alliance illustrates how marketing activity has a dynamic influence on the environment. McDonald's, its franchisees, and their customers each play a significant role in the waste management for the restaurants' packaging and products. The collaboration with EDF enabled the company to strike a win–win strategy that reduced waste and pollution while simultaneously lowering McDonald's production costs.

Although there is a growing interest in examining how individuals and firms affect the environment, there is little agreement concerning how to assess these influences. In Chapters 11 and 14, we elaborate on mechanisms that enable consumers and manufacturers to assess their influences on the ecological environment.

E. Delivering Value to All Stakeholders

Stakeholders refers to the individuals, organizations, and groups that have an interest in the action of an organization and have the ability to influence it.[27] The development of corporate strategy demands consideration of the number of entities that are influenced by the action of the firm. Primary stakeholders include the following:[28]

a) **Consumers.** The purchasers and users of a firm's products are important stakeholders that influence the firm in many ways. Consumers influence the action of a firm when they elect to buy the organization's product offerings or choose to purchase products from competitors. Individuals operating in the marketplace are important sources of new product opportunities for the firm.[29] In addition, consumers provide feedback on their experiences with the firm's products, and these comments influence other consumers as well as corporate product decisions.

b) **Suppliers.** Companies are increasingly finding that their suppliers influence efforts to achieve sustainability. Since the inputs into production influence an organization's ability to achieve sustainable results, suppliers who provide environmentally safe products reduce the buyer's ecological influence.

c) **Employees.** The employees of the firm play a strategic role in the implementation of any strategy. As stakeholders, employees are important sources of sustainable new product ideas. Employees often have industry-specific knowledge and understanding of the market, which enables them to offer insight into product development.

d) **Competition.** The competitors in the market have a strong influence on the activities of the firm. Companies must proactively monitor the action and performance of their competition. Moreover, firms can establish a source of competitive advantage if they raise industry expectations for the environmental standards. For example, in the wake of the Bhopal, India, tragedy, Union Carbide and other companies in the Chemical Manufacturers Association developed the Responsible Care initiative.[30] The CMA established criteria for pollution prevention, process safety, and emergency response, which enabled the firms to improve their competitive positions.

e) **Legal System**. The courts and legal system are stakeholders that influence the firm via the enforcement of laws governing sustainability. For example, in 1989, the *Exxon Valdez* ocean tanker ran aground and spilled 11 million gallons of crude oil into Alaska's Prince Edward Sound.[31] The 1994 class action suit against the firm awarded 33,000 Alaskans $287 million in compensatory damages and $5 billion in punitive damages against Exxon. Although the punitive-damage award was later reduced to $2.5 billion, the example underscores the potentially critical influences of the legal system.

f) **Financial Institutions**. Banks, other lending agencies, and insurance firms are significant stakeholders because they determine the availability and cost of funds to an organization. Financial institutions are increasingly embracing sustainability as an important facet of corporate strategy, and they are developing financial systems to facilitate implementation of the strategy. For example, Standard Chartered is taking a lead role in the financing of renewable and clean energy projects in Asia, Africa, and the Middle East. These projects are slated to have a total value up to US$10 billion over the 2008–2012 horizon.[32]

g) **Government**. Government influences the action of firms via the regulations established to ensure product safety throughout production, use, and postconsumption. The mantle of responsibility falls on government at all levels. Firms must monitor state and local legislation as well as national regulations. In addition, there is increasing pressure from international government, including trade alliances (e.g., EU) and the United Nations. Organizations that fail to track regulatory developments at each of these levels expose themselves to serious competitive disadvantages.

h) **Media**. The *Valdez* disaster offers evidence that media are strategically poised to frame public perception of the events involving the firm. Increasingly, firms recognize that they must manage their interaction with the media in a proactive manner. Moreover, as the firm acts to mitigate its influence on the environment, it must make the media aware that these efforts are taking place.[33]

i) **Stockholders/Owners**. Investors with a variety of levels of ownership in the firm are increasingly taking action to influence the extent to which firms pursue sustainability causes.[34] Individuals influence companies by engaging in dialogue, voting proxies, attending shareholder meetings, and filing resolutions.

j) **Scientific Community**. Evidence developed within the scientific community has a strong influence on other stakeholders and thereby influences firm action. For example, the mounting scientific evidence of a greenhouse effect influenced the Supreme Court ruling that the federal government had the power under the Clean Air Act to regulate carbon dioxide emissions from vehicles.

k) **Nongovernment organizations (NGOs)**. NGO is a term used to describe a broad family of organizations that is not profit oriented or supported by government.[35] Historically, the action of NGOs has been at odds with industry. Increasingly, however, firms such as Starbucks have established relationships with NGOs that enable both parties to achieve objectives.[36]

l) **General Public**. The public at large are also stakeholders that influence operations. For example, urban planners recognize that management of relationships with the public enables them to gain support for land use initiatives.[37] Although the general public may not directly benefit from land development, their participation is essential throughout the design and utilization processes.

F. How This Text Is Organized to Help You Understand Green Marketing

The goal of this text is to drive marketing decision making toward action that is sensitive to the environment. Our general model of the context surrounding marketing action is provided in Figure 2-5. Marketing action is at the core of this model, and it is surrounded by environmental considerations, industrial activity, and marketing strategy. We define **marketing action** as any behavior associated with the procurement, purchasing, sales, consumption, and postconsumption of product offerings. Note that all of this marketing action reflects situations in which there is some sort of exchange between two parties. The purchase of a cup of coffee in a reusable thermos, for instance, involves the exchange of currency for a beverage. Both entities that are involved in the exchange activity are driven by the desire to increase value. The value of an exchange can be expressed in terms of the three related outcomes. To varying degrees, exchange activity provides economic, social, and environmental value. The coffee consumer, for example, may identify economic and environmental value from purchasing coffee in a reusable container, whereas the ambiance and service offered by the restaurant employees may yield social value to the consumer. It is not only meaningful to consider the triple bottom line of the consumer, but it is also increasingly essential for companies to recognize that they must pay attention to the economic, social, and environmental value of their product offerings.[38]

Marketing action is broadly defined to include all action associated with sourcing environmentally sensitive products as well as the activity endemic to using and discarding products. Thus, this definition encompasses all action associated with the supply chain from the procurement of raw materials to the postconsumption treatment products that have outlived their utility. For example, marketing action includes Pepsi's efforts to incorporate clean water into the syrups it sells to local bottlers in India. It also incorporates all the effort to make this product available for sale in the country, and it further includes all efforts to reuse or recycle the packaging of the product.

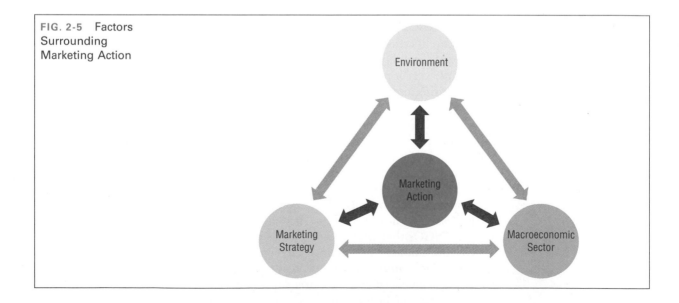

FIG. 2-5 Factors Surrounding Marketing Action

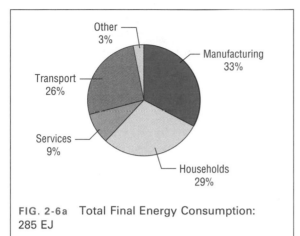

FIG. 2-6a   Total Final Energy Consumption: 285 EJ

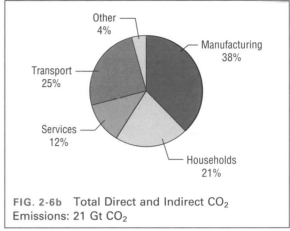

FIG. 2-6b   Total Direct and Indirect CO_2 Emissions: 21 Gt CO_2

Source: *International Energy Agency,* Worldwide Trends in Energy Use and Efficiency *(Paris, France: International Energy Agency)*

Importantly, the marketing action undertaken in a supply chain is influenced by and influences three factors. First, the action undertaken by individuals is influenced by the environment. *The environment* refers to physical and social contexts that provide the potential for marketing activity to occur. Part II of this book focuses on the interaction between the environment and consumption. In Chapter 3, we illustrate how the level of consumption influences the atmosphere, water, land, and biodiversity. In Chapter 4, we examine how the environmental activity influences consumption. Together, these two chapters underscore the interaction between environment and consumption.

In Part III, we examine facets of marketing strategy designed to enhance the sustainability of the firm. The central factor in the pursuit of sustainability is the **value** that market offerings provide to consumers. Sustainable value emerges from analysis of the economic, relational, and ecological returns sought in a market. Consequently, each chapter in our discussion of marketing action focuses on strategies that generate value. In Chapter 5, we outline a process for analyzing markets. This analysis of markets and market segmentation addresses the discovery of value. Promotional efforts by which firms communicate value are examined in Chapter 6. In Chapter 7, we frame product development as the set of processes by which the firm produces value. The effort to deliver value is addressed in the analysis of supply cycles in Chapter 8 and in the analysis of retailing in Chapter 9. Chapter 10 provides an overview of the mechanisms by which the firm proclaims value via its pricing strategy.

In Part IV, we examine the macroeconomic sector in which consumption occurs. This section focuses on sectors of the economy and their consumption of energy. Across the globe, energy consumption and greenhouse gas emissions are associated with four industrial contexts: manufacturing, households, services, and transportation (see Figure 2-6ab). Consequently, Chapters 11 through 14 address the major sources and uses of energy for each of these industrial contexts.

In Part V, we address procedures by which firms monitor and report the pursuit of value.

Summary

A. Green Marketing Planning

The purpose of this chapter has been to provide an overview of strategic green marketing planning. We began by defining *strategic market planning* as the process that outlines the manner in which a business unit competes in the markets it serves.

B. Incorporating a Green Perspective into the Mission Statement

The *mission statement* describes a firm's unique purpose, indicating what the organization intends to accomplish, the markets in which it operates, and the philosophical premises that guide action. If the firm is to have a strategy that meaningfully incorporates green marketing and sustainability, then the mission statement must incorporate green marketing and sustainability.

C. Integrating a Green Mission into Objectives, Strategy, and Marketing Tactics

Organizational objectives are results to be achieved by a specific time; they emerge from the development of the mission statement. First, the objective precisely specifies the goals of the organization. If objectives, strategies, and tactics are precise, measurable, and specific with respect to sustainability goals, management engages in action essential to achieving the mission of the firm.

D. The Interaction Between Strategy and the Environment

Strategic planning refers to the process by which the firm provides a fit between the environment and corporate action. In the strategic planning process, green marketing planning consists of creating and maintaining a fit between the environment and objectives and resources of the firm. By incorporating sustainability into the strategic planning process, the firm increases its likelihood of being able to interact effectively with the environment.

E. Delivering Value to All Stakeholders

Stakeholders refers to the individuals, organizations, and groups that have an interest in the action of an organization and have the ability to influence it.[39] The development of corporate strategy demands consideration of the number of entities that are influenced by the action of the firm. Primary stakeholders include consumers, suppliers, employees, competition, the legal system, financial institutions, government, media, stockholders/owners, and the scientific community.

F. How This Text Is Organized to Help You Understand Green Marketing

This book seeks to outline the relationship among marketing strategy, marketing action, macroeconomic sectors, and the environment. In Part I we introduce green marketing management and strategy. Part II of this book focuses on the interaction between the environment and consumption, and Part III examines facets of marketing strategy designed to enhance the sustainability of the firm. In Part IV, we examine the macroeconomic sector in which consumption occurs. In Part V, we address procedures by which firms monitor and report the pursuit of value.

Keywords

green marketing planning, 21
greenwashing, 23
marketing action, 28

marketing plan, 21
mission statement, 22
organizational objectives, 24

stakeholders, 26
value, 29

Questions

1. Why would a firm like Timberland elect to develop a sustainable strategy when it could effectively compete based on price?

2. How does the strategy of Timberland reflect an effort to achieve sustainability as defined in Chapter 1?

3. To what extent does the incorporation of a green perspective into the mission statement change how the firm will operate and be viewed in the market?

4. Describe a situation under which a firm (other than BP) has been accused of greenwashing. What conditions lead to this evaluation, and what did the firm do to correct it?

5. What did the EDF–McDonald's alliance teach NGOs and CEOs about relationships between NGOs and companies?

6. Consumers and stockholders are two divergent groups of stakeholders for a retailer. How might they differ in their attitudes toward sustainability?

7. Does Timberland consider its suppliers to be important stakeholders? What evidence supports your claim?

8. Describe a situation in which the general public has had an influence on a company's attitude toward sustainability. What events lead the public to become concerned about sustainability in this context?

9. Why would competitors such as the Chemical Manufacturers Association work together to develop sustainability standards? What are the consequences of failing to address sustainability?

10. Why is it necessary to examine the relationship between the macroeconomic industry and marketing action?

Endnotes

[1] K. Galbraith, "Timberland's New Footprint: Recycled Tires," *The New York Times*, March 7, 2009, http://greeninc.blogs.nytimes.com/2009/04/03/timberlands-newfootprint-recycled-tires/?scp=1-b&sq=Timberland&st=nyt.

[2] T. J. Ryan, "Timberland Introduces 'Nutrition Labels,'" *SGB* 39, no. 3 (2006): 14.

[3] M. Frazier, "Timberland 'Walks the Walk,'" *Advertising Age* 78, no. 24 (2007): 8.

[4] Cortese, "Friend of Nature? Let's See Those Shoes," *The New York Times*, March 7, 2007, http://www.nytimes.com/2007/03/07/business/businessspecial2/07label-sub.html?_r=2 (accessed April 28, 2010).

[5] American Marketing Association, "Dictionary," http://www.marketingpower.com/_layouts/Dictionary.aspx (accessed April 28, 2010).

[6] J. D. Thompson and W. J. McEwen, "Organizational Goals and Environment: Goal-Setting as an Interactive Process," *Administrative Science Quarterly* 23 (1958): 23–31; Lee G. Cooper, "Strategic Marketing Planning for Radically New Products," *The Journal of Marketing* 64, no.1:1–16.

[7] C. Daniel, "How to Make Marketing Plans More Effective," *Management Review* 68, no. 10 (1979): 60–61.

[8] See Note 5 above.

[9] G. E. Greenley, "An Understanding of Marketing Strategy," *European Journal of Marketing* 23, no. 8 (1989): 45–58.

[10] D. Ireland and M. A. Hitt, "Mission Statements: Importance, Challenge, and Recommendations for Development," *Business Horizons* 35, no. 3 (1992): 34–42.

[11] P. Kotler, *Marketing Management* (Englewood Cliffs, NJ: Prentice Hall, 2000), 718.

[12] James L. Nash, "Cinergy Agrees to $1.4 Billion Clean Air Penalty," *Occupational Hazards* 63, no. 2 (2001): 29.

[13] R. A. Stone, "Mission Statements Revisited," *SAM Advanced Management Journal* 61, no. 1 (1996): 31–7.

[14] Procter & Gamble, http://www.pg.com.

[15] D. C. Esty and A. S. Winston, *Green to Gold* (New Haven, CT: Yale University Press, 2006), 366.

[16] "Consider the Alternatives," *Economist* 375, no. 8424 (2005, April 30): 21–24.

[17] D. Brady, "Pepsi: Repairing a Poisoned Reputation in India," *Business Week*, June 11, 2007, 46–54.

[18] Adidas, "Our Values," http://www.adidas-group.com/en/ourgroup/values/default.aspx (accessed April 28, 2010).

[19] J. N. DeBonis, E. Balinski, and P. Allen, *Value-based marketing for bottom-line success* (New York, NY: McGraw Hill), 245.

[20] Timberland, "About Timberland," http://www.timberland.com/home/index.jsp (accessed April 28, 2010).

[21] See Note 5 above.

[22] J. P. Peter and J. H. Donnelly, *A Preface to Marketing Management* (New York, NY: McGraw Hill), 280.

[23] See Note 5 above.

[24] J. K. Pinto and J. E. Prescott, "Planning and Tactical Factors in the Project Implementation Process," *Journal of Management Studies* 27, no. 3 (1990): 305–327.

[25] S. M. Livesey, "McDonald's and the Environmental Defense Fund: A Case Study of a Green Alliance," *Journal of Business Communication* 36, no. 1 (1999): 5–39.

[26] C. L. Hartman, "Green Alliances: Strategic Relations Between Businesses and Environmental Groups," *Business Horizons* 39, no. 2 (1996): 50–59.

[27] G. T. Savage and others, "Strategies for Assessing and Managing Organizational Stakeholders," *Academy of Management Executive* 5, no. 2 (1991): 61–75.

[28] M. J. Polonsky, "A Stakeholder Theory Approach to Designing Environmental Marketing Strategy," *Journal of Business and Industrial Marketing* 10, no. 3 (1995): 29–46.

[29] M. J. Polonsky and J. Ottman, "Stakeholders' Contribution to the Green New Product Development Process," *Journal of Marketing Management* 14, no. 6 (1998): 533–557.

[30] F. L. Reinhardt, "Bringing the Environment Down to Earth," *Harvard Business Review* 77, no. 4 (1999): 149–158.

[31] R. G. Edmonson, "Exxon Valdez Spill Reaches High Court," *Journal of Commerce* 8, no. 41 (2007): 26–27.

[32] "Banks Buy Into Green Revolution," *Asiamoney* 18, no. 10 (2007): 3.

[33] See Note 15 above.

[34] "More Stockholders Exert Influence," *Wall Street Journal*, May 15, 2008, D3.

[35] L. M. Salamon and H. K. Anheier, *Defining the Nonprofit Sector: A Cross National Analysis* (Manchester, England: Manchester University Press), 526.

[36] P. A. Argenti, "Collaborating With Activists: How Starbucks Works With NGOs," *California Management Review* 47, no. 1 (2004): 91–116.

[37] L. S. Nelson, "Community Sustainability and Land Use," *Public Administration Review* 61, no. 6 (2001): 741–746.

[38] G. Peters, *Waltzing With the Raptors* (New York, NY: John Wiley), 285; J. Elkington, *Cannibals With Forks* (Gabriola Island, BC: New Society Publishers), 407.

[39] See Note 27 above.

The Consumption– Environment Interface

The Environment and Consumption

A. Understand the Interaction Between Environment and Consumption

ASHKELON DESALINATION PLANT

The Middle East offers a perspective on the increasing need to take water conservation more seriously. This region of the world is one of the most arid areas and is largely devoid of drinking water. In Israel and other countries in the region, water is viewed a natural resource of utmost importance. Israel has faced a chronic water shortage for years, and there is speculation that it will be difficult to supply municipal and household water requirements in the near future. The current cumulative deficit in Israel's renewable water resources amounts to about two billion cubic meters—an amount equal to the annual consumption of the country.[1] Human and nonhuman factors contribute to the country's

© DAVID BUIMOVITCH/AFP/Getty Images

FIG. 3-1a

© DAVID BUIMOVITCH/AFP/Getty Images

FIG. 3-1b

The Ashkelon Desalinization Plant and One of Its Employees Enjoying the Fruits of the Labor

water resource problem. The water deficit has developed due to drought conditions as well as to low precipitation levels. In addition, salt and other pollutants
have invaded existing water sources. Increases in growth and development call
for an additional need for about 60% more water by 2020.[2]

In 2000, the Israeli government launched a master plan designed to alleviate the
water problem. The Ashkelon Desalinization Plant was completed in 2005 at a cost
of $212 million. The facility uses a reverse osmosis technology in which seawater is
pushed at high pressure through a membrane that filters out salt molecules and produces clean water. The facility also has an on-site power plant that enables it to
avoid production disruptions incurred on a grid-based power system. Up to 96%
of the energy associated with concentrated saltwater at the end of the purification
process can be captured and used to generate power. The use of the advanced technologies enables the utility to provide water at 52.7 cents per cubic meter, making
the plant one of the world's cheapest producers of desalinated water.[3]

The Ashkelon facility illustrates how governments and organizations can augment
interaction with the environment. To stimulate interest in making further modifications to our interaction with the environment, we identify current trends in the environment in this chapter. If we have an understanding of our current situation,
then we can monitor environmental conditions to track progress. Furthermore, if
we can identify action that influences the environment, we are equipped to act to
reduce our influence.

It is essential to recognize that all commerce and consumption operate within
natural boundaries. Although some natural assets such as wind power are renewable, others (e.g., crude oil) are not sustainable. Sustainable resources can be regenerated, and they offer ecological advantages that limit the firm's reliance on scare
resources. Consequently, effective green marketers increasingly favor adoption of
sustainable technologies and assets.

Today, there is unequivocal evidence of climate change, and human action is a
primary driver of this change.[4] The Earth's temperature has risen 0.74°C in the
last century, and the best estimate for warming over this century is 1.8 to 4.0°C.
Change of this magnitude will have an enormous influence on many aspects of
life. If firms and individuals wish to quell or stop this trend in climate change,
then it is essential to understand our current environmental situation and identify
marketing factors that influence the environment.

Although many people now agree that climate change is occurring, few recognize
how commerce, industrial activity, and consumption directly affect the environment. As a starting point, we outline the influence of marketing activity on climate
change, energy, the atmosphere, water, and land. Our discussion of the atmosphere
addresses ozone depletion and air pollution. Our examination of water includes reviews of freshwater, oceans and fisheries, and water purity. Our analysis of land
examines urban expansion, land degradation, deforestation, desertification, and
waste management.

We distinguish among climatic, atmospheric, water, land, and biodiversity facets
of the environment to provide background on trends in the environment. These environmental issues are interactive rather than independent. Moreover, factors that
have a primary influence on one facet of the environment likely also influence
others. For example, ozone depletion is an aspect of the atmosphere, but it influences water and biodiversity.[5]

B. Human Activity and Climate Change

In 2007, the United Nations reported that 11 of the last 12 years ranked among the warmest years in global surface temperature since 1850. This report underscores the critical level of climate change faced on the planet. Indeed, climate change is shaping up to be the biggest environmental issue that business has ever faced.[6]

Climate change refers to a change in climate attributed directly or indirectly to human activity that alters the composition of the global atmosphere and that is in addition to natural climate variability over comparable periods of time.[7] The Earth is surrounded by a natural blanket of gases that keeps the planet warm enough to sustain life. Solar enegy in the form of visible light that hits the Earth's surface warms the planet. The Earth emits energy back out to space in the form of thermal radiation. Greenhouse gases block the radiation from escaping, resulting in the **natural greenhouse effect**. This natural effect raises the Earth's temperature by approximately 30°C and is essential for life.[8]

Since the beginning of the Industrial Revolution, increasing emissions of greenhouse gases have been making the blanket thicker. This artificial influence on the environment is known as the **enhanced greenhouse effect**. The Earth must rid itself of energy at the same rate at which it receives energy from the sun. As the blanket of greenhouse gases thickens, less energy is lost to space. The system primarily restores balance through global warming of the Earth's lower atmoshere and surface. Thus, increases in greenhouse gases lead to increases in the Earth's surface temperature.

Climate change has several critical influences on the environment that include the following:[9]

a) *Higher temperatures and increased risk.* The climate takes time to respond to emissions, and the response can take decades. Furthermore, oceans absorb and release heat more slowly than the atmosphere does. The result of these effects is higher temperatures for centuries after stabilization of greenhouse gases. A substantial portion of the strain is associated with higher and more frequent temperature spikes such as those that Europe faced in the summer of 2003. Excess mortality in France alone for the August 1 to 15 period was 11,435 deaths.[10] Evidence also suggests that human influence has more than doubled the risk of European mean summer becoming as hot as 2003, with the likelihood of such events to increase a hundredfold over the next four decades.[11]

b) *Decline in the quantity and quality of freshwater.* Rising temperatures influence the level of moisture in the air. Warmer atmospheres hold more moisture and produce more precipitation, especially in the form of heavy cloudbursts. In addition, greater heat speeds up evaporation. Together, these changes in the cycling of water reduce the quantity and quality of freshwater supplies across all major geographic regions.

c) *Increased health risk.* Although climate change likely reduces the number of deaths due to exposure, it generally has a negative effect on health. Climate change alters distribution patterns of malarial mosquitoes and other carriers of infectious diseases. It also affects the seasonal distribution of allergy-causing pollen.

d) *Rising sea levels.* Climate change associated with higher temperatures is resulting in higher sea levels. Evidence indicates that the Antarctic and Greenland ice sheets are losing mass and contributing to rising sea levels. The rise in sea levels over the last 20 years is twice as fast as the average over the 20th century, and the 20th century experienced a growth rate substantially greater than that of the previous two millennia.[12] These rising sea levels increase coastal flooding and erosion.

e) *Threats to biodiversity*. Biodiversity refers to the animal and plant life that surround us. Climate change over the last 30 years has modified the distribution and location of many species. Increases in average temperatures are associated with increasing levels of species extinction such that 20 to 30% of species face an increased risk of extinction.[13] This trend is attributed to shifts in vegetation zones, shifts in ranges of individual species, interaction between climate change and habitat fragmentation, and changes in ecosystem functioning.[14] Species extinction is likely to occur across regions on the planet.

f) *Affects the most vulnerable*. Exposure to climate change is greatest among the poor and those with limited resources to invest in mitigating and preventing effects of climate change.

g) *Displaced people and environmental refugees*. Changes in climate have potential to force departures from the Arctic climates due to lack of biodiversity and degradation of habitat. Simultaneously, climate change may force departures from tropical areas where inhabitants live just above sea level. These trends will lead to increased displacement and higher numbers of environmental refugees.[15]

Climate change also has several direct influences on business that include the following:[16]

a) *Agriculture*. Rising temperatures and volatile weather patterns adversely affect the agricultural sector and complicate efforts to speculate on future values of agricultural-based commodities (e.g., frozen orange juice, pork bellies).

b) *Tourism*. Winter- and summer-based tourism sites stand to lose considerably due to climate change. Rising temperatures eliminate ski resorts and rising sea levels *drown* beaches. In addition, severe thunderstorms are problematic for airlines and other transportation systems.

c) *Insurance*. The insurance industry is particularly susceptible to climate change. As the premiums and costs associated with underwriting policies become more difficult to assess, costs increase and the number of providers decreases.

d) *Transportation and related costs*. As climate change increases, government will likely act to control greenhouse gas emissions. Consequently, industries that have heavy transportation needs (e.g., automobile production) face higher costs of operation. Similarly, industries that use petroleum-related raw materials (e.g., plastics production) face greater costs.

e) *New product/solution development*. Although climate change has many negative consequences, it presents enormous opportunities for entrepreneurs that develop technologies, services, and products. Consumer demand for products that reduce energy costs or eliminate the need to rely on carbon-based fuels will receive greater attention.

Given its strong influence on the environment, it is essential to examine factors that accelerate the extent of climate change. We distinguish among three types of gases that influence the environment.[17] Gases with a direct influence on climate change include naturally occurring gases and synthetic gases that are the result of industrial activity. The natural gases include carbon dioxide (CO_2), methane (CH_4), and nitrous oxide (N_2O). Synthetic gases include hydrofluourocarbons (HFCs), perflourocarbons (PFCs), and sulfur hexafluoride (SF_6). These fluorinated gases are also referred to as **F gases**.

Some gases do not have a direct effect on global warming but influence the formation and destruction of other greenhouse gases, including carbon monoxide (CO), oxides of nitrogen (NO_x), and nonmethane volatile organic compounds. Figure 3-2 indicates increases in gases with a direct effect on climate change over

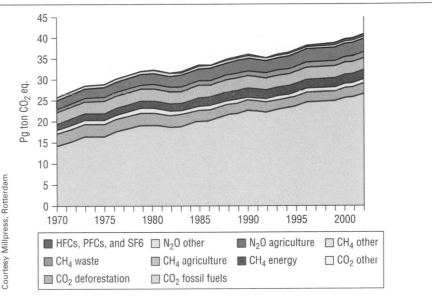

FIG. 3-2 Trend in Global Emissions of Greenhouse Gases 1970–2002

Courtesy Millpress, Rotterdam

Source: *Olivier, Jospeh G.J., John A. van Aardenne, Frank Dentener, and Laurens Ganzeveld "Recent trends in global greenhouse gas emissions: regional trends and spatial distribution of key sources," http://www.mnp.nl/edgar/Images/Olivier2005-FT2000-NCGG4-Utrecht_tcm32-22124.pdf, (February 17, 2010).*

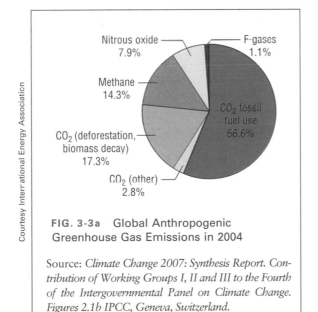

FIG. 3-3a Global Anthropogenic Greenhouse Gas Emissions in 2004

Courtesy International Energy Association

Source: *Climate Change 2007: Synthesis Report. Contribution of Working Groups I, II and III to the Fourth of the Intergovernmental Panel on Climate Change. Figures 2.1b IPCC, Geneva, Switzerland.*

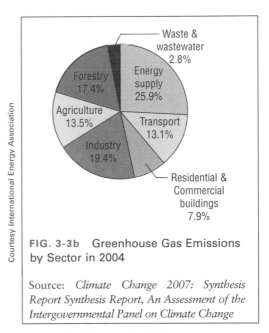

FIG. 3-3b Greenhouse Gas Emissions by Sector in 2004

Courtesy International Energy Association

Source: *Climate Change 2007: Synthesis Report Synthesis Report, An Assessment of the Intergovernmental Panel on Climate Change*

Source: *http://www.iea.org/Papers/2008/Indicators_2008.pdf (February 10, 2010).*

the 1970 to 2002 horizon. Over this 30-year period, greenhouse gas emissions increased by 60%. Figure 3-3a provides an overview of the emissions for each gas with direct influences on global warming.

Figure 3-3b indicates the global sources of these greenhouse gases by industrial sector. Energy accounts for more than 25% of greenhouse emissions, and a

TABLE 3-1	GLOBAL WARMING POTENTIALS (100-YEAR TIME HORIZON)[18]				
GAS		**GLOBAL WARMING POTENTIAL**	**GAS**		**GLOBAL WARMING POTENTIAL**
CO_2	Carbon dioxide	1	HFC-227ea	F-gas	2,900
CH_4	Methane	21	HFC-236fa	F-gas	6,300
N_2O	Nitrous oxide	310	HFC-4310mee	F-gas	1,300
HFC-23	F-gas	11,700	CF_4	F-gas	6,500
HFC-32	F-gas	650	C_2F_6	F-gas	9,200
HFC-125	F-gas	2,800	C_4F_{10}	F-gas	7,000
HFC-134a	F-gas	1,300	C_6F_{14}	F-gas	7,400
HFC-143a	F-gas	3,800	SF_6	F-gas	23,900
HFC-152a	F-gas	140			

Source: United States Environmental Protection Agency.

substantial portion of these emissions are associated with coal. The industrial sector represents the second largest contributor at 19.4%. Forestry, including deforestation and decay from logging and deforestation, accounts for another 17.4%, whereas agriculture accounts for 13.5%. The transportation sector, by contrast, represents 13.1% of greenhouse gas emissions.

In order to compare gases, scientists have developed an index of global warming potential that compares the ability of a greenhouse gas to trap heat in the atmosphere relative to carbon dioxide emissions. Table 3-1 identifies the global warming potential of greenhouse gases with a direct effect on the climate. Thus, sulfur hexafluoride has 23,900 times the warming potential as an equivalent amount of carbon dioxide.

Carbon Dioxide

Carbon dioxide (CO_2) accounts for more than 80% of the greenhouse emissions worldwide. Since 1750, global atmospheric concentrations of carbon dioxide have increased by about 35%.[19] Currently, China has the largest emissions of any country, yet the United States has the largest emissions per capita. The two countries alone account for 40% of carbon dioxide emissions, with Europe providing an additional 15%.[20]

In the United States, emissions have risen by 15.8% over the 1990 to 2004 period.[21] Factors that contribute to this increase include a growing domestic economy as well as significant increases in emissions from electricity generation and transportation. As Figure 3-4 illustrates, the burning of fossil fuels represents the largest source of greenhouse emissions in the United States. Coal used to generate electricity represents the single largest contributor to carbon dioxide emissions. Petroleum used in transportation also contributes substantially to carbon dioxide emissions (see Figure 3-5). Iron and steel production and cement manufacture also contribute significantly to carbon dioxide emissions. Reductions in domestic production of pig iron, sinter, and coal coke contribute to a 40% reduction in iron- and steel-related carbon dioxide emissions since 1990. By contrast, carbon dioxide emissions associated with cement production have risen 37% since 1990.

Waste combustion is also a significant contributor to carbon dioxide emissions. Due in part to the increased amounts of plastics and other fossil carbon-containing materials in municipal solid waste, the amount of waste combustion-based carbon dioxide emissions has increased by 77% since 1990.

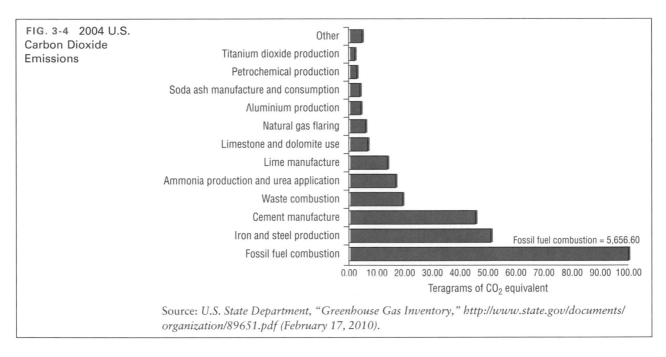

FIG. 3-4 2004 U.S. Carbon Dioxide Emissions

Source: *U.S. State Department, "Greenhouse Gas Inventory," http://www.state.gov/documents/organization/89651.pdf (February 17, 2010).*

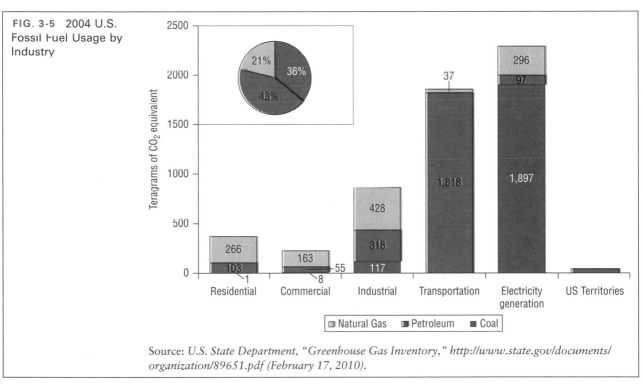

FIG. 3-5 2004 U.S. Fossil Fuel Usage by Industry

Source: *U.S. State Department, "Greenhouse Gas Inventory," http://www.state.gov/documents/organization/89651.pdf (February 17, 2010).*

Methane

Methane (CH_4) is the second-largest contributor to greenhouse gas emissions. As Table 3-1 illustrates, methane is more than 20 times as effective as carbon dioxide at trapping heat in the atmosphere. Since 1750, methane emissions have increased by 143%.[22] Landfills represent the largest manmade sources of methane emissions at 25% of U.S. output. Although the amount of solid waste continues to increase, methane levels are declining due to the portion that is captured and burned at landfills. Similarly, methane emissions from natural gas systems (6% of total CH_4) are in decline due to improvements in technology and management practices. **Enteric fermentation** refers to intestinal processing of methane associated with the digestion process for cattle. This source is also in decline due to decreases in populations of beef and dairy cattle as well as improved feed quality for cattle.[23]

Nitrous Oxide

Nitrous oxide (N_2O) is the third-largest contributor to greenhouse gas emissions. Although emissions are substantially lower than those of carbon dioxide, nitrous oxide is 310 times more powerful than CO_2 in its ability to trap heat in the atmosphere (see Table 3-1). Since the Industrial Revolution (i.e., about 1750), nitrous oxide emissions have increased by approximately 25%. Fertilizer applications and related soil management practices account for 68% of N_2O emissions in the United States. Historical data do not indicate long-term increases or decreases in this source of emissions. The second source of nitrous emissions is in mobile combustion. Over the last decade, control technologies have been developed that yield a steady drop in N_2O emission associated with mobile sources.

Fluorinated Gases

F-gases is a collective term that describes hydrofluourocarbons (HFCs), perflourocarbons (PFCs), and sulfur hexafluoride (SF_6). In contrast to the previous three gases, which occur naturally in the atmosphere, F-gases are produced almost exclusively via industrial activity. These gases represent about 2.0% of U.S. emissions, but they have global warming potentials that range from 140 (HFC-152a) to 23,900 times the potential for carbon dioxide. In addition, sulfur dioxide and

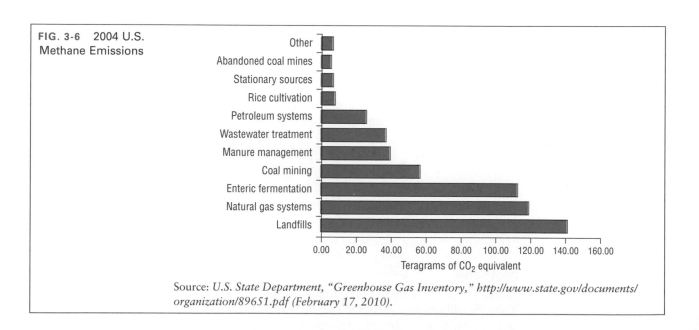

FIG. 3-6   2004 U.S. Methane Emissions

Source: *U.S. State Department, "Greenhouse Gas Inventory," http://www.state.gov/documents/organization/89651.pdf (February 17, 2010).*

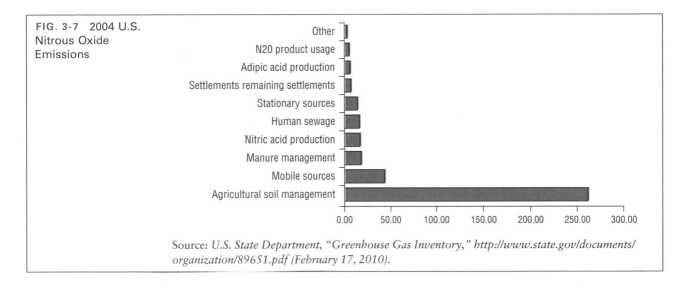

FIG. 3-7 2004 U.S. Nitrous Oxide Emissions

Source: *U.S. State Department, "Greenhouse Gas Inventory," http://www.state.gov/documents/organization/89651.pdf (February 17, 2010).*

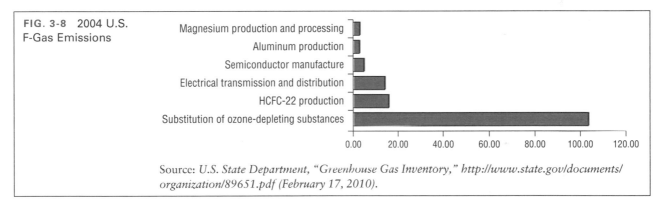

FIG. 3-8 2004 U.S. F-Gas Emissions

Source: *U.S. State Department, "Greenhouse Gas Inventory," http://www.state.gov/documents/organization/89651.pdf (February 17, 2010).*

PFCs have long atmospheric lifetimes that result in nearly irreversible atmospheric accumulation once emitted.

The largest and fastest growing source of HFCs and PFCs is via their use as alternatives to ozone-depleting substances (ODS). Emissions of these gases have increased markedly since the **Montreal Protocol** came into effect, requiring the phase-out of ODSs. Nevertheless, increases associated with substitution for ODSs are offset by decreases in F-gas emissions from other sources. For example, the aluminum industry reduced F-gas production by 85% over the 1990 to 2004 era. In addition, emissions from electrical transmission and distribution fell by 52% from 1990 to 2004. These reductions are associated with industry efforts to reduce emissions and higher purchase prices for sulfur dioxide.

C. Understand Sources of Energy and Their Use Across International Regions

The examination of energy use complements the analysis of climate change because many of the antecedents to climate change are energy related. Figure 3-9 illustrates how the mix of energy sources has evolved worldwide since 1973. Although it

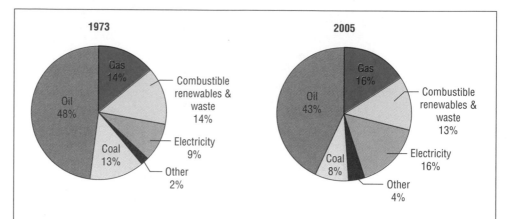

FIG. 3-9 Evolution From 1973 to 2005 of World Total Primary Energy Consumption by Fuel (MTOE = million tons of oil equivalency)

Source: *Key World Energy Statistics* © OECD/IEA, 2007, page 28. *http://www.iea.org/ textbase/nppdf/free/2007/key_stats_2007.pdf (accessed July 31, 2008).*

represents a smaller portion of the energy supply than it once did, at 43.4%, oil remains the primary energy source used worldwide. Oil consumption remains high due to the rising transportation sector (i.e., increasers in passenger travel and freight transport) and expansion in the service economy.[24] Coal and gas together account for another 23.9% of consumption. Electricity usage is increasing and now represents 16.3% of fuel consumption. Combustible renewables and waste that are primarily employed in emerging economies account for 12.9% of consumption. The remaining 3.5% includes geothermal, solar, wind, and heat power. Although there have been substantial strides in these sources of energy, they currently represent a small fraction of consumption.

Review of the data from 1990 through 2005 reveals some intriguing trends. The data underscore the merits of contrasting energy use in OECD (Organization for Economic Co-operation and Development) countries (Australia, Austria, Belgium, Canada, the Czech Republic, Denmark, Finland, France, Germany, Greece, Hungary, Iceland, Ireland, Italy, Japan, Korea, Luxembourg, Mexico, the Netherlands, New Zealand, Norway, Poland, Portugal, the Slovak Republic, Spain, Sweden, Switzerland, Turkey, the United Kingdom, and the United States) and the rest of the world. The final energy usage per unit of gross domestic product has fallen by 26% during this era. Most of these reductions associated with structural changes and efficiency improvements are in non-OECD countries. Although energy use increased by 23%, the associated carbon dioxide emissions rose by 25%. Most of the growth in energy usage and CO_2 emissions occurred outside of OECD countries.

The data outlined in Figure 3-10 also indicate differences between energy use and forms of energy employed in OECD countries versus the rest of the world. Final energy use grew by 19% in the OECD, whereas the growth in energy use outside the region was 27%. Transportation represents the highest percentage of energy use in the OECD at 35%, yet the sector only accounts for 17% of usage outside the OECD. The manufacturing sector in the OECD uses 27% of the energy, but outside of the

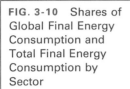

FIG. 3-10 Shares of Global Final Energy Consumption and Total Final Energy Consumption by Sector

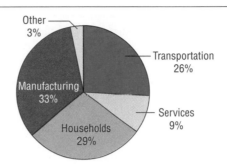

Other
3%

Transportation
26%

Manufacturing
33%

Services
9%

Households
29%

Source: *Worldwide Trends in Energy Use and Efficiency: Key Insights from IEA Indicator Analysis* © OECD/IEA, 2008, figures 2.1 and 2.2, page 17.

OECD this percentage increases to 38%. At 36% of energy consumption, the household sector represents as substantial portion of energy use outside the OECD.

The usage rates are related to the forms of energy that are used in the OECD versus the rest of the world. Due to the importance of transportation, oil represents 47% of energy used in the OECD, yet it only represents 28% outside the bloc. Electricity represents 22% of the energy employed in the OECD, yet only 14% outside of the OECD. Biomass, including wood, agricultural residue, and animal dung, remains an important source of fuel outside the OECD, where more than 2.4 billion people still rely on these energy sources.

D. Human Activity and the Atmosphere

Ozone depletion, and air pollution are facets of the atmosphere influenced by consumption. Consider first the extent of ozone depletion.

Ozone

Ozone is a form of oxygen naturally occurring in the atmosphere. In contrast to the typical oxygen molecule that has two oxygen atoms, the ozone molecule contains three atoms and is labeled O_3. Ozone is observed in two regions of the atmosphere. Approximately 10% of ozone is in the troposphere, the region closer to Earth. This area ranges from the Earth's surface to about 6 miles in altitude.[25] Ozone appearing in this level is an air pollutant that is harmful to breathe and is harmful to crops, trees, and other vegetation. Ozone is the main ingredient in smog.

The remaining 90% of the ozone resides in the stratosphere. This second region ranges from the top of the troposphere to about 31 miles in altitude. The large amount of ozone in the stratosphere is often referred to as the **ozone layer**. Ozone in this layer absorbs some of the sun's biologically harmful ultraviolet (UV) radiation.[26] Depletion of this ozone leads to increased amounts of UV radiation reaching the Earth, which leads to more cases of skin cancer, cataracts, and impaired immune systems. Overexposure to UV radiation is believed to be contributing to the increase in melanoma, the most fatal of all skin cancers. UV radiation can also damage sensitive crops, such as soybeans, and reduce crop yields.[27]

The human activity that contributes to ozone depletion involves use of gases containing the halogens chlorine and bromine. Figure 3-11 provides an overview of

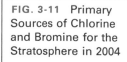

FIG. 3-11 Primary Sources of Chlorine and Bromine for the Stratosphere in 2004

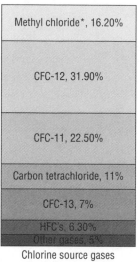

Chlorine source gases

Bromine source gases

*Indicates natural rather than human production.

Source: *From TWENTY QUESTIONS AND ANSWERS ABOUT THE OZONE LAYER: 2006 UPDATE. Lead author: D. W. Fahey. © 2006 United Nations. Reprinted with the permission of the United Nations. http://ozone.unep.org/Assessment_Panels/SAP/Scientific_Assessment_2006/ Twenty_Questions.pdf (accessed February 19, 2010).*

chlorine- and bromine-based ozone-depleting halogens in the stratosphere. Chlorine is a component of CFCs used in refrigerators and air conditioners. Carbon tetrachloride, methyl chloride, and methyl chloroform are also chlorine-based halogens. Bromine-based halogens include halons used in fire extinguishers, large-scale computers, military hardware, and commercial aircraft engines. Methyl bromide used as an agricultural fumigant is also a bromine-based halogen.

After these halogens have been emitted into the atmosphere, they accumulate in the troposphere and are transported to the stratosphere. Once in the stratosphere, these halogen gases are converted to reactive agents by the sun's ultraviolet radiation. The average emission of these gases into the stratosphere is smaller in tropical regions. Emissions in arctic regions are more pronounced, and this effect is more acute during winter and spring. Unique weather and atmospheric conditions in Antarctica result in an ozone hole in this region.

Air Pollution

Air pollution is a global health concern with marked influence on humans and the environment. Regulatory agents use six factors known as **criteria pollutants** to establish air quality levels.[28] These factors include sulfur dioxide, nitrogen dioxide, carbon monoxide, ozone oxygen, lead, and particulate matter (PM). Particulate matter includes chemical compounds (sulphate, nitrate, ammonium, organic carbon, elemental carbon, and soil dust), heavy metals (arsenic, cadmium, mercury), volatile organic compounds (e.g., benzene), polycyclic aromatic hydrocarbons, and persistent organic pollutants (dioxins and furans). Most forms of particulate matter become pollutants through the burning of fossil fuels, biomass, and solid waste, whereas ammonium as a pollutant primarily derives from agriculture.

It is important to distinguish between outdoor and indoor pollution. Outdoor air pollution accounts for 1.4% of total global mortality and amounts to 800,000 deaths annually. Eighty-one percent of the mortality occurs in people 60 years of age or older. The incidence of death is strongly related to geography: 49% of the deaths occur in the region that includes Bangladesh, Bhutan, Democratic People's Republic of Korea, India, Maldives, Myanmar, Nepal, or Timor Leste. Another 19% of deaths occur in Southeast Asia. In addition to the mortality data, outdoor pollution increases hospitalization and emergency room visits, asthma attacks, bronchitis, respiratory symptoms, and lost work days.[29]

Indoor air pollution is the more egregious form of airborne contamination because it is implicated in more than 1.6 million deaths per year.[30] In addition, indoor pollution is associated with higher incidences of acute lower respiratory infections, chronic obstructive pulmonary disease, and lung cancer.[31] The incidence of death related to indoor air pollution is related to geography. Indoor air pollution is responsible for 1.2 million deaths per year in Afghanistan, Angola, Bangladesh, Burkina Faso, China, the Democratic Republic of the Congo, Ethiopia, India, Nigeria, Pakistan, and the United Republic of Tanzania. Moreover, in the 21 most affected countries (Afghanistan, Angola, Benin, Burkina Faso, Burundi, Cameroon, Chad, the Democratic Republic of the Congo, Eritrea, Ethiopia, Madagascar, Malawi, Mali, Mauritania, Niger, Pakistan, Rwanda, Senegal, Sierra Leone, Togo, and Uganda), indoor air pollution is implicated as the cause of 5% or more of the total burden of disease.[32]

The likelihood of experiencing health problems due to indoor air pollution is associated with income, gender, and age. Figure 3-12 outlines the relationship between prosperity and fuel usage. Electricity is used in the most affluent societies and is relatively clean and efficient. By contrast, the crop waste and wood used in emerging economies is relatively unclean and inefficient. These fuels produce indoor smoke with several health-damaging pollutants including particulate matter, carbon monoxide, nitrous oxides, sulfur oxides, formaldehyde, and carcinogens (chemical substances that increase the risk of cancer).[33]

In many countries, women bear the primary responsibility for food preparation. In emerging economies, women typically cook with crop waste or wood.

FIG. 3-12 Relationship of Prosperity With Fuel Cleanliness, Efficiency, Cost, and Convenience.

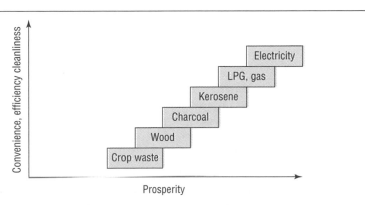

Source: *World Health Organization, http://www.who.int/mediacentre/events/HSD_Plaq_10.pdf (accessed July 30, 2008).*

Wood provides around 15% of energy needs in developing countries, rising to 75% in tropical Africa. In more than 30 countries, wood still provides more than 70% of energy, and in 13 countries it is more than 90%. Because women do the majority of the cooking, they are more susceptible to indoor air pollution than men are. In addition, young children present during cooking are exposed to indoor smoke. This air pollution increases the risk of chronic obstructive pulmonary disease, the leading cause of death among children under 5 years of age in developing countries.[34]

Air pollution has a number of ancillary environmental effects. First, the level of ozone in the troposphere results in crop losses in Europe alone that exceed $5 billion annually. Second, acid rain associated with sulfur and nitrogen historically leads to lake acidification and forest decline in North America and Europe. Although this trend has been markedly reduced, there is growing concern about acidification in other regions, notably Asia. Finally, nitrogen deposits continue to drive losses in the number of species present in sensitive ecosystems. These settings include heaths, bogs, and mires in North America and Europe.

E. Human Activity and Water

Access to Clean Drinking Water

Water is essential for life, yet the influence of consumption on water use is not well understood. Ninety-seven percent of the world's water supply is saline, leaving 3% freshwater.[35] Almost 70% of the freshwater is frozen in the icecaps of Antarctica and Greenland. The remainder is primarily present as soil moisture or lies in deep underground aquifers as groundwater not accessible to human use. Less than 1% of the world's water is available for human use. This water is found in lakes, rivers, reservoirs, and underground sources shallow enough to be tapped at an affordable cost. The three primary uses of freshwater include irrigation (70%), industry (20%), and residential purposes (10%).[36]

The availability of freshwater is related to geographic location. The World Health Organization estimates that one sixth of the world's population does not have access to clean drinking water, whereas two fifths of the world population lacks access to adequate sanitation services.[37] Figures 3-13a and 3-13b illustrate the distribution of this population across the globe. The data underscore the magnitude of the problem in Asia and Africa. These water issues are particularly problematic for people living in rural areas. Sanitation coverage in rural areas is less than half that of urban settings such that 1.3 billion rural inhabitants face poor sanitation in India and China alone.

Although there are deep underground aquifers that can be drilled for human use, only lakes, rivers, reservoirs, and shallow underground sources are renewed by rain and snowfall. Consequently, only this freshwater is available on a sustainable basis.[38]

Several critical consequences of inadequate and unsanitary water include the following:

a) *Falling water tables.* While freshwater derived from lakes, rivers, and shallow underground resources is replenishable, water from connate or fossil aquifers cannot be recharged.[39] The Ogallala aquifer in the United States, the deep aquifer in the North China Plain, and the Saudi aquifer are prime examples of such water repositories. Because these aquifers cannot be replenished, their depletion means

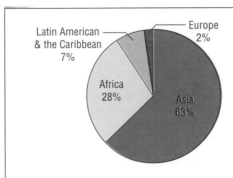

FIG. 3-13a Distribution of Global Population Not Served With Improved Water Supply by Region

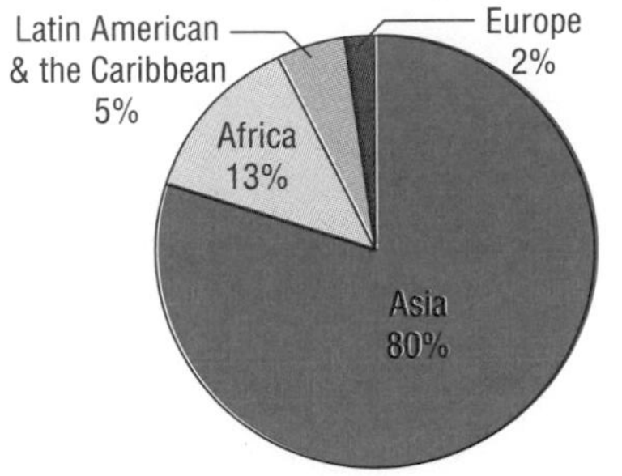

FIG. 3-13b Distribution of Global Population Not Served With Improved Sanitation Supply by Region

Source: *World Health Organization (2000), Global Water Supply and Sanitation Assessment 2000 Report, Geneva, Switzerland: World Health Organization, 7. http://www.who.int/water_sanitation_health/monitoring/jmp2000.pdf (February 10, 2010).*

the end of irrigation and, consequently, a marked change in or end of agriculture in the dependent areas.[40]

b) *Floods and droughts.* Too much water and too little water are the result of variability in the hydrologic cycle influenced by climate change and alterations in land use patterns.[41] Australia, Bangladesh, India, China, Somalia, the United States, and many European countries experienced severe flooding during the last decade of the 20th century, and there is evidence that the number of flood and drought disasters is increasing.[42]

c) *Disease.* Figure 3-14 outlines the global burden of disease associated with lack of adequate water. The World Health Organization estimates that 1.4 million children die every year due to diarrhea acquired due to unsafe water, inadequate sanitation, or insufficient hygiene.[43] Inadequate water supplies raise the number of fatalities associated with malnutrition, malaria, drowning, and other diseases.

d) *Farmers losing to cities.* The economics of production do not favor agriculture over other industries when water is considered. For example, it takes 14 tons of water to make a ton of steel worth $560, yet it takes 1,000 tons of water to

FIG. 3-14 Diseases Contributing to the Water-, Sanitation-, and Hygiene-related Disease Burdens

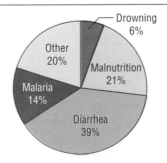

Source: *A. Prüss-Üstün, R. Bos, F. Gore, and J. Bartram,* Safer Water, Better Health: Costs, Benefits and Sustainability of Interventions to Protect and Promote Health, *(Geneva, Switzerland: World Health Organization, 2008): p. 7.*

grow a ton of wheat worth $200.[44] Countries focused on expanding their economies and creating jobs are increasingly favoring industry over agriculture.

e) *Political tension.* The water resources of the 232 international rivers that exist today are ordinarily shared by several countries.[45] The Jordan, Ganges, Colorado, Nile, Zambezi, Amazon, Danube, and Rhine are all examples of international rivers. Conflicts occur between nations due to water scarcity, inadequate distribution, or due to a lack of agreements for distribution.

Factors that contribute to inadequate and unsanitary water include the following:

a) *Population growth and urbanization.* Increases in population are highly related to water resources. As the population increases, land, clean water, and other natural resources become scarce. Moreover, urbanization exacerbates this problem because growing cities demand increases in the water supply.[46] Estimates suggest that the population will increase by 3 billion people by 2050, with the great majority of this increase in urban areas.[47]

b) *Poverty and low human development.* Not surprisingly, the level of poverty and the extent of human development are associated with the water supply. The impoverished are exposed to malnutrition, unclean water, and inadequate sanitation services.[48] Improved education constrains the influences of the environment, yet individuals in many emerging economies do not have access to higher education.

c) *Food security.* Food security refers to access by all people at all times to enough food for an active, healthy life. It includes the ready availability of nutritionally adequate and safe foods as well as the assured ability to acquire personally acceptable foods in a socially acceptable way.[49] Food insecurity affects one out of every six people on the planet.[50] Although food production has increased in many parts of the world over the past few decades, malnutrition remains a problem due to rapid population growth and urbanization.

Oceans and Fisheries

Oceans. Consumption has a marked influence on oceans and fisheries. Mounting evidence indicates that the arctic is warming twice as fast as the rest of the planet is, with the summer sea ice shrinking at 9.1% a decade from 1979 to 2006.[51] At this rate, the sea could be ice free as early as 2030.[52] Nevertheless, substantially more heat is absorbed through water rather than through ice, leading to the melting of the Greenland ice sheet. As the ice melts, some water filters through cracks in glaciers and increases the break-off of icebergs into the ocean. A similar process is occurring in Antarctica, and together these trends indicate potential for rising sea levels. If the sea were to rise 10 meters, one eighth of the world's population would be vulnerable.[53] China, India, Bangladesh, Viet Nam, Indonesia, Japan, Egypt, and the United States would have millions of potential climate change refugees. Some of the world's largest cities—New York, London, Shanghai, and Calcutta—would be partially or totally inundated, and considerable amounts of productive farmland would be lost.

Rivers. Over the past half century, the demand for water has tripled, and the demand for hydroelectric power has grown even faster.[54] Consequently, the worldwide number of dams more than 15 meters high has increased to 45,000 from 5,000. These dams deprive rivers of some of their flow, and the associated evaporation is 10% of their capacities.[55] For example, Colorado River water usage by

Colorado, Utah, California, Arizona, and Nevada results in very little water reaching the Gulf of California. Similar conditions on multiple continents markedly inhibit river ecosystems and their fisheries.

Lakes. On every continent, lakes are shrinking and in some cases disappearing as a result of consumption. The dissolution of lakes is due to excessive diversion of water from rivers and the overpumping of aquifers.[56] For example, the Aral Sea in Central Asia has lost four fifths of its volume since 1960. Expansion of the Soviet cotton industry led to the diversion of two rivers from the sea. As the sea shrank and the water became more saline, the fish died, along with a maritime industry that produced 50,000 tons of seafood annually.

Water Impurities

Unless it has been distilled, water is not pure. Water impurities emerge from naturally occurring substances, agriculture, urbanization, industry, and water treatment.[57] Consider first naturally occurring substances.

Naturally occurring substances. Substances that occur in nature that influence water purity include inorganic and organic materials. Inorganic materials are those that do not contain carbon. These chemicals accrue due to the flowing of water over rocks and soil. Four substances known to be associated with adverse health effects are fluoride, arsenic, selenium, and nitrate. Given their adverse health consequences, it is essential to monitor their levels prior to examining human influence. The pH level of the water should also be monitored because influence of these chemicals is exacerbated by the level of acidity in the water. Organic compounds (i.e., chemicals that contain carbon) emerge from the breakdown of plants or algae and other microorganisms.

Agriculture. The farming sector plays a significant role in the quality of water because agricultural runoff is the leading source of impurities in lakes and rivers.[58] *Fertilizer* in the form of manure or human excrement increases levels of nitrates, ammonium salts, and organic nitrogen compounds, whereas chemical fertilizers increase nitrogen levels when these nutrients are used in excess. Biosolids used as fertilizer are treated residues from industrial or municipal waste or septic soil. These biosolids similarly lead to increased nitrate levels in water. *Animal practices* such as feedlots produce large amounts of waste that also lead to higher levels of nitrates. *Pesticides* refers to a broad mix of chemicals that have chemical and physical properties that contribute to runoff. *Irrigation and drainage* transport pollutants and alter salt balances in soil. Consequently, they raise the level of nitrates and selenium in soil.

Urbanization. The increasing population in urban areas is traced to three categories of contaminant sources. **Point sources** refers to pollution discharged from a specific location and includes on-site sanitation waste disposal locations. These point sources increase levels of nitrate and ammonium in water. **Nonpoint sources** are widely spread and difficult to identify as origins of pollutants. Three primary forms of nonpoint polluters are fuel storage locations, chlorinated solvents, and pesticides. **Diffuse point sources** refers to conditions under which there are many small point sources. For example, urban runoff from small point sources raises levels of nitrates, ammonium, and heavy metals in water.

Industry. Industrial practices include mining and manufacturing. Mining increases multiple types of metals in water, including arsenic, antimony, barium, cadmium, fluoride, and nickel. Manufacturing and processing of materials contribute a variety of chemicals with diverse properties that influence water purity.

Water treatment. Ironically, the efforts to treat water can also contribute impurities. **Chlorine** is used as a disinfectant in the purification process, but in excess it reacts naturally with organic matter to produce unwanted by-products such as chloroform. **Coagulants** such as aluminum and iron salts are important barriers to microbiological contaminants. Although these chemicals are not significant health risks, they may lead to discoloration or sediment. **Conveyors** are the pipes and fittings used to transport water. The most common conveyor is iron, a substance prone to corrosion. Corrosion due to low alkalinity, sediment, and microbes yields to water discoloration. Lead, copper, and zinc are also conveyors that may be present in water. Although lead is more likely to be present at unacceptable levels, copper and zinc are more prevalent in newer buildings. Finally, polyvinyl chloride (PVC) is a form of plastic often used as a conveyor of water. Because lead is often used as a stabilizer for PVC, use of this material may lead to elevated levels of lead.

F. Human Activity and Land

Urban Expansion

Urban expansion refers to the increasing use of land associated with increases in urban populations. In 2007, the urban population on the planet exceeded the rural population for the first time.[59] Current estimates project that the population in developing countries' cities will double in the next 30 years from 2 to 4 billion people. These cities will likely triple their land area. By contrast, the urban population in industrialized countries is expected to grow by 11% from 0.9 to 1 billion people over the same period. Urban land use in these areas is expected to grow by 2.5 times over the next 30-year period.

Research examining of the role of urbanization indicates that many factors are associated with the rise in urban population. Urbanization may be both the cause and the consequence of these factors. Forces that seem to shape expansion include aspects of the local natural environment (e.g., existence of drillable water aquifers), demographic factors (e.g., level of urbanization in a country), economics (e.g., property taxes), prevailing transport systems, consumer preferences (e.g., preference for urbanism), and metropolitan governance. **Greenfield development** refers to construction on a previously unused piece of property. This type of development has been implicated as a factor that yields air pollution, excessive energy use, greenhouse gas production, and traffic congestion. Furthermore, cities draw upon rural areas for water and waste disposal. As cities increase their land masses, the interaction with the environment must remain a central concern.

Land Degradation

Land degradation is a collective term that refers to the long-term loss of ecosystem function and services due to disturbances from which the systems cannot recover unaided.[60] Current estimates indicate significant land degradation of 12% of the global land area over the past quarter century. This land area is home to about 1 billion people. The primary areas of concern for degradation are subequatorial Africa, southeast Asia, south China, north central Australia, Central America, the Caribbean, and southeast Brazil, as well as the boreal forests of Alaska, Canada, and Siberia.

The degradation of land has direct and indirect consequences.[61] The direct effects include losses of organic soil carbon, soil water storage, nutrients, and below-ground biodiversity. The decline in water resources brings about indirect effects that include loss of wildlife habitat and loss of productive capacity.

Two factors that give rise to land degradation are soil erosion and chemical contamination. Soil erosion is a naturally occurring phenomenon that is accelerated by improper land management. Erosion is catalyzed by clearing of forests or grasslands, mining, and urban development. When these activities are improperly managed, topsoil is lost. Consequently, the area experiences losses of soil organic matter, nutrients, water holding capacity, and biodiversity. Chemical pollutants are problematic in industrialized economies and developing markets. Industrial centers of the 20th century in the United States, Europe, and former Soviet Union contain more than 2 million contaminated sites containing cyanide, heavy metals, mineral oil, and chlorinated hydrocarbons. Chemical contaminants also include persistent organic pollutants (POPs) such as the insecticide DDT that persist in the environment for long periods. POPs have been linked to cancer, damage to the nervous system, reproductive disorders, and disruption of the immune system.[62]

Deforestation and Desertification

Forests are important parts of ecosystems that sustain life. Forests prevent soil erosion, maintain soil fertility, support biodiversity, and provide homeopathic and traditional medicines. Furthermore, forests support local economies and provide important sources of fuel. Over the past 15 years, the global forest area has shrunk at an annual rate of 0.2%. Although the forest area has expanded in Europe and North America, deforestation has been observed in Africa, Latin America, and the Caribbean. The 10 countries with the largest net forest loss per year between 2000 and 2005 are Brazil, Indonesia, Sudan, Myanmar, Zambia, United Republic of Tanzania, Nigeria, Democratic Republic of the Congo, Zimbabwe, and Venezuela. These countries had a combined net forest loss of 8.2 million hectares per year. By contrast, Bulgaria, Chile, China, Cuba, France, Italy, Portugal, Spain, the United States, and Vietnam, had a combined net forest gain of 5.1 million hectares per year.

Deforestation is associated with several factors.[63] In many cases, trees are removed from forests for use as fuel or as raw materials in production. Deforestation also occurs due to climate change, disease, invasive species, pests, and air pollution. Economic factors—notably agriculture and mining—increase the level of deforestation. Demographic trends such as changes in population density and urbanization raise demands for timber and firewood, and they increase the demand for water resources. The demographic trends increase the amount of deforestation.

Increased deforestation has several notable consequences for the environment.[64] Reductions in forest acreage result in loss of habitat and consequently lead to limited biodiversity. Deforestation reduces the amount of stored carbon and disturbs biological cycles. In addition, fewer forests mean diminished water resources, lower water quality, and less soil water retention.

Desertification refers to land degradation in arid, semiarid, or dry subhumid areas due to climatic variations and human activities.[65] When individual land degradation processes combine to affect large areas of drylands, desertification occurs.[66] Populations living in poor countries suffer the most due to desertification. Across the globe, drylands cover 40% of the Earth's land surface and support more than 2 billion people. Although 90% of this population lives in developing countries, Western countries are also vulnerable to deforestation. Figure 3-15 provides an overview of global drylands. One third of the Mediterranean and 85% of the rangeland in the United States are susceptible to deforestation.

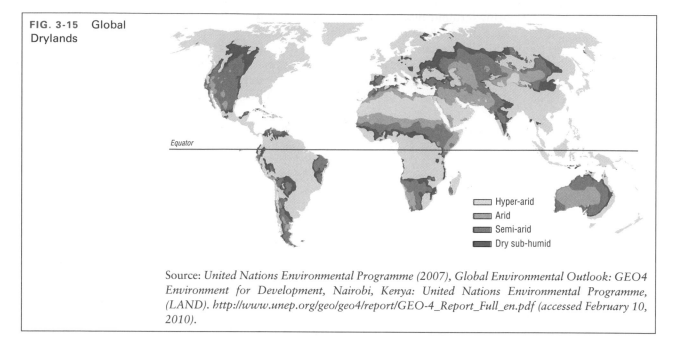

FIG. 3-15 Global Drylands

Source: *United Nations Environmental Programme (2007), Global Environmental Outlook: GEO4 Environment for Development, Nairobi, Kenya: United Nations Environmental Programme, (LAND). http://www.unep.org/geo/geo4/report/GEO-4_Report_Full_en.pdf (accessed February 10, 2010).*

Because desertification occurs over a prolonged period of time in large areas, there is not a consistent measure to chart transition to deserts. The direct cause of deforestation is usually the expansion of cropping, grazing, or wood harvesting. As the level of deforestation increases, ecosystems become less resilient to other environmental conditions.

Global concerns about deforestation have important repercussions for every company that uses wood, paper, or cardboard packaging.[67] Although activists initially targeted prominent retailers about their packaging, today these organizations are focused on a broader mix of companies that use wood-related products in production, marketing, and distribution.

G. Human Activity and Biodiversity

Biodiversity refers to the variety of life on Earth.[68] It includes genetic diversity among individual beings in a population, diversity of species, and diversity of ecosystems and habitats. Biodiversity is the basis of agriculture in that it enables the production of wild and cultivated foods while also contributing to the health and nutrition of humans, animals, and plants.

Biodiversity provides provisional, regulatory, supportive, and cultural services to an ecosystem. **Provisional services** are the supply of food, fuel, or fiber made available for consumption in an ecosystem. For example, the annual world fish catch provides $58 billion in service to the world's ecosystems.[69] The **regulatory services** control interaction between factors in an ecosystem. For example, honeybee pollination of agricultural products is a regulatory service whose global value is estimated at $2 to $8 billion.[70] **Supporting services** maintain the conditions for life on Earth and include soil formation, soil protection, nutrient cycling, and water cycling. **Cultural services** refer to the spiritual, recreational, and aesthetic benefits afforded to an ecosystem through biodiversity. For instance, coral reefs for fisheries and tourism provide worldwide cultural services of $30 billion.[71]

When biodiversity is threatened, the provisional, regulatory, supportive, and cultural benefits enjoyed in the ecosystem are also affected. Unfortunately, 60% of ecosystems that have been assessed are degraded or used unsustainably.[72] Rates of species extinction are 100 times higher than baseline rates based on fossil records. Among the major vertebrate groups that have been examined, 22% of mammals, 12% of birds, 30% of reptiles, 31% of amphibians, and 39% of fishes are threatened with extinction.[73] The percentage among plants is greater—70% of species are threatened (see Table 3-2).

TABLE 3-2[75] THREATENED SPECIES BY MAJOR GROUPS

	NUMBER OF DESCRIBED SPECIES	NUMBER OF SPECIES EVALUATED BY 2007	NUMBER THREATENED IN 2007, AS % OF SPECIES EVALUATED
Vertebrates			
Mammals	5,490	5,490	21%
Birds	9,998	9,998	12%
Reptiles	9,084	1,677	28%
Amphibians	6,433	6,285	30%
Fishes	31,000	4,443	32%
Subtotal	**62,305**	**27,893**	**22%**
Invertebrates			
Insects	1,000,000	2,619	27%
Mollusks	85,000	2,306	45%
Crustaceans	47,000	1,735	35%
Corals	2,175	856	27%
Others	171,075	99	52%
Subtotal	**1,305,250**	**7,615**	**35%**
Plants			
Mosses	16,236	95	86%
Ferns and allies	12,000	211	66%
Gymnosperms	1,021	909	35%
Dicotyledons	281,821	10,876	73%
Monocotyledons	4,053	2	0%
Green algae	6,081	58	16%
Red algae	321,212	12,151	70%
Subtotal	**16,236**	**95**	**86%**
Others			
Lichens	17,000	2	100%
Mushrooms	31,496	1	100%
Brown algae	3,067	15	40%
Subtotal	**28,849**	**18**	**50%**
TOTAL	**1,740,330**	**47,677**	**36%**

Source: IUCN 2009. IUCN *Red List of Threatened Species*. Version 2009.2. *International Union for Conservation of Nature and Natural Resources.*

Five factors that account for reduced biodiversity include habitat conversion, invasive alien species, overexploitation, climate change, and pollution.[74] Habit conversion such as deforestation reduces the amount of available natural habitat, homogenizes species composition, fragments landscapes, and degrades soil. *Invasive alien species* refers to the introduction of new species into an ecosystem. The new species may be competitors or predators of existing species and lead to genetic contamination. Overexploitation, or the harvesting of species above sustainable rates, leads to decreased populations and extinctions. Climate change robs species of their habitats, resulting in contraction of species ranges, changes in species compositions, and extinction. Pollution yields higher mortality rates, influences nutrient availability, and raises levels of acidification in soil and water. Importantly, all these effects on biodiversity constrain the level of provisional, regulatory, supportive, and cultural services in an ecosystem and have significant consequences for the well-being of humans.

Summary

A. Understand the Interaction Between Environment and Consumption

It is essential to recognize that commerce and consumption operate within natural boundaries. Some natural assets such as wind power are renewable, yet many others are not sustainable. Sustainable resources can be regenerated, and they offer ecological advantages that limit a company's exposure to scare resources. Consequently, effective green marketers increasingly favor adoption of sustainable technologies and assets.

B. Human Influences on Climate Change

Climate change concerns changes in climate attributed to human activity that alters the composition of the global atmosphere. Climate change is associated with higher atmospheric temperatures and increased risk, decline in the quantity and quality of freshwater, rising sea levels, and threats to biodiversity. The human-related influences on the environment have direct implications for agriculture, tourism, insurance, transportation, and new product development.

Gases with a direct influence on climate change include naturally occurring gases and synthetic gases that are the result of industrial activity. Carbon dioxide accounts for more than 80% of the greenhouse emissions worldwide. The other natural gases are methane and nitrous oxide. Synthetic gases include hydrofluourocarbons, perflourocarbons, and sulfur hexafluoride.

C. Understand Sources of Energy and Their Use Across International Regions

Fossil fuels in the form of oil and coal dominate energy use across the globe. Oil is the primary energy source used worldwide, and much of this energy usage is associated with increases in the transportation sector. Coal and gas together also account for sizeable percentages of consumption. Consumption in OECD countries is substantially different from emerging economies.

D. Human Influences on the Atmosphere

Ozone depletion, air pollution, and energy are facets of the atmosphere influenced by consumption. Depletion of stratospheric ozone leads to increased amounts of UV radiation, which is associated with more cases of skin cancer, cataracts, and impaired immune systems. Air pollution is a global health concern, and regulatory agents use six factors known as *criteria pollutants* to establish air quality levels.

E. Human Influences on Water

The availability of freshwater is declining in many parts of the world. Current estimates suggest that one sixth of the world's population does not have access to clean drinking water and two fifths of the world population lacks access to adequate sanitation services. The lack of acceptable levels of potable and sanitary water is most serious in Asia and Africa. Lack of water facilities is associated with falling water tables, floods and droughts, disease, and political tension.

F. Human Influences on Land

Human influences on land are attributed to urban expansion, land degradation, and deforestation. Forces related to urban expansion include aspects of the local natural environment, demographics, economics, prevailing transport systems, consumer preferences, and metropolitan governance. The direct effects of land degradation include losses of organic soil carbon, soil water storage, nutrients, and below-ground biodiversity. Reductions in forest acreage result in loss of habitat and limited biodiversity. Deforestation also reduces the amount of stored carbon and disturbs biological cycles.

G. Human Influences on Biodiversity

Human activity is believed to be related to reduced biodiversity: Current rates of species extinction are markedly higher than baseline rates based on fossil records. All vertebrate groups and plant life have substantial percentages of species that are threatened.

Keywords

Questions

1. How did the recognition of the interrelationship between the environment and humankind influence the need to develop the Ashkelon Desalinization Plant?
2. What is the natural greenhouse effect and how does human action influence this effect?
3. What are four industries that are affected by climate change, and how are people in these industries trying to reduce the influence of climate change on their operations?
4. If carbon dioxide represents 80% of the world's greenhouse gases, why is it necessary to consider other greenhouse gases?
5. What is the role of fossil fuels in climate change?
6. How do indoor and outdoor air pollution influence the incidence of disease? How is this incidence of disease related to geography?
7. Is the lack of access to inadequate and unsanitary water a global issue? Why or why not?
8. More people now live in cities than in rural areas. What factors are related to urban expansion?
9. Describe two factors that increase land degradation.
10. What are the consequences of a decline in biodiversity?

Endnotes

[1] Jewish Virtual Library, "Israel's Chronic Water Problem," February 17, 2010, http://www.jewishvirtuallibrary.org/jsource/History/scarcity.html.

[2] Bruno Sauvet-Goichon, "Ashkelon Desalination Plant—A Successful Challenge," *Desalination* 203, no. 1–3 (2007): 75–81.

[3] Jeffrey Marlow, "The Pursuit of Cost-Effective Desalination," *New York Times*, September 21, 2009, http://greeninc.blogs.nytimes.com/2009/09/21/on-the-pursuit-of-cost-effectivedesalination/ NOTE: This blog story does not appear to have been printed by NYTimes.

4 United Nations Environment Programme, *Global Environmental Outlook 4* (Valetta, Malta: Progress Press, 2007), 572.

5 M. D. Lemonick and D. Cray, "The Ozone Vanishes," *Time* 139, no. 7 (February 17, 1992): 60–63.

6 Daniel C. Esty and Andrew S. Winston, *Green to Gold* (New Haven, CT: Yale University Press, 2006), 366.

7 United Nations, "United Nations Framework Convention on Climate Change," 1992, http://unfccc.int/resource/docs/convkp/conveng.pdf (accessed April 28, 2010).

8 United Nations Framework Convention on Climate Change, "The Greenhouse Effect and the Carbon Cycle," http://unfccc.int/essential_background/feeling_the_heat/items/2903.php (accessed April 28, 2010).

9 See Note 8 above.

10 WHO, "The Health Impacts of 2003 Summer Heatwaves," *Briefing Note for the 53 Session of the World Health Organization Regional Committee for Europe*, September 8, 2003, 73.

11 Peter A. Stott, D. A. Stone, and M. R. Allen, "Human Contribution to the European Heatwave of 2003," *Nature* 432, no. 7017 (2004): 610–614.

12 John Church, "Global Sea Levels: Past, Present and Future," *United Nations Educational, Scientific and Cultural Organization*, 2008, 12.

13 Chris D. Thomas, Alison Cameron, Rhys E. Green, Michel Bakkenes, Linda J. Beaumont, Yvonne C. Collingham, Barend F. N. Erasmus and others, "Extinction Risk from Climate Change," *Nature* 427, no. 6970 (2004): 145–148.

14 Maarten Kappelle, Margret M. I. Van Vuuren, and Pieter Baas, "Effects of Climate Change on Biodiversity: a Review and Identification of Key Research Issues," *Biodiversity and Conservation* 8, no. 10 (1998): 1383–1397.

15 See Note 6 above.

16 See Note 8 above.

17 U.S. Environmental Protection Agency, "Inventory of U.S. Greenhouse Gas Emissions and Sinks: 1990–2008," April 15, 2010, http://www.epa.gov/climatechange/emissions/usinventoryreport.html (accessed April 28, 2010).

18 International Energy Agency, *Worldwide Trends in Energy Use and Efficiency* (Paris, France: International Energy Agency, 2008), 17, http://www.iea.org/Papers/2008/Indicators_2008.pdf (accessed April 28, 2010).

19 David Hofmann, *Long-lived Greenhouse Gas Annual Averages for 1979–2004* (Boulder, CO: National Oceanic and Atmospheric Administration, Earth Systems Research Laboratory, Global Monitoring Division, 2004).

20 *Business & the Environment with ISO 14000 Updates*, "Momentum for Greenhouse Gas Cuts Grows," 18, no. 7 (2007): 1–4.

21 US State Department, "Greenhouse Gas Inventory," http://www.state.gov/documents/organization/89651.pdf (accessed April 28, 2010).

22 See Note 21 above.

23 See Note 21 above.

24 International Energy Agency, *Worldwide Trends in Energy Use and Efficiency* (Paris: International Energy Agency), 94,

http://www.iea.org/Textbase/Papers/2008/Indicators_2008.pdf (accessed April 28, 2010).

25 D. W. Fahey, *Twenty Questions and Answers About the Ozone Layer: 2006 Update*, 2006, http://ozone.unep.org/Assessment_Panels/SAP/Scientific_Assessment_2006/Twenty_Questions.pdf (accessed April 28, 2010).

26 See Note 25 above.

27 See Note 25 above.

28 See Note 7 above.

29 B. Osro, *Outdoor Air Pollution: Assessing the Environmental Burden of Disease at National and Local Levels* (Geneva, Switzerland: World Health Organization, 2004), 62.

30 World Health Organization, *Indoor Air Pollution and Household Energy Monitoring: Workshop Resources* (Geneva: World Health Organization, 2005), 20.

31 World Health Organization, "Indoor Air Pollution and Health," http://www.who.int/mediacentre/factsheets/fs292/en/index.html (accessed April 28, 2010).

32 World Health Organization, "National burden of disease due to indoor air pollution," http://www.who.int/indoorair/health_impacts/burden_national/en/index.html (accessed April 28, 2010).

33 World Health Organization, "Pollution and exposure levels," http://www.who.int/indoorair/health_impacts/exposure/en/index.html (accessed April 28, 2010).

34 Nigel Bruce, Rogelio Perez-Padilla, and Rachel Albalak, "The Health Effects of Indoor Air Pollution Exposure in Developing Countries," 78, no. 9 (2000): 1078–1092.

35 U.S. Geologiocal Survey, "Earth's Water Distribution," http://ga.water.usgs.gov/edu/waterdistribution.html (accessed April 28, 2010).

36 Lester R. Brown, "Draining Our Future," *Futurist* (May–June, 2008): 16–22.

37 G. H. Brundtland and C. Bellamy, "Global Water Supply and Sanitation Assessment 2000 Report," 2001, http://www.who.int/docstore/water_sanitation_health/Globassessment/GlobalT C.htm (accessed April 28, 2010).

38 Sandra L. Postel, Gretchen C. Daily, and Paul R. Ehrlich, "Human Appropriation of Renewable Fresh Water," *Science* 271, no. 5250 (1996): 785–788.

39 C. W. Fetter, *Applied Hydrogeology* (New York: Macmillan, 1994).

40 Lester R. Brown, *Plan B 3.0: Mobilizing to Save Civilization* (New York, NY: W.W. Norton, 2008), 691.

41 Laszlo Somlyody and Olli Varis, "Freshwater Under Pressure," *International Review for Environmental Strategies* 6, no. 2 (2003): 181–204.

42 International Federation of Red Cross and Red Crescent Societies, *World Disaster Report* (Geneva, Switzerland: IFRC, 2007), 244.

43 A. Prüss-Üstün, R. Bos, F. Gore, and J. Bartram, *Safer Water, Better Health: Costs, Benefits and Sustainability of Interventions to Protect and Promote Health* (Geneva, Switzerland: World Health Organization, 2008), 60.

44 See Note 43 above.

[45] Ryutaro Hashimoto, "Current Status and Future Trends in Freshwater Management," *International Review of Environmental Strategies* 3, no. 2 (2002): 222–239.

[46] See Note 41 above.

[47] See Note 40 above.

[48] See Note 41 above.

[49] Cathy C. Campbell, "Food Insecurity: A Nutritional Outcome or a Predictor Variable," *Journal of Nutrition* 121, no. 3 (1991): 408–415.

[50] See Note 41 above.

[51] Julienne Holland Stroeve and others, "Arctic Sea Ice Decline: Faster than Forecast," *Geophysical Research Letters* 34, no. 9 (2007): L09501.

[52] David Adam, "Meltdown of Winter Ice Linked to Greenhouse Gases," *Guardian* (May 15, 2006): 12.

[53] Gordon McGranahan, Deborah Balk, and Bridget Anderson, "The Rising Tide: Assessing the Risks of Climate Change and Human Settlements in Low Elevation Coastal Zones," *Environment and Urbanization* 19, no. 1 (2007): 17–37.

[54] John Krist, "Water Issues Will Dominate California's Agenda This Year," *Environmental News Network* (February 21, 2003): 33.

[55] See Note 40 above.

[56] See Note 40 above.

[57] Terrence Thompson and others, *Chemical Safety of Drinking Water: Assessing Priorities for Risk Management* (Geneva, Switzerland: World Health Organization, 2007), 160.

[58] United States Environemntal Protection Agency, "Protecting Water Quality from Agricultural Runoff," http://www.epa.gov/owow/nps/Ag_Runoff_Fact_Sheet.pdf (accessed April 28, 2010).

[59] Shlomo Angel, Stephen C. Sheppard, and Daniel L. Civco With Robert Buckley, Anna Chabaeva, Lucy Gitlin, Alison Kralcy, Jason Parent, and Micah Perlin, *The Dynamics of Global Urban Expansion* (Washington, DC: The World Bank, 2005), 12.

[60] See Note 4 above.

[61] See Note 60 above.

[62] Alexander V. Sergeev and David O. Carpenter, "Hospitalization Rates for Coronary Heart Disease in Relation to Residence Near Areas Contaminated with Persistent Organic Pollutants and Other Pollutants," *Environmental Health Perspectives* 113, no. 6 (2005): 756–761.

[63] Food and Agriculture Organization, *Global Forest Resources Assessment 2005—Progress Towards Sustainable Forest Management*. Forestry Paper 147 (United Nations: Rome, 2006a): 320.

[64] See Note 60 above.

[65] United Nations General Assembly, "United Nations General Assembly Document A/AC.241/27," September 12, 1994, 4.

[66] See Note 60 above.

[67] See Note 6 above.

[68] See Note 60 above.

[69] FAO, *The State of the World's Fisheries and Aquaculture 2004* (Rome, Italy: Food and Agriculture Organization of the United Nations, 2004), 154.

[70] G. P. Nabhan and S. L. Buchman, "Services Provided by Pollinators," in *Nature's Services—Societal Dependence on Natural Ecosystems*, ed. G. E. Daily (Washington, DC: Island Press, 1997), 392.

[71] UNEP, *Marine and Coastal Ecosystems and Human Well-Being: A Synthesis Report Based on the Findings of the Millennium Ecosystem Assessment*. DEW/0785/NA. (Nairobi, Kenya: United Nations Environment Programme, 2006a), 80.

[72] See Note 4 above.

[73] IUCN, "IUCN Red List of Threatened Species. Version 2009.2." 2009, *International Union for Conservation of Nature and Natural Resources*. http://www.iucnredlist.org/documents/summarystatistics/2009RL Stats Table 1.pdf (accessed April 28, 2010).

[74] See Note 70 above.

[75] See Note 73 above.

CHAPTER 4

The Environmental Effects on Consumption

A. Identify Environmental Action Designed to Reduce Climate Change

TUNGU-KABIRI COMMUNITY MICRO-HYDROPOWER

The Meru South District area in central Kenya is an area teeming with beautiful landscapes and rich natural resources. Like much of Africa, however, this region is not adequately served with electrical power. One of the most viable and sustainable ways to bring electrical power to the region is in the form of hydroelectrical power. Hydroelectrical power is a time-proven technology that relies on a nonpolluting, renewable, and indigenous resources. The technology can easily be integrated into irrigation and water supply projects. China, for instance, has more than 85,000 small electricity-producing hydro-power plants.[1]

The potential for hydropower is massive and in many ways an untapped resource. Hydropower accounts for 20% of the world's supply of electricity, and it is an important source of renewable energy in the United States, Canada, and Norway.[2] Nevertheless, 70% of the economically feasible hydro potential in developing countries—and 93% of the potential in Africa—remains unexploited.[3]

Hydropower can be developed on multiple scales ranging from *large-hydro* plants of more than 100 megawatts to *pico-hydro* plants of less than 5 kilowatts. In the Meru South District of Kenya, a micro-hydro plant capable of producing 18 kilowatts was developed to serve 400 households in the Tungu-Kabiri community. Members of the community formed a commercial enterprise by purchasing shares having a maximum value of approximately US$50. The group members also dedicated one day per week to the construction of a run-of-the-river penstock micro-hydropower system (see Figure 4–1). The community also acquired an acre of land from the government, where it built an enterprise center that receives power through the project. The Small Grants Programme of the United Nations also contributed US$63,700 to support project completion.

The construction of this micro-hydropower facility has paid substantial dividends across the triple bottom line of sustainability.[4] Revenue has increased due to the running of the micro-hydro enterprise. Consequently, there is a demand for services such as welding operations, barber shops, beauty salons, and battery changing stations. The environment simultaneously benefits as grain milling is transferred from diesel engines to hydropower and electricity replaces kerosene

FIG. 4-1 Micro-Hydropower Schematic and Photo of the Tungu-Kabiri Facility in Kenya

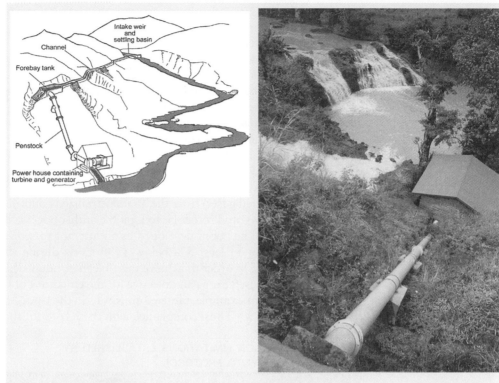

Source: © *Practical Action/Zul*

used for lighting. The notoriety of this successful venture has stimulated interest in building at least two more power plants in the region.

The Kenya example illustrates how people are taking action to confront sustainability issues. In the last chapter, we focused on the influences that consumption has on the environment. In this chapter, we identify activity occurring outside the firm designed to influence consumption. The environment of the firm can be conceptualized as consisting of multiple levels.[5] At one level, the environment concerns entities close to an organization that influence the ability to serve customers. These entities include the company, customers, suppliers, competition, marketing intermediaries, and other groups (i.e., publics) that influence the ability to meet objectives. Because the relationships between these entities and the firm directly influence day-to-day operations, we dedicate the remaining chapters of this book to these relationships. In Part III, we outline the marketing efforts of organizations operating in these macro-environments. In Part IV, we outline the macro-environment of the primary users of energy (industry, households, services, and transportation).

The environment also includes the larger forces that frame the activity of the firm and other participants in a market. These forces include the natural, technological, political, economic, and cultural constraints on operations within a market. Chapter 3 calls attention to influences of technology and culture on the natural environment. Our discussion here considers political and economic forces that shape operations in an industry. We begin by examining efforts to regulate climate change and then engage in a discussion of efforts to influence the supply and demand for energy. In the subsequent sections, we identify macroenvironmental efforts to reduce human influence on the atmosphere, water, land, and biodiversity.

Numerous efforts have been launched to address the influences of consumption and other human activity on the environment, and these activities have taken place at the international, national, regional, and local levels. Although international agencies and national governments enact policies and legislation, local activity determines whether these initiatives are successful.

Consider now macroenvironmental efforts to limit climate change.

The most prominent international effort to reduce climate change is the **Kyoto Protocol**.[6] The Kyoto Protocol was adopted by the United Nations in Kyoto, Japan, on December 11, 1997, and implementation began on February 16, 2005.[7] The Kyoto Protocol limits emissions of greenhouse gases (GHG) (carbon dioxide, methane, nitrous oxide, and fluorinated gases) from the 35 industrialized countries listed in Table 4–1.

The goal of the Kyoto Protocol is to limit the anthropogenic emission of greenhouse gases. The protocol has been developed as an attempt to reduce overall emissions of greenhouse gases by at least 5% below 1990 levels during the commitment period from 2008 to 2012. In order to achieve this objective, countries were designated some percentage of the base year as an objective for the emissions of GHGs during the 2008 to 2012 horizon. For example, targeted emissions in the United States reflected 93% of the emissions in 1990. Thus, compliance with the Kyoto Protocol requires reductions

TABLE 4-1[8]   EMISSION LIMITATIONS ESTABLISHED BY THE KYOTO PROTOCOL

PARTY	EMISSION LIMITATION, %	PARTY	EMISSION LIMITATION, %
Australia	108	Liechtenstein	92
Austria	92	Lithuania*	92
Belgium	92	Luxembourg	92
Bulgaria*	92	Monaco	92
Canada	94	Netherlands	92
Croatia*	95	New Zealand	100
Czech Republic*	92	Norway	101
Denmark	92	Poland*	94
Estonia*	92	Portugal	92
European Community	92	Romania*	92
Finland	92	Russian Federation*	100
France	92	Slovakia*	92
Germany	92	Slovenia*	92
Greece	92	Spain	92
Hungary*	94	Sweden	92
Iceland	110	Switzerland	92
Ireland	92	Ukraine*	100
Italy	92	United Kingdom	92
Japan	94	United States of America	93
Latvia*	92		

*Countries that are undergoing the process of transition to a market economy.
Source: *From Kyoto Protocol to the United Nations Framework Convention on Climate Change, (Kyoto, Japan: © United Nations, 1998), p. 20. Reprinted with the permission of the United Nations.*

in emissions associated with fuel combustion, industrial processes (e.g., mineral products, chemicals, metal production), agriculture, and waste management.

Importantly, the Kyoto Protocol outlines *national* efforts to reduce or limit greenhouse gases. In addition, the protocol introduced three *market* mechanisms that enable countries to engage in international commerce to meet emission targets.[8] These mechanisms stimulate sustainable development via the transfer of technology and investment, and they encourage the private sector and developing countries to contribute to emissions reductions. Furthermore, they help countries to meet their commitments by cost-effectively removing GHGs from the atmosphere in other countries.

A central advantage of the Kyoto Protocol lies in the designation of emissions levels for participating countries. Designation of emission levels created a market for the sale and purchase of greenhouse gas emissions. Three Kyoto mechanisms that facilitate the exchange of emission credits are as follows:

Emissions trading *Emissions trading* refers to the exchange of carbon trading units. The participating countries listed in Table 4–1 allocate carbon trading units to industries such as manufacturing and utilities.[10] Companies in these industries within these countries are required to reduce emissions to the target levels outlined in Table 4–1. If the companies attain emission levels below targeted rates, they can sell the emission credits on an exchange. For example, the European Carbon Exchange (ECX) attracts more than 89% of the global exchange volume with more than 100 participating businesses.[11] If companies surpass their emission levels, they must go to a market and buy **carbon offsets**. These offsets often are investments in developing countries such as China and India. Investments in carbon offsets reduce the emissions in the emerging markets and thereby contribute to lower global emissions.[12]

The European Union's European Trading Scheme (ETS) currently accounts for about two thirds of global **carbon** trading. Because the United States did not ratify the Kyoto Protocol, its carbon exchange market is voluntary. The U.S. market is owned by the Climate Exchange, the parent company of ECX, and is named the Chicago Climate Exchange (CCX).[13] More than 300 parties have become members of this organization since its founding in 2003. A similar market forming in the United States is the Regional Greenhouse Gas Initiative. The initiative is a multistate government program aimed at reducing power plant emissions in the Northeast. This program commenced in 2009.[14]

Clean development mechanism (CDM) The clean development mechanism enables emission reduction or removal projects in developing countries to earn **certified emission reduction** (CER) credits.[15] Each CER is equivalent to one ton of carbon dioxide. CERs can be traded, sold, or used to meet emission targets outlined by the Kyoto Protocol.

Industrialized countries that finance investment projects for greenhouse gas emission abatements in developing countries generate credits used to meet their own commitments. The industrialized countries reduce carbon emissions at a lower marginal cost than domestically. Developing economies gain access to technology more rapidly while simultaneously reducing emissions. They have the opportunity to accelerate technological transfers and to benefit from positive spinoffs in terms of development.[16] Since the beginning of operations in 2006, the clean development mechanism has registered more than 1,000 projects amounting to more than 2.7 billion tons of carbon dioxide.

Joint implementation (JI) Joint implementation is similar to the clean development mechanism given that it relies on collaboration between countries to lower GHG emissions. In contrast to CDMs that involve an industrialized country and a developing country, however, joint implementation projects involve only industrialized countries.[17] Participants to JI arrangements earn **emission reduction units** (ERUs) each equivalent to one ton of carbon dioxide that can be counted toward Kyoto Protocol targets. For example, in 2007 New Zealand established a joint implementation program with the Netherlands to provide a wind farm at Te Apiti on New Zealand's northern island.[18] The project is expected to earn 530,000 ERUs.

JI programs offer benefits to the host country (e.g., New Zealand) and the non-host partner (e.g., the Netherlands). The host country receives foreign investment and technology transfer, while the nonhost country obtains a flexible and efficient means for meeting its Kyoto requirements.

Although 182 Parties of the Convention have ratified the Protocol as of this writing (see Table 4–2), the United States and Australia have refused to participate. While the United States federal government has not endorsed the Kyoto Protocol, 14 U.S. states have adopted the GHG emission targets established by the United Nations. Of the 650 cities worldwide that have adopted Kyoto GHG emission targets, 212 are in the United States. Moreover, the U.S. Environmental Protection Agency (EPA) has established a climate leader partnership that currently includes more than 200 U.S. companies. These corporate partners commit to reducing their impact on the global environment by taking stock of current gas emissions, setting aggressive reduction goals, and annually reporting their progress to the EPA.

B. Understand Efforts to Influence the Supply and Demand for Energy

Many countries throughout the world have established regulations designed to enhance the sustainability and efficiency of energy consumption. The desire to conserve energy is not a new phenomenon, but it is gaining increasing interest due to climate change and rising oil prices. One way to examine energy is on the basis of its supply and demand. Renewable energy sources provide contributions to the supply of energy. To the extent that these sources are employed as substitutes for fossil fuels, the environment does not encounter the negative consequences of oil or other fossil fuel consumption.

Renewable energy sources will increase throughout the world, but the demand for energy will also continue to rise.[19] It is therefore important to consider the mechanisms that influence the demand for energy. While conservation efforts are being undertaken in many industries, we focus attention here on transportation, buildings and construction, and appliance industries due to the amount of regulation and opportunity for substantial reductions in energy usage.

Consider first the role of renewable energy.

Renewable Energy

Energy consumption across the globe is growing at a rapid rate, and current predictions suggest that energy consumption will grow by 60% in the next 25 years.[20] Figure 4–2 indicates the share of energy and electricity use throughout the world. Note that of the 13% associated with renewable forms of energy, 8% of this total is associated with traditional biomass. Other forms of renewable energy account for 5% of usage throughout the world. Renewable energy technologies have made tremendous advances over the last 20 years and offer significant advantages over conventional fuels for meeting energy needs. Research indicates that adding renewable energy to a fossil fuel-dominated energy portfolio reduces generating costs and enhances energy security.[21]

TABLE 4-2 [22]   PARTIES TO THE KYOTO PROTOCOL

Albania	Ecuador	Liechtenstein	Romania
Algeria	Egypt	Lithuania	Russian Federation
Angola	El Salvador	Luxembourg	Rwanda
Antigua and Barbuda	Equatorial Guinea	Macedonia	Saint Lucia
Argentina	Eritrea	Madagascar	Saint Vincent and the Grenadines
Armenia	Estonia	Malawi	Samoa
Australia	Ethiopia	Malaysia	Saudi Arabia
Austria	European Community	Maldives	Senegal
Azerbaijan	Fiji	Mali	Serbia
Bahamas	Finland	Malta	Seychelles
Bahrain	France	Marshall Islands	Sierra Leone
Bangladesh	Gabon	Mauritania	Singapore
Barbados	Gambia	Mauritius	Slovakia
Belarus	Georgia	Mexico	Slovenia
Belgium	Germany	Micronesia	Solomon Islands
Belize	Ghana	Moldova	South Africa
Benin	Greece	Monaco	Spain
Bhutan	Grenada	Mongolia	Sri Lanka
Bolivia	Guatemala	Montenegro	Sudan
Bosnia and Herzegovina	Guinea	Morocco	Suriname
Botswana	Guinea-Bissau	Mozambique	Swaziland
Brazil	Guyana	Myanmar	Sweden
Bulgaria	Haiti	Namibia	Switzerland
Burkina Faso	Honduras	Nauru	Syrian Arab Republic
Burundi	Hungary	Nepal	Thailand
Cambodia	Iceland	Netherlands	Togo
Cameroon	India	New Zealand	Tonga
Canada	Indonesia	Nicaragua	Trinidad and Tobago
Cape Verde	Iran (Islamic Republic of)	Niger	Tunisia
Chile	Ireland	Nigeria	Turkmenistan
China	Israel	Niue	Tuvalu
Colombia	Italy	North Korea	Uganda
Congo	Jamaica	Norway	Ukraine
Cook Islands	Japan	Oman	United Arab Emirates
Costa Rica	Jordan	Pakistan	United Kingdom
Côte d'Ivoire	Kenya	Palau	United Republic of Tanzania
Croatia	Kiribati	Panama	Uruguay
Cuba	Kuwait	Papua New Guinea	Uzbekistan
Cyprus	Kyrgyzstan	Paraguay	Vanuatu
Czech Republic	Laos	Peru	Venezuela
Congo	Latvia	Philippines	Viet Nam
Denmark	Lebanon	Poland	Yemen
Djibouti	Lesotho	Portugal	Zambia
Dominica	Liberia	Qatar	
Dominican Republic	Libyan Arab Jamahiriya	Republic of Korea	

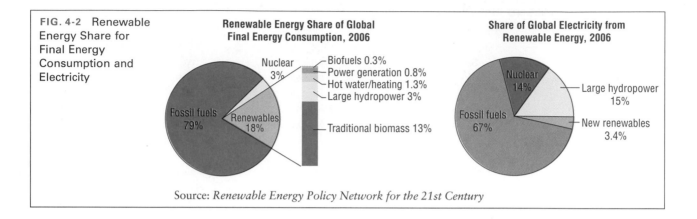

FIG. 4-2 Renewable Energy Share for Final Energy Consumption and Electricity

Source: *Renewable Energy Policy Network for the 21st Century*

The Renewable Energy Policy Network[23] emphasizes the following benefits to renewable energy:

1. Use locally available, renewable resources such as the sun, wind, biomass, geothermal, and hydropower.
2. Reduce reliance on fossil fuels and their associated international trade consequences.
3. Heighten energy security by developing a diverse energy portfolio.
4. Increase price stability during volatile periods for fossil fuel prices.
5. Reduce risk of future energy costs.
6. Increase income, revenue, and job opportunities. Renewable energy supports 2.4 million jobs globally.[24]
7. Conserve the natural resource base in a country.
8. Provide health benefits, notably to women and children, via improved cooking facilities.
9. Contribute to economic and social development via provision of modern energy services, including lighting, heating, cooking, cooling, water pumping, transportation, and communications.
10. Remain environmentally friendly because they lack nitrogen and sulfur oxides that are harmful to humans, animals, and plants, and carbon dioxide and that contribute to climate change.

Due to the simultaneous potential to use local resources and limit climate change, 66 countries have set national targets for renewable energy supply.[25] The European Union, for instance, seeks to have 21% of its electricity and 12% of total energy served through renewable sources by 2010. In the United States, 29 states have developed mandatory renewable energy percentages for utilities, and another four states have voluntary programs[26] (see Figure 4–3 and 4–4). Most national or state targets reflect desires for 5 to 30% of electricity production during the 2010 to 2012 horizon. Brazil, China, the Dominican Republic, Egypt, India, Malaysia, Mali, the Philippines, South Africa, and Thailand are emerging economies that have established renewable energy targets. Developing countries have more than 40% of existing renewable power capacity, more than 70% of existing solar hot water capacity, and 45% of biofuel production. China has targeted 10% percent of total power capacity by 2010, whereas India anticipates that 10% of its electric power capacity will be filled via renewable energy sources by 2012.

In 2007, worldwide renewable electricity generation capacity reached an estimated 240 gigawatts (GW), an increase of 50% over 2004. Table 4–3 outlines

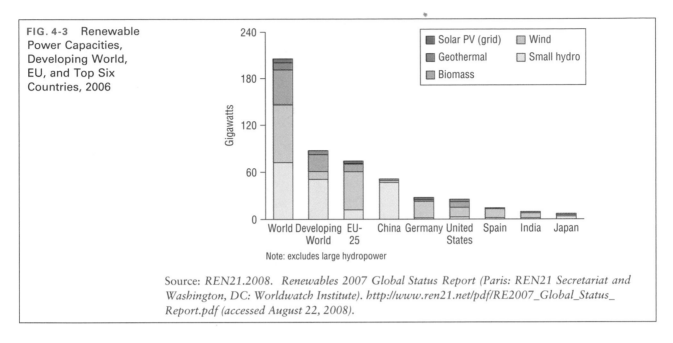

FIG. 4-3 Renewable Power Capacities, Developing World, EU, and Top Six Countries, 2006

Note: excludes large hydropower

Source: *REN21.2008. Renewables 2007 Global Status Report (Paris: REN21 Secretariat and Washington, DC: Worldwatch Institute). http://www.ren21.net/pdf/RE2007_Global_Status_Report.pdf (accessed August 22, 2008).*

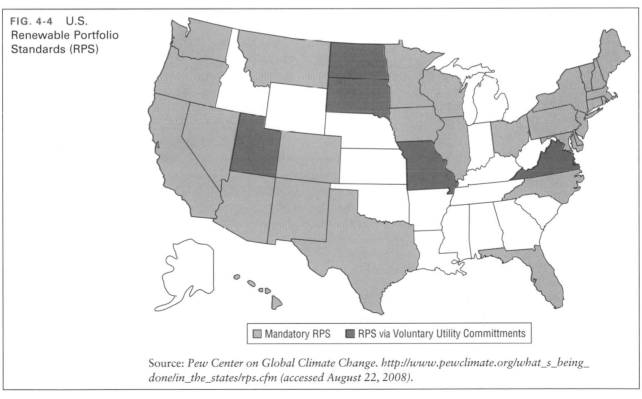

FIG. 4-4 U.S. Renewable Portfolio Standards (RPS)

☐ Mandatory RPS ■ RPS via Voluntary Utility Committments

Source: *Pew Center on Global Climate Change. http://www.pewclimate.org/what_s_being_done/in_the_states/rps.cfm (accessed August 22, 2008).*

several indicators of renewable energy. Renewable energy sources such as hydropower, wind, solar, geothermal, biomass, tidal, and wave technology enable utility companies, individuals, and organizations to meet their energy needs. Note that hydroelectric power, a renewable source that has been in use for decades, generates

TABLE 4-3[25]   INDICATORS OF RENEWABLE ENERGY

SELECTED INDICATORS	2005	2006	2007	(ESTIMATED UNITS)
Investment in new renewable capacity (annual)	40	55	71	Billion US dollars
Renewable power capacity (existing, *excluding* large hydro)	182	207	240	Gigawatts
Renewable power capacity (existing, *including* large hydro)	930	970	1,010	Gigawatts
Wind power capacity (existing)	59	74	95	Gigawatts
Grid-connected solar PV capacity (existing)	3.5	5.1	7.8	Gigawatts
Solar PV production (annual)	1.8	2.5	3.8	Gigawatts
Solar hot water capacity (existing)	88	105	128	Gigawatts
Ethanol production (annual)	33	39	46	Billion liters
Biodiesel production (annual)	3.9	6	8	Billion liters

Source: *Renewable Energy Policy Network for the 21st Century, Renewables 2007 Global Status Report, (Paris, France: REN21 Secretariat and Washington, DC: Worldwatch Institute, 2008), p. 8. Copyright © 2008 Deutsche Gesellschaft für Technische Zusammenarbeit (GTZ) GmbH.*

almost four times as much energy as all other renewable sources. Investments in 2007 in hydropower exceeded $15 billion.

Of the $71 billion invested in other new renewable energy sources during 2007, 47% was for wind power and 30% was for solar photovoltaic (PV). Figure 4–5 illustrates the growth in windpower over the last decade. The 28% growth in global wind generating capacity in 2007 was the largest increase in renewable power. In the United States, more than 25,000 turbines produce enough to power 4.5 million homes (17 gigawatts). Total U.S. capacity rose 45% in 2007 and is forecast to nearly triple by 2012. Wind power only represents 1% of the country's electricity, but government and industry leaders want to see that share hit 20% by 2030. This level of wind power will boost the supply of carbon-free energy and create green-collar jobs.[27]

Three types of solar power include **grid-connected photovoltaic** (PV) **cells, off-grid solar systems,** and **solar water heaters**. Approximately 1.5 million homes worldwide have these rooftop solar PVs feeding into the electric grid. *Grid-connected systems* are connected to the electrical grid in an area and can *sell* unused energy into the grid. For example, programs established in Germany, France, Greece, Italy, and Spain allow consumers to sell power to the national grid at roughly twice the rate (40 to 50 European cents) they pay for it.[28]

Off-grid systems refer to solar power cells employed outside of regional or national electricity grids. Many of these systems are installed in developing economies. One application of off-grid systems is the minigrids designed for rural or island areas. Hundreds of these grids operate in Sri Lanka, Nepal, Vietnam, and India. The largest installed user is China with 1.5 million people using these off-grid systems in rural areas. A second off-grid application is the water pumps that are fueled by solar PV cells. More than 50,000 pumps are installed worldwide, and the largest market is India. Off-grid household solar systems represent a third application. More than 2.5 million people receive electricity from solar home systems. In recent years, China, the largest market, has added more than 400,000 home systems.[29]

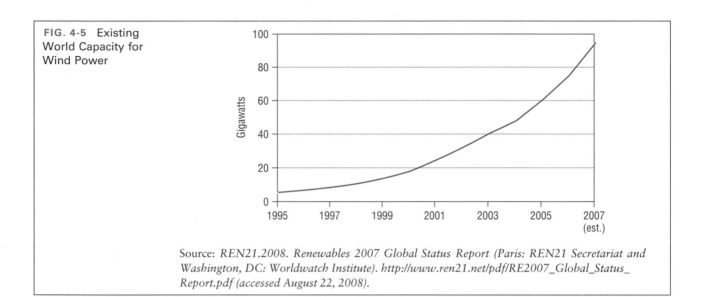

FIG. 4-5 Existing World Capacity for Wind Power

Source: *REN21.2008. Renewables 2007 Global Status Report (Paris: REN21 Secretariat and Washington, DC: Worldwatch Institute). http://www.ren21.net/pdf/RE2007_Global_Status_Report.pdf (accessed August 22, 2008).*

Solar water heaters are heaters that use solar energy to heat water. *Active* heaters use a system of pumps and controls to heat the water, whereas passive heaters do not. Active heaters are more expensive and efficient than passive solar heaters.[30] China is the only major country with a long-term plan for solar water heaters. The country has set goals that would enable one quarter of all Chinese households to use solar water by 2010. Subsidies are employed by countries seeking to establish these devices in national markets. Australia, Austria, Belgium, Canada, Cyprus, Finland, France, Germany, Greece, Hungary, Japan, the Netherlands, New Zealand, Portugal, Spain, Sweden, the United Kingdom, and the United States have established subsidies to encourage solar heater usage. The largest U.S. subsidy was California with a 2007 enactment offering more than $250 million in incentives targeted at 200,000 residents over the next 10 years.[31]

Biofuels refers to a family of fuel products that use some percentage of crops as fuel. Production of biofuels exceeded 53 billion liters in 2007, upto 43% from 2005. *Ethanol* is a fuel made from corn, sugar cane, or wheat that can be used as a substitute for a percentage of fuel in a standard internal combustion engine. Australia, Argentina, Bolivia, Brazil, Canada, China, Colombia, the Dominican Republic, Germany, India, Italy, Malaysia, Paraguay, Peru, Philippines, Thailand, the United Kingdom, the United States, and Uruguay have imposed mandates. These national guidelines typically call for 10 to 15% ethanol in gasoline or 20 to 25% in diesel fuel. Some modified engines provide the ability to use ethanol exclusively. Ethanol production in 2007 represented about 4% of the 1,300 billion liters of gasoline consumed globally.[32]

Biodiesel is a second type of biofuel produced from oilseed crops such as soy or from other vegetable sources such as waste cooking oil. For example, McDonald's converts used cooking oil into biodiesel for delivery trucks in the United Kingdom and Hawaii.[33] Annual biodiesel production increased by more than 50% to more than 6 billion liters in 2006.

Geothermal energy refers to energy available as heat emitted from within the Earth's crust in the form of hot water or steam. It is acquired directly for heating or electricity generation after transformation. Geothermal energy accounts for less than 0.5% of worldwide energy supply, but technological advances are bringing renewed interest to this energy source. More than 2 million ground-source heat pumps are used in 30 countries for heating and cooling of buildings.[34]

At 13% of global fuel usage, biomass represents the largest form of renewable energy in use today. Biomass refers to crop waste, wood, or dung used for home cooking or heating needs. Because of the health consequences associated with biomass, especially from indoor air pollution, efforts are underway to either replace biomass consumption with other forms of energy (e.g., off-grid photovoltaic cells) or to enhance devices employed to process biomass. In developing economies throughout the world, improved biomass techniques are being employed. The stoves are 10 to 50% more fuel efficient, dramatically improve indoor air quality, and reduce greenhouse gases.[35] There are 220 million improved stoves in operation around the world. With 180 million of these stoves, China has supplied 95% of the market for them. By contrast, at 34 million stoves, India has supplied 25% of its market. One third of the African countries have programs in place for enhanced biomass stoves, whereas other countries have promoted access to modern cooking energy for rural populations using traditional stoves.

Although these gains in the use of renewable energy sources are promising, the anticipated 60% increase in demand for energy over the next quarter century is daunting.[36] Fossil fuels will continue to dominate energy consumption, and this consumption will have marked health, environmental, economic, and energy security consequences. The share of renewable energy is growing in absolute terms, but it will remain largely unchanged in the near future. Most long-term projections predict that renewable energy technologies will play a major role in the global energy supply in the second half of the century, but in the first decades the increase in renewable energy will be more modest.

Transportation

Three transportation policies designed to influence energy consumption include cleaner fuels and vehicles, integrated urban road pricing, and bus rapid transit systems.[37] Consider first the cleaner fuels and vehicles.

Cleaner fuels and vehicles In addition to ethanol, compressed natural gas is another alternative to gasoline gaining wider attention in multiple markets. There are currently 11 million propane-powered vehicles operating in the world today.[38] Figure 4–6 indicates, however, that seven countries account for two thirds of consumption. Given that there is great growth potential for other countries to enhance their consumption of this fuel, initiatives are in place in several regions to increase the use of this autogas.[39] Fleet-vehicle purchase mandates or autogas-fuelled public transport program are used in Australia, China, France, Italy, Mexico, and the United States. Canadian legislation provides for mandatory purchases of autogas and other alternative fuels for public fleets. In India, the LP Gas industry succeeded in building very strong relationships with car and three-wheeled vehicle manufacturers. Three-wheeled Asian vehicles are being converted to natural gas to reduce air pollution and enhance energy efficiency.[40] Similarly, Hong Kong has dictated that all new taxis run on liquid propane gas.[41] China's Guangzhou province has converted more than 700 buses to autogas, and 17,000 taxis have been converted to autogas. Similarly, most buses in Beijing run on autogas.[42]

In addition to cleaner fuels, regulations now seek to ensure that vehicles are more fuel efficient. Indeed, automobile fuel economy standards are among the most effective tools in controlling oil demand and GHG emissions from the transportation sector (Table 4–4). As Figure 4–7 illustrates, fuel economy standards for autos have been stagnant in the United States over the past several years. The fuel economy and greenhouse gas emission performance of American cars and light trucks lags behind that of most other nations. The United States and Canada have the lowest standards in terms

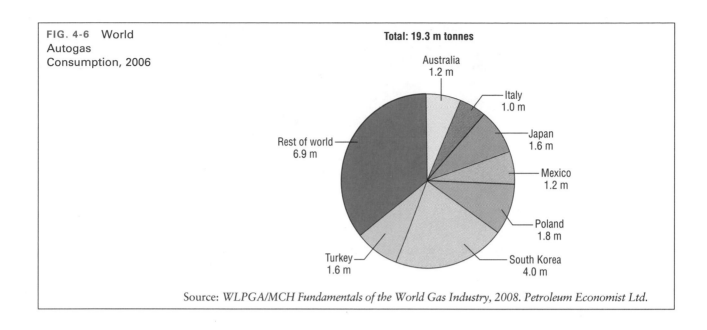

FIG. 4-6 World Autogas Consumption, 2006

Total: 19.3 m tonnes

Australia 1.2 m
Italy 1.0 m
Japan 1.6 m
Mexico 1.2 m
Poland 1.8 m
South Korea 4.0 m
Turkey 1.6 m
Rest of world 6.9 m

Source: WLPGA/MCH *Fundamentals of the World Gas Industry, 2008. Petroleum Economist Ltd.*

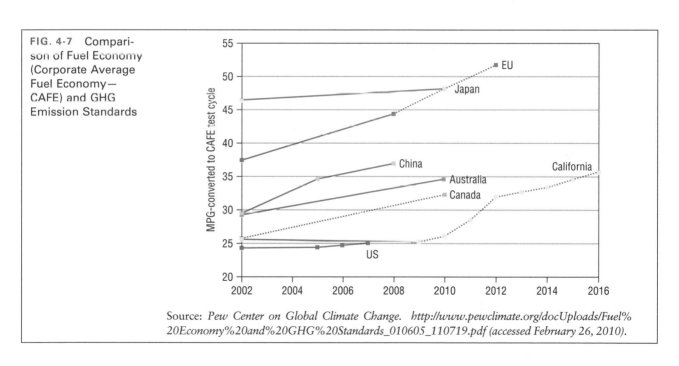

FIG. 4-7 Comparison of Fuel Economy (Corporate Average Fuel Economy—CAFE) and GHG Emission Standards

Source: *Pew Center on Global Climate Change. http://www.pewclimate.org/docUploads/Fuel%20Economy%20and%20GHG%20Standards_010605_110719.pdf (accessed February 26, 2010).*

of fleet-average fuel economy ratings, and they have the highest greenhouse gas emission rates. By contrast, the European Union, Japan, and China have made strides in this area. Japan and the European Union have the most stringent standards in the world. The new Chinese standards are more stringent than those in Australia, Canada, California, and the United States, yet they are less stringent than those in the European Union and Japan. California leads the way in the United States in establishing fuel economy standards. If the California GHG standards went into effect, they would

TABLE 4-4[43] **FUEL ECONOMY AND GHG STANDARDS**

COUNTRY/ REGION	TYPE	MEASURE	STRUCTURE	TEST METHOD[a]	IMPLEMENTATION
United States	Fuel	mpg	Cars and light trucks	U.S. CAFE	Mandatory
European Union	CO_2	g/km	Overall light-duty fleet	EU NEDC	Voluntary
Japan	Fuel	km/L	Weight-based	Japan 10-15	Mandatory
China	Fuel	L/100-km	Weight-based	EU NEDC	Mandatory
California	GHG	g/mile	Car/LDT1 and LDT2[b]	U.S. CAFE	Mandatory
Canada	Fuel	L/100-km	Cars and light trucks	U.S. CAFE	Voluntary
Australia	Fuel	L/100-km	Overall light-duty fleet	EU NEDC	Voluntary
Taiwan, South Korea	Fuel	km/L	Engine size	U.S. CAFE	Mandatory

[a] Test methods include U.S. Corporate Average Fuel Economy (CAFE), New European Drive Cycle (NEDC), and Japan 10-15 Cycle.
[b] LDT1 and LDT2 are categories of light-duty trucks.

Source: *Pew Center on Global Climate Change.*

narrow the gap between American and EU standards. Despite these potential gains, the California standards remain less stringent than the EU standards.

Integrated urban road pricing   *Integrated urban pricing* refers to the use of varied pricing strategies for toll roads based on the time of day one enters a city. These variable pricing strategies are designed to reduce the amount of traffic and limit greenhouse gas emissions. Singapore's automated system charges tolls based on city congestion,[44] and Stockholm uses a similar pricing system in which drivers are charged different amounts depending on the time of day.[45] Bristol, UK; Copenhagen, Denmark; Edinburgh, UK; Genoa, Italy; Gothenburg, Sweden; Helsinki, Finland; Rome, Italy; and Trondheim, Norway also have integrated pricing strategies in place.[46]

Bus rapid transit systems   *Bus rapid transit (BRT) systems* are permanently integrated systems of facilities, services, and amenities designed to improve the speed, reliability, and identity of bus transit. In many respects, BRT is rubber-tired light-rail transit with greater operating flexibility and potentially lower capital and operating costs than rail-based systems.[47] In addition, BRTs can be implemented in a fraction of the time needed to set up rail systems. These systems efficiently modify commuting but require investments in bus running lanes, stations, vehicles, routing, services, and fare collection. BRT has been implemented all over the world. In North America, the best examples of BRT include: Boston, Pittsburgh, Miami, Los Angeles, San Fernando Valley, Las Vegas, Houston, Ottawa, Vancouver, and York. Successful BRTs have also been implemented in Curitiba and Sao Paulo, Brazil; Quito, Ecuador; Leon, Mexico; Bogota, Colombia; Sidney, Adelaide, and Brisbane, Australia; Paris, Nancy, and Rouen, France; and Amsterdam and Eindhoven, Holland.[48] BRT offers a cost-effective way to employ rapid transit operating as rapidly as possible with the least amount of funds, and it also preserves options for latter expansion and upgrading.

Buildings and Construction

Across the globe, 30 to 40% of all energy is consumed in buildings, and the lion's share of this consumption is burned for heating, cooling, lighting, and appliances during the operational phase.[49] Low-energy construction saves money, the climate, and human health.

The construction, maintenance, and refurbishment of buildings is managed by a complex network of stakeholders. Our focus is on the role that government plays in pursuing sustainable buildings. **New construction** represents an opportunity to use technology to develop, install, and maintain component parts that conserve energy and use renewable energy resources. For example, the city of Pune, India, has established an efficient energy housing program that incorporates solar and wind energy, solid and wastewater recycling, and construction materials. The program outlines guidelines for eco-construction and develops financing mechanisms for eco-housing. In addition, eco-housing certificates are issued that result in reduced taxes and promote additional eco-housing development. This program has increased Indian interest in improving environmental facets of construction.[50]

The Landskrona, Sweden, new apartment project is another example of new construction that lowers energy consumption. This southern Swedish program involved the development of 35 new rental apartments. These buildings do not use conventional heating (i.e., no radiators or under-the-floor heating systems) but rely on mechanical ventilation systems with heat recovery. These apartments yield savings of 40 to 70 kilowatt hours per square meter per year over conventional apartments.[51]

Old construction is another opportunity to raise fuel efficiency. Consider, for example, the multifamily dwellings constructed by the Soviets. In 1996, Lithuania embarked on an effort to lower the fuel consumption associated with these buildings. The three primary priorities of these programs are to ensure efficient energy use, sustainable management, and modernization of housing. The goal is to refurbish 70% of housing built before 1993 by 2020. Achievement of this goal will result in savings of €55 million and a reduction of 365,500 tons of carbon emissions.[52]

The citizens of Gårdsten, Sweden, are engaged in similar efforts to raise the performance of existing buildings. Multifamily dwellings have been equipped with prefabricated solar collectors used to heat water for the apartments. In addition, external walls have been insulated with an air gap between the insulation and the wall. These modifications, along with thermal insulation, have reduced energy consumption by 30%.

One benefit of the efforts to enhance sustainability in the developing world is the potential for carbon offsets with mature economies. For example, Cape Town, South Africa, is retrofitting 2,300 low-income housing units with technological enhancements such as energy-efficient lighting and solar water heaters.[53] South Africa benefits from this program through reduced greenhouse emissions, improved health, and new employment opportunities. The project will generate 130,000 tons of carbon credits over its 21-year lifetime. The first 10,000 tons have been sold to the United Kingdom.[54]

The Chinese market represents a significant opportunity to influence sustainability. At the national level, the Chinese government is committed to investing US$193 billion to make buildings more efficient by 2020. An important part of this initiative is to reduce markedly the country's reliance on coal. Government buildings are setting the standard for sustainability. The country's 600 million square meters of government office space represent 6% of the total area of civic buildings. Adding fuel efficiency to these buildings will save the equivalent of 18 million tons of coal. It will, however, take 5 to 10 years to change societal behavior and improve energy efficiency.[55] At the provincial level, the Inner Mongolian and Qinhai Provinces subsidize home expenditures for solar equipment. The program will provide electricity for 23 million people in the region by making use of renewable resources like solar PV and wind generation.[56] At the local level, Shanghai has established a certification and labeling program for energy-efficient housing. Participants enjoy favorable tax policies and have access to special funding for the support of energy-efficient buildings.

Appliances

At 29% of global spending on energy, the household sector represents the second largest contributor to energy spending. One primary area of concern is the use of appliances. Consumers are using more appliances today, and many of these products use more energy than their predecessors did. Consequently, the demand for energy for appliances is the most rapidly growing part of the household sector, with a 57% increase in consumption since 2005. Appliances overtook water heating as the second most energy-consuming category in the late 1990s and now account for 21% of total household energy consumption.[57] Large appliances include refrigerators, freezers, washing machines, dishwashers, and televisions. Since 1990, the share of total energy use by all of these appliances except televisions has decreased in mature economies. The average unit's energy consumption has declined even though the refrigerators and freezers have become larger. Energy efficiency gains for televisions have been outstripped by the consumer trend toward larger screens, which use more energy. Total energy consumption in the EU15 fell for refrigerators and washing machines. For other appliances, improved efficiency has been more than offset by higher levels of ownership and use.[58]

The United Nations works in partnership with the *Collaborative Labeling and Appliance Standards Program* (CLASP) to reduce energy consumption associated with appliance use. Established in 1999 in the United States, CLASP became a global nonprofit corporation in 2005. It is governed by nine directors from six countries on four continents. Working in conjunction with government officials responsible for standards and labeling, CLASP assists in the development of a testing capability for a product and assists in analyzing and setting standards. CLASP also designs and implements label programs along with communications programs designed to inform consumers about product energy usage (Figure 4–8).

FIG. 4-8 Energy Star and EnergyGuide Labels

Source: © Art Directors & TRIP/Alamy

Source: © Federal Trade Commission, www.ftc.gov

CLASP also provides oversight and evaluation to ensure the integrity of the standards. For example, washing machines sold in the United States must meet standards for energy supply, water pressure, agitation and speed settings, and other standards. By coordinating the development of these standards with CLASP, the United States has the ability to compare product efficiencies with those operating in other countries. U.S. law also requires that new appliances display a label that helps consumers compare energy efficiency among similar products. In 1980, the Federal Trade Commission began requiring that *EnergyGuide* labels be placed on all new appliances. These labels indicate a range of energy use among models in a product class, and they provide estimates of the annual cost of operation of a product.

In addition to the EnergyGuide labels, a subset of products in a category can display the **Energy Star** label. This label, which was originally developed in the United States for the computer industry, is now applied to 50 product groups sold in the United States, Canada, Japan, Australia, Taiwan, the European Union, and the European Free Trade Association. The label indicates that the product possessing it is one of the most efficient products in the class. The percentage of products that earn the Energy Star label varies by product class. The Energy Star-qualified appliances in the washing machine group are those that use 10 to 50% less energy and water than standard models.[59] By contrast, televisions sold in the United States that display the Energy Star label use 30% less energy than standard units.[60]

The use of standards to facilitate product comparison offers many advantages. Over the last 10 years, CLASP has assisted with the implementation of 21 new minimum energy performance standards, energy efficiency endorsement labels, and energy information labels that will save 250,000 tons of carbon dioxide by 2014.[61] Participating countries benefit from enhanced institutional capacity for implementing standards and labeling programs, increased production of energy-efficient products by manufacturers, and improved average energy efficiency of appliances. Moreover, these standards yield significant reductions in electricity consumption as well as lower energy-related emissions of greenhouse gases.[62]

C. Environmental Action Designed to Reduce Human Influences on the Atmosphere

Air Pollution

International action focused on controlling air pollution is implemented on a regional basis in Europe, North America, and Asia. In 1947, the United Nations established the United Nations Economic Commission for Europe (UNECE) as one of five regional commissions. The UNECE establishes standards to facilitate international cooperation within and outside the region.[63] Since 1979, this group has developed the Convention on Long-range Transboundary Air Pollution. This treaty has been extended via eight protocols identifying specific measures to be taken by parties to reduce air pollution. Here is a brief synopsis of these protocols:

1. *The 1984 Geneva Protocol on Long-term Financing of the Cooperative Programme for Monitoring and Evaluation of the Long-range Transmission of Air Pollutants in Europe.* This protocol provides for international cost sharing of monitoring programs. The protocol calls for collection of emission data for SO_2, NO_x, VOCs and other air pollutants; air and precipitation quality measurement; and modeling of atmospheric dispersion. About 100 monitoring stations in 24 countries participate in the program.[64]

2. *The 1985 Helsinki Protocol on the Reduction of Sulfur Emissions.* The Helsinki protocol sought sulfur reductions of at least 30% over 1980 levels. The 21 parties to this protocol had reduced 1980 sulfur emissions by more than 50% by 1993.[65]

3. *The 1988 Sofia Protocol Concerning the Control of Emissions of Nitrogen Oxides.* The Sofia protocol seeks a reduction in emissions of NO_x of 9% compared to 1987. Nineteen of the 25 parties to the protocol have reached the target emissions at 1987 (or 1978 for the United States) levels of reduced emissions.[66]

4. *The 1991 Geneva Protocol Concerning the Control of Emissions of Volatile Organic Compounds.* This directive seeks a 30% reduction in emissions of volatile organic compounds (VOCs) by 1999 using a year between 1984 and 1990 as a basis.[67]

5. *The 1994 Oslo Protocol on Further Reduction of Sulfur Emissions.* This protocol augments the 1985 Helsinki directive by adding criteria that led to a differentiation of emission reduction obligations of parties to the protocol.[68]

6. *The 1998 Aarhus Protocol on Persistent Organic Pollutants (POPs).* The goal of this protocol is to eliminate discharges of POPs. The protocol bans the production and use of some products outright (e.g., chlordane), limits the use of POPs and schedules them for elimination at a later stage (e.g., DDT).[69]

7. *The 1998 Aarhus Protocol on Heavy Metals.* This protocol calls for reduced emissions for cadmium, lead, and mercury beyond their levels in 1990. It also requires participating parties to phase out leaded gasoline.[70]

8. *The 1999 Gothenburg Protocol to Abate Acidification, Eutrophication, and Ground-level Ozone.* This protocol sets limits for sulfur, NO_x, VOCs, and ammonia. When the protocol is fully implemented, Europe's sulfur emissions will be cut by at least 63%, NO_x emissions by 41%, VOC emissions by 40%, and ammonia emissions by 17% compared to 1990.[71]

These protocols offer pollution standards adopted by countries outside of Europe. Canada and the United States have participated in several of these protocols. Both countries have ratified the 1984 Geneva Protocol, the 1988 Sofia Protocol, and the 1998 Heavy Metals Protocol. Canada has also ratified the 1985 Helsinki Protocol and the 1998 Aarhus Protocol for heavy metals, whereas the United States has ratified the 1999 Gothenburg Protocol.

In addition to the ratification of these protocols, the United States has been working to enhance air quality since the enactment of the Clean Air Act of 1970. The U.S. Environmental Protection Agency (EPA) sets national air quality standards for common air pollutants (carbon monoxide, ozone, lead, nitrogen dioxide, particulate matter, and sulfur dioxide). As a result, emissions of each of these six pollutants have dropped more than 32% since 1990.[72] The Clean Air Act further required the EPA to issue a series of rules to reduce pollution from automobiles. Emissions from new cars purchased today are well over 90% cleaner than new vehicles purchased in 1970.[73]

In 1990, a new Clean Air Act introduced a nationwide approach to the reduction of acid rain. The law is designed to reduce acid rain and improve public health by reducing emissions of sulfur dioxide and nitrogen oxides. The program sets a permanent limit on the total amount of sulfur dioxide emitted by electric power plants nationwide. As of 2005, emission reductions were 41% below 1980 levels.[74]

Asian countries have also enacted policies to limit air pollution. The Association of Southeastern Nations (ASEAN) has adopted a Haze Fund designed to coordinate response to forest fires and the resulting smoke and fog.[75] In China, a country with tremendous need to curb pollution, environmental law is underdeveloped and neglected.[76] Nevertheless, during the current Five-Year Plan (2006-2010), China will invest 1,375 billion yuan (US$169.5 billion) in environmental protection. Substantial portions of these funds will address air pollution and water shortages.[77]

Ozone

The United Nations and affiliated countries have been taking action to reduce ozone depletion for more than 20 years. In 1987, the United Nations developed the Montreal Protocol.[78] This directive and other regulations banning ozone-depleting substances have reversed the destructive trend toward ozone depletion. CFCs previously used in refrigerants, blowing foams, and solvents have been temporarily replaced with hydro-fluourocarbons (HFCs). Although HFCs also contribute to ozone depletion, their influence is substantially lower (88–98% less effective ozone depletion) than that of CFCs. The UN directives, however, call for the long-term elimination of these chemicals as well. HFCs are also used as substitutes for CFCs. Although these chemicals do not deplete the ozone, they contribute to global warming. Two bromide-based halogens, halon-1211 and halon-1301, represent a substantial portion of bromine from all source gases (see Figure 3–8). Despite the elimination of production in developed nations in 1994, emissions of these gases will remain high into the 21st century due to their long lifetimes and continued release.[79]

Despite the fact that bromide-based emissions continue to be problematic, there is evidence that the Montreal Protocol is working. The concentrations of halogens peaked in the lower atmosphere in 1995 and in the stratosphere in 2001.[80] Recent research indicates evidence of a decrease in the atmospheric burden of ozone-depleting substances in the lower atmosphere. There is also evidence of some early signs of the expected stratospheric ozone recovery.[81] Given that ozone-depleting gases typically last 40 to 100 years in the atmosphere, full recovery is not expected before 2070. Nevertheless, failure to continue to comply with the Montreal Protocol could delay or prevent recovery of the ozone layer.[82]

D. Environmental Action Designed to Reduce Human Influences on Water

Consumption simultaneously influences multiple factors associated with water. We examine three related aspects of water. These include the availability of clean drinking water, the impurities in water, and the oceans and fisheries as bodies of water.

Access to Clean Drinking Water

Efforts to increase the accessibility of freshwater are underway in many parts of the world, yet one sixth of the world's population still does not have access to clean drinking water.[83] The availability of freshwater is increasingly a more significant problem across the globe, but at present it is most pronounced in Asia and Africa.

Over the last decade, Asia has witnessed overall progress in the availability of drinking water (see Figure 4–9). Nevertheless, 655 million people in the region still lack access to safe water. South Pacific states have not made any progress, and conditions in Central Asian countries actually deteriorated. In many megacities, up to 70% of citizens live in slums and generally lack access to improved water and sanitation.

In northeastern Asia, China is developing the Three Gorges Dam. This dam offers a number of environmental benefits but also challenges biodiversity. The

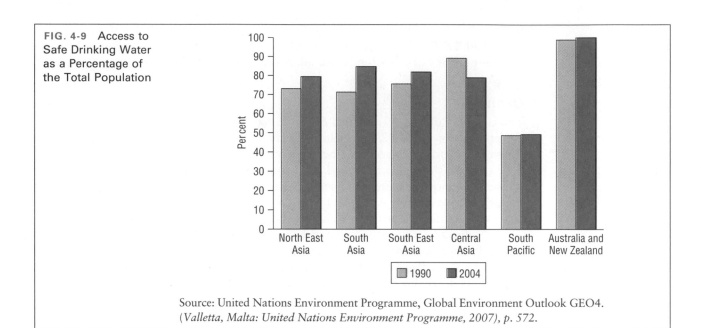

FIG. 4-9 Access to Safe Drinking Water as a Percentage of the Total Population

Source: United Nations Environment Programme, Global Environment Outlook GEO4. (*Valletta, Malta: United Nations Environment Programme, 2007), p. 572.*

dam provides the potential for cleaner drinking water and reduces reliance on coal (and its inherent pollutants) for energy. In addition, China is spending 40 billion yuan (US$5 billion) between 2001 and 2010 on 150 sewage treatment plants and 170 urban garbage disposal centers. This investment is made to prevent water pollution in the Three Gorges Dam and the Yangtze River.

Regrettably, progress toward increased availability of drinking water in Africa has been modest. Although there has been some success such as the shared watercourse systems in the Southern African Development Community (SADC), officials in many countries work in very difficult conditions with minimal resources at their disposal. These resource constraints are due to poor economic conditions as well as low budget allocations to water. Government departments are underresourced, and the number of professionals employed in the water and sanitation sector in public service is inadequate.[84]

Although there are ongoing efforts on each continent to enhance the quality of freshwater, more work is needed to secure suitable drinking water. If appropriate action is not taken, environmental science projects that the majority of the world population will live in conditions of very low water availability by 2025.[85] Science underscores the need for a drastic decrease in water consumption, especially in irrigated land use and industry. In addition, environmental researchers call for reduction of wastewater discharges into the water supply, long-term river runoff regulation, and the redistribution of water resources across territories.[86]

Water Impurities

Whereas the prior section examined the general level of freshwater availability, this section addresses procedures employed to reduce specific impurities in the water supplies. The **World Health Organization** (WHO) has established guidelines designed to limit the impurities in the water supply. The guidelines offer health-based targets implemented by national water authorities. The guidelines indicate generally acceptable levels of biological and chemical (i.e., anthropogenic) water contaminants for water suppliers. For example, the WHO recognizes that manganese in water supplies causes an undesirable taste in beverages and stains laundry. Consequently, the guidelines call for a maximum of 0.4 mg/liter in the water supply. The WHO guidelines also offer background information on microbial, chemical, and radiological aspects of contaminants. In addition, the health-based guidelines indicate procedures for monitoring of control measures for drinking water safety as well as independent surveillance systems to ensure that water supplies remain healthy.

Although the WHO provides the guidelines, the determination of water quality is administered on a national and regional basis. The quality of drinking water is an increasing concern in every region. For instance, the European Union introduced the Water Framework Directive in 2000 with the goal that all water bodies attain good ecological status by 2015. Although there are many international European water agreements, there has been a significant decline in the level of water quality monitoring in parts of Central and Eastern Europe over the last decade.[87] The United States experienced more than 250 disease outbreaks and almost 500,000 cases of water-borne illness from 1985 to 2000. Consequently, the Safe Drinking Water Act has been modified on several occasions to curb exposure to microbial contaminants and disinfectants. In addition, new standards have been developed to eliminate exposure to metals such as arsenic.[88]

Water contaminants continue to be problematic in Asia despite multiple efforts to enhance water quality. There have been attempts to reform the water and sanitation sector in South Asia and Southeast Asia, including large-scale subsidization of water for the poor. For instance, Laos is developing the infrastructure to ensure greater access to safe water and sanitation, especially for the rural population. Similarly, Singapore is recycling wastewater and using new filtration technology to bring it to acceptable drinking standards.[89]

In Africa, suitable water and sanitation facilities have been extended to many more people during the past decade, but there is a strong need to increase the access to clean water and sanitation.[90] South Africa has passed a National Water Act designed to protect ecosystems and enhance the quality of water.[91] Nevertheless, more regulation is needed to ensure that citizens have access to clean drinking water and sanitation. Among countries with available data, almost half had less than 50% coverage for sanitation. Ten countries (Angola, Burkina Faso, Chad, the Democratic Republic of the Congo, Eritrea, Ethiopia, Madagascar, Mauritania, Rwanda, and Sierra Leone) have less than 50% availability of suitable drinking water and sanitation.

Oceans and Fisheries

International governance of oceans is coordinated via the United Nations Convention on the Law of the Sea. This law outlines rights and obligations of countries, and it further provides the international basis for protection and sustainable development of the marine and coastal environment. The Convention entered into force in 1994 and has been ratified by 135 nations. The past 10 years has witnessed substantial progress toward an integrated approach to coastal management. Increasingly, nations are codifying requirements for coastal management. Standards developed by the United Nations and the World Bank provide direction in the development of these regulations. The 1995 Global Programme of Action (GPA) for the Protection of the Marine Environment from Land-based Activities provided additional incentive to develop methods for preventing the degradation of the marine environment. GPA provides conceptual and practical guidance to national water authorities and facilitates cooperation among nations.[92]

Although the level of cooperation among nations has increased, estimates indicate that at least 60% of world fisheries are either fully exploited or overfished. The Food and Agriculture Organization (FAO) of the United Nations Code of Conduct for Responsible Fisheries has influenced many countries to modify fisheries laws. This UN organization developed the Code of Conduct for Responsible Fisheries in 1995. This code is the foundation for promotion of sustainable fisheries and aquaculture. The FAO also has outlined international plans of action to improve shark management and to control fishing. Despite these regulations, illegal, unregulated, and unreported fishing remain severe problems affecting world fisheries.

E. Environmental Action Designed to Reduce Human Influences on Land

Urban Expansion

The year 2007 marked the first year that the population in urban settings exceeded the rural population.[93] Urban expansion is an issue on every continent, but there are varying levels of response to this issue. Interestingly, in Latin America, countries with the lowest percentages of urban citizens are witnessing the fastest urbanization rates. The urban growth rates in Paraguay, Chile, and Bolivia are now faster than in Argentina, Ecuador, and Chile.[94] Africa is the least urbanized inhabited region, but it has the world's highest rate of urbanization.

Increasing urbanization is an issue on every continent, but the primary impetus for change has been in mature economies. The U.S. EPA funds the **Smart Growth Network,** an organization focused on enhancing the quality of living conditions in cities. *Smart growth* refers to a set of policy options that relates the reshaping of urban growth to transportation priorities.[95] This network seeks to enhance urban lifestyles by promoting a range of housing opportunities and walkable neighborhoods. It encourages community and stakeholder collaboration and fosters attractive communities that make fair development decisions. In addition, it seeks to provide transportation alternatives within cities and promotes preservation of open space, farmland, and natural beauty.

In contrast to urban sprawl that follows freeways, smart growth relies on compact urban development and revitalization of older areas in cities in conjunction with renewed public transit systems. Recent evidence indicates that adoption of smart growth principles and guidelines reaps benefits for cities. Research conducted in 44 cities around the world (12 each from the United States and Europe, 6 each from Canada and Australia, and 8 Asian cities) indicate that smart growth is becoming an international trend. Urban districts are beginning to reverse trends toward sprawl, and population densities are increasing or have stopped in many cities. City governments and concerned citizens are revitalizing older areas more than building on the urban fringe.

Land Degradation

Degradation of land is related to several other facets of the environment, especially water quality and biodiversity. One of the primary issues on land degradation is the international movement of hazardous materials. The *Basel Convention on the Control of the Trans-boundary Movement of Hazardous Wastes and Their Disposal* was adopted in 1989 and entered into force in 1992. This convention was created to prevent the economically motivated dumping of hazardous wastes from richer to poorer countries. The *Basel Ban Amendment*, adopted in 1995, prohibits all exports of hazardous wastes from the OECD, EU, and Liechtenstein to all other parties to the convention. The United States is the only OECD country that has not ratified the Basel Convention or the Basel Ban Amendment. China, India, Myanmar, and Pakistan become the home of more than 90% of 20 to 50 million tons of electronic waste produced each year.[96] Export of e-waste to these countries is a violation of the Basel Convention and the Basel Ban Amendment. In other parts of Asia, Japan and South Korea are lowering waste generation through reduced use of natural resources in production and more sustainable consumption.

The New Partnership for African Development (NEPAD) program addresses soil erosion, salinization, declining fertility, soil compaction, and pollution on the continent. Through a network of regional organizations, NEPAD promotes sustainable land use, rational use of rangelands, sustainable agriculture, and integrated natural resource management.[97] Similar problems plague West Asia where poorly managed irrigation systems are associated with higher levels of salinity. Although there are efforts to improve degraded lands, most of this action is focused on 16% of the land mass located in the Arabian Peninsula and Mashriq.

In the European Union, reduction in levels of industrial production and agricultural intensity limits the extent of land degradation. Nevertheless, Eastern Europe faces threats due to Soviet-era accumulation of hazardous materials. These materials include radioactive waste, military and mining waste, and obsolete pesticides (containing persistent organic pollutants). Because funds to dispose of this material are lacking, the environment remains at appreciable risk.

Deforestation and Desertification

Recognizing the worldwide concerns about deforestation, the United Nations has developed some nonbinding instruments for the management of forests. The UN calls for the reverse of loss of forest cover worldwide through sustainable forest development and for enhancement of forest-based economic, social, and environmental benefits. In addition, it calls for increases in the area of protected forests as well as increases in funding for sustainable forest management.[98] Despite this initiative, subregional issues continue to limit the amount of forestation. For example, the European Union has adopted a sustainability strategy for forest management; Eastern Europe continues to try to limit illegal logging as well as human-induced forest fires. Deforestation is rampant in the Middle East, yet the balancing of this activity with reforestation in other areas has resulted in no major changes in the level of forestation over the past 15 years.

Efforts to curb desertification recognize that the increased frequency and severity of droughts (due to climate change) will likely exacerbate desertification. Consequently, the United Nations Convention to Combat Desertification offers a platform for mitigation of this issue. This convention outlines necessary financing, information, and technology to reduce desertification, and it also outlines national action programs.[99]

Implementation of the UN efforts to combat desertification occurs on a regional level with the greatest attention focused on Africa, Asia, the Northern Mediterranean region, Central and Eastern Europe, Latin America, and the Caribbean. Given that two thirds of Africa is desert or drylands, its implementation plan is the most detailed of all regions. The plan calls for adoption on a national basis of legal, political, economic, financial, and social measures to limit desertification.[100]

Asia faces similar problems due to the high percentage of land that is desert. About 27% of China is desertified, and nearly 400 million people live in these areas. China has responded to this environmental threat by passing laws and drawing up a national plan to limit desertification. In the Northern Mediterranean, land degradation is often linked to poor agricultural practices. Thus, Greece, Italy, Portugal, Spain, and Turkey are launching a subregional program for scientific cooperation, exchange of information and documentation, and organization of regional training courses. Similarly, countries in Central and Eastern Europe are coordinating efforts in scientific research, data management, information exchange, training, drought mitigation, and disaster preparedness. The Latin American regional plan outlines the need to eliminate unsustainable practices such as excessive irrigation and inappropriate agricultural practices, inadequate legal issues, inappropriate use of soil, fertilizers and pesticides, overgrazing, and intensive exploitation of forests.

F. Environmental Action Designed to Reduce Human Influences on Biodiversity

Biodiversity concerns variation among species of plant and animal life. In 1992, members of the United Nations signed the *Convention on Biological Diversity*. This document sought to conserve biodiversity, promote sustainable use of the components of biodiversity, and share the benefits of utilization of genetic resources in a fair manner. The Convention offers guidance based on the precautionary principle that where there is a threat of significant reduction or loss of biological diversity, lack of full scientific certainty should not be used as a reason for postponing measures to avoid or minimize such a threat. The convention recognizes that substantial investments are required to conserve biological diversity. Current evaluations of progress of the convention indicate strong increases in the coverage of protected areas for various species. The abundance of species and respected habitats, however, is decreasing. Moreover, threatened species face greater risks than in previous eras.

The Convention on Biodiversity provides guidelines for implementation on a regional or national level. Due in part to rapid development in the region, the Asia Pacific region has encountered tremendous pressure on ecosystems over the past two decades. Asian countries participate in protection of coastal ecosystems by affiliation with one of four Regional Sea Action Plans: East Asia, Northwest Pacific, South Asia, and the Pacific. Despite this affiliation, East Asia and South Asia discharge more than 85% of their wastewater directly into the sea. In the South Pacific, local communities are collaborating through locally managed marine areas designed to protect coastal areas.

The EU initiatives to deter biodiversity loss are more stringent than those established by the UN convention. The Pan-European Ecological Network (PEEN) is a nonbinding framework that promotes cooperative action across Europe, contributing to the evolving international process of developing a stronger strategic component to nature conservation in Europe.[101] The EU Commission on a European Biodiversity Strategy seeks to anticipate, prevent, and attack causes of reduction or loss of biodiversity at the source. It focuses on the reversal of present trends in biodiversity reduction or losses. It also provides a clearinghouse that facilitates public access to information relevant for biodiversity.[102]

Protection of biodiversity is also a vital concern in Latin America. Over the past 15 years, the amount of protected marine and terrestrial land has nearly doubled.

The Mesoamerican Biological Corridor is a nearly 10-year-old project designed to support biodiversity in Mexico, Belize, Guatemala, Honduras, Nicaragua, Costa Rica, and Panama.[103] Similarly, a program designed to conserve the Brazilian rain forest is a joint undertaking of Brazil and the international community that seeks to find ways to conserve the tropical rain forests of the Amazon and Brazil's Atlantic coast.[104]

Although there has been some progress toward biodiversity targets, the UN recognizes that much work is needed to achieve a significant reduction of the current rate of biodiversity loss. To limit biodiversity loss, it is imperative to improve agricultural efficiency and plan for agricultural expansion. Furthermore, the demand for meat by the more affluent sectors of society should be lowered and overfishing should be eliminated. Biodiversity should be integrated with trade liberalization decisions, and it should be integral to poverty-reduction strategies. Finally, regulators should recognize that biodiversity will be better protected through actions that are justified on their economic merits.[105]

G. The Role of Energy Conservation Efforts to Limit Climate Change and Pollution

Energy conservation refers to efforts to limit the amount of resources employed in consumption. Conservation efforts provide a complement to the Kyoto Protocol. **Efficient usage** examines the extent to which organizations and individuals engage efforts to **reduce, reuse, or recycle** resources. Although this strategy is often associated with reductions in pollution, efficient energy use also has important implications for climate change. Since a substantial amount of resources are employed to refine and process materials consumed by individuals, firms, and other organizations, reductions in the amount of material required limit the need for greenhouse gas emissions. For example, use of hybrid automobiles reduces the need for fossil fuels by 30 to 60%.[106]

Reuse of material also constrains energy requirements because there is limited need to process materials that are reused. For instance, Xerox developed a program in 1995 that used components from leased copiers as high-quality, low-cost parts for new machines. This strategy enables Xerox to provide lease customers with the latest technologies while also reducing production costs.[107] Similarly, recycled materials gain economic advantages over new materials to the extent that the costs to process the recycled materials are lower than the costs for new resources. For example, excess aluminum from Ford's Chicago stamping plant is recycled by Alcan. This process requires 5% of the energy used to produce the primary aluminum and reduces GHG emissions by 95%.[108]

Most developed countries promote recycling. For example, Figure 4–10 outlines the sources of waste materials in the United States in 2007. The amount of municipal solid waste (MSW) recovered in 2007 was 33% (85 million tons) of the total MSW generated. American recyclers increasingly pass their materials on to overseas buyers. China, India, and other Asian economies are propelling the markets for recycled paper, metals, and plastics to near-record prices. In addition, they provide a needed outlet for other goods such as newsprint.[109]

Although efforts to reuse–reduce–recycle are promoted in multiple nations, several issues limit the viability of these programs. Economic analyses of household recycling indicate that it usually does not pay for itself. Research illustrates that the typical costs of processing reclaimed materials exceed the revenue generated from

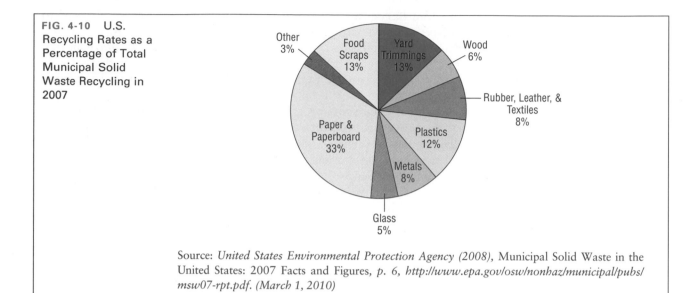

FIG. 4-10 U.S. Recycling Rates as a Percentage of Total Municipal Solid Waste Recycling in 2007

Source: *United States Environmental Protection Agency (2008),* Municipal Solid Waste in the United States: 2007 Facts and Figures, *p. 6, http://www.epa.gov/osw/nonhaz/municipal/pubs/ msw07-rpt.pdf. (March 1, 2010)*

the reclaimed goods.[110] Second, electronic equipment and computers that contain lead, mercury, chromium, cadmium, and other toxic material are an increasing problem for landfills. These products may also contain glass, copper, silver, and gold that raise concern for disposal when the product is no longer useful. In the United States, only 10% of the 2.5 million tons of electronic waste is recycled, yet 70% of the heavy metals in landfills are from this waste.[111]

International conservation efforts are using legislation to control the components that go into products as well the producer's responsibility for a product beyond its useful life. In 2003, the EU also adopted a Directive on Restriction of Hazardous Substances (ROHS) in Electrical and Electronic Equipment. This policy bans the use of lead, mercury, cadmium, hexavalent chromium, and brominated flame retardants used in plastics. China has also adopted regulations banning the same six substances, beginning in 2006, thus ensuring that Chinese products meet EU requirements.[112] Together, this action reduces the amount of hazardous material discarded in landfills. Legislation is also being enacted that requires recycling at the end of the useful life for computers and appliances.[113] In 2003, the European Union adopted the Waste Electrical and Electronic Equipment (WEEE) Directive that requires producers to take responsibility for recovering and recycling electronic waste without charge to consumers. This directive not only promotes recycling and reduces landfill disposal and incineration, but it also is an incentive to producers to design products in ways that reduce waste and facilitate recycling. Dell computers has been active in its efforts to address these requirements. In 2006, the company developed a program that enabled consumers across the globe to return Dell computers, printers, and monitors at no cost.[114]

There are several important business consequences associated with reduce–reuse–recycle strategies.[115] In many cases, organizations must attend to conservation efforts because of legal requirements. Organizations cannot be reckless with hazardous waste, and most countries have laws dictating how these materials may be stored. For example, European Union members must adhere to union legislation for the disposal of hazardous waste.[116] Second, reductions in the amount of consumption and waste lower the firm's overall costs. Shell Oil lowers its waste levels by pumping carbon dioxide into 500 Dutch greenhouses. This action reduces emissions by 325,000 tons per year and saves greenhouses from having to burn millions of cubic meters of gas needed to produce carbon dioxide.[117] Thus, costs are reduced for Shell and the greenhouses.

Although there are some lingering issues with the success of reuse–reduce–recycle strategies, they remain important mechanisms that limit climate change and reduce pollution. Consequently, in the coming chapters addressing various types of consumers, we incorporate discussion of efficient usage into analyses of household, services, transportation, and manufacturing consumers.

Summary

A. Identify Environmental Action Designed to Reduce Climate Change

The Kyoto Protocol outlines national efforts to reduce or limit greenhouse gases. The protocol introduced three market mechanisms (emissions trading, clean development mechanism, and joint implementation) that enable countries to engage in international commerce to meet emission targets. These mechanisms stimulate sustainable development via the transfer of technology and investment, and they encourage the private sector and developing countries to contribute to emissions reductions. They help countries to meet their commitments by cost effectively removing GHGs from the atmosphere in other countries.

B. Understand Efforts to Influence the Supply and Demand for Energy

Renewable energy sources provide contributions to the supply of energy. To the extent that these sources are employed as substitutes for fossil fuels, the environment does not encounter the negative consequences of oil or other fossil fuel consumption. Renewable energy sources will increase throughout the world, but the demand for energy will also continue to rise. Some of the greatest opportunities for energy conservation lie in the transportation, construction, and appliance industries.

C. Environmental Action Designed to Reduce Human Influences on the Atmosphere

International action focused on controlling air pollution is implemented regionally in Europe, North America, and Asia. The United Nations Economic Commission for Europe establishes standards to facilitate international cooperation within and outside the region. This group has developed the Convention on Long-range Transboundary Air Pollution, a document that has been extended via eight protocols identifying specific corrective measures.

D. Environmental Action Designed to Reduce Human Influences on Water

Efforts to increase the accessibility of freshwater are underway in many parts of the world, yet one sixth of the world's population still does not have access to clean drinking water.[118] The availability of freshwater is increasingly a more significant problem across the globe, but at present it is most pronounced in Asia and Africa. Over the last decade, Asia has witnessed overall progress in the availability of drinking water. Nevertheless, 655 million people in the region still lack access to safe water. Progress toward increased availability of drinking water in Africa has been modest. Government departments are underresourced, and the number of professionals employed in the water and sanitation sector in public service is inadequate.

E. Environmental Action Designed to Reduce Human Influences on Land

Increasing urbanization is an issue on every continent, but the primary impetus for change has been in mature economies. The Smart Growth Network, an organization focused on enhancing the quality of living conditions in cities, has established a set of policies designed to reshape urban growth and transportation priorities. This network seeks to enhance urban lifestyles by promoting a range of housing opportunities and walkable neighborhoods. It encourages community and stakeholder collaboration and fosters attractive communities that make fair development decisions.

F. Environmental Action Designed to Reduce Human Influences on Biodiversity

Biodiversity concerns variation among species of plant and animal life. The United Nations has developed a convention designed to conserve biodiversity, promote sustainable use of the components of biodiversity, and share the benefits of utilization of genetic resources in a fair manner. The convention offers guidance based on the precautionary principle that where there is a threat of significant reduction or loss of biological diversity, lack of full scientific certainty should not be used as a reason for postponing measures to avoid or minimize such a threat. The convention recognizes that substantial investments are required to conserve biological diversity.

G. The role of Energy Conservation Efforts to Limit Climate Change and Pollution

Energy conservation refers to efforts to limit the amount of resources employed in consumption. Efficient usage examines the extent to which organizations and individuals engage in efforts to reduce, reuse, or recycle resources. This strategy is often associated with reductions in pollution, but efficient energy use also has important implications for climate change. Because a substantial amount of resources are employed to refine and process materials consumed by individuals, firms, and other organizations, reductions in the amount of material required limit the need for greenhouse gas emissions.

Keywords

biodiesel, 69
biofuels, 69
carbon offsets, 63
certified emission reduction, 63
efficient usage, 83
emission reduction units, 64
Energy Star, 75

grid-connected photovoltaic cells, 68
Kyoto Protocol, 62
new construction, 73
off-grid solar systems, 68
old construction, 73
recycle, 83

reduce, 83
reuse, 83
Smart Growth Network, 80
solar water heaters, 68
World Health Organization (WHO), 78

Questions

1. What sectors of the economy might show favor or disdain for the Kyoto Protocol?
2. How does the Kyoto Protocol facilitate the exchange of emission credits?
3. Why is it important for multinational organizations to be involved in efforts to confront climate change?
4. What is the current role of renewable energy as a source of energy for residential and commercial use?
5. What are the primary types of solar power that are being used in residential settings?
6. The owner of a 40-year-old home claims that sustainable business practices are only important for new housing. How might you respond to such a comment?
7. What are the governing rules concerning air quality, and how effective have they been?
8. What is the magnitude of the clean drinking water and sanitation problem on the globe, and to what extent is this a regional issue?
9. Why is the United Nations concerned about biodiversity, and what efforts has it taken to limit the number species on the endangered list?
10. How are efforts to "reduce, reuse, and recycle" related to climate change?

Endnotes

1 Practical Action, "Micro Hydro Power," http://practicalaction.org/practicalanswers/pdf_thumb.php?s=l&im=micro_hydro_energy.pdf (accessed April 28, 2010).

2 The World Bank Group, "Directions in Hydro Power," http://siteresources.worldbank.org/INTWAT/Resources/Directions_in_Hydropower_FINAL.pdf (accessed April 28, 2010).

3 Peter Browne, "The Rise of Micro-Hydro Projects in Africa," *Green Inc. Blog New York Times*, September 30, 2009, http://greeninc.blogs.nytimes.com/2009/09/30/the-rise-of-micro-hydro-projects-inafrica/#more-25185.

4 United Nations Development Program, "Affecting Electricity Policy Through a Community Micro Hydro Project, Kenya," http://sgp.undp.org/download/SGP_Kenya1.pdf (accessed April 28, 2010).

5 Philip Kotler and Gary Armstrong, *Principles of Marketing* (Upper Saddle River, NJ: Pearson Prentice Hall, 2008), 718.

6 United Nations Framework Convention on Climate Change, *Kyoto Protocol to the United Nations Framework Convention on Climate Change* (Kyoto, Japan: United Nations, 1998), 21.

7 See Note 6 above.

8 See Note 6 above.

9 See Note 6 above.

10 Chris Bartlett, "Carbon Markets Go Global," *Airfinance Journal* (October, 2007): 22.

11 European Climate Exchange, "How to Trade ECX Emissions Contracts," February, 2010, http://www.ecx.eu/media/pdf/ecx%20pres%20-%20february%202010.pdf (accessed April 28, 2010).

12 See Note 10 above.

13 Chicago Climate Exchange, "CCX Offsets Program," http://www.chicagoclimatex.com/content.jsf?id=23 (accessed April 28, 2010).

14 Jonathan Lash and Fred Wellington, "Competitive Advantage on a Warming Planet," *Harvard Business Review* (March, 2007): 94–102.

15 United Nations Framework Convention on Climate Change, "About CDM," http://cdm.unfccc.int/about/index.html (accessed April 28, 2010).

16 Thierry Bréchet and Benoît Lussis, "The Contribution of the Clean Development Mechanism to National Climate Policies," *Journal of Policy Modeling* 28, no. 9 (2006): 981–994.

17 See Note 6 above.

18 Ministry for the Environment, "Notice of Approval of Track One Joint Implementation Projects by the New Zealand Government," http://www.mfe.govt.nz/issues/climate/policies-initiatives/joint-implementation/notice.html (accessed April 28, 2010).

19 The United Nations Department of Economic and Social Affairs, "Increasing Global Renewable Energy Market Share: Recent Trends and Perspectives," December 12, 2005, http://www.un.org/esa/sustdev/sdissues/energy/publications&reports/background_report_birec2005.pdf (accessed April 29, 2010).

20 See Note 19 above.

21 Shimon Awerbuch, "Portfolio-Based Electricity Generation Planning: Policy Implications for Renewables and Energy Security," *Mitigation and Adaptation Strategies for Global Change* 11, no. 3 (2006): 693–710.

22 See Note 6 above.

23 Renewable Energy Policy Network for the 21st Century, "Renewables 2007 Global Status Report," (Paris, France REN21 Secretariat and Washington, DC: Worldwatch Institute, 2008). Copyright © 2008 Deutsche Gesellschaft für Technische Zusammenarbeit (GTZ) GmbH. http://www.ren21.net/pdf/RE2007_Global_Status_Report.pdf (accessed April 28, 2010).

24 See Note 19 above.

25 See Note 23 above.

26 Pew Center on Global Climate Change, "Renewable and Alternative Energy Portfolio Standards," http://www.pewclimate.org/what_s_being_done/in_the_states/rps.cfm (accessed April 28, 2010).

27 Steve Hamm, "Wind: The Power. The Promise. The Business," *Business Week*, July 7, 2008, 46–52.

28 Emma Charlton, "European Consumers Turn to Solar Energy," *Wall Street Journal*, August 13, 2008, 3D.

29 See Note 23 above.

30 U.S. Department of Energy, "Solar Water Heaters," http://www.eere.energy.gov/consumer/your_home/water_heating/index.cfm/mytopic=12850 (accessed April 28, 2010).

31 See Note 23 above.

32 See Note 23 above.

33 Monica Rogers, "Restaurant Chains Find Sustainable Returns," *Chain Leader*, March, 2008, http://www.chainleader.com/article/384064-Restaurant_Chains_Find_Sustainable_Returns.php (accessed April 29, 2010).

34 International Energy Agency, *Renewables in Global Energy Supply* (Paris, France: International Energy Organization, 2007), 34.

35 See Note 23 above.

36 See Note 19 above.

37 United Nations Department of Economic and Social Affairs, *Trends in Sustainable Development* (New York, NY: United Nations, 2006), 33.

38 Byron Pope, "Roush Aims to Create 'Green-Collar' Jobs With Propane-Powered Commercial Vehicles," WardsAuto.com, February 2009, http://wardsauto.com/ar/roush_propane_vehicles_090220/ (accessed April 29, 2010).

39 James Rockwell, "LPG: Clean Energy for a Low-Carbon World," worldlpgas.com, http://www.worldlpgas.com/page_attachments/0000/0330/Petroleum_Economist.pdf (accessed April 29, 2010).

40 See Note 37 above.

41 Clean Air Asia, "Measures Taken by Each City – Vehicle Emissions Control; Regulations and Programs," http://www2.kankyo.metro.tokyo.jp/clean-air-asia/old/forum2002_e/asianrepo_e.html (accessed April 29, 2010).

42 See Note 40 above.

[43] Feng An and Amanda Sauer, "Comparison of Passenger Vehicle Fuel Economy and Greenhouse Gas Emission Standards Around the World," *Pew Center on Global Climate*, December, 2004, http://ww.pewclimate.org/docUploads/Fuel%20Economy%20and%20GHG%20Standards_010605_110719.pdf (accessed April 29, 2010).

[44] See Note 40 above.

[45] Leila Abboud and Jenny Clevstrom, "Stockholm's Syndrome: Hostages to Traffic, Swedes Will Vote on High-Tech Plan to Untangle Snarls with Tolls," *Wall Street Journal*, August 29, 2006, B1.

[46] Progress, "The PRoGRESS Project," http://www.progress-project.org/Progress/pdf/cover_finalbrochure.pdf (accessed April 29, 2010).

[47] Herbert S. Levinson and others, "Bus Rapid Transit: An Overview," *Journal of Public Transportation* 5, no. 2 (2002): 1–30.

[48] Mark A. Miller and others, "Development of Bus Rapid Transit Information Clearinghouse," California PATH Research Report UCB-ITS-PRR-2006-7, http://www.its.berkeley.edu/publications/UCB/2006/PRR/UCB-ITS-PRR-2006-7 (accessed April 29, 2010).

[49] United Nations Environmental Program, "Buildings for a Better Future," http://www.unep.fr/scp/marrakech/taskforces/pdf/Buildings_for_a_Better_Future.pdf (accessed May 3, 2010).

[50] Dinesh Girolla, "Development of Eco-City Concept in Pune City," *Pune Municipal Corporation India*, 2006, http://gec.jp/gec/EN/Activities/2006/Eco-Towns/Pune.pdf (accessed May 3, 2010).

[51] See Note 49 above.

[52] See Note 49 above.

[53] United Nations Framework Convention on Climate Change, "Appendix A1 to the Simplified Modalities and Procedures for Small-Scale CDM Project Activities," February 28, 2005, http://cdm.unfccc.int/UserManagement/FileStorage/FS_292989657 (accessed May 3, 2010).

[54] Helios Centre, "G8 : un sommet qui se veut neuter en émissions de carbone," *Enjeux Energie* 4, no. 12 (2005), 5, http://www.centrehelios.org/downloads/bulletins/Vol4.pdf.

[55] United Nations Environmental Program, "Buildings for a Better Future," http://esa.un.org/marrakechprocess/pdf/Brochure%20_SBC_TF.pdf (accessed May 3, 2010).

[56] National Renewable Energy Laboratory, "Renewable Energy in China," 2004, http://www.nrel.gov/docs/fy04osti/35790.pdf (accessed May 3, 2010).

[57] International Energy Agency, *Worldwide Trends in Energy Use and Efficiency*, (Paris, France: International Energy Agency, 2008), 17, http://www.iea.org/Papers/2008/Indicators_2008.pdf (accessed May 3, 2010).

[58] See Note 57 above.

[59] U.S. Environmental Protection Agency and the U.S. Department of Energy, "About Energy Star," http://www.energystar.gov/index.cfm?c=about.ab_index (accessed May 3, 2010).

[60] U.S. Environmental Protection Agency and the U.S. Department of Energy, "Televisions for Consumers," http://www.energystar.gov/index.cfm?fuseaction=find_a_product.showProductGroup&pgw_code=TV (accessed May 3, 2010).

[61] U.S. Department of Energy, "Collaborative Labeling and Appliance Standards Program," http://eetd.lbl.gov/clasp/ (accessed May 3, 2010).

[62] See Note 61 above.

[63] United Nations Economic Commission for Europe, "About UNECE," http://www.unece.org/about/about.htm (accessed May 3, 2010).

[64] United Nations Economic Commission for Europe, "Protocol to the 1979 Convention on Long-Range Transboundary Air Pollution on Long-Term Financing of the Cooperative Programme for Monitoring and Evaluation of the Long-Range Transmission of Air Pollutants in Europe (EMEP)," http://www.unece.org/env/lrtap/full%20text/1984.EMEP.e.pdf (accessed May 3, 2010).

[65] United Nations Economic Commission for Europe, "Protocol to the 1979 Convention on Long-Range Transboundary Air Pollution on the Reduction Of Sulphur Emissions or Their Transboundary Fluxes by at Least 30 Per Cent," http://www.unece.org/env/lrtap/full%20text/1985.Sulphur.e.pdf (accessed May 3, 2010).

[66] United Nations Economic Commission for Europe, "Protocol to the 1979 Convention on Long-Range Transboundary Air Pollution Concerning the Control of Emissions of Nitrogen Oxides or Their Transboundary Fluxes," http://www.unece.org/env/lrtap/full%20text/1988.NOX.e.pdf (accessed May 3, 2010).

[67] United Nations Economic Commission for Europe, "Protocol to the 1979 Convention on Long-Range Transboundary Air Pollution Concerning the Control Emissions of Volatile Organic Compounds or Their Transboundary Fluxes," http://www.unece.org/env/lrtap/full%20text/1991.VOC.e.pdf (accessed May 3, 2010).

[68] See Note 65 above.

[69] United Nations Economic Commission for Europe, "To the 1979 Convention on Long-Range Transboundary Air Pollution on Heavy Metals," http://www.unece.org/env/lrtap/full%20text/1998.Heavy.Metals.e.pdf (accessed May 3, 2010).

[70] United Nations Economic Commission for Europe, "Protocol to the 1979 Convention on Long-Range Transboundary Air Pollution on Persistent Organic Pollutants," http://www.unece.org/env/lrtap/full%20text/1998.POPs.e.pdf (accessed May 3, 2010).

[71] United Nations Economic Commission for Europe, "Protocol to the 1979 Convention on Long-Range Transboundary Air Pollution to Abate Acidification, Eutrophication and Ground-Level Ozone," http://www.unece.org/env/lrtap/full%20text/1999%20Multi.E.Amended.2005.pdf (accessed May 3, 2010).

[72] U.S. Environmental Protection Agency, "The Plain English Guide to the Clean Air Act: Cleaning Up Commonly Found Air Pollutants," http://www.epa.gov/air/caa/peg/cleanup.html (accessed May 3, 2010).

[73] U.S. Environmental Protection Agency, "The Plain English Guide to the Clean Air Act: Cars, Trucks, Buses, and "Nonroad" Equipment," http://www.epa.gov/air/caa/peg/carstrucks.html (accessed May 3, 2010).

[74] U.S. Environmental Protection Agency, "The Plain English Guide to the Clean Air Act: Reducing Acid Rain," http://www.epa.gov/air/caa/peg/acidrain.html (accessed May 3, 2010).

[75] Association of South Eastern Nations, "ASEAN Agreement on Transboundary Haze Pollution," http://www.aseansec.org/images/agr_haze.pdf (accessed May 3, 2010).

[76] China.org.cn, "Curbing Polluters: *Guangming Daily*," *China Daily*, http://www.china.org.cn/english/environment/239408.htm (accessed May 3, 2010).

[77] China.org.cn, "Fairness Crucial to Environmental Issues," *China Daily*, November 4, 2005, http://www.china.org.cn/english/GS-e/147511.htm (accessed May 3, 2010).

[78] United Nations Environment Programme, *Montreal Protocol on Substances that Deplete the Ozone Layer* (Nairobi, Kenya: United Nations Environment Programme, 1987), 54.

[79] D. W. Fahey, "Twenty Questions and Answers About the Ozone Layer: 2006 Update," United Nations Environment Programme, http://ozone.unep.org/Assessment_Panels/SAP/Scientific_Assessment_2006/Twenty_Questions.pdf (accessed May 3, 2010).

[80] See Note 79 above.

[81] United Nations, *Presentation of the Synthesis Report of the 2006 Assessments of the Scientific Assessment Panel, the Environmental Effects Assessment Panel and the Technology and Economic Assessment Panel* (United Nations Environment Programme, 2007), www.ozone.unep.org/Meeting_Documents/oewg/27oewg/OEWG-27-3E.pdf

[82] National Oceanic and Atmospheric Administration, "Antarctic Ozone Hole Returns to Near Average Levels," November 1, 2007, http://www.noaanews.noaa.gov/stories2007/20071101_ozone.html (accessed May 3, 2010).

[83] Gro H. Brundtland and Caorl Bellamy, "Global Water Supply and Sanitation Assessment 2000 Report," World Health Organization, http://www.who.int/water_sanitation_health/monitoring/globalassess/en/ (accessed May 3, 2010).

[84] Africawater.org. "Water Resources and Poverty in Africa: Breaking the Vicious Circle," April 30, 2002, http://www.africanwater.org/Documents/amcow_wb_speech.pdf (accessed May 3, 2010).

[85] Igor A. Shiklomanov, *World Water Resources and Water Use: Modern Assessment and Outlook for the 21st Century* (Paris, France: IHP/UNESCO, 2000), 37.

[86] Igor A. Shiklomanov, "Appraisal and Assessment of World Water Resources," *Water International* 25, no. 1 (2000): 11–32.

[87] United Nations Environment Programme, *Global Environment Outlook GEO4* (Valletta, Malta: United Nations Environment Programme, 2007), 572.

[88] The Cadmus Group, Inc. "National Drinking Water Advisory Council Meeting Summary," U.S. Environmental Protection Agency, 2005, http://www.epa.gov/ogwdw/ndwac/pdfs/summary_ndwac_1117-18-2005.pdf (accessed May 3, 2010).

[89] See Note 87 above.

[90] Efam Dovi, "Bringing Water to Africa's Poor," *Africa Renewal* 21, no.3 (2007): 7, http://www.un.org/ecosocdev/geninfo/afrec/vol21no3/213-water.html (accessed May 3, 2010).

[91] See Note 83 above.

[92] United Nations Environmental Program, "Global Programme of Action for the Protection of the Marine Environment from Land-Based Activities," http://www.gpa.unep.org/documents/full_text_of_the_english.pdf (accessed May 3, 2010).

[93] Shlomo Angel, Stephen C. Sheppard, and Daniel L. Civco With Robert Buckley, Anna Chabaeva, Lucy Gitlin, Alison Kraley, Jason Parent, and Micah Perlin, *The Dynamics of Global Urban Expansion* (Washington: The World Bank, 2005), 18.

[94] D. L. Dufour and B. A. Piperata, "Rural-to-Urban Migration in Latin America: An Update and Thoughts on the Model," *American Journal of Human Biology* 16, no.4 (2004): 395–404.

[95] Peter Newman, Jeffrey R. Kenworthy, *Sustainability and Cities: Overcoming Automobile Dependence* (Washington, DC: Island Press, 1999), 450.

[96] S. Schwarzer and others, *E-waste, The Hidden Side of IT Equipment's Manufacturing and Use* (Geneva, Switzerland: United Nations Environmental Program, 2005), 4.

[97] United Nations Environmental Programme, "New Partnership for African Development: Action Plan for the Environment Initiative," October 2003, http://www.unep.org/roa/Amcen/docs/publications/ActionNepad.pdf (accessed May 3, 2010).

[98] United Nations, *United Nations Forum on Forests* (New York, NY: United Nations, 2009), 39.

[99] United Nations, *Review of Implementation of Agenda 21 and the Johannesburg Plan of Implementation (JPOI): Desertification* (New York, NY: United Nations, 2008), 21.

[100] United Nations Convention to Combat Desertification, "Combating desertification in Africa," http://www.unccd.int/publicinfo/factsheets/showFS.php?number=11 (accessed May 3, 2010).

[101] The Pan-European Ecological Network, "The ecological network concept," http://www.eeconet.org/eeconet/index.html (accessed May 3, 2010).

[102] Commissions of the European Communities, "A European Community Biodiversity Strategy," http://ec.europa.eu/environment/docum/pdf/com_98_42_cn.pdf (accessed May 3, 2010).

[103] Global Transboundary Protected Areas Network, "Mesoamerican Biological Corridor," http://www.tbpa.net/case_10.htm (accessed May 3, 2010).

[104] World Bank, "Project Follows Chico Mendes' Vision of Conciliating Social and Environmental Development," http://web.worldbank.org/wbsite/external/countries/lacext/brazilextn/0,,contentMDK:22019114~pagePK:141137piPK:141127~theSitePK:322341,00.html (accessed March 1, 2010).

[105] Secretariat of the Convention on Biological Diversity, *Global Biodiversity Outlook 2* (Montreal, QC: United Nations, 2006), 6.

[106] Norma Carr-Rufino and John Acheson, "The Hybrid Phenomenon," *The Futurist* (July–August, 2007): 16–25.

[107] Stuart Hart, "Beyond Greening: Strategies for a Sustainable World," *Harvard Business Review* (January–February, 1997): 66–76.

[108] Jim Johnson, "Ford, Alcan Close Aluminum Recycling Loop," *Automotive News* (November 18, 2002): 20–25.

[109] Bailey Webb, "Passing the TORCH," *Waste Age* 38, no. 10 (2007): 60–66.

[110] Michael D. Peterson, "Improving Productivity at a Materials Recovery Facility: Lessons from a Case Study," *Public Productivity & Management Review* 18, no. 3 (1995): 277–292.

[111] United Nations Environmental Programme, The Marrakech Process, "Integrated Waste and Resource Management," http://esa.un.org/marrakechprocess/pdf/Issue_%20Waste_and_Resource_Management.pdf (accessed May 3, 2010).

[112] See Note 111 above.

[113] Gary Nevison, "Meeting Global Design Legislation Challenges," *Product Design & Development*, 63, March Supplement, 2008, 30–33.

[114] Joe Truini, "Dell Takes 'A Big Step Forward' with Free E-Recycling," *Waste News*, December 12, 2006, 13.

[115] Daniel C. Esty and Andrew S. Winston, *Green to Gold* (New Haven, CT: Yale University Press, 2006), 366.

[116] Albert Weale and others, *Environmental Governance in Europe: An Ever Closer Ecological Union?* (Oxford: Oxford University Press, 2000), 544.

[117] H. Deliser, "Gas for the Greenhouse," *Nature* 442, no. 499 (2006).

[118] See Note 83 above.

Providing Value via Sustainable Marketing Strategies

Discovering Value via Market Analysis

FIG. 5-1 WedVert helps couples choose wedding destinations that support conservation.

A. Introduction

WEDVERT GREEN WEDDINGS

Launched in early 2007, WedVert is the first wedding resource to focus on green efforts as a means to prevent the tons of waste that weddings create each year. The company's Web site, print magazine, and products focus on helping the modern couple turn a traditional wedding into a green masterpiece. WedVert values the importance of saving money and offers plenty of advice to ensure that a wedding is exquisite, economic, and environmentally friendly.[1]

In its efforts to target this group of consumers, WedVert has made interesting strides to change the kinds of consumption associated with weddings. It provides suggestions about making the wedding more ecologically friendly by

Source: © iStockphoto.com/Andre Blais

making changes in the purchase of wedding rings, gifts, and floral arrangements (Figure 5-1). It also outlines ways for couples to buy local products that lower wedding costs, and it recommends sustainable locations for the wedding rite.

Is the green wedding for everybody? Of course not, but there is a growing international target market that places great emphasis on the sustainability of their purchases. Weddings are an important part of life, and they often have substantial carbon footprints. One type of consumer that we will read about in this chapter is focused on trying to limit carbon usage, and this usage is not forgotten on one's wedding day. These lifestyles of health and sustainability (LOHAS) consumers, who are focused on health, the environment, and personal development, spend more than $209 billion in the United States, and the LOHAS market segment is also gaining interest in Japan, Southeast Asia, and Europe.[2] These consumers express concerns about the health of their families, the sustainability of the planet, their personal development, and the future of society. Consumers in the LOHAS segment are also inclined to offset the carbon dioxide emissions associated with the wedding by donating to programs that plant trees or preserve rain forests.[3]

The WedVert example illustrates how companies are using market analyses to help them discover sustainable green strategies. Our analysis of the pursuit of sustainable marketing strategies to this point in the text has focused on the interaction between the market and the environment. In previous sections of this book, we have outlined the interaction between consumption and the environment (Part II), and we have identified the industries that account for most energy consumption (Part III). The market analyses provided in earlier sections of this book support efforts to craft strategies and tactics that enhance sustainability.

In this section, we focus on marketing initiatives that reduce energy consumption and enhance sustainability efforts. Recall that the strategic planning process (see Figure 5-2) underscores the interaction between environmental factors and business strategy. The central factor in the pursuit of sustainability is the *value* that market offerings provide to consumers. Sustainable value emerges from analysis of the

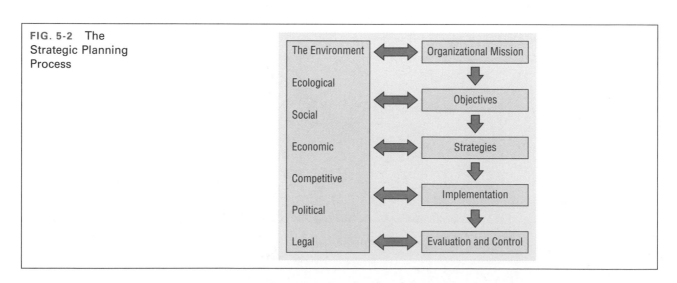

FIG. 5-2 The Strategic Planning Process

The Environment — Organizational Mission

Ecological

Social — Objectives

Economic — Strategies

Competitive

Political — Implementation

Legal — Evaluation and Control

economic, relational, and ecological returns sought in a market. Consequently, each chapter in our discussion of marketing action focuses on strategies that generate value. In this first chapter, we outline a process for analyzing markets. This analysis of markets and market segmentation addresses the discovery of value. Promotional efforts by which firms communicate value are examined in Chapter 6. In Chapter 7, we frame product development as the set of processes by which the firm produces value. The effort to deliver value is addressed in the analysis of supply cycles in Chapter 8 and in the analysis of retailing in Chapter 9. Chapter 10 provides an overview of the mechanisms by which the firm proclaims value via its pricing strategy.

The successful organization must discover and identify the value sought by consumers within a **market**. A market consists of all organizations or people with a need or want and the ability and willingness to make purchases to address these needs and wants.[4] If any of these facets of the market are not present, then the market is also not present. Initial analysis of the market requires the marketer to gain an appreciation of each of these market components. The needs and wants associated with products and services reflect the economic, social, and ecological value derived from a purchase. For example, the commuter that buys a bicycle incurs economic costs that yield financial savings over time. This consumer may also enjoy the camaraderie of other cyclists and will likely acknowledge the environmental benefits of cycling. Note that all three facets of value may not be understood or expressed by the consumer. In many cases, products are marketed to accentuate economic, social, or ecological merits without consideration of the returns associated with each facet of sustainability. The firm that adopts a sustainable orientation, however, has greater capacity to address the breadth of returns sought from purchases.

The firm must also assess the ability and willingness of buyers to make a purchase. Many green marketing propositions fail because the organization does not recognize the consumers' abilities and willingness to invest in sustainable technologies. For example, for many American consumers, hybrid automobiles may not be desirable due to the inability to pay the premium associated with this eco-friendly technology.[5] These consumers may express an interest in the technology, but they do not have the ability to purchase the car at a premium. By contrast, some American consumers of diesel automobiles may not have an interest in the cars because of their previous experience with diesel engines.[6] These consumers may have the ability to buy the car, but their experience makes them unwilling to invest in a diesel car. The consumer must have both the ability and willingness to buy to be part of the market.

After the market has been established, the firm can begin to investigate the extent to which there are subsets of the market with unique value statements. The process of moving from market analysis to marketing mix positioning is outlined in Figure 5-3. After the firm has identified the market, it engages in a series of activities referred to as **STP marketing** characterized by efforts to segment, target, and position.[7] **Market segmentation** refers to the process of dividing a market into distinct segments or subsets of customers that have similar needs or behave in the same way.[8] Every segment of the market has the potential to be reached via a distinct marketing strategy. After the firm has identified the segments in a market, it engages in target marketing. **Target marketing** refers to the organization's efforts to serve a selected segment within the marketplace.[9] The prioritization and selection of various target markets is performed in conjunction with consideration of the competitive and environmental conditions associated with the market. After the firm has selected a target market, it then establishes a positioning strategy. **Positioning** refers to the

FIG. 5-3 Segmentation, Target Markets, and Positioning

Source: *From O'Guinn, Allen, Semenik,* Advertising and Integrated Brand Promotion *(with InfoTrac®), 4E. © 2006 South-Western, a part of Cengage Learning, Inc. Reproduced by permission. www.cengage.com/permissions*

development of the marketing mix to yield a distinctive appeal to the target segment. The positioning approach should reflect the values sought by consumers in the target market.

In the remainder of this chapter, we outline the procedures for identifying market segments, target markets, and positioning strategies. The positioning strategies are further developed and embellished in the chapters that follow that address facets of the marketing mix. For instructional purposes, we present this logic as a step-by-step process. In reality, the analysis of market segments and the development of the marketing mix are dynamic processes that the organization must continue to assess. Consumer preferences shift over time, and these changes in preferences demand that the firm review the market segmentation process and the marketing mix. The positioning theme established as the product is introduced is likely to change over time in response to the needs of the market.

B. Market Segmentation

Segmentation of the market plays a critical role in the development of business strategies that yield desired value for firms, their suppliers, and their customers.[10] Segmentation enables companies to identify groups of consumers with similar needs and enables companies to analyze characteristics and buying behaviors of members of these groups. When the unique needs of a group are identified, the segmentation process also enables the firm to design a marketing mix that reflects the unique requirements of the group. Consequently, segmentation enables companies to address the value sought by consumers while simultaneously achieving the firm's needs.

The segmentation process begins by identifying specific factors that reflect differences in customers' responsiveness to marketing variables or requirements. These differences in levels of responsiveness may be attributed to many factors such as purchase behavior, usage, benefits sought, or loyalty. After the segments are identified, segment descriptors are chosen based on the ability to suggest competitive strategies, to account for variance in the basis for segmentation, or to identify segments.

The process of market segmentation and the design of the marketing mix are activities that the firm performs on a regular basis, and these activities are costly to the organization. The segmentation process can be logically extended to the point at which each consumer in the marketplace is treated as an individual segment of the market. Although this process will identify the unique needs of each consumer, the analysis of the market and the design of the marketing mix would be cost prohibitive in most cases. Segmentation strategies should recognize that proposed segments should be:

Substantial Substantiality is the criterion that emphasizes the need for the segment to be large enough to warrant attention. For example, prior to 2000, most grocers did not view the market for organic goods as substantial enough to warrant their attention.[11] Organic food sales have increased by 20% annually since 1990. As the demand for these products has increased, conventional grocers' interest in the group also increased. The size of the market segment is a particularly salient issue in green marketing given that the interest in sustainability factors is increasing in many markets.[12] As the size of a segment interested in ecological performance increases, there is likely an increase in the amount of competition for the segment.

Identifiable and measurable The identifiable and measurable requirements reflect the need to be able categorize persons within and outside of the market segments. If we cannot identify who is and who is not in a group, then we cannot assess the size of the group, nor can we develop a marketing plan to serve the group. Although personal factors such as demographics (e.g., age, gender) are simple to measure, they are unlikely to be informative in the analysis of the degree to which consumers in a market are interested in sustainability issues. Consequently, many efforts to examine consumer predispositions toward green marketing initiatives rely on personality and motives.

Accessible In many cases, an organization may be able to quantify the size of market segments, but it cannot reach the segment via a customized marketing mix.[13] For example, in emerging economies, the greatest need for drinking water may be among extremely poor, illiterate consumers. The firm may not be able to develop a marketing mix and communication campaign that these consumers can access and understand.

Responsive The responsiveness criterion considers whether the consumers in a market segment are more likely to respond to a marketing mix in a manner that is different from other consumers. If the basis for distinguishing among market segments does not reveal differences in preferences with respect to some factor, then there is no need to treat a segment separately from other groups. Thus, if sustainability is a not a salient issue for a market segment, there is little value in emphasizing the ecological benefits of a product. For example, in 2005, Nike initially promoted the Considered walking boot as an environmentally friendly product. Since consumers were not responsive to this environmental appeal, the promotion shifted to other performance attributes of the footwear.[14]

The process of market segmentation is an attempt to simplify the process of selecting potential buyers for a product. The segmentation for consumer marketing varies somewhat from the strategy for business-to-business marketing. Good segmentation strategies separate potential buyers from people that do not have the needs of the members of a buying group. In consumer markets, firms often use **demographics segmentation** to separate potential buyers based on age, gender, income, or occupation.

For example, cities that are trying to attract Generation Y adults increasingly emphasize the ecological merits of their communities.[15] Because a high percentage of consumers in this age bracket favor environmental causes, the cities recognize that marketing campaigns to this group must emphasize ecology.

Firms also separate groups of consumers based on **geography segmentation**. For example, California is a leading market for green building construction in the United States. The state has aggressively pursued efficiency measures since the oil price escalation era of the 1970s. The state's per capita electricity usage has remained virtually stable over the past 30 years even as per capita consumption has grown across the country. Experts credit state policies that have included establishing state-level appliance efficiency requirements; enacting strict building codes; and giving utilities incentives to help their customers save electricity.[16]

Several analysts of green marketing in the consumer sector have used **psychographic segmentation** to distinguish among consumer groups. *Psychographics* refers to the use of attitudes, opinions, motives, values, lifestyles, interests, or personality to distinguish among consuming groups.[17] Roper Starch Worldwide is a marketing research firm that has pioneered analysis of the consumer's orientation to sustainability in North America. Similar efforts have been conducted in northern European markets.[18] Their research has uncovered the following five market segments:[19]

True blues   True blues are those consumers with strong environmental values that seek to bring about positive change. Individuals that identify with this segment are also inclined to be politically active in their pursuit of sustainability. These individuals are four times more likely to avoid products marketed by companies that are not environmentally conscious. Roper Starch research indicates that 31% of consumers fit this category.

Greenback greens   The greenback greens are also interested in sustainability concerns, but they are not inclined to be politically active. Importantly, these consumers are more willing to purchase environmentally friendly products than average consumers. Prior research suggests that this group represents 10% of the population.

Sprouts   These consumers appreciate the merits of environmental causes, but they do not take this appreciation with them to the marketplace. Although these consumers will be unlikely to spend more for green products, they can be persuaded to do so given the appropriate appeal. Research suggests that sprouts account for approximately 26% of consumers.

Grousers   This group of consumers tends to be cynical about its ability to bring about change, and it is relatively uneducated about ecological concerns. Research suggests that these consumers believe that green products are too expensive and do not perform as effectively as their nongreen counterparts. Approximately 15% of consumers fit the grouser category.

Apathetics   Formerly labeled "basic browns," the apathetics do not concern themselves with sustainability or green marketing practices. The apathetics represent about 18% of the population.

The Roper Starch analysis of green market segmentation has been tracking consumers since 1990 (Figure 5-4). It is interesting to note that the preferences of consumers in the United States population has shifted over time. Although the number of greenback greens and sprouts has remained relatively constant, the percentage of true blue greens has escalated from 11% to 31% of the market. The percentage of

FIG. 5-4 Roper Starch
North American Market
Segments Concerning
Attitudes Toward
Sustainability

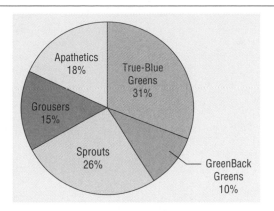

Source: *Based on The Roper segmentation data taken from Wever, Renee, Sophie Lotgering, and Freya Ruijs (2007), "Green Marketing of Consumer Electronics: Applying Kano's Theory of Attractive Quality on EcoDesign" (working paper), Delft University of Technology.*

grousers has moved from 24% in 1990 to 15%. Similarly, the percentage of apathetics has shifted from 35% in 1995 to 18% in 2007. These shifts in the attitudes of consumers reflect a general change in the attitudes and understanding of sustainability. As the number of consumers touting a true blue or greenback perspective increases, the need for green marketing strategies also escalates.

The Roper Starch study of consumer green marketing preferences addresses the attitudes that consumers have toward sustainability. Although attitudes provide insight into the likely action of consumers, behavior provides a stronger insight into market segments. *Behavioral segmentation* refers to the use of consumer behavior or product use to distinguish among market segments.[20] The market analysis provided by the Natural Marketing Institute (NMI) incorporates attitudes and behaviors toward environmentalism and consumption (Figure 5-5).[21] Their research identifies the following five market segments:

The LOHAS consumer *LOHAS* refers to lifestyles of health and sustainability. This term describes an estimated $209 billion U.S. marketplace for goods and services. These consumers are focused on health, the environment, social justice, personal development, and sustainable living, and the future of society.[22] Approximately 17% percent (38 million) of the adults in the United States are considered LOHAS consumers. This group is not limited to the United States; LOHAS is gaining interest in Japan, Southeast Asia, and Europe.

The LOHAS group is based on the *cultural creatives* label developed by sociologist Paul Ray to describe individuals on the cutting edge of social change.[23] He described cultural creatives as slightly more likely than average to live on the West Coast but noted that they are found in all regions of the country. These consumers are altruistic and often less concerned with success or making a lot of money, yet most live comfortably with middle to upper-middle incomes. Cognitive style is a key to understanding the cultural creatives. While these consumers take in a lot of information from a variety of sources, they are good at synthesizing it into a big picture. The environment is central to the LOHAS consumers' belief system. The environment is interconnected with everything, from the way food is grown to the way the workers are treated. It is a holistic world view that recognizes the interconnection between political systems and ecocultures.[24]

FIG. 5-5 Green Marketing Segments from the Natural Marketing Institute

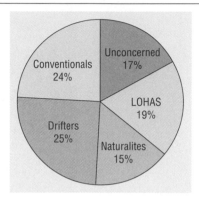

Source: © *Natural Marketing Institute (NMI), 2009. Used with permission.*

LOHAS consumers provide insight into the future of progressive social, environmental, and economic change in multiple markets worldwide. Seventy-three percent buy recycled-paper goods, and 71% buy natural or organic personal care products.[25] They pay more to get food produced without pesticides and want their cars fuel efficient. Although the cultural creatives label describes this group as countercultural, their buying preferences reflect many of the most popular consumer brands. A 2006 LOHAS analysis indicated that these consumers felt that Microsoft, Whole Foods, Kellogg's, McDonalds's, Home Depot, Disney, United Parcel Service, Coca-Cola, Starbucks, and PepsiCo ranked highest in their sustainability and environmental efforts. Thus, these consumers recognize the green marketing efforts of some of the largest consumer brands. Furthermore, the listing of these brands illustrates that these firms have done a good job of incorporating and communicating sustainability efforts to consumers.[26]

NMI further separates this group into two segments.[27] The LOHAS *leaders* are early adopters and opinion leaders for products and concepts that emphasize healthy or green initiatives. They are the first candidates in a market to purchase new and innovative sustainable products. By contrast, LOHAS *followers* are more moderate in their preferences for green products. Like the leaders, however, they are cutting-edge consumers for most purchasing situations.

Naturalites   This second market segment refers to consumers primarily concerned about personal health and wellness. Their preference for food and beverage products is motivated primarily by a strong health focus, not an environmental focus. Although these consumers appreciate that companies should be environmentally conscious, they are not politically committed to the environmental movement, and they are not generally driven to buy eco-friendly durable goods. Naturalites represent 17% of American households (38 million people).

Conventionals   The largest segment in the NMI analysis includes 58 million adults or 26% of the adult population. Because these individuals are practical and enjoy seeing the results of their action, they are likely to recycle and conserve energy.[28] They recognize the value in buying products that save money in the long run, but the ecological merits of consumption are not paramount in their decision making.[29]

Drifters   The drifter category refers to consumers that are not highly concerned about the environment and believe that the problems will eventually be resolved.

Their concerns about the environment focus on things that affect them directly. Because they view sustainability as a trend, they want to be seen in places viewed as environmentally conscious even though they do not make substantial purchases of green products. They are somewhat price sensitive and offer many reasons why they do not make environmentally friendly choices. Drifters include 54 million people or 24% of the American adult market.

Unconcerned   The final group in the NMI analysis is a group that has priorities other than the environment and society. They are not aware of green product choices and are generally unwilling to find out such information. These consumers buy based on convenience, price, quality, and value with little regard for the actions of companies marketing the products. Thirty-six million American adults representing 16% of the population are in the unconcerned market segment.

Business marketing segmentation varies somewhat from the strategies available in the consumer realm. Although geography may be used as a basis for distinguishing among groups, psychographics and lifestyle analysis do not translate well to business marketing.[30] One form of segmentation used frequently in business markets is **benefit segmentation**, which refers to the delineation of segments based on the benefits that buyers hope to derive from a purchase. Thus, delivery truck requirements for florists and dry cleaners may be similar, despite differences in their respective clientele.

A related basis for developing business market segments is the type of industry. In general, the benefits sought by buyers in the same industry can be very similar. In North America, the **North American Industry Classification System (NAICS)** employs a six-digit hierarchical coding system to classify all economic activity into 20 industry sectors. NAICS is the standard used by federal statistical agencies to classify business establishments for the purpose of collecting, analyzing, and publishing statistical data related to the American business economy.[31] NAICS was developed by the U.S. Economic Classification Policy Committee (ECPC), Statistics Canada, and Mexico's Instituto Nacional de Estadistica, Geografia e Informatica, as a means to facilitate comparison of business statistics among these three North American countries.[32] Every effort is made to make NAICS compatible with the Standard Industrial Classification of All Economic Activities of the United Nations.[33]

NAICS is developed based on grouping of producing units using the same or similar production processes. Five sectors are mainly goods-producing sectors and 15 are entirely services-producing sectors. This six-digit hierarchical structure allows for the identification of 1,170 industries compared to the 1,004 found in the SIC (Standard Industrial Classification). In developing NAICS, the governments in the United States, Canada, and Mexico agreed that the five-digit codes would represent the level at which the system is comparable among the countries. The sixth digit allows for each of the countries to have additional detail (i.e., subdivisions of a five-digit category).[34] For example, here is the NAICS for United States new car dealerships:

NAICS	Description
44	Retail sector
441	Retail: Motor vehicles and parts
4411	Retail: Auto dealers
44111	Retail: New auto dealers
441110	Retail: U.S. new auto dealers

Within sectors of the NAICS, industrial-level analyses are being developed to identify best practices, and many of these best practices include sustainability considerations. These industry-level analyses are being developed for many industries outlined in subsequent chapters addressing manufacturing, services, and transportation. For example, the health care industry has been very active in its pursuit of sustainability. The industry has developed a *Green Guide for Health Care* that identifies sustainable and green procedures that enable hospitals to enhance financial performance, improve patient satisfaction, protect health, attract and retain staff, and reduce fossil fuel emissions.[35] Organizations that understand these multiple facets of sustainability can develop strategies tailored to each set of demands associated with green marketing.

The understanding of the various facets of sustainability within an industry can be coupled with the **buygrid framework** to isolate market segments. The buygrid framework describes the organizational buying process based on the type of purchase and the stage of the buying process.[36] The type of purchase may be a new task, a modified rebuy of a former purchase, or a straight rebuy of a product bought previously. Companies or health care facilities that are making their initial investment in sustainable technologies will vary markedly in their preferences from firms that have repeatedly bought such technologies. The stages of the buying process include recognition of need; need definition and description; seller identification; proposal solicitation, evaluation, and selection; ordering procedures; and review. Firms that are just beginning to identify sustainability issues are substantially different from firms that have already placed orders for sustainable technologies.

One facet of the business marketing setting that stands in contrast to consumer marketing is **reverse marketing**. *Reverse marketing* refers to the proactive efforts within the firm to identify potential product providers or vendors.[37] In contrast to consumer markets in which the needs of the buyer can be difficult to establish, in a reverse marketing context, the needs of the buyer are clarified. Thus, sellers can use this information to categorize a buyer into a market segment.

Figure 5-6 provides Walmart's 2009 Vendor Sustainability Criteria used to assess potential sellers to this retail giant. The sustainability criteria can be used initially to classify Walmart as a firm with substantial interest in green marketing activity. Given the firm's size, however, the sustainability criteria also provide the opportunity to classify vendors based on their energy and climate, material efficiency, natural resource utilization, and community involvement.

The market segments identified by Roper Starch and NMI in the consumer setting and the criteria characterized in the business marketing context provide starting points for individuals seeking to increase purchases of sustainable products. These studies underscore an observation made frequently in analysis of green marketing products: Although many consumers will recognize the merits of green products, this recognition is not incorporated into many purchase decisions. Thus, it is incumbent on the marketer to understand the motivations underlying consumer decision making. It is essential to identify the market niches and estimate their size. When the firm has identified these segments, it can then begin to prioritize potential target markets.

C. Target Marketing

After the initial analysis of market segments, it is essential for the firm to select some subset of the market. A *target market* refers to a subgroup of the total market

FIG. 5-6 Walmart
Sustainability
Criteria

Energy and Climate

1. Have you measured your corporate greenhouse gas emissions?
2. Have you opted to report your greenhouse gas emissions to the Carbon Disclosure Project?
3. What is your total annual greenhouse gas emissions reported in the most recent year measured?
4. Have you set publicly available greenhouse gas reduction targets? If yes, what are those targets?

Material Efficiency

1. If measured, please report the total amount of solid waste generated from the facilities that produce your product(s) for Walmart for the most recent year measured.
2. Have you set publicly available solid waste reduction targets? If yes, what are those targets?
3. If measured, please report total water use from facilities that produce your product(s) for Walmart for the most recent year measured.
4. Have you set publicly available water use reduction targets? If yes, what are those targets?

Natural Resources

1. Have you established publicly available sustainability purchasing guidelines for your direct suppliers that address issues such as environmental compliance, employment practices and product/ingredient safety?
2. Have you obtained third-party certifications for any of the products that you sell to Walmart?

People and Community

1. Do you know the location of 100% of the facilities that produce your product(s)?
2. Before beginning a business relationship with a manufacturing facility, do you evaluate the quality of, and capacity for, production?
3. Do you have a process for managing social compliance at the manufacturing level?
4. Do you work with your supply base to resolve issues found during social compliance evaluations and also document specific corrections and improvements?
5. Do you invest in community development activities in the markets you source from and/or operate within?

Source: *Material Handling Management (2009), "Wal-Mart's 15 Questions," Wal-Mart.*

selected as the focal point for the marketing mix.[38] Regardless of how the segmentation was established, the firm must select one or more targets as the basis for a marketing campaign.

One of the primary considerations for selecting a target market is the consideration of the firm's ability to satisfy the needs of the segment. Serving a market demands that the firm make sizeable investments that are often specific to the needs of the market segment. If the firm possesses the resources to satisfy the needs of the market segment, then it is logical for the firm to consider this group as a potential target. For example, Patagonia's recurring investment in organic cotton has enabled it to satisfy the needs of consumers with strong preferences for garments that contain eco-friendly components. In some cases, however, organizations cannot justify the investment needed to satisfy the needs of the market segment. Thus, an airliner may recognize that NMI's LOHAS consumers may respond favorably to jets operated on vegetable oil, but the airliner may not have the capacity to modify its fleet to accommodate the desires of this market segment.

A second consideration in the selection of a target market is the size of a market segment. In general, a large group can be more easily justified as a target due to the sheer amount of consumption. When groups get too large, however, the market segmentation does not offer much insight. Thus, efforts to market to the entire restaurant industry are likely to be unsuccessful due to the failure to consider the multiple buying and consumption patterns across the group. The size of the group must be assessed relative to the amount of consumption within the group. Although there may be few users of engine emissions technology, the massive level of consumption warrants many firms to pursue this target market.

It is not surprising that the growth potential in a market segment is also a consideration when selecting target markets. The recurring research by Roper Starch indicates that the number of *true blue* consumers has increased dramatically over the past few years. Firms such as Stonyfield that anticipated this market growth are well positioned to meet the current needs of this target market. Similarly, developers of alternative auto fuels pursue the auto market primarily for the growth potential rather than current demand. As the volatility in oil prices increases, the consumer interest in alternatives also increases.[39]

In addition to the firm's capabilities, market size, and growth potential, firms must also direct substantial attention to competition. As the number of competitors pursuing a market increases, the potential to serve the market becomes compromised. Large competitors may be able to dedicate sizeable resources to the market that preclude a smaller firm from competing effectively. For example, some question whether Tesla, the upstart Silicon Valley auto company, can compete favorably given the market capitalization of its competition.[40] Small firms, however, may be able to engage in **niche marketing strategies** whereby they serve a selected market better than their competition does. For example, many local farmers are taking advantage of the ability to serve local markets with fresh foods that their multinational competitors cannot provide.[41]

When one considers both the market size and the competitive landscape, one can identify several contrasting opportunities to serve a target market. Figure 5-7 underscores four potential green marketing strategies that vary based on the size of the green market and the ability to differentiate based on the greenness of the product. The **lean green** strategy refers to a situation in which the size of the green market is modest and the firm has limited ability to differentiate based on the greenness of product offerings. Firms in this category are likely to engage in corporate social responsibility, but they do not publicize this action. For example, 2% of the cotton used by Levi Strauss is organic.[42] Since few consumers in the jean market value green products, and this commitment to sustainability could be replicated, the strategy has to limit the emphasis on green products. This competitive position leads to a lean green marketing strategy. In addition, the publicizing of Levi's effort to go green could generate substantial criticism that at 2% of its sourcing, the firm has not done much to promote sustainability. It is likely that firms that face this competitive environment will not be able to engage in a pricing strategy that asks consumers to pay more for products that are sustainable.

The **defensive green** strategy reflects a situation under which the market for green products is large, but the ability to differentiate based on the ecological merits of the product is low. For example, in the bottled water industry, many of the brands focus on health-conscious, environmentally aware consumers.[43] The products in this industry have been singled out due to the carbon footprint of moving water across continents and due to the number of water bottles in landfills. Consequently, many of the marketers of these products have aligned themselves with environmental causes.[44] Thus, this market is highly sensitive to the environment, but it is very difficult to establish one product offering as ecologically superior to other products. Relative to their Pepsi Aquafina and Coca-Cola Dasani competitors, Nestlé's uses a low-price strategy to make the Pure Life brand competitive in the United States market.[45]

The **shaded green** strategy refers to a market in which the demand for ecologically sensitive products is low, but there is a substantial opportunity to differentiate based on ecological viability of a product. For example, the hybrid automobile market represents about 3% of new car sales in the United States. Since demand is relatively soft, marketers often elect to focus on other merits of their product rather than environmental benefits. Thus, the strategy *shades over* the green merits of the product in deference to other benefits that consumers derive from consumption. It is essential for the marketer of these products to have a refined understanding of the complete value sought by the consumer. For example, Toyota's Prius automobile is relatively environmentally friendly, but the marketing of this product focuses on the fuel efficiency of the auto relative to the competition. Promotional strategies used by firms in this competitive setting do not emphasize the ecological merits of the product but focus instead on efficiency considerations. In addition, pricing strategies emphasize the total cost of operations rather than solely the cost of purchasing the product. Value in use over the course of the life of the product is germane to the marketing strategy. Thus, the marketing of products with the Energy Star label emphasizes the cost savings over time rather than at the moment of purchase.

Extreme green refers to a competitive context in which the demand for green products is large, and the ability to differentiate based on product greenness is substantial. The brands in this category often are initiated with a strong desire to promote and foster sustainability.[46] Firms that face this competitive landscape offer

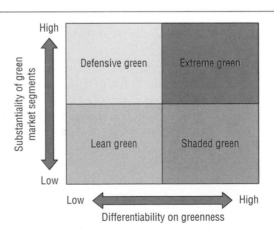

FIG. 5-7 Green Marketing Strategy Matrix

products with premium prices, but the value over the course of the product life is emphasized in marketing campaigns. For example, organic products from Patagonia, the marketer of outdoor gear and clothing, often have higher price points than alternative products.[47] Pricing strategies emphasize how the firm invests in enhancing the natural environment. The founder of Patagonia, for instance, co-founded the 1% for the Planet program. Participants in this program pledge to provide 1% of net sales to environmental causes.[48] Firms such as Patagonia can rely on these pricing strategies because the market for environmentally sensitive products is large, and their opportunities to distinguish themselves from the competition are appreciable.

D. Market Positioning

The third stage of STP marketing is the time during which the firm develops a positioning strategy. The positioning strategy refers to the development of the marketing mix to yield a distinctive appeal to the target segment. When the firm has effectively identified the market and its segments, the market position should flow naturally. Thus, the Body Shop positions itself as a firm that supports self-esteem, fair trade, ecology, human rights, and humane product testing.[49] Effective positioning strategies should contain several elements.[50] First, the organization must be committed to creating substantive value for the consumer. The Body Shop has developed a line of cosmetics that does not rely on animal testing, and the firm has gone to great lengths to develop products in a humane fashion. Consumers in the LOHAS group are inclined to favor such products, and they are willing to pay more to acquire them. Importantly, the shopping experience should reflect this commitment to humane product testing. Note that this position stands in contrast to the product testing strategies traditionally employed by major competitors in this industry.

A vital facet of the positioning strategy is that the value offered to the consumer must be meaningful to that target market. For example, the Segway two-wheeled transportation device offered marked ecological benefits to consumers, but the operation of the device and the initial price did not yield a value proposition that was meaningful to many consumers.[51] By contrast, ultramobile computers such as the MacBook Air have recently been introduced. The MacBook Air offers simplicity and mobility along with an eco-friendly design that is enabling Apple to increase its market share in the personal computer business.[52]

The positioning strategy that a firm selects must be consistent over time and must be internally consistent. Internal consistency is achieved when every member of the organization and every associated message reflect the distinct position that the brand occupies in the eyes of the target market. Starbucks emphasizes the climate of the coffee purchase experience throughout its shops and promotions. Employees are trained to appreciate the issues of fair trade and organic products that are essential elements of the value that the firm offers to consumers.[53] A related factor is that the firm must be consistent with its message over time. For example, Volvo has built a reputation for safe automobiles through a prolonged commitment to research and development and communication strategies that emphasize safety. Brands such as Starbucks that hope to emphasize the organic, healthy nature of their products must offer a prolonged commitment to a product market.

The positioning strategy must also be simple and distinctive. Although a firm's product offerings may rest on highly sophisticated technologies, consumers and industrial buyers make purchases to satisfy needs. The firm that can effectively distill its product message into a simple idea is poised to capture a substantial share of the target market. In 2008, Clorox introduced the Clorox Green Works line of cleaning products that included Green Works Natural Laundry Detergent, Green Works Natural Cleaning Wipes, Green Works Laundry Stain Remover, Green Works Natural Dishwashing Liquid, and other household cleaning products. These products were recognized by the Environmental Protection Agency Design for Environment (DfE) program for their use of environmentally preferable chemical ingredients.[54] The simple logic linking these environmentally friendly products to cleaning has resulted in the brand being rated as the top American green brand in a 2009 survey completed by advertising agency WPP and a consortium of other marketing and consulting firms.[55] The Clorox Green Works brand has been able to capture market share because the sustainability message is easily communicated to consumers. Moreover, the product stands out as a distinctively ecologically friendly product in a household chemical market not known for its environmental appeals.

Effective Positioning Themes

When the positioning strategy is simple and distinctive, it helps the organization to make internal decisions that yield value for consumers, and it further enables the firm to develop a focused communication strategy.[56] The STP marketing approach thus enables the firm to generate positioning themes that are viable in the marketplace. It is essential for the organization to settle on a single idea for the positioning theme. For example, Clorox Green Works drives home the notion that these products are clean and environmentally safe. The selection of this single premise must be made in conjunction with the needs of the target market. If the focal segment is LOHAS consumers, they are inclined to buy based on the premise that a product offers environmental benefits. In such cases, the strategy of firms such as Ben & Jerry's, who regularly invest in carbon reduction and alternative energy products, is salient and meaningful to the consumer. By contrast, Nike continues to market the Considered brand of footwear, but the emphasis on marketing is athletic rather than environmental performance. Thus, the determination of the single idea to be featured in communication must consider the target market.

Three general strategies for a positioning theme include benefit, user, and competitive positioning. **Benefit positioning** refers to an emphasis on a functional, emotional, or self-expressive return realized from product consumption. Since benefits are the basis for most purchases, it is valuable in many markets to focus on the returns derived from consumption. For example, the *functional benefit* of energy-efficient appliances is the reduced fuel consumption and lower fuel costs realized over the life of the product (Figure 5-8). Many green products may be purchased not for their functions, but for emotional benefits. Just as airline passengers can invest in flight insurance to alleviate concerns about air travel safety, they can also balance the environmental influence of their travel by buying carbon reduction services. In many cases, the purchase of the carbon reduction credits provides an *emotional benefit* to consumers. The *self-expressive benefit* addresses the how the product influences the presentation of the individual to relevant others. For example, the drifter category of consumers represents a segment that is generally unconcerned about the environment. Because they see sustainability as a trend, they want to be seen in places viewed as environmentally conscious even though they do not make substantial purchases of green products. Thus, green grocers such as Trader Joe's can attract interest from these consumers because they want to be associated with current trends.

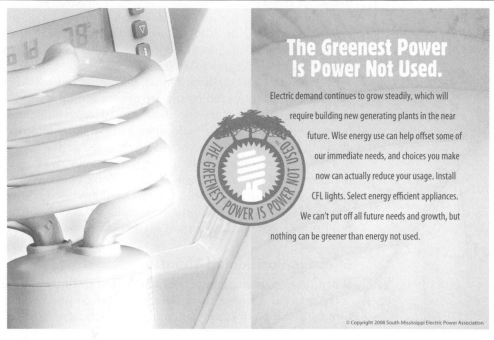

FIG. 5-8 South Mississippi Electric Power Association Ad Exemplifying Benefit Positioning

Source: © *Courtesy South Mississippi Electric, www.smepa.coop.*

User positioning is a second basis for the positioning theme. In this positioning theme, the marketer develops a profile of a specific target user as the focus of the positioning strategy. For example, Woolshire Carpet ads that show a family posing in a natural setting highlight the lifestyle of the target market (Figure 5-9). Such ads seek to make the use of Woolshire carpets consistent with the lifestyle of the target market.

The third fundamental positioning theme is **competitive positioning**, which refers to the direct reference to the competition in order to illuminate the benefits of a firm's brand. In many cases, firms that have developed relatively environmentally friendly products compare the green features of their offerings to the competition. For example, Figure 5-10 reproduces a Kyocera ad that emphasizes the lower operating costs and environmental impact of their Ecosys printers relative to the competition.

The Value Proposition

At the end of the positioning process, the firm is in a position to announce the **value proposition** of a brand. The value proposition is a statement of the emotional, function, and self-expressive benefits delivered by a brand that provide value to consumers in a target market.[57] The value proposition is critical to the ongoing success of the firm because this proposition is the basis for brand choice and consumer brand loyalty. For example, Whole Foods' value proposition emphasizes that they sell organic, natural, and healthy foods to consumers that are passionate about food and the environment.[58]

In order for the firm to develop a value proposition that resonates in the market, it is important to proceed through STP marketing to arrive at a value proposition.

Source: *Courtesy of Woolshire Carpet Mills, Inc.*

Note that STP marketing occurs over time; the participants in the strategy development process are likely to change along with the needs of the consuming market. A carefully selected value proposition gives the firm direction that leads strategic decision making. Importantly, if the benefits derived from the product exceed the price relative to other brands, then there is potential for success. If the relative price exceeds the benefits realized from the brand, the potential for a successful brand is limited. Equally importantly, the developer of the value proposition must consider the extent to which consumers weigh ecological, relational, and economic returns relative to the cost of the product. When each facet of sustainability is incorporated into the development of the value proposition, there is greater potential to serve the needs of the target market successfully.

FIG. 5-10 Kyocera Ad Exemplifying Competitive Positioning

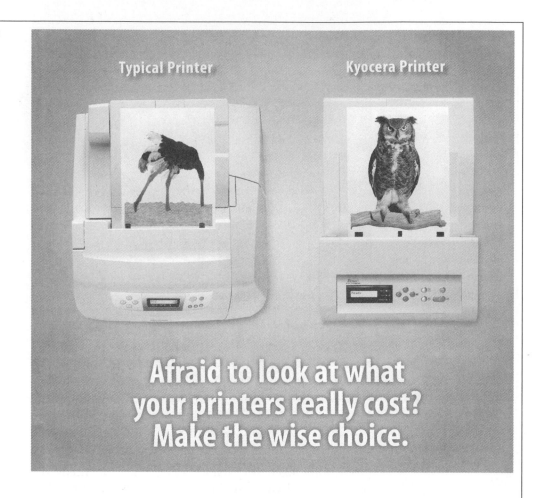

ECO-nomical. ECO-logical.
ECOSYS Printers from Kyocera.

How much did your company spend on printing last month? How about last year? If your company is like most companies, it's probably too much. Switching to ECOSYS Printers from Kyocera could save your company hundreds, even thousands of dollars per year. That's because Kyocera's durable long-life consumables mean less waste, reducing costs—and lowering impact on the environment. Brilliant color, crisp black and white, low Total Cost of Ownership, and environmentally friendly. Now that's a wise choice.

Visit our *TCO Tracker* at www.kyoceramita.com.
Calculate your cost today. Save tomorrow.

Printer's performance is simulated. Cost savings are for similar size printers having comparable prints-per-minute, paper size, memory, processor speed and rated print volume and based upon usage assumptions. Actual cost savings will vary. See our online TCO Tracker at www.kyoceramita.com for assumptions and details underlying specific cost savings calculation for particular comparable printers.

© KYOCERA MITA Corporation KYOCERA MITA America, Inc. 2010 Kyocera Corporation.

Source: © *Kyocera Mita America, Inc.*

Summary

A. Introduction

The purpose of this chapter has been to outline the facets of the market segmentation process. We initially outlined the elements of the segmentation–target–positioning framework. The segmentation process involves dividing a market into distinct segments or subsets of customers that have similar needs or behave in the same way. After the firm has identified the segments in a market, it engages in target marketing characterized by efforts to serve a selected segment within the marketplace. After the firm has selected a target market, it then establishes a positioning strategy in which the marketing mix is crafted to yield a distinctive appeal to the target segment. The positioning approach is designed to reflect the values sought by consumers in the target market.

B. Market Segmentation

Segmentation enables companies to identify groups of consumers with similar needs and enables companies to analyze characteristics and buying behaviors of members of these groups. The segments identified in the market must be substantial, identifiable, and measurable, as well as accessible and responsive to the marketer. Two common methods of segmentation include classification based on geography and demographics. Green marketing analysts have also classified consumers based on psychographics and consumer behavior.

C. Target Marketing

Target marketing refers to the selection of a subgroup of the total market as the focal point for the marketing mix. Identification of a target market demands consideration of the firm's ability to satisfy the market as well as the size of the target and the level of competition. Simultaneous analysis of size and competition yields defensive green, shaded green, extreme green, and lean green potential approaches to the target market.

D. Market Positioning

The *positioning strategy* refers to the development of the marketing mix to yield a distinctive appeal to the target segment. Three general strategies for a positioning theme include benefit, user, and competitive positioning. *Benefit positioning* refers to an emphasis on a functional, emotional, or self-expressive return realized from product consumption. *User positioning* is a positioning theme in which the marketer develops a profile of a specific target user as the focus of the positioning strategy. *Competitive positioning* refers to the direct reference to the competition in order to illuminate the benefits of a firm's brand. At the end of the positioning process, the firm is in a position to announce the value proposition of a brand. The value proposition is a statement of the emotional, functional, and self-expressive benefits delivered by a brand that provides value to consumers in a target market.

Keywords

apathetics, 98
benefit positioning, 107
benefit segmentation, 101
buygrid framework, 102
competitive positioning, 108
conventionals, 100
defensive green, 104
demographics segmentation, 97
drifters, 100
extreme green, 105
geography segmentation, 98
greenback greens, 98

grousers, 98
lean green, 104
LOHAS, 99
market, 95
market segmentation, 95
naturalites, 100
niche marketing strategies, 104
North American Industry
Classification System
(NAICS), 101
positioning, 95

psychographic segmentation, 98
reverse marketing, 102
shaded green, 105
sprouts, 98
STP marketing, 95
target marketing, 95
true blues, 98
unconcerned, 101
user positioning, 108
value proposition, 108

Questions

1. Why is it necessary for the firm to analyze the market for segments and targets?
2. What are the elements of STP marketing?
3. What are the criteria for determining market segments?
4. Describe four types of market segmentation used by green marketing firms.
5. What insight does the Roper Starch Worldwide research provide?
6. What is LOHAS? Contrast LOHAS with other market segments identified by the Natural Marketing Institute.
7. What criteria are used to select target markets?
8. How do market segment size and the level of competition influence target market selection?
9. Describe the positioning themes.
10. What is the importance of the value proposition?

Endnotes

[1] Wedvert, "Seaside Oasis," http://portovert.com/node/1413 (accessed May 3, 2010).

[2] LOHAS Online, "About LOHAS," http://www.lohas.com/about.html (accessed May 3, 2010).

[3] Mireya Navarro, "How Green Was My Wedding," *The New York Times,* February 11, 2007, 1.

[4] Charles W. Lamb, Joseph F. Hair, and Carl McDaniel, *Marketing* (Mason, OH: Cengage Publishing, 2009), 671.

[5] Mana Sangkapichai and Jean-Daniel Saphores, "Why are Californians Interested in Hybrid Cars?" *Journal of Environmental Planning and Management* 52, no. 1 (2009): 79–96.

[6] Thomas S. Turrentine and Kenneth S. Kurani, "Car Buyers and Fuel Economy?" *Energy Policy* 35, no. 2 (2007): 1213–1223.

[7] Thomas C. O'Guinn, Chris T. Allen, and Richard J. Semenik, *Advertising and Integrated Brand Promotion* (Mason, OH: Thompson Higher Education, 2006), 781.

[8] American Marketing Association, "Dictionary" http://www.marketingpower.com/_layouts/Dictionary.aspx (accessed May 3, 2010).

[9] Peter D. Bennett, *Dictionary of Marketing Terms* (Chicago, IL: American Marketing Association, 1988), 220.

[10] Charles W. Lamb, Joseph F. Hair, and Carl McDaniel, *Marketing* (Mason, OH: Cengage Publishing, 2009).

[11] G. Philip Robertson and Scott M. Swinton, "Reconciling Agricultural Productivity and Environmental Integrity: A Grand Challenge for Agriculture," *Frontiers in Ecology and the Environment* 3, no. 1 (2005): 38–46.

[12] Joel Makower, *Strategies for the Green Economy* (New York, NY: McGraw Hill, 2009), 290.

[13] Philip Kotler and Gary Armstrong, *Principles of Marketing* (Upper Saddle River, NJ: Pearson Prentice Hall, 2008), 718.

[14] Jeena Rana, "Nike Goes Green Quietly," *Business Week*, June 22, 2009, 56.

[15] Lisa Belkin, "What Do Young Jobseekers Want? (Something Other Than the Job)," *The New York Times*, September 6, 2007, 2, http://www.nytimes.com/2007/09/06/fashion/06Work.html.

[16] Kate Galbraith, "Governments Can Promote Energy Efficiency," *The New York Times*, August 2, 2009, 2, http://www.nytimes.com/2009/08/03/business/energy-environment/03iht-green03.html

[17] O. C. Ferrell and Michael D. Harline, *Marketing Strategy* (Mason, OH: Thompson Higher Education, 2008), 717.

[18] Renee Wever, Sophie Lotgering, and Freya Ruijs, "Green Marketing of Consumer Electronics: Applying Kano's Theory of Attractive Quality on EcoDesign," (Working paper, Delft University of Technology, Netherlands, 2007), 6.

[19] Jacquelyn A. Ottman, "Know Thy Target," In Business, *GreenBiz.com* (November, 2003): 30–31; Jill M. Ginsberg and Paul N. Bloom, "Choosing the Right Green Marketing Strategy," MIT Sloan Management Review (Fall, 2004): 79–84.

[20] O. C. Ferrell and Michael D. Harline, *Marketing Strategy* (Mason, OH: Thompson Higher Education, 2008).

[21] See Note 2 above.

[22] See Note 2 above.

[23] Paul H. Ray, "The Emerging Culture," *American Demographics* 19, no. 2, (1997): 29–35.

[24] Laura Everage, "Understanding the LOHAS Lifestyle," *The Gourmet Retailer*, October, 2002, 82–86.

[25] Steven Waldman, "Lohasians," Newsweek, 2006, 10.

[26] See Note 12 above.

[27] Natural Marketing Institute "NMI Announces LOHAS Consumer Segments," http://www.nmisolutions.com/lohasd_segment.html (accessed May 3, 2010).

[28] See Note 12 above.

[29] See Note 27 above.

[30] See Note 4 above.

[31] U.S. Department of Labor Occupational Safety and Health Administration, "North American Industry Classification System (NAICS)," http://www.osha.gov/oshstats/ (accessed May 3, 2010).

[32] U.S. Census Bureau, "North American Industry Classification System (NAICS)," http://www.census.gov/eos/www/naics/ (accessed May 3, 2010).

[33] United Nations Department of Economic and Social Affairs, *International Standard Industrial Classification of All Economic Activities* (New York: United Nations Publication, 2008), 307.

[34] U.S. Census Bureau, "2007 NAICS Codes and Titles," 2007, http://www.census.gov/naics/2007/NAICOD07.HTM (accessed May 3, 2010).

[35] "Green Guide for Health Care (2008) Version 2.2 Operations Section, 2008 Revision," http://www.gghc.org/PilotDocsPub//2008%20GGHC%20Ops%20Revision/GGHC-Ops-08Rev-clean.pdf (accessed May 3, 2010).

[36] American Marketing Association, "Dictionary," http://www.marketingpower.com/_layouts/Dictionary.aspx?dLetter=B (accessed May 3, 2010).

[37] Michiel R. Leenders and David L. Blenkhorn, *Reverse Marketing: The New Buyer–Supplier Relationship* (New York, NY: The Free Press, 1988), 198.

[38] See note 7 above.

[39] Thomas L. Friedman, *Hot, Flat, and Crowded: Why We Need Green Revolution—And How It Can Renew America* (New York, NY: Farrar, Straus and Giroux, 2008), 448.

[40] David Welch, "Can Tesla Become a Real Automaker?" *Business Week*, June 24, 2009, 2.

[41] Brian Halweil and Thomas Prugh, *Home Grown* (Danvers, MA: World Watch Institute, 2002), 83.

[42] See Note 12 above.

[43] Hank Behar, "Let's Drink to Bottled Water," *Beverage Aisle* 13, no. 4 (2004): 46.

[44] "Bottled Water Companies Adopt Eco-Friendly Causes," *Drug Store News*, 2008, 33.

[45] Natalie Zmuda, "Why Bottled Water Is Not All Washed Up," *Advertising Age* 79, no. 45 (2008): 16.

[16] Jill M. Ginsberg and Paul N. Bloom, "Choosing the Right Green- Marketing Strategy," *MIT Sloan Management Review* (October, 2004): 79–84.

[47] Jordan K. Speer, "Patagonia: Shearing the Edge of Innovation," *Apparel Magazine* 47, no. 9 (2006): 44–47.

[48] One Percent for the Planet, "History," http://www.onepercentfortheplanet.org/en/aboutus/history.php (accessed May 3, 2010).

[49] The Body Shop, "Our Values," http://www.thebodyshop.com/_en/_ww/services/aboutus_values.aspx (accessed May 3, 2010).

[50] See Note 7 above.

[51] John T. Horn, Dan P. Lovallo, and S. Patrick Viguerie, "Beating the Odds in Market Entry," *The McKinsey Quarterly*, 4 (2005): 35–45.

[52] Cybernetnews, "Apple Computer Market Share Progress Report," http://cybernetnews.com/apple-computer-market-share-progress-report/ (accessed May 3, 2010).

[53] Paul A. Argenti, "Collaborating with Activists: How Starbucks Works with NGOS," *California Management Review* 47, no. 1 (2004): 91–116.

[54] Green works Presskit.com, "Home," http://www.greenworkspresskit.com/ (accessed May 3, 2010).

[55] Dimitra Defotis, "Clorox Isn't Recession-Proof, But it May Be Close Enough," *Wall Street Journal*, May 10, 2009, 2, http://online.wsj.com/article/SB124190163049204003.html.

[56] See Note 7 above.

[57] David Aaker, *Building Stronger Brands* (New York, NY: Free Press, 1996), 400.

[58] Michael E. Porter and Mark R. Kramer, "Strategy and Society: The Link Between Competitive Advantage and Corporate Social Responsibility," *Harvard Business Review* (December 2006): 78–101.

CHAPTER 6

Communicating Value via Integrated Marketing Programs

A. Introduction

MERRELL FOOTWEAR AND APPAREL

In 1981, Merrell Footwear introduced the Randy Merrell Cowboy Boot as the original fitted boot. Since that time, the company has evolved considerably, but the firm's message has always been about urging people to go out and enjoy the outdoors. The footwear products offered by this company have grown from cowboy boots to include hiking boots, sandals, slip-ons, and shoes for men, women, and children. The company has also successfully introduced lines of men's and women's apparel as well as backpacks, bags, and accessories. As part of the company's ongoing efforts to encourage and equip outdoor activity, Merrell supports the National Park Foundation, Appalachian Trail Conservancy, American Hiking Society, Bay Area Wilderness Training, Conservation Alliance, Project Athena, and Youth Outdoors Legacy Fund.[1]

Two ways that Merrell can increase its revenues are via selling more footwear and apparel to current customers and by selling more of these products to new customers. Some of these efforts have focused on consumers that spend time outdoors but have spent less time enjoying backpacking, hiking, and other traditional outdoor sports. In support of this desire to broaden its market share, Merrell has used its promotional strategy to communicate its participation in outdoor events that emphasize the need for sustainability in consumption. For example, Merrell has become a primary sponsor of the Rothbury Music Festival in Western Michigan (Figure 6-1).

The Rothbury Music Festival is a four-day music event attended by more than 30,000 people each year for the past two years. Headliners at this event have included the String Cheese Incident, Dave Matthews, Snoop Dog, Keller Williams, and many other musical groups.[2] Beyond the well-known headliners, Rothbury is also guided by an environmental sustainability mission. The festival is dedicated to running as close to a zero-waste event as possible, and it supports companies that favor environmentally friendly products. The festival attempts to reduce trash via recycling and the replacement of disposable products with compostable products. The festival's power is primarily provided via renewable sources of energy and uses carbon offsets to account for energy that cannot be eliminated. The festival also promotes the use of public transportation and carpooling.

Merrell has developed a series of promotions and advertisements designed to bring attention to Merrell and the Rothbury Music Festival. Before the event,

Source: © Romain Blanquart/Detroit Free Press/MCT/Newscom

Merrell sponsored a **sweepstakes** in which the grand prize winners received air transportation to and from the festival, admission to the four-day event, Merrell gift certificates, camping gear, and pocket money. **Advertisements** prior to the festival provided consumers with information about Merrell, the sweepstakes, and the festival. In addition, seven weekly prize drawings of gift certificates and outdoor gear were picked each week leading up to the festival. At the Rothbury Music Festival, Merrell made its presence known by featuring ads and brand placement materials strategically throughout the grounds of the event. In addition, the Rothbury general store sold many types of Merrell shoes and hiking boots, and **point-of-sale displays** outlined the merits of these footwear products.

In this chapter, we will examine alternative forms of promotion, and we will examine a variety of creative strategies. The Merrell example illustrates how companies communicate the value associated with their products and brands. Companies seeking to promote a sustainable message use a variety of promotional messages and media. Since many companies have different objectives in promotion and have different means to distribute their products, companies in the same industry may develop very different promotional strategies.

Recall that in the last chapter, we completed a process for the development of a value proposition designed to serve the needs of a target market. In this chapter, we examine a series of strategies that marketers employ to *communicate* value to the consumer. We begin by introducing integrated marketing communication as a series of processes that add continuity to the promotional strategy. We then identify a number of message strategies used to achieve alternative objectives in promotion. We illustrate that the effectiveness of these strategies is related to the target market, product, and environmental considerations. In the next part of this chapter, we explore the use of brands and accreditation labeling to communicate value. Brands reflect an effort on the part of the firm to illustrate a unique value proposition, whereas accreditation labeling reflects an effort to distinguish a firm's products based on the firm's achievement of some industry-level or environmental standard. We conclude by discussing deconsumption as a strategy employed to illustrate the value of consuming less.

B. Integrated Marketing Communication

Think about the number of advertisements that a person witnesses on a daily basis. Because consumers are confronted with many messages from many companies, it is essential that marketers offer a consistent message. Thus, companies such as Merrell that want to associate their brands with the outdoors should offer a consistent message in advertising on the Internet, in magazines, and on television. Similarly, sales promotion and personal selling should also reflect the same message. **Promotion** refers to all communication from the marketer designed to persuade, inform, or remind potential buyers of a product in order to elicit a response or influence an opinion.[3]

The **promotional mix** includes advertising, personal selling, public relations, sales promotion, and direct marketing. **Advertising** refers to one-way, impersonal mass communication about a product or organization that is paid for by a marketing organization. By contrast, **personal selling** refers to personal, face-to-face interaction with a potential customer. The effort of Merrell's sales force to gain shelf space at Bass Pro Shops exemplifies personal selling. **Public relations** involves the use of publicity and other nonpaid forms of promotion and information to influence attitudes about a company, its products, or the values of the organization. Merrell's press releases and publicity about their participation in the Rothbury Music Festival provide examples of public relations. **Sales promotion** includes all marketing communication action other than advertising, personal selling, public relations, and direct marketing designed to influence consumer purchases and relationships with intermediaries in distribution channels. The sweepstakes developed by Merrell is one type of sales promotion focused on increasing consumer purchases.

Direct marketing refers to direct efforts to target an audience via the Internet, direct mail, telemarketing, direct-action advertising, and catalog selling.[4] Companies such as Merrell engage in direct marketing when they use e-mail to invite consumers to enter a sweepstakes. Note that direct marketing serves as both a form of promotion and a means of retailing. As we will see in Chapter 9, retailing refers to all activities directly related to the sale of goods and services to the ultimate consumer. Direct marketing used to inform customers about an upcoming sale is a form of promotion because it provides information to potential buyers about an opportunity to buy. By contrast, mail received by consumers that asks them to purchase a product or service warranty is a retailing activity because it asks the consumer to make a purchase. Since marketers can combine these objectives in a single communiqué to consumers, we include direct marketing as a means of both promotion and retailing.

When marketers deliberate about the degree to which promotional expenditures will be dedicated to various forms of promotion, it is in their best interest to examine the goals of the promotion as well as the costs and returns associated with each form of promotion. The company must determine the promotional objectives. Some companies use promotions to raise brand awareness and inform consumers, yet other companies use the promotional mix to generate sales. In the evaluation of the promotional mix, it is germane to identify the stage of the purchasing process and the goals of the promotion. Because one can modify the presentation made by a sales representative, there is a greater opportunity to change the presentation to focus on the specific needs of consumers at the time they are making purchases. By contrast, advertising is an impersonal medium in which the marketer ordinarily cannot make changes to the presentation. Although the effectiveness of advertising may be somewhat lower than that of personal selling when the sale is about to be made, advertising is more effective at gaining broad consumer awareness of a company's products and brands. In general, personal selling and sales promotion are most effective at the moment of a purchase decision, whereas other forms of promotion tend to be more effective before and after the purchase.

In addition to considering the consumer's stage in the purchasing process, marketers also examine the relationship between the returns and costs of alternative forms of promotion. In 2000, the average cost of a personal sales call for an industrial marketing firm was estimated at more than $260.[5] Not only has this cost increased over time, but the consideration of cost has been broadened to include ecological costs. Personal selling is not only labor intensive, it often also demands that sales representatives use substantial amounts of energy to get a message to the consumer. Advertising often is associated with substantially lower costs to reach the consumer, and it may require relatively little energy to deliver the message to the consumer. As marketer concerns about the environmental cost of communication increase, there will undoubtedly be increased evaluation of the ratio between the costs of promotion and the revenue generated from the promotion.

Although companies must make tough decisions about the allocation of resources across advertising, personal selling, public relations, direct marketing, and sales promotion, most companies value having a common message across components of the promotional mix. Since consumers are exposed to multiple promotions on a daily basis, companies find that consumer response to promotions is heightened when the promotional mix provides a consistent message. **Integrated marketing communication** refers to coordination among the elements of the promotional mix to ensure the consistency of the message delivered at every contact point between the consumer and the company. For example, Merrell used an integrated marketing communication approach in the days leading up to the Rothbury Music Festival. Print ads in magazines and banner ads on the Internet featured the Merrell brand as well as the logo for Rothbury. Point-of-sale placards, provided via sales and distribution channels, used the same design. Press releases by public relations offered the same message about Merrell and the Rothbury Festival's commitments to the environment and sustainability.

Integrated brand promotion is a related term used to describe efforts to bring consistency to the presentation of the *brand* to consumers. **Integrated brand promotion** refers to the use of the promotional mix to build brand awareness, identity, and preference.[6] Merrell, for instance, strives to have a consistent message about the brand's efforts to market outdoor products in an environmentally friendly manner. Whereas *integrated marketing communication* refers to coordination in the communication effort of a firm, *integrated brand promotion* addresses coordination in order to build brand awareness, identity, and preference for a specific brand. In a world in which firms rely heavily on brands, integrated brand promotion is essential to building the value of the brand in the marketplace. Consequently, firms today strive to achieve consistency in the messages sent as well as the brands associated with these advertisements and other promotions.

C. Message Strategy

Promotion strategies are developed to obtain a consumer response or influence a consumer opinion. One of the essential responses that the firm seeks is a product purchase. For example, India's treesforfree.org (Figure 6-2) has point-of-purchase advertisements that ask consumers to contribute to reforestation.

Although increased consumption is often the motivation underlying promotion and advertising, select groups are now also presenting promotional campaigns that emphasize reduced consumption. For instance, the advertisement in Figure 6-3 was developed by ClimateMaster to promote reductions in the costs associated with home heating and cooling. These advertisements often focus on the environmental or economic returns associated with conservation of resources.

The second objective of promotion involves influencing the opinion that a consumer has about a brand, product, product attribute, or behavior. In many cases, promotional strategies designed to influence a consumer are in place well before a potential buyer is able or ready to buy. The promotional or advertising manager seeks to develop some association with the brand so that the association with the brand becomes relevant at the time of purchase. Thus, when Siemens advertising illustrates their wind turbines operating in the countryside, they are trying to foster an opinion about the firm rather than influence an immediate purchase.

FIG. 6-2
Treesforfree.org
Point-of-Purchase
Display Seeking
Immediate
Contributions

Source: © *Vinod lal Heera Eshwer*

FIG. 6-3
AMSOIL Ad Calling for Reductions in the Number of Oil Changes

Source: © *Courtesy of AMSOIL INC.*

The **promotional strategy** refers to a plan for the optimal use of advertising, sales promotion, public relations, direct marketing, and personal selling. To varying degrees, firms use each of these elements to communicate the value of their brands and products to the target audience. The strategy that underlies each of these forms of promotion should be focused on a particular target market and the associated value proposition developed by the firm. The **message strategy** refers to the objectives established by the promotional manager and the methods employed to achieve these objectives.[7] Messages have verbal, nonverbal, and technical components that are employed to enhance the communication process and gain consumer acceptance.

In their analysis of advertising message strategies, O'Guinn, Allen, and Semenik identify several objectives associated with advertising and promotion, and they identify several different procedures employed to achieve these objectives.[8] The objectives and the techniques ordinarily employed to achieve these objectives include:

1. *Promote brand recall.* The initial objective employed by many firms involves getting consumers to remember the service or brand name. If a consumer can remember the brand or some attribute, they are more inclined to buy the brand or engage in an activity associated with the message. The seemingly ubiquitous "reduce, reuse, and recycle" motto exemplifies an attempt to get the consumer to remember this activity. If consumers are unaware of these practices, they are unlikely to engage in them. Recurring use of a message builds retention that increases the likelihood that the consumers will reduce, reuse, and recycle.

Firms and organizations also promote their ideas and brand names via jingles and slogans. These communications to the consumer attempt to increase the likelihood that a consumer will remember the idea, product, or service. For example, Waste Management uses the copyrighted slogan *Think Green*. This brand association with a renewed vision of waste is supported by the firm's efforts to create clean, renewable energy from ordinary waste, efforts to convert solid waste into renewable electric power, and efforts to redevelop land for wildlife.[9]

2. *Link a key attribute to the brand name.* In some cases, the firm seeks to associate particular attributes of a brand with the consumption decision (Figure 6-4).

FIG. 6-4 Siemens Ad Illustrating Commitment to the Environment

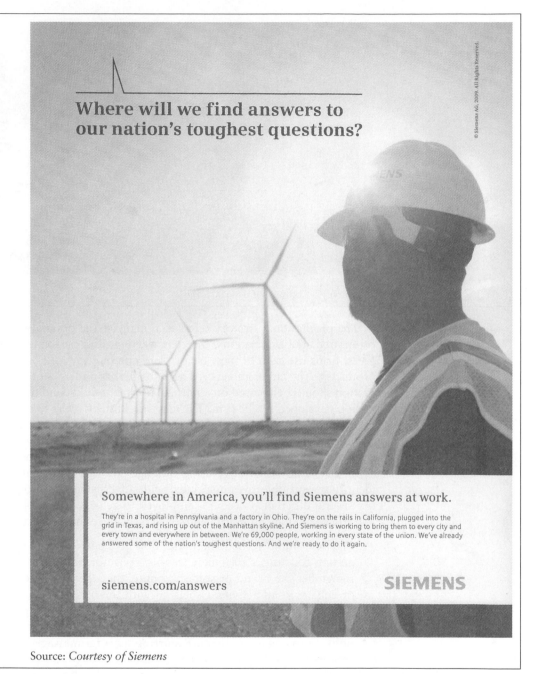

Where will we find answers to our nation's toughest questions?

Somewhere in America, you'll find Siemens answers at work.

They're in a hospital in Pennsylvania and a factory in Ohio. They're on the rails in California, plugged into the grid in Texas, and rising up out of the Manhattan skyline. And Siemens is working to bring them to every city and every town and everywhere in between. We're 69,000 people, working in every state of the union. We've already answered some of the nation's toughest questions. And we're ready to do it again.

siemens.com/answers

SIEMENS

Source: *Courtesy of Siemens*

A properly developed value proposition identifies self-expressive, emotional, or functional benefits delivered by a brand that provide value to consumers in a target market.[10] The ability to achieve these benefits should be, in some way, superior to the competition. The firm must therefore develop advertisements that emphasize the unique selling proposition of the brand. For example, consumers have many alternatives with respect to the purchase of bottled water. The ads for

FIG. 6-5 Repetitive Use of the Reduce, Reuse, and Recycle Theme Designed to Increase Sustainability

Source: © *Kellie L. Folkerts/Shutterstock.com*

Bangalore, India-based Bisleri water emphasize that the company has made substantial commitments to reforestation. In contrast to brand recall ads, such ads require the consumer to learn somewhat more about the brand and the product class. A single viewing of a Bisleri water bottle will not likely project the message of the firm's commitment to reforestation, but viewing multiple ads with this same message provides greater insight into the efforts of this water bottling company.

FIG. 6-6 Bisleri Water Ad Illustrating a Reminder from Treesforfree.org that Bottled Drinking Water Comes from Rain, and That Trees are Necessary for Rain.

Source: © *Vinod lal Heera Eshwer*

In many cases, firms seeking to link a key attribute to a brand name will focus on a single attribute of the product. Thus, Bisleri repeatedly states that purchases of their products lead to more money being invested in the planting of trees in Bangalore (Figure 6-6). When the firm has made a long-term commitment to this single brand attribute (e.g., reforestation), it often finds the strategy to be superior to a series of ads addressing multiple brand attributes. In addition, being the first to make a claim makes it difficult for the competition to make the same statement. Thus, competitors to Bisleri water will have some challenge making an association between their brands and reforestation in India.

3. *Convince the consumer.* In many cases, the marketer seeks to influence the buyer to make a purchase. Whereas the earlier strategies offered one or two reasons to buy, efforts to convince the consumer to make a purchase involve several logical arguments. Marketers use this approach when they feel the consumer is highly involved in the purchase. These consumers are willing to listen to cogent arguments about branded products. For ads and other promotional vehicles of this nature to work, the consumer must understand the logic presented in the ad, and the consumer must also agree with the logic. Advertisements that explicitly offer reasons to buy a product embody this strategy. For example, the American Public Transportation Association has developed newspaper and magazine ads that inform commuters that they can save money by taking public transportation (Figure 6-7).

The success of the strategies to persuade or convince consumers is contingent on the consumer's involvement in the purchase process. On some occasions, companies draw attention to the relative advantage of their products. By illustrating the superior performance of a product, the marketer hopes to convince the consumer to buy. This method has been found to be effective for brands with low market share when compared with high–market-share brands, and it has been shown to be effective when consumers have not demonstrated a brand preference.[11] Thus, many consumers faced with purchasing a new faucet are likely to have no brand preference. The Delta ad for

Source: *Courtesy of the American Public Transportation Association*

the Dryden brand draws attention to the money-saving benefits of this efficient-flow-rate faucet (Figure 6-8).

Another means that marketers use to convince the consumer to buy is via ads that express a sense of urgency. For example, sellers of solar panels for homes may post a

FIG. 6-8   Delta's Ad for Dryden Faucets

Source: *Courtesy of Delta Faucet Company*

newspaper ad that indicates a limited-time offer of a reduction in the price of goods. This form of ad is particularly effective when the consumer is comfortable with the benefits of a product but is looking for additional motivation to buy now.

4. *Instill brand preference.* In many cases, the goal of communication is not to influence an immediate purchase but to nurture preferences for the brand. These ads and promotions often emphasize the development of positive feelings toward the brand rather than rational thoughts about the salience of a product. One means of fostering these feelings is through ads that attempt to make the

consumer **feel good** about the brand. The logic rests on the presumption that consumers who like a brand will prefer the brand to alternatives. For example, Clorox's Green Works brands (see Figure 6-9) attempt to foster positive feelings for the brand prior to purchase.

Two of the most common methods used to foster positive feelings toward a brand are via the use of humor and sex appeals. Humorous ads ordinarily attempt to create a memorable and pleasurable association with a product or brand. Humor is particularly effective when the punch line or payoff from the humor is directly associated with the product or brand. For instance, ads for the MINI featured a play on the carbon footprint terminology through the vehicle's fuel efficiency and the fun go-kart feeling of a MINI by referring to MINI's Carfun Footprint (Figure 6-10). The humorous mention of the footprint shaped like a MINI vehicle draws attention to the MINI advertisement. Sexy ads similarly draw attention to the product with the hope that this attention will lead to brand preference. The Body Shop, for example, uses attractive models in their campaigns to draw attention to the firm's health care and beauty products (Figure 6-11).

5. *Change behavior by inducing fear or anxiety.* Marketers operating in some situations have found that they can get a consumer to act—or convince the consumer *not to act*—by instilling fear or anxiety in the consumer. Fear apparently is most effective when consumers have engaged in some thought about the issue, and under such circumstances, fear can be an effective way to induce consumer action. In the world of green marketing, fear is more likely to be used in a public service announcement than in ads for specific products. Aspen/Snowmass ads, for example, that treat snow as an endangered species are designed to instill in the consumer a desire to act in an environmentally responsible manner (Figure 6-12).

FIG. 6-9 Green Works Ad With "Feel-good" Quality

Source: © *Jeff Greenberg / Alamy*

FIG. 6-10   MINI Ad associated with the Carfun Footprint initiative

The Aspen/Snowmass ad shown below illustrates an effort to instill fear that one is leaving a less than desirable climate for future generations. The use of anxiety is related to the use of fear because both methods attempt to call attention to the negative consequences of certain activities or consumption practices. Anxiety is not as strong an emotion as outright fear, and it can last longer. For example, the World

FIG. 6-11 The Body Shop Ad Using Sex Appeal

Source: © *Image courtesy of The Advertising Archives*

FIG. 6-12 Aspen/ Snowmass Ad Using Fear Appeal

Source: © *Aspen Skiing Company*

Wildlife Federation (WWF) has repeatedly employed ads that use destruction of habitat for polar bears to generate anxiety over global warming (Figure 6-13).

6. *Situate the brand socially.* The social nature of humans is at the core of this strategy that situates the brand socially. Products have social meaning such that by putting them in the proper context, the marketer can gain awareness and, hopefully, adoption of a product. Many ads use a **slice of life** appeal that

FIG. 6-13 World Wildlife Federation Ad That May Generate Anxiety About Global Warming

"When it comes to climate change, the time has come for us to do more than mind our own business."

- Muhtar Kent, CEO, The Coca-Cola Company

LET THE CLEAN ECONOMY BEGIN

碳减排先锋
Defensores do Clima
クライメート・セイバーズ
Climate Savers

Johnson&Johnson   Nike   LAFARGE   The Collins Companies   SAGAWA   Xanterra   Catalyst   novo nordisk   Tetra Pak   SONY

NOKIA   hp   Nokia Siemens Networks   JohnsonDiversey   The Coca-Cola Company   SOFIDEL   Fairmont   ELOPAK   NATIONAL GEOGRAPHIC

Source: © AP Images/PRNewsFoto/WWF

situates the brand in an ideal usage setting. While this method is used extensively in television and print media, it is also used when marketers engage in **product placement**. Product placement refers to efforts on the part of brand owners to feature their products in films, movies, plays, or other performances. By linking the brand to a seemingly real activity, the marketer hopes to foster awareness of the brand. Figure 6-14 illustrates the use of Coca Cola on the TV show *American Idol*. Coca Cola gains increased awareness of its product, and the TV show receives revenue from the product placement.

7. *Transform the consumption experience.* Ads that transform the consumption experience seek to operate in a manner quite different from the strategies outlined previously. In most ads, the goal is to provide information about the product or enhance perceptions of the brand. When the firm elects to transform consumption, it is trying to make the consumption experience better. The marketer tries to make expectations about the experience or memories of the experience better. For instance, Starbucks has attempted to transform the mundane experience of buying coffee into something else. The claim that *Starbucks is not just coffee* (Figure 6-15) reflects the idea that Starbucks is trying to frame the experience of its coffee as different and superior to alternatives.

8. *Define the brand image.* The final strategy refers to action taken by the marketing organization to define the brand. In this type of advertising, the goal is to project an image of what the marketer hopes the consumer will associate with the brand. Regardless of whether the ad relies solely on visual images or lengthy copy, the objective is to link specific attributes to the brand. The Toms ad (Figure 6-16) defines the brand image as consisting of environmentally conscious, high-quality footwear.

The strategies outlined in this section are representative of most advertisements and promotions, but they certainly do not include all strategies employed by firms. The selection of these various strategies is driven by the goals of the firm as well as

FIG. 6-14 Product Placement of Coca Cola

Source: © *Photo by F. Micelotta/American Idol 2009/Getty Images for Fox*

FIG. 6-15
Starbucks Ad
Exemplifying
Transformation of
the Consumption
Experience

Source: © *Richard Levine/Alamy*

FIG. 6-16 Toms Ad
That Helps to Define
the Brand Image

Source: © *AP Images/PRNewsFoto/TOMS Shoes*

by the corporate and environmental context faced by the organization. In addition, it is not uncommon for firms to use multiple appeals in the same ad. Many humorous ads, for example, also are competitive promotions that link the product to specific attributes. The competitive position of the firm also influences the strategy employed. Well-established firms are likely, for instance, to place less emphasis on achieving brand awareness, but they are more inclined to invest in promotional strategies that promote a brand image.

D. Green Branding

The last strategy identified in the previous section addressed the development of a brand image. We define a **brand** as a name, term, design, or symbol that identifies a seller's products and differentiates them from competitors' products.[12] Firms are heavily focused on branding because at the product-market level, brand equity increases channel effectiveness and communications and decreases price sensitivity associated with the brand.[13] In some cases, firms are aggressively developing reputations for products that outperform the competition with respect to environmental concerns.[14] For example, the Body Shop brand emphasizes natural ingredients designed to enhance natural beauty while striving to achieve sustainability. By contrast, other brands may pursue sustainability efforts within the firm, but this message is not integral to the manner in which they present the brand to consumers. Nike, for instance, has made a commitment to reduce deforestation in the Amazon basin, but the reduction of the firm's carbon footprint and its commitment to rain forests are not central to the promotion of its brands.

In this section, we consider ways in which a brand can be differentiated from the competition based on appeals to sustainability or the environment. Firms that establish well-defined brand identity are substantially more likely to yield brand value.[15] The value of a brand expressed as brand equity has been examined from a *customer*, *corporate*, and *financial* basis.[16] *Customer-based brand equity* considers the attraction to a particular product from a particular company generated by factors other than the product's attributes. *Corporate-based brand equity* refers to the additional value that accrues to a firm because of the presence of the brand name that would not accrue to the equivalent, unbranded product. *Financially based brand equity* is the price the brand brings in the financial market.

The levels of company-based and financially based equity are driven by customer-based brand equity. Customer-level brand equity can be captured by five factors that form a hierarchy from lowest to highest. This hierarchy is consistent with the awareness–interest–desire–action framework developed to describe and influence consumption.[17] These factors include:

Awareness. The initial step for a brand often involves positioning the brand and its promotion to increase the likelihood that consumers will remember the brand. Awareness of the brand fosters interest that prompts desire and ultimately action. Consumer awareness of the brand can be evaluated based on **brand recall,** the ability to retrieve the brand when given the product category, the needs fulfilled by the category, or some other type of cue. For example, Toyota is likely to monitor the extent to which consumers recall the Prius brand name when prompted with the hybrid automobile product category. **Brand recognition** refers to the consumers' ability to confirm exposure to the brand when given the brand as a cue. Thus, Toyota could show consumers the product or brand logo and assess recognition.

Associations. Firms that establish brand associations in the minds of customers differentiate the brand and have potential to establish competitive superiority.[18] The tangible components of products are obvious ways to instill associations with the firm. Thus, Patagonia's use of organic cotton in its clothing products provides an association between this brand and environmental sustainability. Tangibles include product features, price, service reliability, style, design, and other factors incorporated into a product offering that provide superior performance relative to competition.

Intangibles are also germane to the development of associations with the brand. Intangibles develop **brand imagery** that influences how consumers think about a brand rather than their objective assessment of product attributes.[19] One source of imagery involves user profiles that describe the type of organization or person that uses a brand. A Patagonia ad, for instance, may paint a picture about the type of athlete that wears the brand. Imagery can also inform the consumer about the appropriate usage situation for a green product. For example, advertisements for compact fluorescent light bulbs illustrate the utility of these lights. Imagery can also be derived from personalities and values associated with the brand. Research identifies five dimensions of brand personality that include sincerity, excitement, competence, sophistication, and ruggedness.[20] Subaru ads, for instance, espouse the rugged durability of the company's automobiles. Finally, the history and heritage associated with a brand fosters imagery about the firm. Eddie Bauer's trademark, for instance, indicates the long-term dedication of the firm to the environment (Figure 6-17).

A third means for developing associations with the brand lies in the reputation and image of a brand. In a world in which greenwashing is rampant, it is essential

 FIG. 6-17 Eddie Bauer's Trademark

Source: © *RICK WILKING/Reuters/Landov*

that the firm establish credibility in the eyes of the consumer. **Corporate credibility** refers to the degree to which consumers believe that a company is willing and able to provide products and services that satisfy the needs and wants of consumers.[21] Credibility can be developed in a number of ways. For example, Merrell's support of the Rothbury Music Festival lends credence to the company's claims about its concerns for the environment.

Attitude. Brand attitude refers to the consumer's overall assessment of the brand. Attitudes are important because they form the basis for brand choice. Research indicates that attitudes toward brands are associated with beliefs a consumer has about a product and evaluative judgment about those beliefs.[22] In their efforts to market BlueTec diesel automobiles, Volkswagen may seek to assess consumer beliefs and assessments of this technology.

Attachment. The emotional bond that may exist between a consumer and a brand embodies brand attachment.[23] The attachment that consumers have toward a brand is embodied in affective, warm feeling for a brand, passionate intense feelings toward the brand, and the consumer's feelings of being connected with the brand.[24] Attachment is important because it can lead to brand loyalty and a willingness to spend more for a brand. For example, Starbucks has developed many loyal customers by fostering an affiliation with the company through a unique, retail dining experience.

Activity. The activity associated with the brand addresses the purchase and consumption frequency of a brand as well as the consumer's involvement with the marketing program. In general, higher levels of activity should foster stronger consumer brand equity. Frequent buyer programs, for instance, enable consumers to take active parts in the marketing programs of the firm. For example, Staples ink cartridge recycling program is an activity that bolsters the environmental reputation of the brand while simultaneously stimulating brand loyalty and store traffic.

The five factors listed above reflect ways in which firms have increasingly nurtured brand equity among consumers. Each level implies increasing interaction and involvement with the brand, thereby yielding higher levels of brand equity. **Green brand identity** refers to a specific set of brand attributes and benefits associated with reduced environmental influence of a brand and the perception of being environmentally sound.[25] Positioning a brand as green or sustainable involves communication and differentiation of the brand through its environmental attributes. Companies specifically interested in enhancing their affiliations with green practices and sustainability have focused on the functional and emotional benefits derived from the brands. Similar to the tangible brand associations addressed above, functional benefits are based on the relevant environmental advantages of the product compared to competing products. For example, Brita markets the functional benefits of lower costs and reduced landfills of its water purifiers over conventional bottled water.

As many analysts have indicated, the functional, ecological benefits alone of a product can have a limited influence on consumption. In many cases, the environmental benefit is not realized by the consumer, and these benefits can be easily replicated by competitors.[26] The benefit of smaller landfills may not resonate with many consumers, and other marketers could make the same claims about landfills.

Emotional brand benefits can serve as alternative complementary strategies to nurture green brand identity in three ways.[27] First, a brand can enhance its green equity by engaging in altruistic acts that contribute to the environment. Celestial Seasonings, for example, has partnered with Trees for the Future to plant one tree in a developing country for every box of Celestial Seasonings tea purchased.[28] This benevolent activity enriches sentiments toward the brand. Second, consumers can express green benefits through socially visible consumption of green brands. Thus, the purchase and operation of a Prius sends a message to other consumers that one is acting in an environmentally conscious manner.[29] Third, a brand can espouse a green identity when it enables consumers to get in contact with natural environments. Thus, the Siemens ad in Figure 6-4 associates the company's wind power products with a pastoral setting.

E. Certification Labeling

Businesses and consumers that want to act environmentally responsible are looking for ways to do so when they go to market. Consequently, a wealth of certification labels has been developed in a variety of industries and contexts. For example, the Energy Star label is a joint program of the U.S. Environmental Protection Agency and the U.S. Department of Energy. This certification is designed to save money and protect the environment through energy-efficient products and practices. Certification labels include **eco-labels** that reflect adherence to some standard associated with food safety and environmental performance and **social labels** that concern human rights and labor standards.[30] Although traditional labels focused on a single aspect of the useable life cycle of a product, these labels increasingly incorporate multiple criteria. For example, Food Alliance certification ensures that United States farms, ranches, and food handlers engage in both sustainable agricultural and facility management practices.[31]

Retail Product Terminology. In the retail sector, consumers are increasingly interested in purchasing healthy and sustainable products.[32] Research suggests that 60% of consumers in the United States market select foods for health purposes, regardless of age or gender.[33] The challenge for many consumers, however, is to determine the meaning associated with high-quality products. Three terms are used to varying degrees to describe and classify products. Although these terms may be viewed as interchangeable by the consumer, they have different meanings, cost structures, and marketing implications. The terms include:

Natural. Few terms employed in consumer marketing are as confusing as the term **natural**. Since essentially all products derive from nature, every competitor can claim to have natural products. Although the definition of this term varies based on the type of product under consideration, there remains a lack of agreement on the meaning of this term. Since products are produced in a variety of ways that include new technologies such as genetic modification, the ability to label a product as natural continues to be problematic and confusing to consumers. Moreover, the *natural* term alone is likely to offer little competitive advantage in comparison to *organic* or other healthy claims.

Organic. Organic production refers to the pesticide-free farming of locally produced ingredients typically grown in a small farm setting. Due to the different interpretations of the term, many standards have developed in different markets and states. In 1990, passage of the Organic Foods Production Act (OFPA) required that the United States Department of Agriculture (USDA) establish national standards for U.S. organic products. The USDA definition uses the term **organic** to refer to food that is generally free of synthetic substances; contains no hormones or antibiotics; has not been irradiated or fertilized with sewage sludge; was raised without the use of most conventional pesticides; and contains no genetically modified ingredients.[34] The USDA legislation (1) established standards for marketing organically produced products, (2) assured that organic products met a consistent standard, and (3) facilitated interstate commerce. The legislation targeted environmental quality by requiring that organic producers address soil fertility and regulate manure application to prevent water contamination. The act also included environmental and human health criteria to evaluate materials used in organic production. The USDA organic logo and the USDA National Organic Standards (NOS) were implemented on October 21, 2002, replacing the prior patchwork system of organic standards in various American states.[35] Organic certification is performed via state-run or accredited private agencies that see whether farms conform to the standards of the National Organic Program (NOP). Farmers that meet these requirements can market their products as "USDA Certified Organic" and display the USDA organic seal on their packaging.[36]

It is important to recognize the merits and limitations of organic farming. Note that research performed over several decades indicates that organic farming is usually associated with reduced soil erosion, lower fossil fuel consumption, less leaching of nitrate, greater carbon sequestration, and marked reductions in pesticide use.[37] Despite these merits of organic farms, the organic label, per se, does not mean food is necessarily healthier than nonorganic food. The label applies to the manner of production, yet it says nothing about the nutritional value.[38] There remains some debate as to whether food produced in an organic manner is necessarily *better* for the consumer.[39] While some studies indicate added nutritional value and flavor for organic products, the results vary somewhat from product to product. Making organic junk food does not alleviate any of the health problems associated with a regular diet of such food. In addition, some farmers are wary of the future potential of organic farming. For example, Stonyfield no longer markets many of its products as organic. Because production of organic ingredients has not kept pace with the demand, companies like Stonyfield are increasingly finding it difficult to find enough organic feed, organic cows, and organic fruit to make genuinely organic yogurt.[40]

Biodynamic. As the rapid commercialization of organic products has developed, there has been a complementary interest in developing and marketing products that exceed the organic criteria. Biodynamics is a farming orientation based on the teachings of Austrian philosopher Rudolph Steiner. **Biodynamics** refers to a specific form of organic farming that augments organic processes with consideration of the time of year, location, soil type, existing flora and fauna, and other factors.[41] Biodynamic farms are virtually complete ecosystems such that livestock create manure to fertilize fields and natural predators, such as insects, provide pest control. Since biodynamics does not use artificial settings such as greenhouses, seasonality becomes a major issue. For example, the United States vintners using biodynamic techniques must plant grapes at the seasonally appropriate time rather than use hothouses.

Demeter International is a Brussels-based nonprofit organization that oversees use of the term *biodynamics*. In order to gain eligibility, a farm must first meet the National Organic Program standards for organic farms for at least three years. Given the variation among farms, a single threshold is not employed. On the contrary, certification is based on existing environmental and social conditions with the goal that each farm evolves toward its maximum potential.

Certification labels help reduce the asymmetry of information between producers and consumers by allowing communication of credible characteristics of products.[42] Consequently, these labels are employed to inform consumers of product quality issues and the environmental processes used in production. The premise behind using these labels is that this information will be used in consumer decision making. The consumer must know what the label means and the issues associated with the label must be meaningful to the consumer. Consider, for example, the purchase of a microwave oven. If the Energy Star label is to be instrumental to the purchase, consumers need to know that Energy Star is awarded to the most efficient products in this product class, and efficiency must be important to consumers.

Increasingly, certification labeling is not only used to indicate diverse criteria, but it is further associated with complete life cycle usage assessment. **Life cycle assessment** refers to accounting for production and processing as well as resource energy usage, emissions, and waste. Because of life cycle assessment, labeling criteria increasingly require firms to track products throughout the entire supply chain. The **life cycle inventory assessment** identifies the sum amount of resources and emissions associated with a product or service over its life.[43] The eco-Leaf label used in Japan uses a life cycle assessment that quantitatively evaluates environmental information for all stages of the product's life.

Given that there are more than 400 eco-labels in use, it is meaningful to distinguish among the types of certification.[44] One can distinguish initially between labels that area mandatory versus voluntary.[45] The Energy Guide label, for example, is a required label for appliance sales in the United States. It provides the average yearly operating cost of an appliance as well as the average operating cost for all other products in the class. Not only are these types of labels required in many markets, but the credibility of these governmental labels is also higher than the level of credibility for labels developed by retailers.[46]

Among voluntary labels, one can distinguish between standards affiliated with the International Standards Organization (ISO). ISO 14000 certification is the international management standard associated with environmental management, and ISO 14020–29 address labeling. There are three types of labels associated with ISO 14000. First, labels can be based on *self-declarations* made by producers and suppliers without the direct authorization of a third party. For example, the "recycled content" label is featured on many supermarket products. Since corporately developed labels may lower levels of credibility more than other labels,[47] it is germane for the marketer to consider whether these labels will lead to product associations that generate revenue. The credibility of these labels is likely to be associated with the overall credibility of the firm. These labels are used on the product and are featured in advertisements and other promotions.

A second type of label is awarded by agencies external to the firm. For example, USDA certified organic labels are awarded to products that adhere to recognized standards for organic farming and food processing (Figure 6-18). Another such certification is the *Blue Angel*, which is awarded to products and services that are of considerable benefit to the environment and that further meet high standards of serviceability. They must also achieve high ratings for health and occupational protection. Economical use of raw materials during production and use, a long service life, and a sustainable disposal are also factors of great importance in making this award. The Blue Angel is awarded in Germany by the government after a review by an independent decision making body[48].

It is noteworthy that there are many standards that are not directly associated with the International Standards Organization. For example, the Energy Star label used in the United States is not, per se, based on ISO criteria. In many cases these standards are focused on a single industry. There are standards and associated

FIG. 6-18 USDA Certified Organic label

Source: © *Canadian Press via AP Images*

labels designed for assessment of buildings, carbon, electronics, energy, food, forest products, retail goods, textiles, tourism, and other industries. For example, Leadership in Energy and Environmental Design (LEED) certification is focused on the construction and building industry. To use the fair trade label in the coffee industry, a company must buy coffee directly from certified small coffee producers, and it must offer long-term contracts beyond one annual harvest. The company must agree to pay a price premium of $1.26 per pound, and it must offer producers prefinancing covering at least 60% of the annual contract.[49]

A third type of label is awarded based on quantitative life cycle environmental data provided in an extensive report format.[50] In this case, an organization external to the firm provides extensive reporting and assessment of the sustainability efforts by a company. For example, Environmental Product Declaration (EPD) has developed integrated systems that enable companies to help communicate the environmental performance of their products in a credible and understandable way. Upon verification, companies qualify to use the EPD trademark label on products as well as in advertisements and packaging materials.

Since there are many types of labels, it can be overwhelming to decipher which labels are most informative in a particular context. The development of a certification label involves many challenges and trade-offs. At one extreme, the label must be simple and distinctive to enhance consumer awareness. At the same time, however, the certification must also be supported by significant investment in sustainable business practices. The label must therefore convey complex efforts in an uncomplicated way. The Blue Angel, for instance, offers an efficient way to communicate sustainable practices associated with responsible management of health, climate, water, and resources.[51]

Several criteria should be accessible regarding any label associated with an environmental claim or standard.[52] First, it is germane to consider the *coverage* of the standard. The developer of the standard needs to establish the breadth and extent of the environmental coverage associated with the standard. Over its life, a product uses resources and exerts influences on water, air, land, and energy. The degree to which a label is associated with concern for each of these factors should be addressed. Standards offer varying levels of attention to each of these factors that may be affected by products bearing a certification label.

In addition to the coverage of a standard, it is also important to know how the achievement of the standard is verified. The basis for *verification* should be available, as should the length of time during which a company may use the label.[53] In addition, it is germane to report how often companies are audited with respect to the criteria associated with the award. For example, the Nordic Swan label is granted in 66 product categories based on environmental, quality, and health factors. The label is usually valid for three years, after which the criteria are revised and the company must reapply for a license.[54] Information on environmental coverage and verification for a multitude of labels is provided at ecolabelling.org.[55]

In addition to the coverage of the label, it is also relevant to examine who is involved in developing and managing the standard. There is tremendous variation in the extent to which groups are included in the development and maintenance of standards and related labels. Government, producers and processors, NGOs, and consumers are included in the development of standards and labels to varying degrees. The extent to which these groups are involved in the labeling process is related to the credibility of the label. Research suggests that consumers have greater trust in labels developed by consumer and environmental groups than those developed by other third-party groups, government, or retailers.[56]

To this point, our review of labels has examined how the label is developed and the extent of environmental coverage associated with the standard. The logic of standards suggests that they inform the consumer, and the consumer thereby makes purchases of products developed in sustainable ways. The ultimate question of the label, then, is its effectiveness in generating consumption and thereby increased revenues to the firm. If the label is effective, then revenue should increase after it is in place. For example, research has illustrated that under some conditions, the use of the organic and free trade labels can be associated with increased willingness to pay for related products.[57]

Although we value measuring the effectiveness of a label in driving consumers toward green products, results do not illustrate a strong relationship between labeling and consumption.[58] Consequently, few labels can illustrate a direct link between their application and performance. Although people want to act in an environmentally friendly way, in many cases the environment is not a top priority in making a purchase.[59] The purchase process may also be driven by habit or heuristics such that the consumer gives it little thought.[60] In addition, the information overload can be overwhelming to consumers. As the amount of information increases, it becomes increasingly more difficult to process the information.[61] When this information is not processed, it is unlikely that behavior will change.

F. Demarketing

The role of certification labels, like most marketing efforts, is to increase the amount of product consumed. By contrast, **demarketing** refers to action undertaken by marketers to discourage consumption.[62] Consumers may be asked to refrain from consumption on a permanent or temporary basis. For example, water is an increasingly scarce resource, and industry, consumers, and government benefit from water conservation. Research investigating the response to government efforts to reduce water consumption indicates that minority groups are less responsive than the majority population in reducing water consumption.[63]

The firm can demarket in three contrasting ways:

General demarketing occurs when companies such as utilities try to shrink the level of total demand. The effort to reduce consumption can be on short-term basis, such as the efforts to limit water consumption during a drought, or on a long-term basis, such as oil company promotions to conserve energy.[64]

Selective demarketing occurs when an organization discourages demand from certain classes of consumers. Urban governments in some countries seek to fight congestion by raising toll prices at selective times of the day. In Stockholm, a road pricing trial implemented was to reduce congestion by 10 to 15%. A congestion fee was differentially employed depending on the time one chose to enter the zone where the fee was being charged. The highest fee was set to 20 SEK (around $3) for the time period 7:30 until 7:59 in the morning and the period from 4:00 to 4:30 in the evening. The fee was SEK 10 from 9:00 to 3:29, no fee was charged on weekends, and the maximum fee per car per day was SEK 60. Environmentally friendly vehicles, vehicles owned by disabled drivers, motorcycles, taxis, buses, and other essential vehicles (e.g., police, military) were exempt from congestion fees. This selective demarketing effort in Stockholm yielded a 10% total travel reduction and a 17% reduction in travel for shopping purposes.[65]

Ostensible demarketing refers to a strategy that involves limiting consumption for the purpose of increasing sales. Note that in contrast to the general and selective demarketing, the goal of this strategy is to stimulate additional demand. Companies sometimes use ostensible demarketing to increase brand awareness and attractiveness by claiming overwhelming demand for a product. Limited availability of a good is often used to stimulate consumers to act immediately to ensure product ownership. For example, the rising gas prices in the summer of 2008 led some Hyundai dealers to offer to pay for a buyer's gas for a year.

In many situations, marketers use the logic of ostensible demarketing to stimulate increased consumption of new, energy-efficient technologies and products. These ostensible demarketing campaigns emphasize that investments in new technologies can yield less consumption, lower costs, and greater benefits to the community. The Lexmark Corporation, for instance, engages consumers in sustainability by encouraging them to print less. This developer of printers and related computer technologies has developed document scanning technologies, duplex and multipage printing capabilities, and print preview, as well as draft print and quick print modes. Each of these technologies enables consumers to print less and, consequently, use less paper, energy, toner, and ink.[66] Higher levels of sustainability accrue due to greater financial performance, better working relationships with consumers, and relatively lower influences on the environment.

Demarketing practices are related to sustainability and green marketing practice because they are employed to influence the financial, relational, and ecological returns associated with consumption. For example, low-flow showerheads can save homeowners more than US$100 per year over earlier technologies. Many of the promotions that emphasize demarketing are focused on the long-term health and relational benefits of reduced consumption. The American Lung Association, for instance, runs multiple programs and promotions designed to limit tobacco consumption. The ecological returns associated with limited consumption are also featured in promotions. The Peace River Water Authority in Florida, for example, has developed promotions designed to stimulate water conservation.

A recurring theme in promotions that feature calls for environmental responsibility is that the consumer is often more interested in other issues associated with product consumption and use.[67] Marketers that recognize this fact use multiple motivations to encourage reduced consumption. For example, Brita uses all three forms of demarketing in its ads for water filters. It emphasizes the cost savings from reusing a single bottle, the health and relational merits of filtering water, and the environmental savings associated with limiting the number of water bottles.

Summary

A. Introduction

The purpose of this chapter is to illustrate how marketers communicate value through the promotional mix. We used logic based on the marketing efforts of Merrell to illustrate an integrated marketing communication strategy developed to promote a relatively sustainable brand and its related products.

B. Integrated Marketing Communication

Integrated marketing communication is concerned with coordination among the elements of the promotional mix to ensure the consistency of the message delivered at every contact point between the consumer and the company. The promotional mix includes advertising, sales promotion, personal selling, public relations, and direct marketing. Integrated brand promotion is a related term that refers to the use of the promotional mix to build brand awareness, identity, and preference. Many firms today that seek to promote the sustainability of their brands engage in integrated marketing communication along with integrated brand promotion.

C. Message Strategy

Since there are multiple communication objectives associated with a promotional campaign, marketers have developed a series of strategies designed to help realize these objectives. Firms use jingles and slogans to increase brand recall, and they develop unique selling propositions to link a key attribute to a brand. When consumers are more involved in the purchase process, marketers use cogent logic or positive sentiment to stimulate brand interest. Positive feelings toward the brand are also generated through promotions and advertisements that use humor or sex appeal. Anxiety and fear have also been found to be effective strategies to induce consumption. Advertisements that situate the brand socially attempt to shape the meaning of the brand, whereas promotions that transform the consumption seek to make the consumption experience better. Promotional campaigns that attempt to define the brand image link certain attributes of the product class to the brand.

D. Green Branding

Green branding addresses the degree to which firms associate their brands with sustainability and sustainable business practices. The value of the brand can be expressed on a customer, corporate, or financial basis, yet many assessments of corporate or financial brand equity are derived from customer-based brand equity. The customer based value of the brand is based on consumer brand awareness, associations made with the brand, attitudes and attachments toward the brand, and consumer involvement with the brand.

E. Certification Labeling

Labels are used by marketers to increase consumer awareness of the product and brand attributes. They help reduce the asymmetry of information between producers and consumers by allowing communication of credible characteristics of products. Certification labels include eco-labels that reflect adherence to some standard associated with food safety and environmental performance and social labels that concern human rights and labor standards.

The labels may be based on self-proclamation by a firm, or they may involve evaluation by a third party. Certification labeling is used to account for production and processing as well as for resource energy usage, emissions, and waste.

F. Demarketing

Demarketing refers to action undertaken by marketers to discourage consumption. General demarketing refers to efforts by organizations such as power companies that seek to reduce the overall amount of energy usage. Selective demarketing is employed when a company seeks to limit the amount of consumption by target markets within a community. Ostensible demarketing refers to strategies that use limited consumption as a means for increasing revenue.

Keywords

advertisements, 115
advertising, 116
biodynamics, 136
brand, 132
brand imagery, 133
brand recall, 132
brand recognition, 132
corporate credibility, 134
demarketing, 139
direct marketing, 116
eco-labels, 135
feel good, 125

general demarketing, 140
green brand identity, 134
integrated brand promotion, 117
integrated marketing communication, 117
life cycle assessment, 137
life cycle inventory assessment, 137
message strategy, 119
natural, 135
ostensible demarketing, 140
personal selling, 116

point-of-sale displays, 115
product placement, 129
promotion, 116
promotional mix, 116
promotional strategy, 119
public relations, 116
sales promotion, 116
selective demarketing, 140
slice of life, 128
social labels, 135
sweepstakes, 115

Questions

1. The introduction of this chapter characterizes Merrell as a company that engages in integrated marketing communication to present its brands and products. Describe the marketing mix of another firm that uses integrated marketing communication to promote sustainability.

2. Is direct marketing a component of the promotional mix? Under what circumstances would direct marketing be classified as either promotion or retailing?

3. What are the benefits that companies realize when they elect to develop integrated brand promotions?

4. One of the purposes of promotion is to generate consumer responses in the form of immediate purchases. Describe an ad or point-of-sale display that has been used to spur immediate consumer purchases of relatively environmentally friendly products.

5. The Green Works ad campaign uses a feel-good strategy to foster preferences for the brand. Describe another ad for an environmentally friendly product that is marketed using this strategy.

6. It is relatively easy these days to instill consumer anxiety about the environment. Under what conditions do you believe that such a strategy will be either effective or ineffective?

7. Distinguish brand recognition from brand recall as message objectives. Which of these strategies is more challenging to achieve?

8. What is the difference between eco-labels and social labels? Describe a certification label that incorporates both ecological and relational components.

9. The logic of labels suggests that the presence of a certification label should lead to increased awareness and ultimately increased sales. How successful have labels been in stimulating sales of sustainable products?

10. Why would a company use a demarketing strategy when this strategy is designed to reduce consumption? Will this strategy necessarily mean lower revenues for the firm?

Endnotes

1 Merrell.com, "Outreach," http://www.merrell.com/US/en-US/Home/FlexPage.mvc.aspx#meet_merrell/outreach/ (accessed May 4, 2010).

2 Gary Graff, and David J. Prince, "Latest Buzz," *Billboard*, 2009, 26.

3 Charles W. Lamb, Joseph F. Hair, and Carl McDaniel, *Marketing* (Mason, OH: Cengage, 2008), 708.

4 American Marketing Association, "Dictionary," http://www.marketingpower.com/_layouts/Dictionary.aspx? (accessed May 4, 2010).

5 "Sales Call Costs," *Controller's Report*, 1(2000): 9.

6 Thomas C. O'Guinn, Chris T. Allen, and Richard J. Semenik, *Advertising and Integrated Brand Promotion* (Mason, OH: Thompson Higher Education, 2006), 736.

7 Yehoshua Liebermann and Amir Flint-Goor (1996), "Message Strategy by Product-Class Type: A Matching Model," *International Journal of Research in Marketing* 13, 3:237–249.

8 See Note 6 above.

9 Waste Management, "How We Think Green," http://www.thinkgreen.com/home (accessed May 4, 2010).

10 David A. Aaker, *Building Strong Brands* (New York, NY: Free Press, 1996), 400.

11 See Note 6 above.

12 See Note 3 above.

13 Kevin Lane Keller and Donald Lehmann, "Brands and Branding: Research Findings and Future Priorities," *Marketing Science* 25, no. 6(2006): 740–759.

14 Jill M. Ginsberg and Paul N. Bloom, "Choosing the Right Green Marketing Strategy," *MIT Sloan Management Review*, (October, 2004): 79–84.

15 David A. Aaker and Eric Joachimsthaler, *Brand Leadership* (New York, NY: The Free Press, 2000), 368.

16 See Note 13 above.

17 Edward K. Strong, "Theories of Selling," *Journal of Applied Psychology* 9, no. 1(1925): 75–86.

18 Kevin Lane Keller, Brian Sternthal, and Alice Tybout, "Three Questions You Need to Ask About Your Brand," *Harvard Business Review* 80, no. 9(2002): 80–89.

19 Kevin Lane Keller, "Building Customer-Based Brand Equity: A Blueprint for Creating Strong Brands," (Working paper, Marketing Science Institute, 2001): 1–107.

20 Jennifer L. Aaker, "Dimensions of Brand Personality," *Journal of Marketing Research* 34, no. 3(1997): 347–356.

21 Kevin Lane Keller and David A. Aaker. "Corporate-level Marketing: The Impact of Credibility on a Company's Brand Extensions," *Corporate Reputation Review*, 1 (August, 1998): 356–378.

22 Martin Fishbein and Icek Ajzen, *Belief, Attitude, Intention, Behavior: An Introduction to Theory and Research* (Reading, MA: Addison-Wesley Publishing Company, 1975), 314.

23 John Bowlby, *The Making and Breaking of Affectional Bonds* (London, England: Tavistock, 1979), 184.

24 Matthew Thomson, Deborah J. MacInnis, and C. Whan Park, "The Ties That Bind: Measuring the Strength of Consumers' Emotional Attachments to Brands," *Journal of Consumer Psychology* 15, no. 1(2005): 77–91.

25 Patrick Hartmann, Vanessa Apaolaza Ibáñez, and F. Javier Forcada Sainz, "Green Branding Effects on Attitude: Functional Versus Emotional Positioning Strategies," *Marketing Intelligence and Planning* 23, no. 1(2005): 9–29.

26 See note 10 above.

27 See note 25 above.

28 Environmental Leader, "Celestial Sees Sales Bounce From Tree Planting Program," http://www.environmentalleader.com/2009/02/11/celestial-sees-sales-bounce-fromtree-planting-program/ (accessed May 5, 2010).

29 Micheline Maynard, "Toyota Hybrid Makes a Statement, and That Sells," *New York Times*, July 4, 2007, 2, http://query.nytimes.com/gst/fullpage.html?res=9C0DE0D8153EF937A35754-C0A9619C8B63&;sec=&spon=&&scp=1&sq=%20Toyota%20Hybrid%20Makes%20a%20Statement,%20and%20That%20Sells&st=csc (accessed May 5, 2010).

30 Ulrike Grote, Arnab Basu, and Nancy Chau, *New Frontiers in Environmental and Social Labeling* (Heidelberg, Germany: Springer-Verlag, 2007), 241.

31 Ecolabelling.org, "Food Alliance Certified," http://ecolabelling.org/ecolabel/food-alliance-certified (accessed May 5, 2010).

32 Joel Makower, *Strategies for the Green Economy* (New York, NY: McGraw Hill, 2009), 290.

33 J. A. Milner, "Functional Foods and Health: a US Perspective," *British Journal of Nutrition* 88, no. 2(2002): S151-S158.

34 Mark Pittman, "Eating Food That's Better for You, Organic or Not," *New York Times*, March 22, 2009, 3.

35 Carolyn Dimitri and Lydia Oberholzer "EU and U.S. Organic Markets Face Strong Demand Under Different Policies," *U.S. Department of Agriculture: Amber waves* http://www.ers.usda.gov/Amberwaves/February06/Features/Feature1.htm.

36 George Kuepper and Lance Gegner (2004), "Organic Crop Production Overview," *U.S. Department of Agriculture: National Center for Appropriate Technology*, http://attra.ncat.org/attra-pub/PDF/organiccrop.pdf (accessed May 5, 2010).

37 See Note 36 above.

38 Katy McLaughlin, "Is Your Tofu Biodynamic? Making Sense of the Latest Organic Food Terminology," *Wall Street Journal*, April 19, 2005, D1.

[39] See Note 35 above.

[40] Diane Brady, "The Organic Myth," *Business Week*, October 16, 2006, 50–56.

[41] Kyle Shadix, "Biodynamic Agriculture May Slowly Gain Fans Among Chefs," *Nation's Restaurant News* (September 24, 2007): 26.

[42] Morven G. McEachern, "Guest Editorial: The Consumer and Values-based Labels," *International Journal of Consumer Studies* 32, no. 5(2008): 405–406.

[43] G.Rebitzer and others, "Life Cycle Assessment: Part 1: Framework, Goal and Scope Definition, Inventory Analysis, and Applications, *Environment International* 30, no. 5 (2004): 701–720.

[44] Ecolabelling.org, "Food Alliance Certified," http://ecolabelling. org/ecolabel/food-alliance-certified (accessed May 4, 2010).

[45] Ralph E. Horne, "Limits to Labels: The Role of Eco-labels in the Assessment of Product Sustainability and Routes to Sustainable Consumption," *International Journal of Consumer Studies* 33, no. 2(2009): 175–182.

[46] Renate Gertz, "Eco-labelling—A Case for Deregulation?" *Law, Probability and Risk* 4, no. 3(2005): 127–141.

[47] See Note 46 above.

[48] Blue Angel, "The Blue Angel – Who is behind it?" http:// www.blauer-engel.de/en/blauer_engel/who_is_behind_it/index. php (September 5, 2009).

[49] Sarah Lyon, "Evaluating Fair Trade Consumption: Politics, Defetishization and Producer Participation," International Journal of Consumer Studies 30 (5, 2006): 452–464.

[50] See Note 46 above.

[51] Blue Angel, "The Blue Angel – What's behind it?" http:// www.blauer-engel.de/en/blauer_engel/whats_behind_it/protec-tion-goals.php.

[52] See Note 51 above.

[53] Sara Stroud, "The Great Eco-Label Shakedown," *Sustainable Industries*, August, 2009): 29–33.

[54] Nordic Ecolabel, "About the Nordic Ecolabel," http://www. svanen.nu/Default.aspx?tabName=aboutus&;menuItemID=7069 (September 5, 2009).

[55] Ecolabelling.org, http://ecolabelling.org/

[56] See Note 46 above.

[57] Tagbata Didier and Sirieix Lucie, "Measuring Consumer's Willingness to Pay for Organic and Fair Trade Products," *International Journal of Consumer Studies* 32, (2008): 479–490.

[58] See Note 42 above.

[59] Daniel C. Esty and Andrew S. Winston, *Green to Gold* (New Haven, CT: Yale University Press, 2006), 366.

[60] Daniel Kahneman and Amos Tversky, "On the Psychology of Prediction," *Psychological Review* 80, (1973): 237–257.

[61] Paul Hemp, "Death by Information Overload," *Harvard Business Review* 87, (September, 2009): 82–89.

[62] Philip Kotler and Sidney Levy, "Demarketing, Yes, Demarketing," *Harvard Business Review*, 49 (November–December, 1971): 74–80.

[63] Amir Grinstein and Udi Nisan, "Demarketing, Minorities, and National Attachment," *Journal of Marketing* 73, no. 2 (2009): 105–122.

[64] See Note 62 above.

[65] Sven-Olov Daunfeldt, Niklas Rudholm, and Ulf Rämme, "Congestion Charges and Retail Revenues: Results from the Stockholm Road Pricing Trial," *Transportation Research Part A: Policy and Practice* 43, no. 3(2009): 306–309.

[66] Lexmark International, "2007 Environmental Sustainability Report," http://www.lexmark.com/environment/Environmental-SustainabilityReport.pdf (accessed May 5, 2010).

[67] See Note 60 above.

Producing Value via Innovation

FIG. 7-1 3M's MPro 120 Projector

A. Introduction

Watching a movie on a mobile phone screen can be somewhat of an eyesore, and it is quite difficult to watch the movie with someone else. A new breed of projectors, however, is ushering in a new age for mobile phones, mp3 players, and other devices. For example, 3M's MPro120 Pocket projector is a handheld device that can project high-quality images from 8 to 50 inches (Figure 7-1). A device that is approximately the size of a small TV remote control, this innovative product uses LED lamp technology that enables the device to run without any internal cooling system. Moreover, this technology enables the projectors to run for four hours while still keeping the total weight at 5.6 ounces.[1] Compatibility with personal computer formats, DVD players, iPods/iPhones, and other mobile phones ensures that this product will be enjoyed by many consumers.

The development of all new 3M products follows a long-established commitment to the environment by 3M. The company's Pollution Prevention Pays (3P) program, which is now in its fourth decade, underscores the company's high visibility regarding environmental management systems and eco-efficiency. The company continues to reduce emissions, and the eco-design of its products responds to customer demand for environmentally lean products.[2] 3M employs a life cycle management program that requires all business units to conduct life cycle management reviews for all new products.[3] This strategy enables the firm to commercialize new products like the MPro projector that incorporate environmental advantages in component procurement, production, customer use, and product disposal.

Source: *Courtesy of 3M Company*

As the 3M example illustrates, innovative companies are incorporating sustainability concerns into the design of new products. The purpose of this chapter is to identify strategies that enable firms to develop innovations that offer sustainable competitive advantages. We view **innovation** as the effort to create purposeful, focused change in an enterprise's economic, social, and ecological potential.[4] If organizations are to attain sustainability, it is essential for them to develop innovations that attend to each facet of the triple bottom line. They must recognize that focused change can occur to meet a variety of sustainability needs. Firms invest in new ideas in order to address growing populations, provide affordable products and services, serve growing unmet needs, and reduce environmental influences.[5]

As emerging markets mature and mature markets continue to develop, the need for sustainable innovations continues to escalate. Current estimates, for instance, suggest that if per capita consumption rates in the developing economies mirror the rates in developed markets, it will take the equivalent of three Earths to support resource consumption.[6] Innovations are necessary that promote sustainability by finding new ways to do old things as well as new ways to do new things.[7]

We focus our analysis of innovation on practices associated with developing innovative new products. It is essential, however, to recognize that firms innovate in a number of ways that include new channel development, new business models, and novel product ideas.[8] We distinguish between product and process innovation as two components of development. **Product innovation** refers to new goods and service that offer improvements in technical abilities, functional characteristics, ease of use, and other dimensions.[9] By contrast, **process innovation** refers to novel techniques for producing goods and services. These production enhancements are often designed to yield higher levels of triple bottom line effectiveness. Understanding of the innovation process demands consideration of both activities within the firm. In many cases, the process innovations developed by one firm become the product innovations of a second organization. For example, the innovations that UPS has made in its package tracking technology have enabled the firm to market these capabilities to its clients.[10]

In the following text, we begin by outlining the new product development process. We subsequently address the preliminary assessment, business case analysis, product development, and marketability of innovative product offerings. We then provide an overview of process development. Consider first a general framework for the development of new products.

B. Product Innovation Framework

Firms engage in an interactive process in their efforts to develop new product and service offerings. The stage-gate process outlined in Figure 7-2 elucidates the series of activities involved in designing new products.[11] *Stage-gate* recognizes that firms engage in a number of activities between idea conception and the market launch of a product. These phases are multifunctional and require interaction among marketing, R&D, production, and other activities internal and external to the firm.[12] Research indicates that technical flaws account for about 20% of product failures, whereas marketing- and management-related deficiencies account for 75% of product failures. The last 5% is not addressed in the reviewed literature. The various

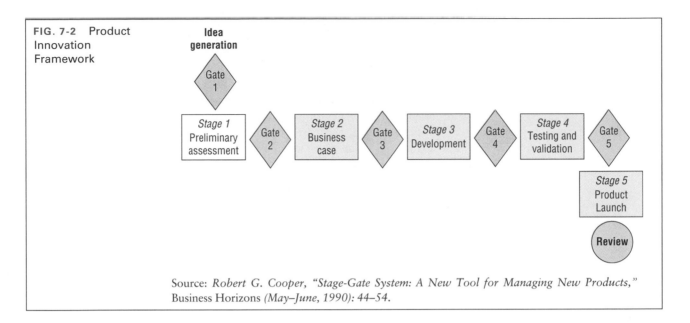

FIG. 7-2 Product Innovation Framework

Source: *Robert G. Cooper, "Stage-Gate System: A New Tool for Managing New Products,"* Business Horizons *(May–June, 1990): 44–54.*

departments within the firm must work together to increase the likelihood of new product success.[13]

Each phase and stage of the development framework is accompanied by a complementary gate. **Gates** are the points in the development process at which the firm evaluates the potential for a product. The gates are predetermined and specify *must meet* requirements of a project and *should meet* requirements of a product. At each stage in the process, firms deliberate whether to *kill* the project or allow it to *go* forward to the next stage. Firms make substantial investments in new product development, and the benefits of successful new products and the costs of failure are staggering. Estimates indicate that products released in the past three years account for at least 25% of a firm's revenue.[14] By contrast, failed product launches in the electronics industry are estimated at more than $20 billion per year.[15] By devising an appropriate series of gates or checkpoints, firms increase the likelihood of success and reduce the potential for failure. As the product develops toward full market launch, the costs associated with the product increase. Consequently, each stage of the process demands more stringent gates that serve as barriers to advancement of the new product project. Decisions that are made to *kill* products should be made as early as possible in the development process. The early elimination of products destined for market failure prevents the firm from spending valuable resources needlessly. Nevertheless, the decision to eliminate a known unsuccessful project benefits the firm regardless of the stage at which the project is killed.

We next outline the various phases of the new product development process. We begin with a discussion of idea generation.

C. Product Innovation: Idea Generation

The initial activity in the new-product development process is the generation of an idea. The stakeholders associated with an organization are at the forefront of this phase of the new-product development process, and it is essential to treat stakeholders as partners throughout product innovation. New ideas can emerge from virtually any aspect of the environment, and it is important to work with stakeholders to understand their vantage points for innovations. Participation in product development should therefore include employees, consumers, vendors, government, nongovernment organizations, and the general public.

Employees are often valuable sources of information because they have the potential to understand the market as well as the production and strategic objectives of the firm. Note, however, that this understanding can also be limiting to employees. The logic of "business as usual" may detract from the ability to offer ideas that genuinely challenge current operations. In many situations, organizations develop teams of employees involved in new-product development. These individuals come from the marketing function as well as from other technical areas of the firm.[16]

If these teams are to generate ideas successfully, it is imperative for them to recognize some of the inherent challenges in group development. The group process may generate **production blocking** characterized by the inability to offer opinions simultaneously. In addition, the firm should recognize that the group process may be hindered by employee concerns about evaluations drawn from the idea generation process. Research indicates that the influence of these problems can be quelled by electronic idea generation sessions. Asynchronous interaction enables multiple responses without blocking, and anonymous participation precludes management from using the idea generation sessions in employee evaluations.[17] The organization must also contend with the possibility that some team members free-ride in the development process by failing to offer ideas. This failure to participate in idea generation can be lowered by offering employees incentives for their participation.[18]

Beyond the organization, it is also clearly essential to poll the activity of consumers of the firm's product. Although the typical process in the firm has been to survey the breadth of consumers in a market, recent studies emphasize the need to look at lead users. **Lead users** are consumers that expect attractive innovation-related benefits from a solution and experience needs for an innovation earlier than most participants in a target market.[19] A representative sample of the target market customers that is familiar with existing product uses may have difficulty conceiving of novel product uses and attributes. By contrast, future-oriented lead users are more inclined to face issues today that most users will face in the coming months.[20] These lead users tend to have more consumer product knowledge and experience than other consumers. Relative to other users, they more frequently commit to risky, innovative, and difficult tasks, and they are more likely to be predisposed to innovation.[21]

Vendors, the organizations that market to one's firm, can also be a source of new product ideas. Competitive suppliers operating close to the firm provide shortened communication lines that facilitate the exchange of ideas that yield innovations.[22] Furthermore, sales organizations can take the innovative ideas generated in one context and adopt this logic in a novel setting. Nevertheless, vendors operate in a mixed-motive model and may not have the best interests of the seller in mind. In some cases, firms have therefore elected to develop teams of personnel including vendors as well as users.[23] These interfirm teams can increase the quality of new product ideas by reducing the misunderstanding that arises from working across corporate boundaries. Similarly to their intrafirm counterparts, cross-functional teams that share information early and throughout their operations can identify problem areas early in the development process.[24]

Government at all levels—from local operations to multinational alliances—is also a valuable source of new ideas. For example, the United States Department of Commerce supports efforts to bring new technology to market via the National Institute of Standards and Technology (NIST). NIST promotes innovation in the United States through high-risk, high-reward research in areas of critical national need.[25] Scientists affiliated with NIST conduct breakthrough research that leads to the innovations, but the range of NIST effort does not extend to product development in any of its research areas. The work needed to exploit NIST technologies for commercial viability requires innovation on behalf of the private sector. Commercially promising patents are identified together with the technological gaps that impede their direct transition to the marketplace. For example, recently supported NIST research has fostered the development of flexible computer chip technology. Innovators that gain an understanding of this technology can develop marketable processor chips for a variety of applications.[26]

Nongovernment organizations (NGOs) are similar to government in the sense that they serve as sources of information for the development of new ideas. Organizations such as McDonald's, IBM, and Walmart have recognized that interaction with these organizations can provide a wealth of information that is relevant to the generation of new ideas.

While it is insightful to examine the source of an innovation, it is also illuminating to examine the events that serve as the impetus for developing an innovation. Prior research suggests seven possible sources of innovation that vary based on whether they are associated with events occurring within or outside of an industry.[27] Internal events that yield innovation include:

Unexpected occurrences Unexpected occurrences are situations in which customers find novel unanticipated uses for a product. For example, backpackers that hike long distances are reluctant to carry many items in their backpacks because each item increases the burden of the journey. Many backpackers will therefore forego the use of a pillow when a makeshift one can be made from clothing and a nylon bag. When the utility of an item can broaden to include multiple functions, a new use for a product emerges. In addition, by enabling a single product to do the work of multiple items, the economic and ecological costs associated with the activity decline.

Incongruities Incongruities are situations in which there is an inconsistency concerning the prevailing logic in the industry. These incongruities can be associated with manufacturing processes as well as with economic incongruities. For example, the personal computing industry has been characterized by an incongruity between market growth and falling profits. The introduction of netbook computers is partially attributable to the desire to overcome this incongruity.[28] These netbooks enable firms to generate revenue and profits at price levels lower than most personal computers equipped with a hard drive.[29]

Process needs Process needs are modifications in the operations of a product to enhance its performance. For instance, the QWERTY typewriter keyboard was developed in response to the cost of fixing typeface machines that were jammed. Because users of the alphabetic keyboard often jammed the machines at substantial cost, the new keyboard design was developed to slow down users.[30]

Market changes Market changes are situations in which the nature of the industry or market changes. In the television industry, for instance, the basic operation of the product changed from an analog to a digital device in 2009. This change in the product requirements occurred despite recognition that more than 3.5 million American homes were not ready for digital broadcasting.[31]

External events refer to factors happening outside of the industry that prompt innovation. These include:

Demographic changes Demographics is the study of vital statistics such as race, age, gender, and income. Changes in these factors within a population can have a dramatic effect on innovations. In the developing world, for instance, many countries face a situation in which rapid population growth yields higher levels of poverty, and poverty yields higher levels of population growth. These demographic changes are being partially addressed through innovations in irrigation and water recycling.[32]

Changes in perception Changes in perception occur when consumers modify their opinions about some factor in the marketplace. For example, grocery shoppers have begun to modify their perceptions of the environmental costs associated with disposable paper and plastic bags. Consumers are increasingly using reusable canvas bags that are less harmful to the environment.[33]

New knowledge New knowledge is the use of new technical, scientific, or social information that can be instrumental in addressing a market problem. For example, the advent of hybrid automobile engines was prompted in part by new knowledge associated with fuel cell and electric motor technologies.[34]

After the initial generation of an idea, the firm implements its first assessment of the viability of the topic. Throughout the development process at each stage of the model, many firms use checklists or scorecards to determine the degree to which the idea fulfills "must-meet" and "should-meet" criteria. The product development evaluations are a *funnel rather than a tunnel* used to assess products that move toward the market.[35] Thus, the initial screening of the product is less stringent than later in the process. Although there are must-meet and should-meet criteria at this stage, there are no financial criteria at this juncture. The evaluation focuses on project feasibility, strategic alignment, synergy, market attractiveness, and synergy with the company's core resources and business. If the decision is made to move forward, the firm begins the preliminary assessment.[36]

D. Product Innovation: Preliminary Assessment

The preliminary assessment is the first stage of the new-product development process. At this stage, the firm performs an initial market assessment in which the organization determines the market potential and size. The firm will ordinarily perform a online and library search for related products and use focus groups and interaction with key users to assess the likelihood of marketplace acceptance of the product.[37] The market analysis is complemented by a preliminary technical analysis in which the firm assesses the manufacturing and development feasibility of a project. The organization will seek to quantify the time and costs associated with manufacturing the product.[38]

Because the firm will move forward in multiple directions that may include marketing, procurement, logistics, manufacturing, and R&D, it is essential to build effective project teams at the beginning of the development process. Effective new-product teams must have clear goals and unified commitment among the team members.[39] Team members should collectively possess the capabilities to achieve the project's objectives, and they should be supported by resources and psychological support needed to maintain a high level of motivation and focus. Furthermore, the team structure should emphasize a collaborative work environment that promotes effective communication. Team leaders should provide a consistent focused message that directs all team members to achieve high levels of performance.[40]

Gate 2 is the screen used to evaluate potential products at the end of the first stage. Although the *Go/Kill* decision will not be markedly different from the initial screen, the should-meet criteria now incorporate considerations brought to the process by customers and sales representatives. Financial criteria at this point are not substantial, but they do address the potential break-even point for the venture. If the project adequately addresses the should-meet and must-meet criteria, the project moves forward to the business case preparation.[41]

E. Product Innovation: Business Case Preparation

The business case preparation phase is the last stage in the process before substantial investment is made in product development. Consequently, it is essential for the firm to identify the attractiveness of the product associated with manufacturing, marketing, legal, and financial constraints.[42] The manufacturing assessment must address the investment required to engage in production as well as the costs of manufacturing. Since organizations that do not address sustainability concerns face increased social and economic liability, it is important for the manufacturing cost analysis to consider triple bottom line costs associated with manufacturing and the supply chain.[43]

The marketing component of the business case requires the organization to assess consumer needs and wants to determine customer expectations for the ideal new product. In addition, the firm will propose new products to customers to determine their likely acceptance of a new product. Firms that engage in dialogue with potential consumers gain input that enables them to make product enhancements prior to the product development stage.[44] This dialogue enables the firm to identify the economic, social, and ecological merits of the product as they relate to potential consumers. The marketing analysis will also require a competitive analysis to determine the relative advantage of a new product. Similarly, the firm will assess the patentability of a new product as well as a review of legal and regulatory constraints. Increasingly, the legal requirements are embracing technologies that are more beneficial or less harmful to the environment. For example, prevailing EU law prevents firms from marketing electrical or electronic components made from mercury, lead, cadmium, and hexavalent chromium.[45]

The third gate in the new-product development process is critical because it is the last chance to eliminate the idea prior to a sizeable investment. Research within the stage-gate model indicates the need to incorporate the following considerations before advancing to product development:[46]

Product competitive advantage The value proposition for the new product must be compelling and superior with respect to some facet of the triple bottom line. This benefit should be recognized and viewed as favorable by the consumer. If the value proposition is based on ecological merits, then the trade-offs associated with this benefit should be greater than any associated limitations with respect to the social and economic benefits of the product.

Strategic fit   It is essential that the new product be consistent with the firm's business strategy. Furthermore, the importance of the product to the business strategy must be recognized.

Market attractiveness   The attractiveness of the market includes consideration of the market size and growth potential. The margins realized by competitors in this market should be established, and the intensity of the competition in the market must also be determined.

Core competencies relatedness   New projects should reflect the core strengths in the firm. The attractiveness of new products should increase when they enable a firm to leverage strengths in marketing, production, technology, and distribution.

Technical feasibility   The feasibility of the technology is addressed by identifying the results to date of a technology and the complexity of the technology associated with a new product. The firm should also identify the degree to which it is familiar with the technology inherent to a new product.

Financial risks and rewards   The financial assessment should consider the level of risk associated with a product as well as the ability of the firm to address the risk. The organization should also examine the financial reward in terms of the net present value, productivity index, and size of the financial opportunity.

F. Product Innovation: Product Development

When a product concept successfully passes through the third gate in the development process, it then moves into product development.[47] Marketing and manufacturing activities move in parallel at this stage. The marketing function must continue to track the potential for the product and continue to obtain customer feedback concerning the ecological, social, and economic value associated with the new offering. It is essential to determine the extent to which consumers understand, recognize, and value the benefits derived from the product. On the manufacturing side, the firm develops a product prototype. In the process, the firm assesses the technical feasibility of the new product.

At the close of this stage, the firm faces Gate 4 in the development process. The criteria outlined in Gate 3 are reviewed to evaluate the attractiveness of the product. Although the evaluative criteria do not change much from the previous gate, new information concerning the marketplace attractiveness and financial merits of the project are incorporated into the decision calculus. If the decision is made to go forward, the firm mobilizes to perform a market test.

G. Product Innovation: Test Market and Validation

In the final stage before full market launch of the product, the firm examines whether the product can be manufactured and marketed in a profitable manner. The firm will engage in pilot production during which it will determine the production rates and costs.[48] Importantly, the triple bottom line criteria identified previously must be observable in the test runs of the production process. The firm cannot determine the total amount of by-products that emerge from production, but it will be able to observe which by-products are provided by manufacturing. The firm can determine whether these products can be used in alternative operations as well as the costs and returns associated with the by-product. For example, steel manufacturers identify the amount of slag produced that can be marketed to the cement industry. The assessment of by-products should also examine the amount of greenhouse gases produced in the manufacturing process. Firms that identify greenhouse gas production can act to offset the cost of this operation by making carbon dioxide available to industry or via carbon offset trading.

The marketing activity at this stage focuses on determining the level of interest and acceptance among consumers. If the firm can adequately determine demand, it can accurately determine the resources needed in production and marketing. Test marketing of the product is one activity that provides substantial insight into resource constraints. In a test market, the firm implements a complete market strategy in a single market over a short-term horizon. The test market provides new information about consumer responses to products, and it provides an estimate of sales and profitability.[49] For example, in October 2006, Procter and Gamble began test marketing its concentrated liquid laundry detergent in Cedar Rapids, Iowa.[50] When used in the proper amount, concentrated detergents produce fewer chemical by-products than traditional-strength detergents.[51] The test also provided the opportunity to learn about consumer acceptance and use of this new technology. Thus, the firm could observe whether consumers used the proper dose of the product and the proper water temperature.

Gate 5 at the end of the test market is a crucial point at which to assess whether the product should go into full production. Given the overall costs of producing and selling the product, it is important to be frank in the evaluation at this stage. Many organizations grapple with the desire to be objective at this stage because many individuals have dedicated substantial effort to product development.[52] Projects that will not obtain profitable levels of sales that are eliminated at this stage save the firm sizeable investments. Financial projections are paramount at this stage, and the market test and pilot production provide great insight into these projections. The market test illuminates the potential sales, whereas the market test and pilot production inform the firm about the ecological, social, and economic costs of the product. Consequently, the firm is poised to offer a more precise prediction of the sales and profit potential of a product. This information is essential because it enables the firm to project human resource needs for production and marketing. This information further enables the firm to estimate its resources requirements as well as the by-products of production. If the profit potential of a product is sizable, then the firm begins full product production.

H. Product Innovation: Full Production and Follow-up

When the product reaches the commercialization stage, the production staff commits resources to full-scale manufacturing. Similarly, marketing and sales must be fully committed to the product. Review of operations, regardless of the level of performance germane to this stage of operations, must be performed. Despite the detailed analysis associated with the new-product development process, roughly half of all new products still fail to achieve commercial success.[53] It is incumbent on the firm to review the product development process to reconcile marketplace and production realities against the projections. Sustainability assessments associated with the ecological and social returns of a project necessarily should augment the economic costs and benefit considerations.

Data associated with expenditures, revenues, profits, and timing should be compared to related projections so that the firm can identify opportunities to learn from the new-product development process. This exercise should be performed regardless of the degree of success with the project. Recognizing individuals that made high-quality projections and evaluations likely reinforces their predisposition to continue to perform adequately. Critiques that identify potential areas for improvement similarly enable members of the new-product development team to refine their evaluation and assessment of future projects.

I. Process Innovation

Process innovation refers to a technical system that generates value by transforming resources into products. These products contain physical and service components.[54] Several factors contribute to the desire to develop uniform, standard processes.[55] Standardized processes enhance communication and information systems operating across departments and firms. In addition, standardized processes provide the opportunity to hand off subcomponents and products more efficiently between functional groups. The standardization of processes also enables organizations to outsource activities associated with a process more easily. For example, specification of component requirements enables Dell to focus its internal operations on final assembly and pass component-related production to its suppliers.[56]

Organizations that develop operational standards may evaluate the operations associated with the process in three ways.[57] First, standards emerge due to the simultaneity of this activity in numerous organizations and locations. The movement toward standardization is occurring simultaneously across multiple organizations, and as this transformation occurs, process standards and performance guidelines for these standards are emerging. The Supply Chain Council, for example, has developed the Supply Chain Operations Reference (SCOR) model.[58] This model provides detailed visibility of how work is accomplished. It promotes team building and facilitates process improvement by addressing the entire supply cycle. Second, the development of standards facilitates **process performance evaluation**. When companies in an industry develop consensus about the activities and flows associated with a process, they can begin to compare their results to external service providers and competitors. Version 9.0 of the SCOR standards, for instance, incorporates industry best practices with respect to the environment. The standards address energy consumption and efficient resource utilization, and they identify environmental metrics such as carbon footprint, energy costs, and emissions per unit of production. The emerging standards also identify procedures for the management of waste and other by-products of manufacturing.[59] These standards enable the firm to compete more effectively while lowering costs, reducing cycle times, and enhancing reliability. Third, **process management standards** provide the opportunity to assess how well processes are managed. By outlining the key activities and resource demands of a process, a firm can evaluate the performance of alternative providers of a process. For example, firms can decide whether it is more efficient to have a process performed in-house or by a third-party vendor.

FIG. 7-3 Framework for Examining Process Innovations

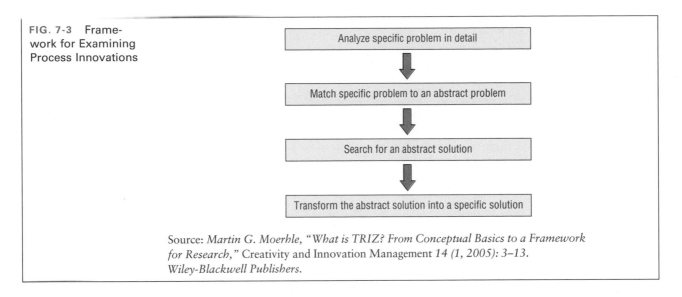

Source: *Martin G. Moerhle, "What is TRIZ? From Conceptual Basics to a Framework for Research,"* Creativity and Innovation Management *14 (1, 2005): 3–13. Wiley-Blackwell Publishers.*

Given the potential to augment efficiencies and raise performance via innovation, firms continue to evaluate the processes associated with production and supply. The *theory of inventive problem solving* recognizes that action dedicated to solving one issue often has negative outcomes for another aspect of the system.[60] A **contradiction** includes anything that limits the performance of a system relative to its goal. For example, increases in the number of functions performed on a computer likely yield higher costs of computer maintenance. When such contradictions are managed effectively, the overall performance of a process should increase. The evaluation of a process to enhance its productivity can be achieved via a four-phase procedure outlined in Figure 7-3.[61]

Analyze specific problem in detail   In the initial phase, the firm begins by illustrating how the present process addresses a problem. The firm identifies how a process works, and it identifies the materials, information flows, and energy associated with a process. Importantly, the firm specifies the input materials used in a process as well as the tool that transforms the process and the action undertaken by the tool. For example, the removal of impurities from water involves a water source (input), a gauze filter (tool), and purified water (output). The action of the tool can be expressed in terms of the operations it performs on the input material. The output materials may be useful or harmful, and in many cases the analysis of the process examines the utility of the outputs. Whereas some outputs are likely harmful, firms are increasingly searching for useful purposes for all output materials. For example, the steel production process outlined in Chapter 14 underscores efforts made within this industry to use most outputs from each production stage. Note that the desired and harmful outcomes associated with a process may reflect different performance outcomes associated with the economic, ecological, and social outcomes sought in a process. For example, the social returns from having mobile telephone service must be weighed against the economic and ecological cost incurred in production and service.

After the operation of a process and its associated inputs and outputs have been identified, one can determine whether there are resources within the process that are not fully exploited. Resources include the materials endemic to operations (e.g., input materials, desired outputs, by-products), but they also include spatial requirements (e.g., physical footprint of the tool), temporal considerations (e.g., just-in-time considerations), energy demands, and information requirements. Since all of these resources influence productivity, firms that consider each of these factors have greater potential to raise productivity.

Analysis of the resources associated with an operation enables the firm to evaluate the productive use of currently employed resources as well as alternatives to current operations. In the evaluation of their refinery operations, Shell isolates substantial levels of carbon dioxide that they market to Dutch greenhouses. Note that this evaluation of manufacturing processes also enables firms to assess whether there are available external resources. The carbon dioxide provided by Shell, for instance, is an external resource made available to the floral industry. Sale of this compound reduces emissions by 325,000 tons per year and saves greenhouses from having to burn millions of cubic meters of gas.[62]

In addition to identifying the resources in a process, this initial evaluation also examines the goals of the operation. This consideration demands that the firm balance the best possible solution against conditions that restrict one from recommending the best solution. Consider, for example, the design of computers used to verify production quality of automobiles rolling off an assembly line. The design of these machines must consider the trade-off between the convenience of uninterrupted power versus the weight of the device. Efforts to enhance power capabilities must be assessed in light of the market attractiveness of a relatively heavy computer.

Match specific problem to an abstract problem   After the current operations have been clarified, the organization then matches the specific problem associated with a process to an abstract problem. Theory of inventive problem solving calls for the inventor to develop a **contradiction matrix**.[63] According to this approach, a series of 39 factors represent the potentially favorable or harmful outcomes associated with a process. These factors include weight, length, area, power and energy considerations, operational issues, and productivity. The matrix matches each of these factors against all other factors in the matrix. At 39 factors, the number of potential constraints is 1,482 (39^2 – 39). A partial contradiction matrix is provided in Figure 7-4. By developing this matrix, the inventor identifies all trade-offs between desired and harmful outcomes. In the personal computer example, the desired outcome of uninterrupted power is treated as a component of the need to limit the amount of energy lost. By contrast, the weight of the batteries within the computer is represented by the *weight of the moving object* in the contradiction matrix. Note that at this point in the analysis, the contradiction (in the specific problem) between power convenience and computer weight has been transformed to an abstract problem between loss of energy and weight of a moving object.

Search for an abstract solution   In the third phase of process innovation, the firm searches for technologies that enable them to overcome the constraints identified in the prior phase. In the development of theory of inventive problem solving, researchers observed that 40 abstract principles have previously been applied to address the series of contradictions in the matrix. Importantly, these principles have historically been successfully associated with selected contradictions in the matrix. For example, firms and inventors that have faced the trade-off between loss of energy and weight of a moving object have used the principles of dynamics, universality, periodic action, and mechanics substitution. By shifting the problem to the abstract, the inventor gains the ability to consider the multiple ways in which others have successfully addressed this type of issue. Thus, the computer developer for quality control at the

FIG. 7-4
Contradiction Matrix

Worsening feature ⟹ Improving feature ⬇	1. Weight of moving object	...	22. Loss of energy	...	39. Productivity
1. Weight of moving object	+		6, 2, 34, 19*		35, 3, 24, 37*
...					
22. Loss of energy	15, 6, 19, 28*	,	+		28, 10, 29, 35*
...					
39. Productivity	35, 26, 24, 37*		28, 10, 29, 35*		+

*The numbers represent 40 abstract principles previously used to address the 1,482 abstract problems in the matrix:[63]

2. *Taking out*
Separate an interfering property or part from an object.

3. *Local quality*
Change an object's structure from uniform to nonuniform, or make each part fulfill multiple functions.

6. *Universality*
Make a part or object perform multiple functions, or eliminate the need for other parts.

10. *Preliminary action*
Before it is necessary, perform the required change of an object; or arrange objects so that they can come into action from the most convenient place and without time loss.

15. *Dynamics*
Design characteristics of an object to be optimal; divide an object into parts capable of movement relative to each other; or make inflexible objects adaptive.

19. *Periodic action*
Use periodic or pulsating action instead of continuous action.

24. *Intermediary*
Use an intermediary process or an intermediary carrier article, or temporarily merge one object with another.

26. *Copying*
Replace unavailable, expensive, fragile objects with simpler and inexpensive copies.

28. *Mechanics substitution*
Replace a mechanical means with a sensory means, or use magnetic and electric fields to interact with the object.

29. *Pneumatics and hydraulics*
Use liquid or gas parts of an object instead of solid parts.

34. *Discarding and recovering*
Eliminate or modify objects that have fulfilled their functions, or restore consumable parts during operations.

35. *Parameter changes*
Change an object's physical state (e.g., to a liquid); change the concentration, consistency, flexibility, or temperature.

37. *Thermal expansion*
Use thermal expansion and contraction of materials.

Source: *Based on Features of the Contradiction Matrix, by Ellen Domb, Joe Miller, and Ellen MacGran.* TRIZ Journal, *(November 1998.), http://twin-spin.cs.umn.edu/files/matrixwordversion .pdf (accessed June 10, 2009).*

end of an assembly line may elect to investigate the degree of universality as an abstract solution to the contradiction. This principle suggests that objects associated with a process perform multiple functions. When components offer multifunctional versatility, other components can be reduced or eliminated.

Transform the abstract solution into a specific solution In the final phase of the process, the abstract solution is transformed into a specific solution. The computer developer pursuing the principle of universality may consider increasing the functionality of selected components. Thus, photovoltaic cells placed on the back of the display add marginal weight, but they also add a source of energy.

The theory of inventive problem solving provides a strong framework for the analysis of enhancements to production processes. The breadth of the favorable and unfavorable outcomes associated with the contradiction matrix enables the organization to apply this logic across elements of the triple bottom line. Organizations must augment consideration of social and economic returns with consideration of ecological returns from these processes. When all three outcomes are considered, the potential for sustainable processes and designs should increase.

Summary

A. Introduction

The goal of this chapter has been to develop strategies that enable firms to develop innovative products and product strategies. New products are important to success, yet many products fail to enhance the performance of the firm. We presented the stage-gate model of new-product development as a framework for product development. We augmented the discussion of this framework by outlining a process by which firms can enhance process innovations.

B. Product Innovation Framework

The *stage-gate process* refers to a series of activities involved in designing new products. Stage-gate recognizes that firms engage in a number of activities between idea conception and the market launch of a product. These phases are multifunctional and require interaction among marketing, R&D, production, and other activities internal and external to the firm.

C. Product Innovation: Idea Generation

The initial activity in the new product development process is the generation of an idea. Since new ideas can emerge from virtually any aspect of the environment, it is important to work with stakeholders to understand their vantage points for innovations. Participation in product development should include employees, consumers, vendors, government, and other stakeholders.

D. Product Innovation: Preliminary Assessment

The preliminary analysis is the stage in which the firm performs an initial market assessment to determine the market potential and size. The firm will ordinarily perform an online and library search for related products and use focus groups and interaction with key users to assess the likelihood of marketplace acceptance of the product. The market analysis is complemented by a preliminary technical analysis in which the firm assesses the manufacturing and development feasibility of a project.

E. Product Innovation: Business Case Preparation

The business case preparation phase is the stage in which the firm evaluates the attractiveness of the product given manufacturing, marketing, legal, and financial constraints. The manufacturing assessment must address the investment required to engage in production as well as the costs of manufacturing. The marketing component of the business case requires the organization to assess consumer needs and wants to determine customer expectations for the ideal new product. The firm also assesses the patentability of a new product and reviews other regulatory constraints.

F. Product Innovation: Product Development

During this stage, marketing and manufacturing work in tandem to bring the product closer to market. The marketing function tracks the potential for the product and obtains customer feedback concerning the ecological, social, and economic benefits derived from the product. On the manufacturing side, the firm develops a prototype and assesses the technical feasibility of the new product.

G. Product Innovation: Test Market and Validation

In this final stage before full market launch of the product, the firm examines whether the product can be manufactured and marketed in a profitable manner. The firm will engage in pilot production during which it will determine the production rates and costs. The marketing activity at this stage focuses on determining the level of interest and acceptance among consumers. When the firm adequately determines demand, it can accurately determine the resources needed for production and marketing.

H. Product Innovation: Full Production and Follow-up

At this stage, the production staff commits resources to full-scale manufacturing, and marketing similarly commits to the product. Review of operations, regardless of the level of performance germane to this stage of operations, must be performed. It is essential for the firm to review the product development process to reconcile marketplace and production realities against the projections. Sustainability assessments associated with the ecological and social returns of a project necessarily should augment the economic costs and benefit considerations.

I. Process Innovation

Process innovation refers to a technical system that generates value by transforming resources into products. The theory of inventive problem solving enables firms to examine whether enhancements to one process influence other outcomes associated with a system. The evaluation of a process includes analysis of a specific problem in detail, matching the specific problem to an abstract problem, searching for an abstract solution, and transforming the abstract solution into a specific solution.

Keywords

contradiction, 155
contradiction matrix, 156
gates, 147
innovation, 146

lead users, 148
process innovation, 146
process management
   standards, 154

process performance
   evaluation, 154
product innovation, 146
production blocking, 148

Questions

1. How is sustainability relevant to new product development?
2. Figure 7–2 outlines a series of processes that precede the development of new products. Why is it necessary for the firm to pass through each phase?
3. What are gates, and why are they important to new-product development?
4. Explain why the decisions made at each gate should involve sustainability considerations.
5. Who are the stakeholders that should be consulted during idea generation, and how does each inform the development process?
6. Describe a situation in which internal events lead to the development of an innovation.
7. What are the potential consequences to the firm that does not adequately engage in business case preparation?
8. What critical decision is made after test marketing, and what information contributes to this decision?
9. Distinguish process innovation from product innovation, and explain why both forms are necessary.
10. What are the four stages of the theory of inventive problem solving, and how do these phases help to develop process innovations?

Endnotes

[1] 3M, "The 3M MPRO120," http://www.3m.com/mpro/ (accessed May 6, 2010).

[2] Carl-Johan Francke, "Dow Jones Sustainability Index: 3M Company," *Dow Jones Sustainability Index*, http://www.sustainability-index.com/djsi_pdf/Bios07/3M_07.pdf (accessed May 6, 2010).

[3] 3M, "Life Cycle Management," http://solutions.3m.com/wps/portal/3M/en_US/global/sustainability/product/life-cycle-management/ (accessed May 6, 2010).

[4] Peter F. Drucker, "The Discipline of Innovation," *Harvard Business Review* 63, no. 3 (1985): 67–72.

[5] Chad Holliday, DuPont, and John Pepper, *Sustainability Through the Market; Seven Keys to Success* (Geneva, Switzerland: World Business Council for Sustainability, 2001), 60.

[6] Marylynn Placet, Roger Anderson, and Kimberly Fowler, "Strategies for Sustainability," *Research Technology Management* 48, no. 5 (2005): 32–41.

[7] See Note 5 above.

[8] Nicholas G. Carr, "Visualizing Innovation," *Harvard Business Review*, 77, no. 5 (1999): 16.

[9] Jakki Mohr, Sanjit Sengupta, and Stanley Slater, *Marketing of High-Technology Products and Innovations* (Upperaddle River, NJ: Prentice Hall, 2010), 538.

[10] Lea Soupata, "Managing Culture for Competitive Advantage at United Parcel Service," *Journal of Organizational Excellence* 20, no. 3 (2001): 19–26.

[11] Robert G. Cooper, "How Companies Are Reinventing Their Idea-to-Launch Methodologies," *Research Technology Management* (March–April, 2009): 47–57.

[12] Doug Ayers, Robert Dahlstrom, and Steven J. Skinner, "An Exploratory Investigation of Organizational Antecedents to New Product Success," *Journal of Marketing Research* 34, no. 1 (1997): 107–116.

[13] Christopher O. Clugston, "Product Failures: Why Are We Implementing Wrong Solutions?" *Electronic News* 41, 1995, 50.

[14] Vijay Mahajan and Jerry Wind, New Product Models: Practice, Shortcomings, and Desired Improvements, Report Number 91-125, (Cambridge, MA: Marketing Science Institute, 1991), 35.

[15] See Note 13 above.

[16] Gary L. Lilien and others, "Performance Assessment of the Lead User Idea-Generation Process for New Product Development," *Management Science* 48, no. 8 (2002): 1042–1059.

[17] Joseph S. Valacich, Alan R. Dennis, and Terry Connolly, "Idea Generation in Computer-based Groups: A New Ending to an Old Story," *Organizational Behavior and Human Decision Processes* 57, (1994): 448–467; R. Brent Gallupe and others, "Electronic Brainstorming and Group Size," *Academy of Management Journal* 35, no. 2 (1992): 350–369.

[18] Olivier Toubia, "Idea Generation, Creativity, and Incentives," *Marketing Science* 25, no. 5 (2006): 411–425.

[19] Eric von Hippel, "Lead Users: A Source of Novel Product Concepts," *Management Science* 32, no. 7 (1986): 791–805.

[20] See Note 16 above.

[21] Martin Schreier and Reinhard Prügl, "Extending Lead-User Theory: Antecedents and Consequences of Consumers' Lead Userness," *Journal of Product Innovation Management* 25, no. 4 (2008): 331–346.

[22] Michael Porter, "The Competitive Advantage of Nations," *Harvard Business Review* 68, no. 2 (1990): 73–93.

[23] Cornelius Herstatt and Eric von Hippel, "From Experience: Developing New Product Concepts via the Lead User Method: A Case Study in a 'Low-Tech' Field," *Journal of Product Innovation Management* 9, no. 3 (1992): 213–221.

[24] Frank Q. Fu, Eli Jones, and Willy Bolander, "Product Innovativeness, Customer Newness, and New Product Performance: A Time-Lagged Examination of the Impact of Salesperson Selling Intentions on New Product Performance," *Journal of Personal Selling & Sales Management* 28, no. 4 (2008): 351–364.

[25] U.S. Department of Commerce: National Institute of Standards and Technology, "Technology Innovation Program," http://www.nist.gov/tip/index.cfm (accessed May 6, 2010).

[26] Chad Boudin, "Memory with a Twist: NIST Develops a Flexible Memristor," *U.S. Department of Commerce: National Institute of Standards and Technology*, http://www.nist.gov/eeel/semiconductor/memristor_060209.cfm (accessed May 6, 2010).

[27] See Note 4 above.

[28] Justin Scheck and Loretta Chao, "Leaner Laptops, Lower Prices," *Wall Street Journal*, April 22, 2009, D1.

[29] Hewlett-Packard, "Solid State Disks for HP StorageWorks: Array Whitepaper," http://h20195.www2.hp.com/V2/GetPDF.aspx/4AA2-4509ENW.pdf (accessed May 6, 2010).

[30] Everett Rogers, *Diffusion of Innovations* (New York, NY: Free Press, 1995), 453.

[31] Amy Shatz, "FCC to Hold National Digital-TV Test Before Switch," *Wall Street Journal*, http://online.wsj.com/article/SB124154664161288223.html.

[32] Lester R. Brown, *Plan B 3.0; Mobilizing to Save Civilization* (New York: W.W. Norton & Co., 2008), 398.

[33] Jeffrey Ball, "Paper or Plastic? A New Look at the Bag Scourge," *Wall Street Journal*, June 12, 2009, A11.

[34] Karim Nice and Julia Layton "How Hybrid Cars Work," *How Stuff Works.com*, http://auto.howstuffworks.com/hybridcar.htm.

[35] See Note 11 above.

[36] Robert G. Cooper, "Stage-Gate System: A New Tool for Managing New Products," *Business Horizons*, (May–June, 1990): 44–54.

[37] Robert G. Cooper and Elko J. Kleinschmidt, "An Investigation Into the New Product Process: Steps, Deficiencies and Impact," *Journal of Product Innovation Management* 3, (1986): 71–85.

[38] Tony Fairlie-Clarke and Mark Muller, "An Activity Model of the Product Development Process," *Journal of Engineering Design* 14, no. 3 (2003): 247–252.

[39] Carl Larson and Frank LaFasto, *Teamwork: What Must Go Right/What Can Go Wrong* (Thousand Oaks, CA: Sage Publications, 1989), 150.

[40] Paul J. Componation and others, "A Preliminary Assessment of the Relationships Between Project Success, System Engineering, and Team Organization," *Engineering Management Journal* 20, no. 4 (2008): 40–46.

[41] See Note 36 above.

[42] See Note 37 above.

[43] Michael Bernon and John Cullen, "An Integrated Approach to Managing Reverse Logistics," *International Journal of Logistics Research and Applications* 10, no. 1 (2007): 41–56.

[44] Victor P. Seidel, "Concept Shifting and the Radical Product Development Process," *Journal of Product Innovation Management* 24, no. 6 (2007): 522–533.

[45] Oladele A. Ogunseitan, "Public Health and Environmental Benefits of Adopting Lead-Free Solders," *Journal of the Minerals, Metals and Materials Society* 59, no. 7 (2007): 12–17.

[46] See note 11 above.

[47] Lawrence Miller, Ruth Miller, and John Dismukes, "The Critical Role of Information and Information Technology in Future Accelerated Radical Innovation," *Information Knowledge Systems Management* 5, no. 2 (2005–2006): 63–99.

[48] See Note 36 above.

[49] American Marketing Association, "Dictionary," http://www.marketingpower.com/_layouts/Dictionary.aspx (accessed May 6, 2010).

[50] The Soap and Detergent Association, "Procter & Gamble Announces Cedar Rapids Test Market Launch of New 2X-Compacted Liquid Laundry Detergents as a Full Replacement of their Existing Lineup," http://www.sdahq.org/sustainability/Procter_and_Gamble_new_detergents.pdf (accessed May 6, 2010).

[51] "Laundry Detergents Clean & Green Options," *Consumer Reports* 72, no. 1 (2007): 43–44.

[52] See Note 9 above.

[53] Susumu Ogawa and Frank T. Piller, "Reducing the Risks of New Product Development," *MIT Sloan Management Review* 47, no. 2 (Winter, 2006): 65–71.

[54] G. Cascini, P. Rissone, and F. Rotini, "Business Re-Engineering Through the Integration of Methods and Tools for Process Innovation," *Journal of Engineering Manufacturing* 222, no. 12 (2008): 1715–1728.

[55] Thomas H. Davenport, "The Coming Commoditization of Processes," *Harvard Business Review* 83, no. 6 (2005): 100–108.

[56] Jayashankar M. Swaminathan, "Enabling Customization Using Standard Operations," *California Management Review* 43, no. 3 (2001): 125–135.

[57] See Note 55 above.

[58] Joe Francis, "Team Building with the SCOR Model," *Supply Chain Management Review* 11, no. 2 (2007): 60–65.

[59] David Blanchard, "SCOR Goes Green," *IndustryWeek* 257, no. 5 (2008): 79.

[60] Martin G. Moerhle, "What Is TRIZ? From Conceptual Basics to a Framework for Research," *Creativity and Innovation Management* 14, no. 1 (2005): 3–13.

[61] See Note 54 above.

[62] H. Deliser, "Gas for the Greenhouse," *Nature* 442, (August, 2006): 499.

[63] Genrikh S. Altshuller, *Creativity as an Exact Science* (New York, NY: Gordon and Breach Science Publishers, 1984), 319.

Delivering Value via Sustainable Supply Cycle Strategies

A. Introduction

STARBUCKS

Consumers can buy coffee anywhere, but there is no mistaking the ambiance and aroma that surround a Starbucks. The company that revolutionized the way we buy coffee has also been working behind the scenes to ensure that its rich coffee will continue to be available in more than 40 countries across the globe for a long time. The company is committed to minimizing its impact on the planet, and it is passionate about sharing this commitment with its partners throughout the supply chain.

The Starbucks Shared Planet program is an environmental commitment that recognizes that conservation should occur throughout the supply chain—from coffee growers in Guatemala to recyclers in Seattle (Figure 8-1). On the supply side, Starbucks has worked in conjunction with Conservation International for 10 years to develop Coffee and Farmer Equity (C.A.F.E.) Practices. CAFE consists of 24 comprehensive, measurable standards designed to enable suppliers and farmers to become sustainable sources of coffee. Growers are required to meet criteria for product quality, ethical accounting, social responsibility, and environmental leadership. The program has paid huge dividends for growers, who become able to strengthen their marketplace positions and exercise some control over transformation of their organizations and operations.[1]

In 2008, 77%—295 million pounds (651 kilograms)—of the coffee Starbucks bought was purchased from suppliers verified and approved under C.A.F.E Practices guidelines.[2] The average cost of $1.49 per pound ($3.28 per kilogram) is 5% above the average price for C-grade Arabica. This price enables producers to increase their quality of life in terms of improved housing, enhanced education, and increased investments in their farms. Moreover, the stability realized through stable incomes reduces the need to migrate for employment.[3]

The premium price on the supply side has enabled the company to refund some portion of the price back to suppliers. In contrast to many performance standards, growers are rewarded (rather than penalized) for meeting sustainability standards. Growers must have third-party verification of their performance on the C.A.F.E. Practices Generic Scorecard, and this performance is reviewed annually.[4] In 2008, for example, 13% (38 million pounds/17 million kilograms) of the coffee purchased from C.A.F.E. Practices suppliers came from new and existing suppliers who had improved their scores by 10 percentage

FIG. 8-1 Starbucks Shared Planet Program

Source: © *Terri Miller/ E-Visual Communications, Inc.*

points or more. These suppliers were rewarded with an additional $1.9 million in premiums over contract prices.

Starbucks' ecological commitment has enabled the company to establish sustainable sources of supply to meet its rapidly growing demand while simultaneously providing a systematic response to consumer concerns about social and environmental facets of production[5]. The environmental commitment is carried throughout its distribution channels. The company takes stock of its greenhouse gas emissions and recognizes that 75% of its footprint is associated with electricity for stores, offices, and roasting plants; 24% is associated with store operations and coffee roasting; and less than 1% is related to corporate jets and vehicles. Starbucks is also aggressive about postconsumer waste and has a goal to use 100% recycled cups by 2015.[6]

The Starbucks example illustrates how companies can take command of their supply chains to deliver value to consumers. In this chapter, we examine the role of distribution as a central facet of efforts to achieve sustainability. Consistent with our focus on marketing as the means by which firms offer value to consumers, we focus in this chapter on the distribution function as the way by which the firm delivers value to consumers. We begin by diagnosing the elements of the supply cycle, from raw materials procurement to postconsumption disposal. We then outline several benefits that firms realize when they attempt to raise the sustainability of their distribution efforts. We subsequently outline green marketing activity associated with logistics. We close the chapter by describing the role of ISO 14000 in the firms' efforts to attain sustainability.

B. Diagnosing the Elements of Sustainable Supply Cycles

Supply cycles support virtually every marketing product delivery across industries. The supply cycle for textbooks, for example, includes the timber industry, soybean farmers (who supply raw materials for ink), paper producers, ink manufacturers, printers, book binders, wholesalers, retailers, teachers, students, and recycling centers. An understanding of supply cycles requires that one appreciate both the *organizations* involved in making a product available for sale and the *functions* performed by these organizations. An understanding of the functions performed within the cycle is highly germane to efforts to raise sustainability. In efficient supply cycles, these functions offer benefits to some member of the supply chain. As discussed in Chapter 1 in the treatment of the *triple bottom line*, these benefits may be associated with heightened economic, social, and financial performance. The sustainability of the organization, however, derives from the simultaneous pursuit of these alternative facets of performance in the triple bottom line. When one has an understanding of the benefits derived from each function, then one can work toward developing environmentally friendly supply channels that offer heightened benefits throughout the value chain.

In many industries, the functions performed within the channel are ascribed to specific organizations. For example, the auditing function to some degree is associated with accounting firms. Although in many cases one can eliminate an organization from the supply cycle, one cannot eliminate the value derived from the activities performed by an organization. Thus, a textbook manufacturer may elect not to use retailers, but then the sale of books to students must be achieved via the Internet or other means. In the following section, we outline a series of activities performed in a supply cycle, and we treat these entities as separate organizations. We present these activities as separate but recognize that in many cases, one organization will elect to perform multiple functions in the supply cycle. For example, Starbucks Coffee is a retailer that owns most of the supply cycle from coffee bean processing to retail operations[7].

Academic research offers a number of definitions for the delivery of value. The marketing definition of a **channel** describes it as a set of organizations involved in the process of making a product available for consumption.[8] Similarly, logistics frames the supply chain as a set of organizations linked directly to the flow of products and information from a source to the consumer.[9] Both of these definitions incorporate the specific entities that direct products to consumers, but they do not emphasize the value that derives from product offerings. By contrast, Porter describes a value chain as the set of primary and support activities performed by the firm to serve as sources of competitive advantage.[10] A company achieves a competitive advantage by understanding how its channel provides value to the consumer. Although this perspective provides keen insight into efforts to deliver value to consumers, it does not specifically address the relationship between value and the environment.

We define **supply cycles** as the "set of entities associated with yielding environmental, social, and economic value from resource procurement through resource processing, consumption, and postconsumption." Our definition incorporates the logic of the value chain described by Porter, and it incorporates the logic of supply chains and distribution channels in logistics and marketing strategy. This definition calls for understanding of the input–output process at each stage of the supply cycle

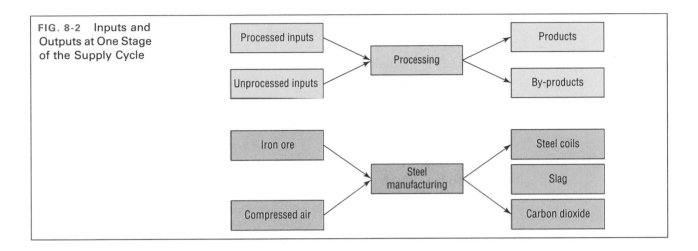

FIG. 8-2 Inputs and Outputs at One Stage of the Supply Cycle

as well as an understanding of the value chain (Figure 8-2). The input–output process presumes that each level of the supply cycle (manufacturer, retailer, consumer) engages in some sort of processing. There are inputs to processing and there are outputs.

Every entity in the supply chain has two forms of input and output. Inputs include those factors processed by an entity higher in the supply chain, and they further include resources (e.g., water, air) obtained from the environment. Every entity in the supply cycle has two types of outputs—products and by-products. Products are the focal outcomes of processing, and by-products refer to all other results of processing. For example, the steel manufacturing process outlined in Chapter 14 describes iron ore and compressed air as input to steel production. These inputs are combined in a series of processes that yield steel coils as the product output and by-products that include slag and carbon dioxide. To the extent that the steel manufacturers find uses for these by-products, they are able to increase revenues and lower their costs of operations. Thus, if the steel manufacturer is able to market the slag to the concrete industry, the steel manufacturer eliminates the costs of slag disposal while achieving increases in revenue. In addition, the slag by-product of steel production lowers the carbon footprint cost of the road production industry.

We refer to the process of delivering value as a supply cycle due to the relationship between the environment and the product development process. Ultimately, inputs are derived from the environment and outputs are returned to the environment. Product outputs are the motivation to engage in the supply cycle, and these outputs become inputs to the next stage of the supply cycle. The by-products either become inputs to other supply chains or they are returned to the environment.

Since the environment is both the source and result of supply chain activities, the complete cycle of the value chain must incorporate consideration of the environment. For example, Figure 8-3 describes a simple (one raw material) supply cycle for bicycle production. At each stage of the process, the entities involved in the

FIG. 8-3 Inputs and Outputs Across a Supply Cycle

Iron ore ⟶ Steel ⟶ Bicycle ⟶ Retailer ⟶ Consumer ⟶ Disposal

Environment

supply cycle provide product inputs to the next stage of the cycle. These entities derive their value either from processing at an earlier stage of the supply cycle or from the environment. Thus, the bicycle manufacturer gets steel from a metal producer, but bicycle production also relies on water derived from the environment. At each stage of the supply cycle, an entity interacts with the environment, both collecting and sending materials. An entity such as a retailer produces by-products that are either employed in other supply chains or returned to the environment. To the extent that these outputs are incorporated into other supply chains, the entity can derive revenue from the by-product. In contrast, by-products that do not have value in supply chains must be transferred back to the environment. These outputs do not generate revenue, but they increase the cost of operations.

Viewing the delivery of value as a supply cycle provides the opportunity to examine the specific outputs and their inherent costs and benefits. Consistent with this perspective, Walmart developed a **sustainability scorecard** in 2007 that identifies 14 categories of products or processes with the greatest environmental impact.[11] These 14 categories are associated with the firm's goals to use 100% sustainable energy, achieve zero waste, and market sustainable products. The firm has subsequently increased its use of solar panels and natural lighting as forms of sustainable energy, and it has pioneered innovations in material handling in its efforts to reduce waste. The firm has also adopted many sustainable technologies such as the exclusive sale of ultraconcentrated detergents.

C. Benefits of Sustainable Supply Cycles

The focus on the triple bottom line provides the opportunity to address multiple advantages that accrue due to sustainable supply cycles. Consider the following benefits associated with responsible supply cycle management.[12]

Better Working Conditions, Reduced Turnover, and Improved Product Quality
When an organization takes the time to investigate the firms and activities within its supply cycle, it has the opportunity to identify the conditions under which raw materials are transformed into consumer products. For example, the Mayflower Vehicle System PLC is a Birmingham, England-based subcomponent assembler in the British auto industry.[13] In its analysis of the sustainability of operations, it addressed the waste associated with shop floor operations. Consideration of waste included defective parts (per million), personal productivity, frequency of stock turns, delivery schedule achievement, equipment effectiveness, value added per person, and floor space utilization. Change agents realized that these waste reductions goals were more palatable to employees when the employees were endowed with a sense of ownership over processes and equipment associated with the jobs. Thus, the review of operations to achieve heightened levels of sustainability yielded better working conditions, a social facet of the triple bottom line. Better working conditions also yield economic returns in the forms of lower employees turnover[14] and enhanced product quality.[15]

Improved Efficiency and Profitability The pursuit of sustainability in the delivery of value calls attention to the inputs and outputs associated with every level of the supply cycle. By focusing on efforts to reduce inputs and maximize the productivity of outputs, the firm has tremendous opportunity to raise profitability. Packaging exemplifies a number of ways in which sustainability can influence profits. By employing efficient packaging, the firm reduces warehouse, distribution, and transportation costs. Efficiency can be achieved by lowering the amount of fiber in packaging via package designs that are lighter in weight and use less corrugated board. Efficiency can also be realized by using reusable packaging and through the automation of case forming and stretch wrapping of pallets of materials.

Another innovative example of packaging sustainability is in club stores such as Sam's Club. The packaging that is employed at these stores often functions as a shipping container and display package. Optimal packaging in these stores ensures defect-free delivery, enhanced shelf appeal, and lowered store waste. Together, these benefits raise the productivity of retail space while simultaneously reducing overhead.

Better Management of Risk Firms that understand their liabilities are better positioned to limit their exposure to risk. *Risk* refers to variations in possible outcomes and their likelihoods.[16] Assessment of liabilities includes analysis of supply cycle disturbances and their negative consequences.[17] Lowered risk can be associated with cost avoidance, lower insurance premiums, reduced legal and regulatory costs, and preferred rates on loans.[18]

In the supply cycle, risk emerges from the value stream, asset considerations, interfirm networks, and macroenvironmental issues. Analysis of risk in the value stream takes into consideration the flow of materials, information, and money in the supply cycle. Firms evaluate the sourcing and processing of products and by-products (including waste) by upstream partners in the value cycle. In addition, organizations also assess the consumption and postconsumption practices of consumers of their products. **Asset considerations** refers to conditions under which a firm invests in specific technologies that have limited use outside of their intended purpose.[19] When organizations embrace global supply specialization of processes, they face greater risk associated with quality control and security of component supplies.[20] Interfirm networks call attention to the degree to which one is dependent on other organizations in the supply cycle. When firms are highly dependent on other organizations, they face greater levels of risk that should be controlled via contracts or strong working relationships with stakeholders. The **macroenvironmental issues** refer to the overall level of risk encountered in the social, economic, and natural environments.

Although these four levels of risk may be viewed independently, there is an interaction among these contingencies. For example, cash flow in the personal computer industry is influenced by the investments that software companies make in the dedicated operating systems of Microsoft and Apple. As these investments appreciate, the software firms become more dependent on the architects of the operating system.

Enhanced Brand Reputation Firms that invest in sustainable practices in the supply chain develop positive brand reputations that pay dividends in multiple relationships. For example, Cisco Systems has developed a strong reputation as an industry supply chain leader. In this firm's supply network, almost 90% of the production is delivered by someone other than a Cisco employee.[21] Cisco's proactive approach to the supply chain fosters strong working relationships with a few suppliers. Their supply strategy also involves listening carefully to customer requests, monitoring technological advancements, and offering customers a range of options.

Stakeholder Returns Increased Organizations that focus on the triple bottom line have the ability to anticipate and monitor risk associated with economic, social, and environmental returns. By engaging dialogue with both upstream partners and downstream consumers, Cisco has been able to establish strong interfirm relationships. In addition, it is able to maintain a very low level of turnover in volatile high-technology markets.[22] Consequently, this firm and others that nurture strong supply cycles are more attractive to investors because they are better equipped to manage these multiple facets of risk than their competitors.[23] Attention to supply chain sustainability also reduces the likelihood of a firm encountering criticism or other reprisals from NGOs and communities.

D. Sustainable Logistics

Logistics refers to the process of planning, allocating, and controlling human and financial resources dedicated to physical distribution, manufacturing support, and purchasing operations.[24] Distribution communications, inventory control, materials handling, order processing, parts and service support, plant and warehouse site selection, procurement, packaging, return goods handling, salvage and scrap disposal, traffic and transportation, warehousing and storage, customer service, and demand forecasting are activities associated with the logistics function. To gain an appreciation of the role of logistics, consider the fact that this function represented almost 10% of the United States' gross domestic product in 2006. On average, logistics represent 9.9% of the costs to the firm,[25] and these expenditures are primarily associated with transportation, warehousing, order entry/customer service, administration, and inventory carrying costs (see Figure 8-4). Firms gain competitive advantage from the assets they possess and via capabilities that enable them to deploy these assets advantageously.[26] Analysis of the logistics function provides the opportunity to assess these assets as well as their deployment from their point of origin to consumption.

Although logistics has traditionally been associated with the flow of goods toward consumption, **reverse logistics** that trace products back from the point of consumption have increasingly been addressed in supply chains.[27] The interest in reverse logistics has been prompted by concerns about returned goods, proper disposal of end-of-life products, production planning and inventory management, and supply chain management.[28] In 2005, the total cost of returns was estimated to be

FIG. 8-4 2007
Average Company
Logistics Costs

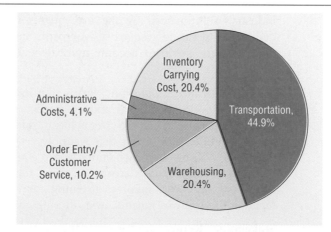

Source: *Based on Hoffman, William (2007), "Logistics Redraws Efficiency,"* Traffic World, *271 (51/52), 19–21.*

$100 billion, and roughly 70% of this merchandise was not defective but was returned for some other reason (e.g., wrong color, size, minor package defect). Recognizing the high cost of returns, Walmart set a goal in 2008 to end defective product returns among its largest 1,000 suppliers in less than four years. The company plans to use on-site audits, enforcement of social and environmental standards, and the threat of lost business to support efforts to realize this goal.[29] A perspective on reverse logistics provides the opportunity to examine the influence of return goods, and it further provides the opportunity to determine the extent to which promotional campaigns, product life cycle issues, and retail inventory levels influence supply chain decisions.[30]

Given the magnitude of logistics and the effect of logistics management on the cost of operations, it is imperative that the firm view this function as a source of sustainable competitive advantage. Increasingly, firms interested in enhancing triple bottom line performance examine the following facets of logistics:[31]

Fleet Optimization   The costs associated with product transportation are extensive, and since most forms of transportation rely heavily on fossil fuels, this facet of logistics is highly germane to sustainability concerns. Organizations are making a host of efforts to curb this function carried out either within the firm or via third-party suppliers. Importantly, optimization of the fleet cost is achieved by limiting the cost of transportation as well as by limiting the amount of travel undertaken by these vehicles. For example, in 2007 Staples installed governors on all of its fleet vehicles. These governors capped the speed of delivery trucks at 60 miles per hour. After installing these devices, the company realized a 25% savings in fuel economy and cut diesel fuel costs by 500,000 to 750,000 gallons. Similarly, UPS implemented a system several years ago that trained drivers to map their routes to turn right whenever possible. This simple strategy saves fuel, reduces emissions, and yields safety advantages because drivers do not have to cross traffic. In addition, left turns require more idling time waiting for oncoming traffic, whereas right-on-red regulations help save fuel. UPS estimates that in 2007 the company saved 3.1 million gallons of fuel and eliminated 32,000 metric tons of emissions via the right-turn policy.[32]

A second means by which to lower transportation costs is associated with the planning of the distribution function. When organizations take into consideration the relative location of the ultimate consumer and the firm's distribution centers, they can get aggressive about the costs to deliver product to consumers. For example, Procter and Gamble reassessed its staging and distribution costs and reduced the number of distribution centers by 200 locations.[33] In the process, the firm was able to deliver products to consumers in a more timely fashion.

Energy Efficiency   Beyond the costs of transportation, firms can also achieve higher levels of efficiency by controlling the energy utilization at distribution and production centers. Enhanced efficiency is realized due to the use of advanced building materials. New construction that focuses on the design of airtight facilities enables companies to limit waste associated with heat and cooling losses.[34] For example, in the United Kingdom, ProLogis has developed a warehouse for Sainsbury's, one of England's largest grocers. This facility features wall-mounted photovoltaic panels that generate electricity, solar walls that produce heat from sunlight, an on-site power plant that reuses the heat produced by air conditioning, an on-site recycling facility, energy-efficient lighting, and air-tight construction that minimizes energy loss.

Innovative Technology   Several innovative technologies provide enormous opportunity to manage the logistics function. Four technologies that influence operations include *routing and tracking computer systems, inventory management software, RFID (radio frequency identification)*, and *GPS (global positioning system)*.

In the global courier services and shipping industry, UPS faces a marketplace characterized by increased need for time-definite services.[35] UPS has expanded its reputation as a leading package distribution company by developing an equally strong capability as a mover of electronic information. The company has developed an information processing system designed to provide a competitive advantage in this challenging market. UPS delivery specialists capture the signature of every package and document recipient using handheld, pen-based custom computers. The system collects electronic data on more than 9.5 million packages each day. This system is supported by the largest IBM D-baseII installation in the world. The system has been designed to allow simple introduction of future technologies into the network. In addition, reporting capabilities provide the opportunity to deliver customized reports to UPS patrons about their products and customers. The **routing and tracking computer system** has improved the company's efficiency and price competitiveness while simultaneously offering improved information handling and customer service.

Inventory management software is a second innovative technology that provides a source of competitive advantage. Inventory represents a sizeable investment to many organizations. Money invested in inventory does not provide the return that is realized when this money is invested in a financial institution. Organizations therefore prefer to minimize inventory to levels that meet the service expectations of customers. The cosmetics industry exemplifies a market characterized by highly volatile demand along with potential risks of inventory obsolescence and, simultaneously, out-of-stock conditions. Procter and Gamble markets Olay skin care products, CoverGirl cosmetics, Aussie shampoo, and many other products in this setting. Five years ago, the firm began implementing *multi-echelon inventory* (MEI) tools designed to optimize inventory throughout the supply chain.[36] This MEI software has been designed to accommodate increasingly global supply chains, contract manufacturing, dynamic product life cycles, and multichannel distribution systems. This software incorporates mathematical models that enable managers to plan around complex market scenarios. The software uses probabilistic optimization techniques that identify demand and supply variability to make better decisions about inventory policy and strategy. The software has enabled P&G to work with suppliers to cut materials inventories and has enabled them to collaborate with customers to reduce retail inventories. These reductions have been implemented while improving materials and production planning along with improved responsiveness of the firm's manufacturing and distribution systems. Importantly, this system primarily focuses on the optimization of inventory rather than on the reduction in inventory. In the initial installation at P&G, the Beauty Care division trimmed total inventory by 3 to 7% while maintaining service levels greater than 99%. Net earnings increased by 13%, sales increased by 7%, and the number of inventory days on hand dropped by 8 days. These results have prompted P&G to implement the inventory management software across all of the firm's strategic business units.

RFID or **radio frequency identification** is an innovative technology that has significant applications in logistics and retailing.[37] The RFID technology consists of a radio frequency tag with a printed antenna and a radio frequency emitter/reader.[38] The signal from the tag provides a unique 96-bit product identification code. In contrast to bar codes, the RFID tag can be read without line-of-sight reading.

Some of the most insightful initial research on RFID was performed at the Auto-ID Center at MIT[39] by a consortium that included the Uniform Product Code, P&G, Gillette, Coca-Cola, the Department of Defense, and Walmart. In manufacturing, these readers offer a number of benefits. The presence of these tags ensures that all items associated with an assembly are in fact present. Similarly, RFID readers simplify the process of confirming the accuracy of plant deliveries by eliminating the need to corroborate physical delivery of product with a driver's bill of lading. These systems also enable management to determine the appropriate positioning of products in storage. For example, out-of-stock items that arrive at the loading dock can be immediately positioned on the assembly line to increase manufacturing throughput. Because the devices do not require line of sight to read the contents of a container, the warehousing of inventory can be performed with considerable flexibility. RFID devices also provide the ability to identify compatibility issues between two chemical reagents and therefore allow warehousing staff to store such products in separate locations. The tracking capability of RFID also reduces the potential for employee theft by identifying any item leaving a distribution facility.

The RFID readers also offer a number of important benefits to retailers, and the importance of these benefits is reflected in Walmart's 2005 decision to require its top 100 vendors to implement RFID chips.[40] This technology enables retailers to allocate inventory accurately among various locations in the store and to price products variably based on their location. Thus, refrigerated soft drinks could be priced higher than those located on normal shelves. In addition, because the products each possess information that links the date sold with the date of delivery, retailers can be more focused in their efforts to rotate stock in their stores. The ability to track products also provides the opportunity to reduce shrinkage at the retail level.[41]

The implementation of RFID technology has strong implications for the supply cycle. The information accessible to retailers likely increases their power relative to suppliers. The retailer can use the RFID technology to develop its own category management system without the aid of manufacturers. The retailer can also use this information to negotiate higher compensation for obsolescence and spoilage, and it can also be used to urge manufacturers to develop retail-ready displays. These displays fuel additional costs to manufacturers and lower the product stocking cost to retailers.

Global Positioning Systems (GPS) represent another technology that has the potential to transform logistics. GPS is an American radio-navigation system that provides free positioning, navigation, and timing service on a continuous worldwide basis. GPS consists of satellites orbiting the Earth, control and monitoring stations on Earth, and GPS receivers owned by users. The satellites broadcast signals from space that are picked up and identified by GPS receivers. Each receiver provides the location (latitude, longitude, and altitude) plus the time.[42]

Two primary benefits of GPS in the supply chain involve the ability to monitor delivery drivers and their vehicles. GPS allows managers to track every vehicle in their fleet at any given moment. They can study a driver's behavior to determine whether he is driving safely, off-route, or too fast or slow. In addition, GPS ensures that the most optimal routing is taken, resulting in more efficient use of gasoline and diesel. The tracking units also enable managers to assess vehicle performance. Management can determine whether the optimal speed, tire air pressure, and others factors that affect fuel usage are in place.[43]

Packaging As the underlying means for ensuring that products are delivered in usable formats, packaging represents an important element of logistics. Manufacturers and retailers have made some important modifications to packaging procedures that reduce package costs while reducing the amount of damaged goods in the supply cycle. Over the 1995 to 2005 era, Dow Chemical reformulated its packaging in a way that saved more than $3 billion and reduced energy usage by 22%. Similarly, Walmart set a goal in 2008 to reduce packaging by 5%. Walmart estimates this reduction keeps 667,000 metric tons of carbon dioxide out of the air, keeps 213,000 trucks off the road, saves 66.7 million gallons of diesel fuel, and saves the retailer $3.4 annually.[44]

A critical look at the role of packaging must consider the overall supply cycle rather than a single level of the distribution channel. The packaging needs of products vary based on whether rail or truck transportation is involved in moving the product to its destination.[45] Truck-based transportation requires balanced, stackable pallets that maximize the use of trailer space. By contrast, secure and stable packaging is essential for the rigors of rail transportation. Stretch hoods that cover product on five sides provide a higher level of protection than the stretch wrap that secures only the sides of a pallet.

Supply cycle managers recognize that carton optimization and other freight packaging techniques limit packaging to minimal levels necessary to deliver product free of damage. Implementation of these strategies can yield savings of 10 to 50% of the total transportation and packaging cost. In addition, supply cycle managers are increasingly reusing materials within the supply chain. For example, Amerisource Bergen, the medical supply company, saved more than $22,000 a year and cut 30,000 pounds of paper boxes a year by reusing vendor supply boxes to ship orders.

Interorganizational Relationships Due to the volatility and rate of change in logistics, firms are increasingly recognizing the opportunities and insight acquired through relationships established with other participants in the supply cycle. Third-party logistics firms enable manufacturers and retailers to enhance their sustainability in the supply cycle in several ways:

Enhance vehicle performance. Third-party suppliers have the expertise to consolidate shipping routes and reduce inventory levels. In addition, they can train and monitor driver efforts to use fuel-efficient behaviors that lead to better vehicle performance. These vehicle performance enhancements lower personnel costs, lengthen the useful life of vehicles, reduce fuel costs, and lower the firm's carbon footprint.

Reduce total supply cycle costs. Cost is a sensitive issue in the supply cycle because consideration of cost immediately requires evaluation of the value added by the third-party supplier. Third-party logistics companies implement several strategies to optimize fuel economy and enhance environmental performance. For example, a recent trend among third-party providers is the replacement of standard, two-tire configurations on long-haul trucks with single wide-based tires. These tires save more than 400 gallons of fuel per year and lower carbon emissions by more than four metric tons annually. In addition, third-party logistics companies that use tractor-trailer aerodynamic devices to monitor trailer performance can eliminate more than 5 metric tons carbon emissions annually.[46]

Enhanced customer service. Due to experience with a variety of users and applications, third-party logistics agents can optimize distribution networks and consolidate routes. Importantly, third-party vendors that approach the supply cycle as a chain of events—rather than discrete processes—can provide synergy to distribution by focusing efforts on maximizing sustainability throughout the supply chain. Manufacturers enjoy greater product availability rates, improved order accuracy, and fewer customer complaints. These activities enhance the level of customer service and preclude the firm from engaging in special deliveries and other accommodations associated with inefficiency. Collectively, this enhanced customer service lowers the environmental influence of the entire supply cycle.[47]

It is important to recognize that the ability of these third-party providers to raise sustainability is linked to the incentives and monitoring practices implemented by retailers and manufacturers.[48] Firms increasingly will reward suppliers with additional business when they pursue these sustainability efforts. Former arms'-length agreements are being replaced with joint process improvements whereby the manufacturer and supplier collectively work to address the sustainability concerns in the supply cycle. Manufacturers and retailers are asking suppliers to provide sustainability metrics and tracking this performance over time.

E. ISO 14000

Managers of supply cycles are increasingly asking suppliers to provide sustainability metrics, and they are requiring third-party certification of major suppliers.[49] In response to these calls for systematic assessment of a firm's influence on the environment, companies of all sizes have implemented **environmental management systems (EMS)**. An EMS is a set of regulations established to achieve environmental goals.[50] The ISO 14000 standards are voluntary standards established by the International Organization for Standardization (ISO). The ISO family of standards has emerged as a family of standards applied across industries to monitor and control interaction with the environment. ISO has more than 100 member countries represented primarily by government and industry standards groups.[51] ISO generates more than 1,100 new standards every year and currently has developed more than 17,500 international standards on a variety of subjects. Given the potential for enhanced performance, many organizations have implanted these standards. The Ford Motor Company, the first automaker to embrace ISO 14000, credits the standard with saving millions of dollars since implementation in 1998.[52]

Two of the primary standards associated in the ISO 14000 family are 14001 and 14004. These standards were updated in 2004.[53] ISO 14001:2004 provides a framework for an organization to control the environmental influence of its activities, products, and services and to improve its environmental performance continually. ISO 14001:2004 outlines the guidelines associated with the firm's approach to sustainability, and it provides a strategic approach to the organization's environmental policy. The standard is broad enough to enjoy application in a variety of contexts that include restaurants, construction firms, hotels, manufacturers and their suppliers, and airports.[54] In addition, small and medium-sized enterprises are also recognizing that they can benefit from ISO 14001:2004 certification.[55] ISO 14004:2004 provides guidelines on the elements of an EMS, its implementation, and the principal issues involved.

In many cases, organizations desire to make their pursuit of ISO management standards a matter of public record. ISO does not offer certification, but it does provide criteria for determining certification. Certification of ISO 14001:2004 is performed via independent environmental auditors. The accreditation of these auditors is based on their work experience, education, personal attributes (communication and decision-making skills), and auditor training.[56] External auditors offer consultation over the sustainability efforts of the firm. Certification refers to the auditor's written assurance that it has audited an EMS and verified that it conforms to the standard. Registration, however, occurs when the auditor records the certification in its company register.[57] Certification of ISO 14001:2004 is valid for three years.[58]

Some of the benefits of adoption of ISO 14001:2004 accrue externally. Evidence suggests that, relative to firms with similar assets and performance, companies that implement it realize a competitive advantage over other firms in a market.[59] This advantage is associated with relatively lower toxic emissions among firms that have implemented the standard. The firm also enjoys lowered resource usage, higher energy savings, and lowered costs of waste disposal as a result of ISO 14001:2004 certification.[60] The merits of certification also provide assurance to stakeholders that the firm is committed to sustainability. Certification provides evidence to the local community that the firm is an environmental leader. Government and nongovernment organizations as well as private consumers are more likely to be favorably disposed toward firms that adopt the ISO 14000 standards. Adoption of the standards supports the firm's claim about its own environmental policies. Moreover, it illustrates and enumerates plans and actions that demonstrate conformity to environmental guidelines.[61]

Adoption of this standard provides a strong response to customers and suppliers that place environmental demands on the firm. Among United States firms, for example, those organizations with capital investments or strong ties to Japanese or European firms are more likely to adopt ISO 14001:2004. Because attitudes associated with sustainability tend to be more pronounced in these geographic markets, American firms with strong relationships with firms in these markets are likely to adopt the standards.[62] In addition, the adoption process—complete with an assessment of conformity by a third-party auditor—reduces the need for verification among trading partners.

There are appreciable merits of ISO 14001:2004 certification to stakeholders within the firm. Top management gains confidence that it is monitoring and regulating processes within the firm that influence the environment.[63] Consequently, the firm can support claims about sustainability and provide a strong response to criticisms that focus on *greenwashing*. Employees gain confidence that their firms are environmentally responsible. Given the costs of employee recruitment and turnover,[64] firms that illustrate empathy for environmental concerns provide additional incentives that attract and retain employees.

Summary

A. Introduction
The goal of this chapter has been to examine the role of distribution as a central facet of efforts to achieve sustainability. We focused on distribution as the firm-level function that delivers value to consumers. We diagnosed the elements of the supply cycle, provided several benefits firms realize via efforts to enhance sustainability, and outlined green marketing activity associated with logistics. Given the multi-industry benefits of environmental management systems, we also outlined the role of ISO 14000 certification.

B. Diagnosing the Elements of Sustainable Supply Cycles
We presented supply cycles as the entities associated with yielding environmental, social, and economic value from resource procurement through resource

processing, consumption, and postconsumption. This approach calls for understanding of the input–output process at each stage of the supply cycle as well as an understanding of the value chain. The input–output process presumes that each level of the supply cycle engages in some sort of processing that yields products and by-products.

C. Benefits of Sustainable Supply Cycles

Sustainable supply cycles offer benefits that include better working conditions, reduced turnover, and improved product quality. In addition, these supply cycles yield improved efficiency and profitability, better management of risk, enhanced brand reputations, and increased stakeholder returns.

D. Sustainable Logistics

Logistics refers to the process management of human and financial resources associated with physical distribution, manufacturing support, and purchasing operations. When this vital strategy is managed with sustainability as a goal, the firm has potential to optimize fleet operations, manage energy more efficiently, employ innovative technologies such as RFID, reduce packaging costs, and strengthen interfirm relationships.

E. ISO 14000

The ISO 14000 standards provide firms with the ability to monitor and control interaction with the environment. Companies that implement these standards can realize competitive advantages over other firms in a market. This advantage is associated with relatively lower toxic emissions, lowered resource usage, higher energy savings, and lowered costs of waste disposal. Certification provides evidence to the local community that the firm is an environmental leader. Adoption of ISO 14000 standards provides a strong response to customers and suppliers that place environmental demands on the firm. In addition, the adoption process and the assessment by a third-party auditor reduce the need for verification among trading partners.

Keywords

asset considerations, 167
channel, 164
environmental management systems (EMS), 173
global positioning systems (GPS), 171

inventory management software, 170
ISO 14000, 163
logistics, 168
macroenvironmental issues, 167
radio frequency identification (RFID), 170

reverse logistics, 168
routing and tracking computer system, 170
supply cycles, 164
sustainability scorecard, 166

Questions

1. To what extent does Starbucks' sourcing strategy enable it to secure long-term commitments from suppliers and consumers?
2. What is the ultimate source for resources entering a supply cycle? How does this differ from the output of the supply cycle?
3. Why is it necessary for firms to assess the by-products of their supply cycles?
4. Why would a manufacturer take time to learn about Walmart's sustainability scorecard even though it does not do business directly with the retailer?
5. What is fleet optimization and why is it relevant to assessing sustainability in the supply cycle?

6. What benefits can a company realize from incorporating RFID technology into the supply chain?
7. How can GPS technology enable a firm to lower its distribution costs?
8. How do relationships with suppliers and customers benefit from sustainable logistics?
9. If firms can increase their levels of sustainability without ISO guidelines, why is it valuable to engage in the cost of certification?
10. What is the value of third-party verification of ISO 14000 certification?

Endnotes

[1] Kate McDonald, "Globalising Justice within Coffee Supply Chains? Fair Trade, Starbucks and the Transformation of Supply Chain Governance," *Third World Quarterly* 28, no. 4 (2007): 793–812.

[2] Starbucks.com, "Responsibility to Grow Coffee," Ethical Sourcing, http://www.starbucks.com/sharedplanet/ethicalinternal.aspx?story=sspprinciples (accessed May 7, 2010).

[3] See Note 1 above.

[4] Starbucks.com, "C.A.F.E. Practices Generic Scorecard" http://www.starbucks.com/sharedplanet/assets/cafePracticesScorecard.pdf

[5] See Note 1 above.

[6] Starbucks.com, "Environmental Stewardship," http://www.starbacks.com/responsibility/environment (accessed May 7, 2010).

[7] See Note 1 above.

[8] Anne T. Coughlan and others, *Marketing Channels* (Upper Saddle River, NJ: Prentice Hall, 2001), 590.

[9] Robert Monckza, Robert Trent, and Robert Hadfield, *Purchasing and Supply Chain Management* (Mason, OH: Thompson-Southwestern, 2005), 744.

[10] Michael E. Porter, *Competitive Advantage* (New York, NY: The Free Press, 1985), 557.

[11] "Wal-Mart's Supply Chain Goes 'Green,'" *Packaging Digest* 44, no. 10 (2007): 63–64

[12] United Nations Environment Program, *Unchaining Value: Innovative Approaches to Sustainable Supply* (Paris, France: United Nations Environmental Programme, 2008), 24; B. Willard, *The Sustainability Advantage: Seven Business Case Benefits of a Triple Bottom Line* (Gabriola Island, BC: New Society Publishers, 2002), 236.

[13] Barbara Tilson, "Success and Sustainability in Automotive Supply Chain Improvement Programmes: A Case Study of Collaboration in the Mayflower Cluster," *International Journal of Innovation Management* 5, no. 4 (2001): 427–456.

[14] Rodger W. Griffeth, Peter W. Hom, and Stefan Gaertner, "A Meta-Analysis of Antecedents and Correlates of Employee Turnover: Update, Moderator Tests, and Research Implications for the Next Millennium," *Journal of Management* 26, no. 3 (2000): 463–488.

[15] Alexandre Mas, "Labour Unrest and the Quality of Production: Evidence from the Construction Equipment Resale Market," *Review of Economic Studies* 75, (2008): 229–258.

[16] James G. March and Zur Shapira, "Managerial Perspectives on Risk and Risk Taking," *Management Science* 33 (1987): 1404–1418.

[17] H. Peck, "Reconciling Supply Chain Vulnerability, Risk and Supply Chain Management," *International Journal of Logistics: Research and Applications* 9, no.2 (2006): 127–142.

[18] B.Willard, *The Sustainability Advantage: Seven Business Case Benefits of a Triple Bottom Line* (Gabriola Island, BC: New Society Publishers, 2002), 236.

[19] Oliver E.Williamson, *The Economic Institutions of Capitalism* (New York, NY: The Free Press, 1985), 450.

[20] Reinier de Man and Tom R. Burns, "Sustainability: Supply Chains, Partner Linkages, and New Forms of Self-regulation," *Human Systems Management* 25, no.1 (2006): 1–12.

[21] Eugenia Corrales, "Cisco Builds a Supply Chain," *World Trade* 20, no. 3, (2007): 34–40.

[22] Charles A. O'Reilly and Jeffrey Pfeffer, "Cisco Systems: Acquiring and Retaining Talent in Hypercompetitive Markets," *Human Resource Planning* 23, no. 3 (2000): 38–52.

[23] Claire Galea, "Selling Sustainability," *Money Management* 22, no. 24 (2008): 14–15; David Blanchard, "Green is the New Black," *IndustryWeek (IW)* 258, no. 3 (2009): 46–47.

[24] American Marketing Association, "Dictionary," http://www.marketingpower.com/_layouts/Dictionary.aspx (accessed May 7, 2010).

[25] William Hoffman, "Logistics Redraws Efficiency," *Traffic World* 271, no. 51/ 52 (2007): 19–21.

[26] Meng Zhao, Cornelia Dröge, and Theodore P. Stank, "The Effects of Logistics Capabilities on Firm Performance: Customer-Focused Versus Information-Focused Capabilities," *Journal of Business Logistics* 22, no. 2 (2001): 91–107.

[27] Dale Rogers, and Ronald S. Tibben-Lembke, *Going Backwards: Reverse Logistics Trends and Practices* (USA: Reverse Logistics Executive Council: 1999), 280.

[28] Sergio Rubio, Antonio Chamorro, and Francisco J. Miranda, "Characteristics of the Research on Reverse Logistics (1995–2005)," *International Journal of Production Research* 46, no. 4 (2008): 1099–1120.

[29] William Hoffman, "Reversing Returns," *Traffic World* 272, no. 45 (2008): 16.

[30] Michael Bernon and John Cullen, "An Integrated Approach to Managing Reverse Logistics," *International Journal of Logistics: Research and Applications* 10, no. 1 (2007): 41–56.

[31] Perry A. Trunick, "Green is Good Business: In Logistics, Best Practice is Green," *Outsourced Logistics* 1, no. 6 (2008): 22–23.

[32] Tom Long, "Right Turns Make the Most Out of Gas," *Boston Globe*, July 10, 2008, 18, http://www.boston.com/news/local/articles/2008/07/10/right_turns_make_the_most_out_of_gas/ (accessed May 7, 2010).

[33] See Note 25 above.

[34] See Note 31 above.

[35] Nabil Alghalith, "Competing With IT: The UPS Case," *Journal of American Academy of Business Cambridge* 7, no. 2 (2005): 7–15.

[36] John Kerr, "P&G Takes Inventory Up a Notch," *Logistics Management* 47, no. 2 (2008): 24–26.

[37] Stephen Rutner, Matthew A. Waller, and John T. Mentzer, "A Practical Look at RFID," *Supply Chain Management Review* 8, no. 1 (2004): 36–41.

[38] Mark Vandenbosch and Niraj Dawar, "Beyond Better Products: Capturing Value in Customer Interactions," *MIT Sloan Management Review* 43, no. 4 (2002): 35–42.

[39] Ephraim Schwartz, "RFID About to Explode," *InfoWorld* 25, no. 5 (2003): 28–29.

[40] See Note 38 above.

[41] Sydney D. Howell and Nathan C. Proudlove, "A Statistical Investigation of Inventory Shrinkage in a Large Retail Chain," *International Review of Retail, Distribution & Consumer Research* 17, no. 2 (2007): 101–120.

[42] U.S. Coast Guard Navigation Center, "Global Positioning System," *USA.gov*, http://www.gps.gov/ (accessed May 7, 2010).

[43] Stephen Colwell, "Go Green with GPS," *GPS World* 19, no. 10 (2008): 30–31.

[44] William Hoffman, "Repackaging Savings," *Traffic World* 272, no. 2 (2008): 14.

[45] Greg Bunker, "Five Tips for Improving the Effectiveness and Efficiency of Your Logistics Operations," *Logistics Today* 48, no. 9 (2007): 34.

[46] Brewster Smith, "Outsourcing to a Sustainable 3PL," *Outsourced Logistics* 1, no. 3 (2008): 20.

[47] David Blanchard, "Making Effective Use of 3PLs," *IndustryWeek*, June, 2007, 78–80.

[48] William Hoffman, "The Greening of Logistics," *Traffic World* 271, no. 25 (2007): 10–13.

[49] See Note 49 above.

[50] Michal Syzmaski and Piysuhi Tiwari, "ISO 14001 and the Reduction of Toxic Emissions," *Policy Reform* 7, no. 1 (2004): 31–42.

[51] Vildan Korul, "Guide to the Implementation of ISO 14001 at Airports," *Journal of Air Transportation* 10, no. 2 (2005): 49–68.

[52] Tim O'Brien (2000), *Ford & ISO 14001 — The Synergy Between Preserving the Environment and Rewarding Shareholders* (McGraw Hill: New York), 291.

[53] "Improved Versions of ISO 14000 EMS Standards Published," *Business & the Environment with ISO 14000 Updates* 15, no. 12 (2004): 12–13.

[54] "ISO 14001 for Restaurants? — The Green Restaurant 4.0 Standard (Part 1)," *Business & the Environment with ISO 14000 Updates* 20, no. 4 (2009): 12–14; Ahmet Murat Turk, " The Benefits Associated with ISO 14001 Certification for Construction Firms: Turkish Case," *Journal of Cleaner Production* 17, no. 5 (2009): 559–569; Wilco W. Chan and Kenny Ho, "Hotels' Environmental Management Systems (ISO 14001): Creative Financing Strategy," *International Journal of Contemporary Hospitality Management* 18, no. 4 (2006): 302–316.

[55] Mari Elizabete Bernardini Seiffert, "Environmental Impact Evaluation Using a Cooperative Model for Implementing EMS (ISO 14001) in Small and Medium-sized Enterprises," *Journal of Cleaner Production* 16, no. 14 (2008): 1447–1461.

[56] Robert C. Wilson, "The Professional Credentials for an ISO 14000 Consultant," *Pollution Engineering*, (May, 2002): 38–39.

[57] International Organization for Standardization, "Certification," http://www.iso.org/iso/iso_catalogue/management_standards/certification.htm (accessed May 7, 2010).

[58] Deepa Aravind and Petra Christmann, "Institutional and Resource-Based Determinants of Substantive Implementation of ISO 14001," *Academy of Management Proceedings* 54, (annual, 2008): 1–6.

[59] Charles J. Corbett and Michael V. Russo, "ISO 14001: Irrelevant or Invaluable?" *ISO Management Systems* (December, 2001): 23–29.

[60] See Note 51 above.

[61] International Organization for Standardization, "ISO 14000 Essentials," http://www.iso.org/iso/iso_catalogue/management_standards/iso_9000_iso_14000/iso_14000_essentials.htm (accessed May 7, 2010).

[62] Timothy Gutowski and others, "Environmentally Benign Manufacturing: Observations From Japan, Europe and the United States," *Journal of Cleaner Production* 13, no. 1 (2003): 1–17.

[63] See Note 58 above.

[64] Keith Townsend, "Recruitment, Training and Turnover: Another Call Centre Paradox," *Personnel Review* 36, no. 3 (2007): 476–490.

Delivering Value in Retailing

CHAPTER
9

A. Introduction

IKEA

In May 2007, IKEA announced plans for premium parking for consumers that drive hybrids or other highly fuel-efficient automobiles to its Canadian store.[1] The company subsequently began providing premium parking at all 11 locations in Canada. The parking spots are located near handicapped and family parking areas at the entrance of IKEA stores. Green signage at ground and eye levels reminds drivers of the preferred spaces. The attractiveness of this idea has prompted the company to bring the idea to its stores in the United States (Figure 9-1).[2]

The subtle incentive behind this simple parking plan is to reward consumers for acting in a sustainable manner. Founded by Ingvar Kamprad in Agunnaryd,

FIG. 9-1 Reserved Parking for Hybrid Vehicles

Source: © Meghan McCarthy/The Palm Beach Post/Newscom

Sweden in 1943, IKEA's business philosophy is to offer a wide range of products of high-quality design and function at prices that enable the majority of people to afford them. Today IKEA is a leading home furnishings retailer with 285 stores in 37 countries worldwide. Each year, IKEA stores receive more than 631 million visitors.[3] IKEA Group has grown into a major retail experience with 128,000 workers and annual sales of more than €21.1 billion.

IKEA's decision to provide premium parking to hybrid vehicles is part of its environmental commitment to finding business solutions that have an overall positive influence on the people and the communities in which the company operates.

Sustainable retailing is at the center of this company's mission and operations.[4] This commitment is reflected in the firm's management of transportation, supply chains, and product packaging. The hybrid parking arrangement is one facet of transportation. Since hybrid and fuel-efficient cars help the company realize its environmental objectives, IKEA rewards consumers for their commitments via preferred parking and more convenient shopping experiences. The firm also ensures that all stores are located close to public transit for workers and customers. In some markets, the firm even manages a bus system that routes consumers and employees to the store at no cost to the riders. IKEA has shuttle bus routes servicing stores in Richmond, British Columbia, as well as the North York and Etobicoke locations in Ontario. These services have been set up adjacent to central public transit hubs for the convenience of customers.

IKEA's commitment to efficient supply chains is reflected in its transportation and product shipping policies. The company seeks to minimize the route from supplier to customer with as little effect on the environment as possible. The efficiency of product shipping is addressed via the product packaging and the containers. Most IKEA furniture is distributed in flat packs that enable larger quantities to be transported with less environmental impact.[5] Flat packaging reduces the amount of space required on a pallet. For example, when the Helmer chest of drawers is completely flat packed, the number of products that can be shipped on a single pallet jumps from 6 units to 39. Consequently, carbon dioxide emissions are reduced by 79%.[6]

Getting product and consumers to the store is not the end of this company's commitment to the environment. On the consumption side, the company has many initiatives that include waste minimization and postpurchase packaging. IKEA stores provide collection points for electrical and electronic equipment, discarded packaging, spent batteries, and low-energy bulbs. Where possible, returned products are repaired and used as spare parts or sold at reduced prices.[7] In addition, the company has a bagging policy that charges consumers for bags as they check out of the store. Consumers quickly learn that they can purchase IKEA bags made of recycled material or bring their own bags with them on the shopping trip. Regardless of which strategy the consumer employs, the environment is served by this policy.

The action of IKEA underscores the sustainability efforts currently being undertaken in the retail sector. Our review of sustainability in retailing begins with a discussion of the central role of retailers in supply cycles. We subsequently examine the sustainability of the product lines offered by retailers. We conclude by addressing the merits of marketing of sustainable consumption at the retail level.

B. The Central Role of Retailing in Supply Cycles

Several factors combine to make retailing the epicenter of the supply cycle in many industries. The first of these factors reflects the change in access to information within the industry. Historically, market research conducted for the retail sector was often completed by manufacturers.[8] Although the retailer is typically closer to the customer, retailers often lacked the financial and human resources needed to gather market information. The cost to collect data on more than just a small fraction of the products sold in a retail store was infeasible. The **universal product code** (UPC) that was introduced in 1974 changed the way business was conducted. The universal product codes provided retailers with access to market information on product movement, consumer purchasing behavior, and the use of marketing mix variables by manufacturers and retailers.[9] Consequently, retailers no longer relied on the market research provided by manufacturers to the same degree they once did. The retailers now had available a tool that not only provided them with inventory management capabilities but also enabled them to study consumer demographics, psychographics, and demand elasticity.

The second factor that makes retailing central to the supply cycle reflects the increasing market power of selected retailers. The increase in access to information—due to the UPC—has been accompanied by the development of larger retail outlets and the growing concentration of market share among a few retailers.[10] Walmart's development of the superstore echoes the trend toward larger retail outlets. The company's superstores that were introduced in 1988 are roughly 75% larger than their regular store counterparts.[11] The retail market share is also edging toward fewer competitors. Walmart is the largest competitor in the United States, Mexico, and Canada, and it controls a large and increasing share of the business done by most every major U.S. consumer-products company.[12] As the share of the market becomes more concentrated among fewer retailers, there is potential for the retailers to gain a lion's share of the profit at the expense of their suppliers. Research suggests, for instance, that Walmart suppliers holding a small share of their respective markets do not perform relatively as well financially when Walmart is one of their primary customers. Large-share suppliers to Walmart, however, perform better than their large-share counterparts reporting other retailers as their primary customers. Thus, suppliers that seek Walmart's broad market reach may derive benefits from using this association if it can be used to strengthen their market positions.[13]

As large companies with substantial visibility associated with large stores in many communities, retailers have become easy targets for concerns about sustainability. For example, Walmart has been attacked for its international environmental record as well as for the treatment of workers and shoppers.[14] The visibility of large retailers makes them easy targets for criticism and results in their receiving a substantial amount of scrutiny in the media. In addition, the focus on these companies provides an opportunity to receive mammoth returns from getting them to reconsider their procurement, processing, and waste disposal systems.

Over the past few years, retailers have begun to recognize that there are appreciable ecological, social, and financial rewards from embracing sustainability. For example, Walmart invited former vice president Al Gore to meet with 800 retail employees at its Bentonville, Arkansas, headquarters in July 2006. Mr. Gore echoed the sentiments of Walmart management when he stated that the company will illustrate that economic objectives and environmental goals can be reached in tandem. Walmart also vowed to enhance efficiency of its vehicle fleet by 25% over the next three years, eliminate 30% of the energy used in stores, and reduce solid waste from U.S. stores by 25% in three years. The company further invested $500 million in sustainability projects, and it began developing more sustainability targets. The firm quickly became the world's biggest seller of organic milk and the biggest purchaser of organic cotton.

The Walmart example illustrates how retailers have begun to recognize that they are accountable for the consumption associated with their entire supply chain from the procurement of raw materials to the postconsumer waste. Retailers are quantifying their supply chains' influences on the environment so that they can take action to reduce these influences. In addition, they are seeking third-party certification to ensure that the accuracy of the reporting. Retailers are actively assessing five areas of the supply chain that include:

Energy and climate.   The energy and climate concerns refer to the amount of greenhouse gas emissions associated with the supply chain. Given the amount of disparity in wages across the globe, there are some tremendous cost advantages from product processing in emerging economies. For example, cod caught off the coast of Norway is shipped to China, where it is turned into filets and then shipped back to Norway.[15] Although the overall processing cost is lowered under such circumstances, greenhouse gas expenditures are magnified due to this strategy. Retailers that recognize these trade-offs have begun to ask suppliers to report the amount of greenhouse gases produced by suppliers. In addition, they have asked suppliers to set greenhouse gas reduction targets and make these targets available to the public. In some cases, retailers and their suppliers are reporting this information to the Carbon Disclosure Project (CDP). CDP is a nonprofit organization that collects and distributes information designed to motivate investors, corporations, and governments to take action to prevent dangerous climate change. The data collected by CDP provides insight into the strategies used by many of the largest companies in the world to address climate change.[16] For example, Carrefour, the French retailer, employed product life cycle analyses to identify that the most important greenhouse gas emissions occurring in the extraction of raw materials, the production of semifinished and finished goods, and downstream with the use and disposal of products.[17]

At the retail level of the supply chain, the three greatest culprits for energy use are lighting, heating/cooling, and equipment.[18] Increasingly, retailers are taking measures to reduce each of these expenditures. Firms are aggressively using alternative lighting sources that include light-emitting diode (LED) technologies.[19] LEDs are very efficient and, unlike compact fluorescent lights, they do not contain mercury. In addition, modern stores are likely to use direct sunlight where possible on the shop floor. In general, one watt of power used in an electronic device creates one watt of heat.[20] Thus, for every watt used by a cash register, computer, or other device, two watts of energy are required. The installation of energy-efficient appliances and climate-control products, however, enables retailers to lower their cost of operations at the store level.

Land and soil.   The treatment of land and soil throughout the retail supply chain is being assessed by most large retailers. Suppliers increasingly recognize that retailers require adherence to ISO 14000 land requirements or other environmental specifications.[21]

The retailer, rather than its predecessors in the supply chain, is the focus of many discussions about land use. Retailers receive criticism about their own land use and its relationship to urban sprawl.[22] **Urban sprawl** refers to the widespread movement of households and private firms from city centers and inner suburbs to very low-density suburbs.[23] Ten factors endemic to urban sprawl include:[24]

1. Seemingly unlimited extension of new development
2. Low-density commercial and residential settlements, particularly in new-growth areas
3. *Leapfrog* development that jumps out beyond established settlements
4. Fragmented power over land use distributed among many small localities
5. Private automobile dominance of transportation
6. Absence of centralized planning or control of land uses
7. Widespread strip center commercial development
8. Large fiscal disparities among localities
9. Segregation of types of land uses in different zones
10. Reliance on filtering or trickle-down processes to provide housing to low-income households

Sprawl generates substantial environmental concerns that include increased traffic congestion, large-scale absorption of open space, extensive use of energy for movement, and air pollution.[25] Moreover, suburban sprawl concentrates poor households in certain high-poverty neighborhoods. These neighborhoods subsequently suffer from high crime rates, poor-quality public services and public schools, and fiscal resources that are inadequate for the services needed.

Three strategies that have emerged as alternatives to urban sprawl involve regional development that selectively permits growth.[26] The first strategy involves the development of tightly bounded higher-density development typical of many Western European metropolitan areas. The second strategy involves a loosely drawn growth boundary that permits some development outside the boundary. This strategy raises population densities above sprawl levels and relies on increased use of public transit and carpooling. The third strategy is the development of new outlying communities and green spaces surrounded by tightly drawn urban growth boundaries.

Regardless of the strategy, there are opportunities for retailers to work with state and local government that contribute to development while simultaneously increasing revenues and limiting urban sprawl. Retailers and other citizens that are active participants in the development process can actively work to realize the firm's objectives while reducing their influences on sprawl.[27] For example, Subway is a retail franchise that requires very little space and can therefore easily be implemented in existing manufacturing plants, hospitals, and appliance stores.[28]

Air.   The influence of retailing on air quality is assessed at the retail and supply chain levels. At the retail level, a substantial portion of the influence on air quality is associated with the transportation costs involved with getting product to the stores and procuring products within the stores. It is not surprising that air pollution is also related to increases in retailing that accompany sprawl.[29] Consequently, retailers interested in enhancing air quality should benefit from working together with government-based planning organizations that seek to develop unified plans for development.

Water.   The use of water in the supply chain is gaining increasing interest in several parts of the world. Processors of water within the supply chain are increasingly being asked to report on their efforts. ISO 14000 standards require firms to report their use of water in the supply chain,[30] as water usage is an essential consideration in agriculture and production.

The sale of water at the retail level and the processing of this water are highly contested issues in many markets. The U.S. market share leader at the retail level is private-label products, yet branded products incur much of the scrutiny over water.[31] In Michigan, for instance, Nestlé is facing environmental challenges for its use of spring water. Pepsi (Aquafina water) and Coca-Cola (Dasani water), however, have already switched to processing of municipal water for the sale of water at the retail level.[32]

Community and people.   Community and people considerations refer to retailers' responsibility for fair treatment of employees throughout the supply chain, including their own operations. In the supply chain, many retailers have begun to engage in fair trade in their interaction with their trading partners. *Fair trade* refers to a family of principles that include guaranteed minimum floor price for products; safe working conditions and living wages; direct transactions between producer and retailers, community development; and environmentally sustainable farming methods.[33] Fair trade yields reduced debt, more economic options for producers, and increasingly sustainable agricultural practices.[34]

To varying degrees, retailers are working with their supply chains to enhance the sustainability of the distribution channel. Since 2006, Walmart has substantially enhanced its commitment to sustainability. In 2009, the company developed a supplier survey that focuses on energy and climate, material efficiency, natural resources, and people and community.[35] The questions are provided in Figure 9-2. Ultimately, the 100,000 worldwide suppliers to the firm will answer these questions, but initially U.S. suppliers provided answers to each of the criteria. After the survey data has been developed, the company will create a consortium of universities that will collaborate with suppliers, retailers, nongovernmental organizations, and governments to develop a global database of information on the life cycle of products from raw materials to disposal. This data will be shared globally as a common database designed to prompt environmentally competitive efforts by suppliers. The index also has potential to raise product quality, lower products costs, and fuel innovation throughout the supply cycle. The final step of this initiative will involve transforming this sustainability information into a simple rating for consumers.

C. Marketing Sustainable Product Lines

In the previous section, we examined efforts to enhance the sustainability of the upstream supply chain and retail operations. In this section, we examine a number of ways in which the marketer can make sustainable products available at the store level. Our discussion of sustainable product lines focuses on two issues, the incorporation of green technology into the product mix and the appropriate distribution of products. Although retailers are beginning to grapple with these issues, very few empirical studies have been developed that provide insight into these decisions.

Green technology in the product mix.   Consider, first, the producer of a product that recognizes that some technologies can be incorporated into the product mix that markedly enhance product sustainability. For example, over the past decade, automobile manufacturers have developed hybrid fuel technologies that significantly lower gas consumption. Firms can elect to market these technologies in existing brands or they

FIG. 9-2 Walmart Supplier Survey

Energy and Climate

1. Have you measured your corporate greenhouse gas emissions?

2. Have you opted to report your greenhouse gas emissions to the Carbon Disclosure Project?

3. What is your total annual greenhouse gas emissions reported in the most recent year measured?

4. Have you set publicly available greenhouse gas reduction targets? If yes, what are those targets?

Material Efficiency

1. If measured, please report the total amount of solid waste generated from the facilities that produce your product(s) for Wal-Mart for the most recent year measured.

2. Have you set publicly available solid waste reduction targets? If yes, what are those targets?

3. If measured, please report total water use from facilities that produce your product(s) for Wal-Mart for the most recent year measured.

4. Have you set publicly available water use reduction targets? If yes, what are those targets?

Natural Resources

1. Have you established publicly available sustainability purchasing guidelines for your direct suppliers that address issues such as environmental compliance, employment practices and product/ingredient safety?

2. Have you obtained third-party certifications for any of the products that you sell to Wal-Mart?

People and Community

1. Do you know the location of 100% of the facilities that produce your product(s)?

2. Before beginning a business relationship with a manufacturing facility, do you evaluate the quality of, and capacity for, production?

3. Do you have a process for managing social compliance at the manufacturing level?

4. Do you work with your supply base to resolve issues found during social compliance evaluations and also document specific corrections and improvements?

5. Do you invest in community development activities in the markets you source from and/or operate within?

Source: *Material Handling Management* (2009) "Wal-Mart's 15 Questions," Wal-Mart.

may develop new brands. In the small-car market, for instance, Toyota introduced the Prius hybrid vehicle in 2000.[36] The third generation of the model is now being sold in North America, Europe, and Japan. Toyota also markets hybrid versions of its Highlander, Camry, and Lexus RX 400, yet each of these other models is available in conventional internal combustion engine models as well. In 2008, 66% of all hybrid vehicles sold by the company were Priuses. Although many factors contribute to these numbers, the model that is sold exclusively as a hybrid has sales that exceed all other models combined. Recent research suggests that desire to be seen doing something for the environment is an important motivator among some consumers.[37] While purchase of any model illustrates to others that one is concerned about the environment, the clarity of this message is diluted among cars that are sold via both internal combustion and hybrid models. Drivers, for instance, will notice that a fellow motorist is driving a Camry, but the fact that this car is a hybrid will likely go unnoticed. By contrast, motorists necessarily recognize the Prius as a hybrid. Since the commitment to the environment is more visible with the Prius, one might expect that consumers interested in gaining recognition for their purchases would buy a model sold exclusively as a hybrid.

Distribution of sustainable products. A second facet of establishing sustainable product lines at the retail level concerns the distribution of products. Regardless of

FIG. 9-3 Light of Day Organic Teas and Tisanes

Source: © *Courtesy of Light of Day Organic Teas, Traverse City, Michigan, USA.*

whether a product is sustainable, the level of competition on the grocery shelf is quite large. Retailers stock, on average, more than 45,000 unique products,[38] and they are approached with thousands of new products every year. Retailers typically want to carry sufficient numbers of products that enable them to serve customers and generate a profit. Because shelf space is limited, introductions of new products often come at the expense of other products in the merchandise category. New products must be justified by demand so that the cost of carrying inventory for the new brand is relatively low. To be successful in this setting, producers of new branded products need to illustrate that the demand for the new product is substantial. If the demand for the new product and its related profitability are not appreciable, the retailer will not be able to justify adding the new product to the retail product mix.

Consumer demand for products influences the form of distribution sought by producers of sustainable product lines. Consider, for example, a company such as Light of Day Organic Teas and Tisanes of Traverse City, Michigan (Figure 9-3).[39] This entrepreneurial firm would like to increase the distribution of its products. The company is an organic, biodynamic producer that incorporates sustainability logic into its supply chain and operations. It also engages in fair trade with its international suppliers of tea and related products. Firms of this type that seek to market their products through grocery stores can pursue one of three paths. They can market their brand through grocers that market predominantly sustainable and organic brands. A second option is to market their branded products through full-line grocers that market products supported and developed with varying levels of sustainability. The third option is to focus on production technologies and serve as a private-label brand for a retailer.

Although large firms may be able to support marketing through all three forms of distribution, young entrepreneurial companies may find it advantageous to market through just one of these distribution channels. Several advantages accrue to the firm that elects to market branded products through specialty grocery retailers such as Whole Foods and Trader Joe's. The first advantage to marketing through these retail chains is their size. These stores have grown rapidly in the past decade and now represent a significant portion of the retail grocery market. For example, Whole Foods has 275 stores in the United States, Canada, and the United Kingdom, and it has become the world's largest retailer of natural and organic food.[40] As the 10th largest food and drug store in the United States, Whole Foods employs 54,000 people and ranks 369th on the Fortune 500 list.[41] As the size of these retail chains has increased, the visibility of brands marketed through these locations has also increased.

A second advantage associated with these retail locations is the credibility that affiliation with these retailers brings to the brand. Sustainable operations and natural products are at the heart of the marketing strategy for these retailers, and they prefer to work with producers that share these dispositions toward consumer marketing. For example, Whole Foods is the only multistore retailer in North America that markets the Herve Mons brand of French cheese.[42] The relationship between these companies was established over a five-year period that preceded the decision to begin marketing Herve Mons products at Whole Foods. Since the retailer has a core mission and values statement that emphasizes green marketing and sustainability, it goes to great lengths to ensure that its suppliers have the same philosophy. Whole Foods found Herve Mons to be an attractive supplier because the company sells high-quality, traditional products that are sustainability developed by farmers in the Normandy region of France. Although the review process for Whole Food was prolonged, the wait was worth it. Consumers at Whole Foods understand the natural and organic emphasis throughout the product mix and are likely to make purchases without engaging much effort to scrutinize the brand.

It is interesting to note the challenge associated with electing to market via the specialty retailers. Although the inclusion of a product in the Whole Foods or Trader Joe's product line immediately brings recognition as a product of some natural, organic, or sustainable character, the brand is surrounded by other products that have similar attributes. The competitive advantage of the product is unlikely to be sustainability because virtually all the competition offers this benefit. The savvy marketer has to illustrate the sustainability of the product, but it cannot rely on this attribute exclusively. In addition, the target market of these specialty stores is likely to be *LOHAS*[43] or true blue consumers.[44] Although these market segments are growing, a substantial portion of the consuming public may not frequent specialty grocery stores.

The branded alternative to marketing through specialty retailers is marketing via a general grocery merchandiser such as Walmart or Kroger. General grocery merchandisers have always had a strong emphasis on product quality, and in recent years these firms have made substantial investments in sustainable business practices and green marketing. One of the advantages of working with these larger firms is the economies of scale in their operations. For example, Walmart is the largest marketer of organic milk and organic cotton in the world.[45] Products that are welcomed to the product line of these general-merchandise grocers have greater distribution that in some cases leads to greater sales and revenue.

Several issues complicate the sale of products through these grocers. Products of high sustainability may be placed either in a special part of the store or alongside products in the same category. For example, Kroger stores often feature a healthy foods section that stands outside of the regular offering for a product class. The product offerings from a company such as Light of Day teas could be sold in either location. Sale of the product in the healthy choice section of the store has some of the advantages and disadvantages of the specialty retail alternative. The products may be seen primarily by LOHAS consumers, and the differential advantage of the product cannot solely reside in the sustainability of its production and distribution. Consequently, labeling should feature advantages associated with product quality, nutrition, or other potential competitive advantages.

If the sustainable product is marketed alongside all products in the class, there is greater potential for it to reach a broader audience. This broader audience that includes the unconcerned and drifter market segments, however, may not appreciate the benefits associated with sustainable operations. Many consumers will also be unwilling to dedicate the time to understand the benefits of the sustainable product. The price-sensitive consumer will often select the product with the lowest sticker price regardless of the product's sustainability. To the extent that sustainable products are more expensive than their alternatives, price-sensitive consumers should be less willing to purchase the sustainable products. In addition, companies run the risk of cannibalizing sales of nonsustainable product offerings by offering sustainable products in the same location. For example, a company that sells organic, sustainably produced and conventionally produced strawberries may witness some cannibalization of sales by offering the products together. Although the increase in sales of the sustainable product is beneficial to the consumer, it could yield lower profits for the firm. The retailer that is interested in maximizing financial and ecological performance will be reluctant to sell these products at the same place in the store.

The third alternative for the entrepreneur is to market the brand as a private-label product. A **private label** refers to a product in which the brand is owned by the retailer or wholesaler rather than by the producer. For example, Kroger offers more than 14,000 private-label products sold in a multitier strategy that includes Private Selection, Private Selection Organics, Naturally Preferred, Kroger brand, Active Lifestyle, Comfort Brand, and Kroger Value brand products.[46] Whole Foods similarly offers more than 2,150 store-branded products. Sales of private-label brands have been growing rapidly in recent years, and they represent more than 15% of supermarket sales. In some categories, private-label brands have higher unit market share than the top national brands.[47]

The private-label alternative also involves trade-offs for the producer and retailer. Because companies such as Kroger and Whole Foods have hundreds of outlets, the sale of these products enables the producer to operate with economies of scale. Although the producer gains efficient access to a large distribution channel, the identity of the product is entirely associated with the retailer. Over time, retailers can establish specific production criteria that enable them to select the lowest-cost producer of the product. In the absence of a brand or other means by which to distinguish one's product, the producer is subject to greater price scrutiny.

D. Marketing Sustainable Consumption

The need to promote and ensure sustainable use of products is extensive. Our analysis at this juncture addresses two facets of sustainability that are most prominent after a purchase at a retail store. Our treatment of sustainable consumption in retailing, therefore, focuses on postretailing packaging and efforts to reclaim products and restrict component part usage. In both cases, marketers have made tremendous strides to reduce the carbon footprint of the retail sector.

Postretail packaging. We use the term **postretail packaging** to refer to the form of packaging used by the consumer to transport product away from a retail establishment. The amount of this material is substantial. In Massachusetts alone, more than 1.5 billion paper or plastic bags are thrown away every year.[48] The form of packaging used in retailing varies by the culture and by the form of retailing. In the American grocery store, for example, consumers are accustomed to hearing "Paper or plastic?" at the cash register, and traditionally, consumers bear no direct cost for these bags because the merchandise is packed for them. By contrast, in many parts of Europe, consumers pack their own groceries at the register, and they pay a fee for each bag they purchase.

Postretail packaging is changing in many markets. Consumers are beginning to recognize substantial limits to using either paper or plastic bags. Paper is the traditional packaging material made from a renewable source. Paper, however, consumes more energy and water in its production and further yields higher levels of pollution and more greenhouse gases.[49] Plastic bags were introduced to the market 30 years ago as a low-cost alternative to paper. The lightweight nature of plastic means that it is less expensive to transport. Plastic is also longer lasting and less expensive. Nevertheless, plastic is rarely recycled, and it is a formidable trap for fish, birds, and other wildlife. For example, while filming a documentary on Midway Island in the Pacific Ocean, Rebecca Hoskins encountered hundreds of albatross carcasses with plastic bags lodged in their stomachs.[50] When she returned home, she convinced her hometown of Modbury and 80 other English towns to ban plastic bags. Her action led to a reduction in the 200 million bags that litter Britain's parks and beaches every year.[51]

There is a clear trade-off between plastic and paper. Plastic is lighter and less expensive, but it is rarely recycled and a threat to wildlife. By contrast, paper has a larger carbon footprint, and it is heavier and more expensive to produce, but it is more often recycled. Recognizing these trade-offs, consumers, government, and retailers have begun to explore other packaging options. Some consumers have taken this charge on themselves and have begun to use reusable bags. A study conducted by French retailer Carrefour in 2004 indicated that a reusable bag was better for the environment—regardless of the material—so long as the bag was used at least four times.[52]

In order to influence consumer behavior associated with postretail packaging, government has also intervened. For example, the city of San Francisco became the first U.S. city to ban conventional plastic bags in grocery stores in 2007. Similarly, China banned the distribution of free grocery bags in 2008. In other markets, government has imposed a tax on plastic bags. Ireland, for instance, imposed a tax on plastic bags in 2002 as a means of maintaining the country's clean, green image. On August 18, 2009, the residents of Seattle, Washington, voted down a referendum that would have required grocers to charge 20 cents for each plastic bag provided at the checkout counter. Stores with annual revenues of less than $1 million would have kept the bag receipts to cover their costs, while those grossing more would have kept 25% and passed the remainder on to the city for recycling, environmental education, and reusable bags for low-income consumers. Many residents indicated that they opposed the bill as an unnecessary tax rather than a preference for current levels of sustainability in the city.[53]

Government has also placed restrictions on the type of paper and plastic used in restaurants. This retail industry is entertaining the use of some novel forms of packaging made from sugar cane, corn, and other replenishable sources. The Federal Trade Commission has set guidelines for the claims manufacturers can make regarding their recycled products. **Biodegradable** materials refers to packaging that will break down and return to nature within a reasonably short time after the usual disposal. **Compostable items,** however, break down organically into humus-like material and return nutrients to the earth.

Retailers have also made strong strides to reduce the amount of postretail packaging. In 2007, IKEA began charging 5 cents for each plastic bag that was used at the checkout counter in North America. The store also enables shoppers to walk away with a reusable blue bag for 59 cents.[54] The response to this action has been a substantial reduction in the number of single-use bags sold. In 2009, the Canadian branch of the firm was able to phase out the single-use bag completely.[55] Similarly, the Kroger company in the United States has begun to offer incentives to customers that use reusable bags. Consumers earn discounts on in-store purchases or price discounts on gasoline when they bring reusable bags.[56]

Restaurateurs are also employing new materials to reduce the carbon footprints of their packaging. The dining-in option has been revolutionized through plates and bowls made from plant-based materials that are compostable or biodegradable.[57] EATware International, for instance, produces a line of 100% biodegradable tableware made from bamboo, sugar cane pulp, water, and cellulose.[58] The company claims its microwave- and oven-safe plates will decompose in 180 days in a landfill. The Sugar Cane Paper Company combines the residue left over after sugar cane is crushed with 15% recycled paper to make napkins.[59] Solo similarly offers the Bare collection *of* hot cups lined with a plant-based polylactic acid resin.[60] The cups are compostable, made 100% from renewable resources, and range from 8 to 20 ounces. Even plastic silverware has been replaced with ECO Products cutlery made from cornstarch.[61]

Together, these examples illustrate the measures that the retailing industry is taking to lower its cost of operations while simultaneously lowering the carbon footprint of its operations.

Reclamation and component restriction. **Reclamation** refers to the responsible collection of products once they no longer offer value to consumers. For example, the Environmental Quality Company provides retailers with means for handling hazardous electronics (including lighting and batteries), pharmaceuticals, and medical waste.[62] Land and soil considerations also prompt retailers and their suppliers to develop programs that facilitate product reclamation. **Component restriction** refers to limits placed on the ingredients that can be incorporated into a product. For example, asbestos has been banned from new application use in the United States since 1991.[63] Since the regulations associated with reclamation and restriction often address the same materials (e.g., iron ore) and end products (e.g., personal computers), these issues are examined in tandem.

The historical perspective on reclamation is the *cradle-to-grave* logic used in the 1980s to ensure that manufacturers and users properly disposed of chemicals and other hazardous materials. This logic has been replaced with a **cradle-to-cradle** perspective that emphasizes recovery, recycling, and reuse.[64]

Some industries face legislation that compels companies to reclaim products and modify components. Automobiles, electronics, and appliances face regulations in several geographic markets, notably the European Union. Firms from America, Japan, and other non-EU countries must adhere to these directives if they wish to conduct business in the EU. Moreover, firms use the mandates of progressive regulation as preconditions that influence product design, manufacture, and reclamation. Four regulatory acts that influence reclamation and component restrictions include:

End-of-Life Directive. Established in 2000, the EU's **End-of-Life Directive** requires automotive manufacturers and component suppliers to reclaim auto products.[65] Specifically, this directive requires all manufacturers to take back and dismantle all motor vehicles for domestic use at the end of their useful lives. Component parts are then either reused or recycled. The goal is for all motor vehicle manufacturers to have a reuse or recyclable content of 85% at the end of their products' useful lives now and move toward 95% by 2015. This directive requires manufacturers and their component manufacturers to innovate and design for disassembly. This requirement can be at odds with the goal of trying to limit carbon emissions and enhance fuel efficiency. Nevertheless, it has also fostered stronger relationships among component producers, manufacturers, disassemblers, and recyclers.[66] Figure 9-4 illustrates how the various parts of an automobile are reintroduced into the supply chain. This directive has also opened up entrepreneurial opportunities for disassemblers. For example, there are more than 10,000 companies of this type in the United States alone.

Restriction of Hazardous Substances (RoHS). **Restriction of Hazardous Substances (RoHS)** is an EU directive that severely restricts the use of lead, hexavalent chromium, mercury, cadmium, and some flame retardants. RoHS's regulations apply to large and small household appliances, information technology and telecommunications equipment, consumer equipment, electrical and electronic tools, toys, leisure equipment, and other devices.[67] Compliance with this directive is required for manufacturers, resellers marketing under their own brand names, and importers or exporters of electrical and electronic equipment. The primary implication of RoHS is the need to comply with the directive or face punitive charges. Producers and retailers must therefore request documentation from suppliers regarding supplies, components, subassemblies, and equipment to ensure compliance. Companies can be convicted and fined for failing to comply with the directive and for failing to submit technical documentation.

Waste Electrical and Electronic Equipment Directive (WEEE). **Waste Electrical and Electronic Equipment Directive (WEEE)** is a directive designed to reduce the amount of electronic waste in landfills. It addresses all the products in RoHS, and it further includes medical devices and monitoring and control instruments. WEEE and RoHS were adopted in 2003 and began to take effect in 2005. Adherence to WEEE requires the seller to demonstrate that it will cover the cost of disposal in an environmentally friendly manner.[68] The producer is also required to educate consumers regarding the recycling and recovery options available to them. Before a new product enters the market, producers are required to provide "do not landfill" labels on each package.

The retailer's role in WEEE administration is substantial given that consumer participation is crucial to the success of this directive. Although producers can set up recovery facilities anywhere, in many cases these collection sites are at retail locations. For example, Best Buy and Staples enable consumers to return used equipment at their stores. In addition, retailers provide incentives to consumers to return used equipment. These incentives include store rebates, coupons, and other store credit. Upon receipt of a product, the retailer sends it to the producer or its affiliate that determines whether recycling, reuse, or disposal is appropriate for the product.

Registration, Evaluation, Authorization and Restriction of Chemical Substances (REACH). **Registration, Evaluation, Authorization and Restriction of Chemical Substances (REACH)** was adopted by the EU in 2006 to provide information

**FIG. 9-4
Automobile
Disassembly**

End-of-Life Vehicle → Fluid Removal → Gasoline, Engine oil, Antifreezing Solution → Recycler → Reuse, Parts Recycling

Fluid Removal → 1st Dismantlement → Used Parts Supplier → Reuse, Parts Recycling

1st Dismantlement → Tire → Recycler → Reuse, Parts Recycling

1st Dismantlement → 2nd Dismantlement → Battery, Wire → Recycler

2nd Dismantlement → Seat, Synthetic Rysins → Recycler

2nd Dismantlement → 3rd Dismantlement → Engine, Transmission → Cutting → Ferrous Metal, Non-ferrous Metal

3rd Dismantlement → Spring

3rd Dismantlement → Compress/Cutting → Shredder → Ferrous Metal / Non-ferrous Metal → Incineration at Site

Shredder → Shredder Dust → Incineration → Landfill

Material & Chemical Recycling

Source: Reprinted from *International Journal of Production Economics* 115, 305–315. Kumar, Sameer and Valora Putnam (2008), "Cradle to Cradle: Reverse Logistics Strategies and Opportunities Across Three Industries," with permission from Elsevier.

on chemicals that are used and to phase out chemicals that pose unacceptable risks.[69] The health-related consequences of exposure to toxic chemicals are substantial. The incidence of cancer, for instance, is in part related to exposure to toxins.[70] In the United States alone, the annual cost of treating cancer is over $210 billion, and this number is increasing at 7% annually.[71] Reductions in the amount of toxic chemicals have the potential to enhance the environment and the quality of life.

REACH regulation is designed to protect human health and the environment while enhancing innovation and competitiveness. REACH approaches this goal by requiring businesses to register the substances in their products and make public any potential risks from the use of these chemicals. In order to manage REACH, a firm must assess its product portfolio. This assessment should identify products either sourced from or imported into the European Union. The substances contained in these products should then be inventoried. After the firm has inventoried the components of its products, it develops a plan to achieve heightened sustainability by phasing out restricted substances.[72]

Although the legal requirements associated with reclamation and restriction are substantial, there are marketplace opportunities that arise from these requirements. Several benefits accrue to the firm that adopts this perspective toward reclamation and component restrictions.[73] First, there is substantial potential for cost reductions. Because component parts are reused and restored, production costs are lowered. For example, the cost of recycling aluminum is roughly 5% of the cost to refine it from raw materials. Second, constraining the firm's influence on the environment also enables the firm to manage risk effectively. Because the firm that adheres to regulations has a lower likelihood of facing litigation or marketplace criticism, the overall level of risk is reduced through copious attention to regulations.

A third benefit of reclamation and component restrictions is the brand differentiation that it affords to the firm. Since only brands that adhere to standards can compete, the brands that meet regulatory requirements open themselves to market opportunities unavailable to the competition. The adherence to environmental standards is viewed as favorable by many consumers, and this same track record for sustainability fosters an image that is preferred by some employees and stockholders. Retention of loyal consumers and employees can be achieved through adherence to regulation.

Another inherent benefit to sustainability regulation is that it fosters innovation in the supply chain and in product components. The institution of a new regulation requires the firm to review the complete supply chain for a product. In many cases, firms engage in *reverse logistics* whereby a manufacturer accepts previously shipped products or parts from the point of consumption for recycling, reuse, or disposal.[74] Firms have developed **close-looped systems** in which manufacturers work with downstream channel partners to ensure the reclamation of products. For example, Ford Motor Company and Alcan established the first closed-loop recycling system for auto aluminum in 2002.[75] Innovations also accrue in product design as a result of regulation. The firm that can no longer offer a toxic product must find a new solution that meets addresses the product need at a reasonable cost. Thus, regulations also foster innovations in product design.

The final benefit of regulation is that it enables firms to respond to economic realities of supply and demand. Because the supply of landfills is limited, companies that reduce their need for landfills lower their costs of operations. Similarly, the demand for steel and aluminum is strong, yet the supply of raw materials (and costs of refining) provide ample opportunities to recycle these materials. Since the costs of mining and refining bauxite (for aluminum) and iron ore (for steel) are appreciable, there are substantial opportunities to reclaim these products after products have reached the end of their productive lives.

Summary

A. Introduction

The purpose of this chapter has been to underscore the importance of the retailing sector to sustainability. Since by definition retailing addresses the interface between producers and consumers, analysis of retailing offers substantial opportunities to limit the carbon footprint of manufacturers, distributors, retailers, and consumers.

B. The Central Role of Retailing in Supply Cycles

Several factors place retailing at the heart of the supply cycle in many industries. The first of these factors reflects the change in access to information within the industry. The universal product code provides retailers with access to market information on product movement, consumer purchasing behavior, and the use of marketing mix variables. The increase in access to information has been accompanied by the development of larger retail outlets and the growing concentration of market share among a few retailers. As large companies with substantial visibility operating large stores in many communities, retailers have become easy targets for concerns about sustainability. Retailers are therefore developing solutions that limit their carbon footprints and enhance relationships with communities where they source and sell products.

C. Marketing Sustainable Product Lines

The incorporation of green technology into the product mix and the appropriate distribution of sustainable products are two of the most salient issues facing retailers. Firms can elect to market green technologics in existing brands, or they may develop new brands. When firms have developed new products that incorporate green technologies, they can market these products through specialty retailers, general merchandise retailers, or via private-label arrangements.

D. Marketing Sustainable Consumption

Since a sizeable portion of the greenhouse gases associated with products occurs after their purchase, this chapter also examined sustainable postpurchase practices. The discussion of postretail packaging illustrated limitations to paper and plastic bags and the sustainability related benefits of reusable bags. In addition, retailers have adopted a cradle-to-cradle perspective in which they attempt to reclaim as many products as possible and refrain from using products that have substantial negative influences on the environment.

Keywords

biodegradable, 189
close-looped systems, 192
component restriction, 189
compostable items, 189
cradle-to-cradle, 189
End-of-Life Directive, 190
postretail packaging, 188

private label, 187
reclamation, 189
Registration, Evaluation, Authorization and Restriction of Chemical Substances (REACH), 190

Restriction of Hazardous Substances (RoHS), 190
universal product code, 180
urban sprawl, 182
Waste Electrical and Electronic Equipment Directive (WEEE), 190

Questions

1. How has the access to consumer purchasing information changed, and how has this changed the role of retailers?
2. Over the past decade, has retailing become more or less important to the supply chain? What factors support your conclusions?
3. To what extent is urban sprawl a retailing problem, and how does sprawl influence the carbon footprint of a community?
4. Name and describe four ways in which retailers are actively assessing sustainability in supply chains.
5. Is the revenue stream of a firm favorably enhanced by incorporating sustainable features into existing brands, or are firms better off to incorporate these features into new brands?
6. What are the advantages and disadvantages of promoting sustainable or organic brands in a specialty aisle of the store rather than with other items in a product class?
7. Why might a large consumer products company prefer marketing of its branded products to private-label products?
8. Regarding shopping bags, which is preferred—paper or plastic?
9. What steps can retailers take to increase product reclamation?
10. Why should retailers participate in discussions about the components and ingredients in the products they market?

Endnotes

[1] CBC NEWS, "IKEA to introduce anti-idling program, hybrid preferential parking," *CA spots,* http://www.cbc.ca/consumer/story/2007/05/10/ikea-hybrid.html (accessed May 8, 2010).

[2] Kate Galbraith, "Priority Parking for Hybrids?" *The New York Times,* http://greeninc.blogs.nytimes.com/2009/07/14/priority-parking-forhybrids/ (accessed May 8, 2010).

3 Inter IKEA Systems B. V., "Facts and Figures," http://franchisor.ikea.com/showContent.asp?swfId=facts1 (accessed May 8, 2010).

4 IKEA, "Drivers of Hybrid and Fuel Efficient Vehicles Get Preferred Green Parking at IKEA Stores in Canada," *New* http://www.ikea.com/ms/en_CA/about_ikea/press_room/press_release/national/hybrid_parking.html (accessed May 8, 2010).

5 Sven Rosenhauer, *Profit is a Wonderful Word: IKEA's Strategy Behind the Profit* (Norderstedt, Germany: Grin Verlag für Akademische Texte, 2005), 28.

6 See Note 4 above.

7 IKEA, "Products and Materials," http://www.ikea.com/ms/en_US/about_ikea/our_responsibility/products_and_materials/index.html (accessed May 8, 2010).

8 Robert J. Dolan, "Note on the Marketing Information Industry," *Harvard Business School Note 9-588-027* (Boston, MA: Harvard Business School Publishing Division, 1987).

9 Wujin Chu and Paul R. Messinger, "Information and Channel Profits," *Journal of Retailing* 73, no.4 (1997): 487–499.

10 Michael Wahl, *In-Store Marketing: A New Dimension in the Share Wars* (New York, NY: Sawyer Publishing Worldwide, 1992), 220.

11 Walmartstores.com, "About Us," http://walmartstores.com/AboutUs/ (accessed May 8, 2010).

12 Anthony Bianco and others, "Is Wal-Mart Too Powerful?" *Business Week*, October 6, 2003, http://www.businessweek.com/magazine/content/03_40/b3852001_mz001.htm.

13 Paul N. Bloom and Vanessa G. Perry, "Retailer Power and Supplier Welfare: The Case of Wal-Mart," *Journal of Retailing* 77, no. 3 (2001), 379–396

14 Charles Fishman, *The Wal-Mart Effect: How the World's Most Powerful Company Really Works—And How It is Transforming the American Economy* (New York, NY: Penguin Press, 2006), 336.

15 Elisabeth Rosenthal, "Environmental Cost of Shipping Groceries Around the World," *The New York Times*, April 26, 2008, http://www.fco.cat/files/imatges/Butlleti%20135/NYT.pdf (accessed May 8, 2010).

16 "What We Do," *Carbon Disclosure Project,* http://www.cdproject.net/aboutus.asp (accessed May 8, 2010).

17 Carrefour.com, "At the Heart of Life, 2008 Sustainability Report" http://www.carrefour.com/docroot/groupe/C4com/Commerce%20responsable/Publications/RGG2008GB.pdf (accessed May 8, 2010).

18 Bob Thompson, "Green Retail: Retailer Strategies for Surviving the Sustainability Storm," *Journal of Retail and Leisure Property* 6, no. 4 (2007): 281–286.

19 Naoki Kimura and others, "Extra-high Color Rendering White Light-emitting Diode Lamps Using Oxynitride and Nitride Phosphors Excited by Blue Light-emitting Diode," *Applied Physics Letters* 90, (2007): 051109–051109–3.

20 See Note 18 above.

21 Javier González-Benito and Oscar González-Benito, "An Analysis of the Relationship between Environmental Motivations and ISO14001Certification," *British Journal of Management* 16, (2005): 133–148.

22 Michael J. Hicks, "Wal-Mart's Impact on Local Revenue and Expenditure Instruments in Ohio, 1988–2003," *Atlantic Economic Journal* 35, no. 1 (2007): 77–95.

23 Anthony Downs, "Suburban Ecosystem Inner-city," *Journal of Property Management* 62, no. 6 (1997): 60–66.

24 Anthony Downs, "The Big Picture," *Brookings Review* 16, no. 4 (1998): 8–11.

25 Institute of Community Preservation, "An Overview of Sprawl," http://www.preservationist.net/sprawl/overview.htm (accessed May 8, 2010).

26 See Note 24 above; "Wal-Mart's 15 Questions," *Material Handling Management* (2009): 8.

27 Anthony Downs, "Break Down Those Barriers," *Planning* 71, no. 9 (2005): 20–23.

28 Emily Bryson York, "While Competitors Shut Doors, Subway is Still Growing," *Advertising Age* 79, no. 28 (2008): 24–25.

29 Matthew E. Kahn and Joel Schwartz, "Urban Air Pollution Progress Despite Sprawl: The 'Greening' of the Vehicle Fleet," *Journal of Urban Economics* 63, (2008): 775–787.

30 International Organization for Standardization, "ISO 14000 Essentials," http://www.iso.org/iso/iso_catalogue/management_standards/iso_9000_iso_14000/iso_14000_essentials.htm (accessed May 8, 2010).

31 "Bottled Water's Perfect Storm," *Beverage Industry*, 100, no. 7 (2008): SOI8.

32 Jyoti Thottam and others, "War on the Water Front," *Time* 166, no. 25, (2005): 60.

33 Fair Trade Certified, "Fair Trade Overview' http://www.transfairusa.org/content/about/overview.php (accessed May 8, 2010).

34 Katie Cameron, "Brewing Justice: Fair Trade Coffee, Sustainability, and Survival," *Berkeley Journal of Employment and Labor Law* 29, no. 1 (2008): 267–268.

35 Doris De Guzman and Joseph Chang, "Responsible Retailing," *ICIS Chemical Business* 276, no. 3 (2009): 16.

36 Kathryn Kranhold, "Toyota Makes a Bet on New Hybrid Prius," *Wall Street Journal*, July 20, 2000, 18.

37 Dan Ariely, Anat Bracha and Stephan Meier, "Doing Good or Doing Well? Image Motivation and Monetary Incentives in Behaving Prosocially," *American Economic Review* 99, no. 1 (2009): 544–555.

38 Jeongwen Chiang and Ronald T. Wilcox, "A Cross-Category Analysis of Shelf-Space Allocation, Product Variety, and Retail Margins," *Marketing Letters* 8, no. 2 (1997): 183–191.

39 Light of Day Organics, "About US," http://www.lightofdayorganics.com/wp/ (accessed May 8, 2010).

40 Whole Foods Market, "About Whole Foods Market," http://www.wholefoodsmarket.com/company/index.php accessed May 8, 2010).

41 Sam Gwynne "Born Green," *Saveur,* "http://www.saveur.com/article/Our%20Favorite%20Foods/Born-Green (accessed May 8, 2010).

42 Whole Foods Market, "Whole Foods Market's Exclusive Herve Mons Camembert" http://wholefoodsmarket.com/pressroom/blog/2009/05/06/whole-foods-markets-exclusiveherve-mons-camembert/ (accessed May 8, 2010).

[43] Laura Everage, "Understanding the LOHAS Lifestyle," *Gourmet Retailer* 23, no. 10 (2002): 82–86.

[44] Joel Makower, *Strategies for the Green Economy* (New York, NY: McGraw Hill, 2009), 290.

[45] Marc Gunther "The Green Machine," *Fortune*, http://www.business.uiuc.edu/aguilera/Teaching/The%20Green%20Machine%20(Wal-Mart)%20August%2006.pdf (accessed May 8, 2010).

[46] Kroger, "Our Exclusive Brands," http://www.kroger.com/in_store/corporate_brands/Pages/default.aspx (accessed May 8, 2010).

[47] Rajeev Batra and Indrajit Sinha, "Consumer-level Factors Moderating the Success of Private Label Brands," *Journal of Retailing* 76, no. 2 (2000): 175–191.

[48] Jim Johnson, "Paper or Plastic?" *Waste and Recycling News* 14, no. 24, (2009): 1–2.

[49] Jeffrey Ball, "Currents—Power Shift: Paper or Plastic? A New Look at the Bag Scourge—Improved Recycling Options Lessen Plastic's Stigma, Even as Cities and States Consider Imposing Bans or Taxes," *Wall Street Journal*, June 12, 2009, A11.

[50] Rebecca Hoskins, *Ban the Plastic Bag: A Community Action Plan for a Carrier Bag Free World* (London: Alistair Sawday Publishing, 2007), 240.

[51] William Lee Adams, "Banning Plastic Bags," *Time* 174, no. 11 (2009): 52.

[52] See Note 49 above.

[53] Marc Ramirex "Seattle Voters Don't Buy Shopping-bag Charge," *Seattle Times*, http://seattletimes.nwsource.com/html/politics/2009686467_elexseabagfee19m.html (accessed May 8, 2010).

[54] David Roberts "An Interview with IKEA Sustainability Director Thomas Bergmark," *Grist*, http://www.grist.org/article/ikea/ (accessed May 8, 2010).

[55] Karen Hawthorne "Ikea Canada to eliminate plastic bags," *National Post.com*, http://network.nationalpost.com/np/blogs/posted/archive/2009/04/14/ikea-canada-to-eliminate-plasticbags.aspx (accessed May 8, 2010).

[56] Kroger, "Kroger Rewards," http://www.kroger.com/rewards/Pages/rewards_nfo.htm (accessed May 8, 2010).

[57] Tom O'Brien, "The Greening of Paper and Plastic," *Restaurant Business* 108, no. 3 (2009): FSB13.

[58] Eatware.com, "Welcome to Eatware," http://www.eatware.com/ (accessed May 8, 2010).

[59] The Sugar Cane Paper Company, "The Sugar Cane Paper Company, Inc.," http://www.thesugarcanepapercompany.com/ (accessed May 8, 2010).

[60] Bare by Solo, "Our Products," http://www.barebysolo.com/products.html (accessed May 8, 2010).

[61] Eco products, "Cutlery," http://www.ecoproducts.com/va-cms/cutlery.html (accessed May 8, 2010).

[62] The Environmental Quality Company, "Retail Solutions," http://www.eqonline.com/services/RetailSolutions.asp (accessed May 8, 2010).

[63] U.S. Environmental Protection Agency, "Asbestos Ban and Phase Out," http://www.epa.gov/asbestos/pubs/ban.html (accessed May 8, 2010).

[64] Sameer Kumar and Valora Putnam, "Cradle to Cradle: Reverse Logistics Strategies and Opportunities Across Three Industries," *International Journal of Production Economics* 115, no. 2 (2008): 305–315.

[65] "Directive 2000/53/EC of the European Parliament and of the Council of 18 September 2000 on End-of-Life Vehicles" *Official Journal of the European Communities*, http://eur-lex.europa.eu/LexUriServ/LexUriServ.do?uri=OJ:L:2000:269:0034:0042:EN:PDF.

[66] Jo Crotty and Mark Smith, "Strategic Responses to Environmental Regulation in the U.K. Automotive Sector: The European Union End-of-Life Vehicle Directive and the Porter Hypothesis," *Journal of Industrial Ecology* 10, no. 4 (2008): 95–111.

[67] Robin Wright and Karen Elcock, "The RoHS and WEEE Directives: Environmental Challenges for the Electrical and Electronic Products Sector," *Environmental Quality Management* 15, no. 4 (2006): 9–24.

[68] See Note 67 above.

[69] See Note 64 above.

[70] Ohio Department of Health, "Exposure to Toxic Chemicals and Cancer," http://www.odh.ohio.gov/ASSETS/1B0335A0D-C374A65A89857791EC8E6CD/chemexp.pdf (accessed May 8, 2010).

[71] Doug Lockwood, "The REACH Regulation: Challenges Ahead for Manufacturers of Articles," *Environmental Quality Management* 18, no. 1 (2008): 15.

[72] Joyce Borkhoff, "European Union's REACH Regulation," *Paint and Coatings Industry* 24, no. 5 (2008): 88–89.

[73] Ken Alston, "Cradle to Cradle Design Initiatives: Lessons and Opportunities for Prevention Through Design (PtD)," *Journal of Safety Research* 39(2008): 135–136.

[74] Shad Dowlatshahi, "Developing a Theory of Reverse Logistics," *Interfaces* 30, no. 3 (2000): 143–155.

[75] Paul Millibank, "Aluminum Recycling Vital to Global Supply Chain," *Aluminum International Today* 16, no. 5 (2004): 44–49.

Proclaiming Value via Sustainable Pricing Strategies

A. Introduction

SUSTAINABLE TRAVEL INTERNATIONAL

The flight from Los Angeles to New York is a five-hour red-eye evening flight that can cost the traveler well over $1000. The financial and physical costs of this flight are tremendous, but many people forget about the substantial carbon cost of such an excursion. Clever marketers, however, are now enabling consumers to offset the cost of their travel. A recent review of the emerging industry examined 11 different firms that provide such a service.[1] While these companies use different methods to determine offset prices and offer contrasting ways to offset carbon, the development of these firms is in response to a consumer need to reduce the environmental burden of travel.

Although the number of passengers willing to make this commitment is small, there is a growing number of true blue and LOHAS consumers that are willing to pay to offset the environmental cost of travel. Furthermore, there is also a growing breed of environmental entrepreneurs in the travel and hospitality industry. Hoteliers with conservation programs, taxi companies with hybrid automobiles, restaurateurs with large-scale recycling plans, and other eco-entrepreneurs are using new technologies to limit the toll that travel and tourism take on the environment.[2]

Sustainable Travel International (STI) is among this group of environmental entrepreneurs committed to enabling consumers to lower the carbon cost of travel (Figure 10-1). Founded in 2002, STI is a not-for-profit organization created to reduce the toll that travel and tourism take on the environment and local

FIG. 10-1
Sustainable Travel International

Source: © *Sustainable Travel International*

cultures. Founding sponsors include Continental Airlines, United Airlines, Enterprise Car Rental, and several other firms. This firm estimates that the carbon cost of the Los Angeles–New York trip at 1.78 tons of carbon dioxide per person, and the cost to offset this price is around $45. This pricing strategy enables passengers to offset the carbon cost of this flight by making contributions to sustainable forests in the United States, China, Ghana, India, Madagascar, or Turkey. STI's commitment to offsetting activity is not limited to airline travel; the company also offers similar offset programs for auto travel, gifts, events and conferences, home energy usage, and hotel stays.[3] The company also provides a host of travel tools and tips designed to reduce the environmental cost incurred whenever anyone travels.

The Sustainable Travel International example underscores the role of pricing in the firm's efforts to deliver sustainable product offerings to consumers. Although the components of the marketing mix are often presented independently, these marketing decisions must flow from organizational objectives and work together to yield desired outcomes for the firm. The proper pricing of an organization's product offerings enables the firm to achieve its objectives, and the development of the pricing strategy must be derived from the overall strategy of the organization.

The development of the pricing strategy can be viewed as the multistage process[4] outlined in Figure 10-2. The result of this process is the proclamation of value. The organization begins this process by determining the corporate mission and objectives. Once the objectives are established, then the organization develops a series of pricing objectives that complement the overall goals of the firm. These objectives are then converted to specific action that the firm will take to achieve pricing goals and the overall objectives of the firm. Before this conversion occurs, however, the firm must consider the internal and external constraints on this process. Internal constraints include costs of production, sales, and delivery; external constraints include customer demand, legal considerations, and competition influence. When all of these factors have been considered, the firm is in the position to proclaim the value of its product offerings in the form of pricing strategies. As a preface to our development of the pricing objectives and strategy, we outline these internal and external constraints on the price planning process.

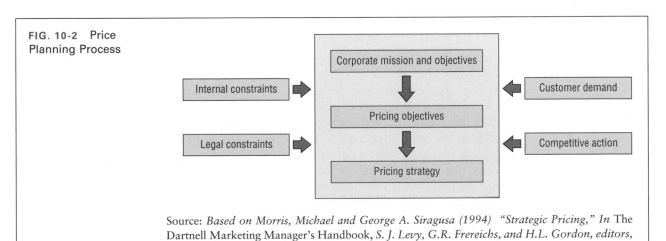

FIG. 10-2 Price Planning Process

Source: *Based on Morris, Michael and George A. Siragusa (1994) "Strategic Pricing," In* The Dartnell Marketing Manager's Handbook, *S. J. Levy, G.R. Frereichs, and H.L. Gordon, editors, Chicago, IL: The Dartnell Corporation, 835–854.*

B. Internal Pricing Constraints

The constraints within the firm reflect the costs incurred to produce, sell, and deliver a product. Many firms use cost as the basis for determining price, and costs must be covered if the firm is to generate a profit. Thus, it is essential to understand the components of cost. One can distinguish between fixed and variable costs associated with a product. **Fixed costs** refer to cost factors that do not change in the short run, whereas **variable costs** refer to costs that fluctuate with the amount of product sold. Fixed costs are exemplified by investments in real estate and equipment. By contrast, the electricity consumed on an auto assembly line is a variable cost that fluctuates with the number of cars produced. Efforts to enhance the sustainability of product offerings must consider both cost elements.

In addition to the fixed–variable cost dichotomy, it is also relevant to consider how costs are allocated among the products manufactured at a specific location. Ford's efforts to enhance the sustainability of its operations and products exemplify these allocation considerations. In the Rouge River plant, for example, Ford has invested more than $2 billion to raise the sustainability of this facility.[5] These investments accommodate the concerns of many interest groups related to the manufacturer such as employees, communities, and NGOs. The costs associated with the Rouge River plant are allocated across products that leave this assembly line. Regardless of their sentiments toward green marketing and production, buyers of cars from this facility must pay some portion of the cost of raising the sustainability. By contrast, Ford has also invested €332 million in a joint agreement with Peugeot to develop diesel engines.[6] The investment in diesel engines is not carried to a large degree by all products coming off the assembly line, but it is allocated to the diesel vehicles. The investment in diesel engines can be allocated among a variety of users that have motivations to purchase fuel-efficient cars that produce relatively few carbon emissions. Given the breadth of consumer preferences in the auto industry, Ford faces a much tougher challenge to assess the consumer response to enhanced production sustainability in the Rouge River facility. By contrast, the consumer response to adding sustainable components to products enables the firm to estimate returns from specific segments of the auto market. Although the assembly line challenge is more daunting, in both cases the firm must consider customer demand in its allocation and pricing decisions.

C. Customer Demand

Grocery stores offer consumers a variety of products that offer differential levels of value. Most large retailers offer competitively priced private-label products that deliver the same ingredients as the nationally advertised brands. Private-label products such as Walmart's Equate brand are sold at lower cost to the consumer, yet these products have higher gross margins than the advertised brand counterparts.[7] The variety at the retail level enables the consumer to select among products with different levels of value, and this diversity enables the retailer serve multiple segments of the market. Grocers recognize that they can increase their revenues by offering multiple products directed at different market niches that desire different levels of value.

In order to assess the potential of a market or market segment, it is necessary to understand what is valued by the customer. Note that this call for understanding of the value derived from consumption *does not* necessarily include green marketing or sustainability considerations. The marketer of ecologically friendly products must recognize that consumers *rarely* cite green marketing issues as the primary motivation for consumption. Traditional selling considerations such as price, quality, and performance are often central motivations that are expressed prior to sustainability concerns.[8] For example, Brita water filtration products offer consumers clean water that offers health, fitness, and vitality benefits to the body. In addition, the combined costs of tap water and these filtration products is frequently lower than the cost of bottled water. These biological and economic benefits are likely to prompt consumers to invest in Brita filtration devices. One primary sustainability benefit is the reduction in the size of landfills associated with fewer purchases (and disposals) of bottled water. While it is likely that consumers would have a strong interest in the stamina-related and biological benefits of the product without the sustainability benefit, it is unlikely that the reduction in landfills alone would prompt substantial purchases. The sustainability benefit does not stand alone and requires consideration of the broader value assessment.

An understating of value is necessary if one is to understand how green marketing benefits can be incorporated into product offerings. **Value** may be defined in the following manner:[9]

$$\text{Value} = \frac{\text{Desired benefits}}{\text{Relative costs}}$$

The expression of value in this equation illuminates several important facets of consumption. Value inherently is associated with trade-offs. Purchase decisions ask the consumer to forego something of value (e.g., money) for something of superior value (product). Desired benefits refer to things that matter to the consumers. They are willing to pay for these things that they genuinely want. The benefits of a product speak to what the product does for the consumer rather than to the product components. The turbo diesel is a feature offered by many automobile companies, but the benefits of this component are the fuel savings and speed of the product.

Effective marketing campaigns move beyond the mere proclamation of product attributes and focus on the aspects of the product that are meaningful to the consumer. The green product proposition often fails to recognize that the promotion of green benefits alone will not stimulate consumption. The Ford plant on the Rouge River in Dearborn, Michigan, offers one example of the promotion of green benefits that do not resound with consumers. This 90-year-old plant was rebuilt to sustainability specifications at a cost of $2 billion.[10] Although Ford's investment in sustainability is admirable, improvements to the plant do not address the primary environmental issue in the industry: the burning of fossil fuels. More importantly, this benefit does not address issues at the heart of auto purchase and consumption decisions.

The analysis of benefits derived via purchasing must consider the breadth of motivations related to the purchase. Many consumers are concerned about the environment, yet they are also concerned about other matters at the point of purchase. The Tesla automobile, for example, may offer substantial ecological benefits, but the $109,000 base price makes the car infeasible for most consumers. The green benefits of products do not stand on their own but are incorporated into the value assessment made by the potential consumer. Marketers must understand the reasons behind consumption and present green benefits as they relate to these motivations for purchase.

Understanding of the purchase criteria enables the marketer to develop a sustainable competitive advantage that focuses on purchase, usage, and sustainability.

A *sustainable competitive advantage* refers to a company's performance relative to competition and the ability to outperform competition along one or more aspects. The development of competitive advantage requires the firm to take stock of its product offerings and those of the competition. Importantly, this assessment should focus on the aspects of consumption most relevant to the consumption. The firm will realize that certain aspects of its product offerings will be superior to the competition's, yet the competitive landscape usually presents alternatives that outperform the firm's product along some dimension.

Consider, for example, the replacement of a worn-out water heater for the home. The purchase of this product presents the buyer with a number of options with respect to fuel alternatives and energy efficiency. The marketer of these products should understand that consumers seeking to replace this appliance face a unique set of circumstances. Because most homes have a single heater and the water heater purchase is only considered when this appliance fails, consumers are immediately aware of the benefits of heated water. The purchase decision is likely to give strong consideration to the heating capability of the alternative appliances. Consumers often rate gas heaters as superior to alternatives due to the consistency in their abilities to generate hot water. Marketing of the efficiency of solar power will not resonate with many consumers if other salient benefits are discounted. In short, the analysis of desired benefits must focus on the merits of the product for the consumer.

Importantly, the relative cost of a product is substantially more than the price. To determine the value proposition, one must examine the acquisition, possession, usage, and opportunity costs.[11] **Acquisition cost** refers to the energy expended to make the purchase as well as to the *purchase price*. This cost component includes the time dedicated to learning about the salient criteria associated with a purchase as well as the time dedicated to evaluating alternatives. Brands that have established themselves within a product class require less time for evaluation,[12] and these reductions in cost are associated with increased revenue. If a new, fuel-efficient technology is presented to the consumer at the point of sale, the consumer will ordinarily need to develop an understanding of the technology prior to purchase. Effective advertising campaigns that make the consumer aware of the merits of the technology prior to purchase should lower acquisition costs and increase revenues.

Possession cost includes all expenditures associated with gaining possession of the product after the purchase decision has been made. These include taxes, insurance, and transportation. Possession is a substantial facet of cost in the water heater example. After the consumer realizes that the current heater is not working, there is an immediate desire to get a replacement as soon as possible. The transition from an electric device to more fuel-efficient alternatives may not be relevant to many consumers when the installation is prolonged. Although solar water heaters are highly efficient, the installation is likely to take more time and require more space on the consumer's property. The consumer faced with making this purchase will be reluctant to consider alternative fuel sources or technologies.

Usage cost is the third facet of cost and includes the cost of operations as well as the disposal cost. In many cases, new technologies provide energy efficiency that yields lower costs in usage relative to alternatives. The marketer of such new technologies should present its products to illustrate the trade-off between acquisition costs and usage costs. The marketer of this product should prompt the consumer to consider the cost of use of the product over its lifetime rather than the initial purchase price. Promotion online and at the point of sale can illustrate to the consumer that an Energy Star appliance will be a less expensive alternative in the long run.

The disposal facet of cost is an increasingly important factor in many industries. The European Union and the United States have implemented regulations requiring electronics manufacturers to reclaim products.[13] Because these products may still be functional, or contain valuable metals, policy makers in many countries have implemented policies requiring the end-of-life take-back of these products.[14]

Many industries understand that they must either establish industry standards for waste or face regulatory action by government. **The Product Stewardship Institute (PSI)** is a United States-based NGO that seeks to reduce the health and environmental impacts of consumer products.[15] PSI takes a unique product stewardship approach to solving waste management problems by encouraging product design changes and mediating stakeholder dialogues. PSI is supporting product end-of-life legislation in several American states. One initiative associated with this legislation concerns proper disposal of paint. In the United States alone, approximately 10% of the amount sold, or 64 million gallons of used paint, is left over annually. The disposal cost associated with proper handling of this product is $8 per can.[16] PSI has similar initiatives addressing reclamation of medical waste, pharmaceuticals, fluorescent lamps, thermostat manufacturers, and phonebooks.

The final element of cost is the **opportunity cost** associated with one product over alternatives. Opportunity costs are forfeited by the consumer that incurs a cost. The purchaser of a gas appliance forfeits the chance to invest and learn about efficient solar water heaters. Since the average automobile lasts 17 years, the purchase of a new internal combustion engine commits to older technology and forfeits the opportunity to use more fuel-efficient transportation alternatives.

When the firm has properly identified the desired benefits and relative costs of a product, then the value assessment can be determined. For a product offering to be successful, it must be real, superior, and profitable.[17] For the product to offer real value, it must have relevance to an identifiable market that has specific customers and segments. The desired benefits of a product offering must exceed the perceived costs of ownership. Note that although the ratio of benefits to costs must exceed one, different consumers have different value ratios. Research of the market should provide insight into the various market segments associated with different benefits and relative costs. The buyers of a Toyota Prius, for example, may be distinguished based on the perceived importance of the ecological performance of the vehicle as a benefit that augments its fuel efficiency merits.

Although a product may reflect the desired benefits sought by the consumer, the value offered by a product must also be superior to the value of competitive products. For example, the traveler between New York and Boston may consider alternative forms of mass transportation. Although the cost of the airline flight may be less than that of rail transportation, the consumer may elect to take the train because it is more convenient and has a lower carbon footprint. The advocate of sustainability that understands the breadth of benefits and costs of alternative product offerings is more likely to influence consumers to choose one product offering over another.

When the value of a product offering is real and superior to the competition, the marketer must also examine whether the value proposition is profitable. A value proposition that is profitable is consistent with the firm's mission and objectives. The for-profit organization has a responsibility to earn a financial profit for the ownership. If the value of an offering does not help the firm realize its mission and objectives, then the firm needs to re-examine the offering.

An important facet of the value proposition is the recognition that different consumers have different value ratios. It is therefore salient to consider devising multiple products with multiple value offerings and targeting different market segments. The green market segments described by the Roper Starch (i.e., true blues, greenback greens, sprouts, grousers, and basic browns) provide a starting point for analysis of the relevant green segments in a market.[18]

D. Legal Constraints

The *legal constraints* refer to the regulatory requirements associated with the marketing of products. To varying degrees, industries face regulations concerning sourcing of component parts, promotions, and postconsumption product disposal. The need to adhere to these regulations can result in higher costs of sourcing, production, distribution, promotion, and disposal. These constraints are established and regulated at the international, federal/regional, state, and local levels. The Kyoto Protocol discussed in Chapter 4 illustrates the influence of international environmental agreements.[19] Adherence to Kyoto standards within in the EU has resulted in new regulation in 182 participating countries, and new standards for greenhouse gas emissions have been incorporated into municipal planning in more than 600 cities worldwide.

The U.S. Environmental Protection Agency (EPA) provides an illustration of national environmental regulation. The EPA creates and enforces regulations concerning environmental issues. The enforcement of environmental concerns is derived from the Clean Air Act (CAA) of 1970 and the Clean Water Act of 1972. The Clean Air Act placed control of air pollution and enforcement of air pollution regulations in the hands of the EPA.[20] CAA regulates stationary and mobile sources of air emissions. Thus, the pollution control associated with auto assembly and auto operations are regulated as a result of the CAA. In 2007, the Supreme Court ruled that the CAA gives the EPA the authority to regulate carbon dioxide as a pollutant.[21] The EPA also regulates vehicle emissions for hyrdocarbons, carbon monoxide, and nitrogen oxides.

The Clean Water Act (CWA) provides standards, technical tools, and financial assistance to limit water pollution and enhance water quality. CWA requires major industries and municipalities to adhere to standards for water quality and pollution control. It sets state-level specific water quality criteria and provides funding to states and communities to help them meet their clean water infrastructure needs. In addition, it employs a permitting system that is designed facilitate development while simultaneously protecting wetlands and other aquatic ecosystems.[22]

Organizations must also monitor and adhere to the regulations established at the state and local levels. For example, the state of California enacted the California Global Warming Solutions Act in 2006.[23] This act strives to achieve gas emissions levels of 1990 throughout the economy by 2020. This goal represents approximately an 11% reduction from current emissions levels and nearly a 30% reduction from projected business-as-usual levels for 2020.[24] The act also requires annual monitoring and reporting of greenhouse gas as well the accounting for greenhouse gas emissions from all electricity consumed in the state. The pursuit of these goals and requirements demands that firms operating in every sector of the California economy invest in energy-efficient technologies. These organizations must also attend to the regulations at the municipal level. San Francisco, for example, has implemented a green building ordinance that requires new buildings to meet or exceed the requirements established by Build It Green in the GreenPoint Rated (GPR) system or the U.S. Green Building Council's Leadership in Engineering and Environmental Design (LEED) building rating system.[25]

These regulatory conditions—from the Kyoto Protocol to the San Francisco green building ordinance—underscore the influence of legal requirements on pricing decisions. It is incumbent upon the firm to recognize current sustainability standards for operations in each geographic market it serves. In addition, organizations that monitor or participate in developing regulations have a greater opportunity to anticipate changes in environmental law.

E. Competitive Action

Our pricing model (see Figure 10-2) recognizes that pricing decisions must take into account the environment in which the firm operates. Decisions about the pricing strategy must consider the nature of the market as well as the nature of the competition.[26] In Chapter 5, we characterized five segments of the consumer's orientation to sustainability. This segmentation research illustrates the multiple orientations to the market, and it underscores the need to examine the extent to which consumers in a market value product offerings that offer heightened ecological benefits.

The organization should evaluate the size of the green consumer segment in the marketplace. Some markets are characterized by a strong preference for green products. For example, Starbucks recognizes that a strong portion of the retail coffee consumers have a preference for fair-trade, sustainably produced coffee.[27] Because many of these consumers are willing to pay more for these coffees, Starbucks can retain a premium price for fair-trade coffee. By contrast, some markets are characterized by negative predisposition toward sustainability concerns.

The competitive landscape should be considered in conjunction with the consumer's attitude toward green products. Thus, the organization must examine the differentiability based on greenness. To varying degrees, companies have resources that enable them to compete favorably based on the ecological sensitivity of the strategy. The competition to the firm also has resources that could be (or are already) committed to achieving sustainability. Thus, the Body Shop's commitment to sustainability makes it difficult to compete with this firm based on the green marketing and production practices.

Analysis of the competitive landscape should incorporate consideration of the market factors outlined in Chapter 5. These factors include the ability to differentiate based on sustainability and the size of the green market segments. *Lean green* and *defensive green* marketing strategies are appropriate where the ability to distinguish market offerings based on ecological considerations is modest. For example, consumers in the heavy-duty pickup truck market may not be favorably disposed to hybrid technology. Although there may be many consumers with strong (favorable or unfavorable) attitudes toward sustainability, consumers are indifferent to green marketing concerns when making purchases. In such cases, the firm is likely to benefit from a pricing strategy that does not ask the consumer to invest more for green technology. Similarly, Nike introduced the Considered brand of footwear in 2005. This environmentally friendly shoe made from brown hemp fibers was marketed at $110 per pair. Ecological concerns were not salient to consumers in this marketplace. The consumers in the market purchased shoes to make them feel slick, fast, and hip. Nike learned from this product launch that most consumers do not use sustainability criteria when they purchase footwear. Nike continues to enhance the sustainability of its product offerings, but new products do not emphasize green factors.[28]

In markets characterized by marked opportunities to distinguish product offerings based on sustainability, the firm must also consider the size of the green market. The *extreme green* strategy reflects a competitive situation in which there is substantial demand for green products and the firm has appreciable ability to differentiate based on the green qualities of its products.

Consider, for example, Stonyfield Farms, the New Hampshire producer of organic dairy products. This firm has the fourth largest market share in the yogurt industry, trailing only Yoplait, Dannon, and private-label products.[29] Stonyfield recognizes that one segment of the yogurt market is highly cognizant of the merits of organic food, and it has crafted its product line to address the demand in this segment. The organic label is a form of sustainable differentiation that enables the firm to offer products at a price premium.[30] The average price of their products is $1.56 per unit—greater than twice the price of Yoplait at $0.71 per unit. The price premium of such a firm must exceed the cost incurred to differentiate based on the organic quality of the products. It is therefore essential for a firm that uses this pricing strategy to monitor its cost position. The firm using this strategy attempts to achieve price parity by reducing costs in areas other than the source of the differential competitive advantage. Firms such as Stonyfield can pare down promotional and supply chain costs relative to their competition. Companies that are able to control these costs and maintain their competitive advantages can be strong performers in the industry.

The *shaded green* strategy refers to a market in which the demand for ecologically sensitive products is low, yet there is a substantial opportunity to differentiate based on the environmental merits of a product. For example, in the clothing market, roughly 0.1% of the cotton products sold are organic. Organic products tend to be more expensive than competitive products that use inorganic fertilizers.[31] Nonorganic cotton farming has substantial implications for the environment. The nonorganic industry covers 2.4% of the world's farmland, but it uses 25% of the world's pesticides and 10% of the world's synthetic fertilizers. Large quantities of defoliants, fungicides, and herbicides are sprayed into fields, causing harm to other crops, farm workers, and neighbors.

Patagonia serves this niche market by marketing jeans, hats, shirts, and undergarments made exclusively from organic cotton.[32] The firm's products command prices roughly 20% higher than those of other outdoor wear specialists. Patagonia customers tend to be better educated and have higher incomes than most consumers in the markets served by the firm. Patagonia earns revenues of about $250 million per year and donates 1% (or 10% of pretax profits if they are greater than 1% of revenue) to environmental organizations.[33] It also tries to reduce the environmental impact of its products and processes. The majority of Patagonia's costs of goods sold are attributable to the garments' raw materials. Fabric accounts for about 80% of the total costs of raw materials, and the firm estimates that its fabric costs can be as much as 20% to 30% higher than those of its competitors. Patagonia's primary marketing vehicle is a series of catalogs that display men and women using the products in spectacular settings. The catalogs also offer essays about environmentalism and cultural values. In contrast to competition that uses less than 10% of catalog space for nonselling activities, Patagonia dedicates roughly 50% of the catalog space to nonselling activities.

In 1996, Patagonia made the decision to convert to organic cotton. This decision demanded attention to consumer attitudes, retail prices, and costs of goods sold. The spring 1996 catalog featured an opening article from Patagonia's founder concerning the switch to organic cotton, and the description of such organic products offered repeated references to organic components. The firm recognized that its consumers were sensitive to organic products, but it also modified prices. Patagonia reduced margins on most cotton sportswear products so that the retail price on an organic product would not be more than 20% more than the price of the conventional product. Products that could not meet the goal were eliminated, resulting in organic cotton garments selling for not more than 8% above comparable garments made from conventional cotton. Although the cost of goods sold increased, the additional average willingness to pay for the organic cotton exceeded the costs incurred.

The Patagonia example underscores a situation in which the market for green products is modest, yet the firm has the ability to offer a product with sustainable competitive advantage to the market. By understanding the needs of the consumer base and its responsiveness to price and quality modifications, firms can successfully implement strategies to accommodate shaded green markets.

F. Corporate Mission and Pricing Objectives

It is vital to recognize that the outcome of the marketing mix embodies the only manner by which the firm can achieve objectives. If each element of the mix, and notably price, does not reflect the mission and objectives of the firm, then there is little likelihood that these goals of the firm will be obtained. When the firm establishes a clear mission and objectives, the pricing strategy must be designed to complement these goals. For example, Procter and Gamble places a heavy emphasis on the desire for the firm to grow via innovation.[34] Across the multiple brands of this firm, the goal is increased revenues by a steady flow of innovative ideas with respect to products, their delivery, and their consumption. In many markets, price is an important means for differentiation among branded products and retailers' private-label brands. The constant pursuit of innovation enables Procter and Gamble to compete with premium and mid-tier-priced products. Thus, the pricing strategy can be implemented because it is consistent with the innovation goals of the firm.

The pricing strategy should be consistent with the overall objectives of the firm. The specific pricing strategy may focus on multiple objectives and varying levels of these potentially inconsistent objectives.[35] Organizations that have corporate objectives that revolve around the targeted return on investment or targeted profit levels are likely to adopt pricing objectives that are consistent with these corporate objectives. One objective of the pricing strategy concerns the extent to which the firm seeks a targeted *return on investment*. Firms that focus on this objective determine their costs and then establish prices based on a desired rate of return. Similarly, some firms rely on targeted *level of profitability*. These firms estimate costs and then add a margin designed to yield a level of profit.

The organizational goal to achieve some level of market share may not be compatible with targeted ROI or profits. Firms with a market share objective will have pricing strategies that ensure they attain or maintain a presence in the market. Companies with a targeted market share are likely to charge lower prices than firms that are focused on the return on investment. Note that firms can either engage in these strategies to maintain a position in the market, increase market share, or prevent competition from gaining a foothold in the market.

In addition to targeted returns and market share, an organization also seeks to covey an image about the firm and its products. Thus, pricing objectives are developed that focus on the image that firm seeks to convey.[36] Some firms such as Gucci are inclined to price to convey the luxury associated with the company's product offerings. In contrast, firms such as Costco seek to convey that they are the low-price leader in a market.

Firms are increasingly incorporating sustainability goals into their objectives, and this enhancement to strategy has strong implications for the pricing objectives of the firm. For example, Timberland's mission is to equip people to make a difference in the world, and it seeks to approach this mission by becoming carbon neutral.[37] Firms with the objective to achieve higher levels of sustainability can engage in multiple strategies that must take into consideration other aspects of the competitive marketplace and consumer preferences.

G. Pricing Strategies

Because different market segments have different value ratios, one needs to prepare a wide arsenal of strategies for approaching a market. In this section, we address several strategies that enable firms to increase revenues and simultaneously address the firm's sustainability objectives.

We distinguish among three pricing strategies. First, we discuss the use of carbon offset pricing. We then outline pricing strategies associated with the competitive position and product line pricing.[38]

Carbon Offset Pricing

Carbon offset pricing refers to situations under which the marketer of a product enables the purchaser to compensate for the greenhouse gas emissions associated with consumption. This pricing strategy places the cost of sustainability directly in the hands of the consumer.[39] Two parameters associated with determining the offset price are the determination of the carbon-related cost of a product and the determination of the cost of the offset investment. For example, Continental Airlines has joined the joined Sustainable Travel International (STI) and offers passengers the opportunity to offset the carbon dioxide-related costs of air travel. To determine the carbon-related cost of air travel, STI determines the average quantity of greenhouse gases emitted per passenger. It estimates that on short-distance domestic flights, approximately 0.64 metric tons are discharged per passenger, whereas 2.75 metric tons of carbon dioxide (CO_2) are emitted per passenger on long-distance flights.[40] The second consideration is the cost of the offset. STI offers different offset programs that vary based on the location of the offset and the form of service. The Conservation Carbon offset supports reforestation projects in Africa and Asia and costs whereas the Green Tag program for renewable energy projects in North America is more than twice as expensive per unit of travel.

Competitive Pricing

In many cases, the specific strategies the firm will use are based on the firm's position in the market. Consider how these pricing strategies have been used in conjunction with products that offer sustainability advantages:

Break-even pricing. The break-even pricing strategy attempts to establish a price that covers all costs of operations. To use this pricing strategy, the firm must determine its fixed and variable costs. The organization then estimates demand for the product. The price is then determined as the sum of the fixed and variable costs divided by the number of units sold. This strategy is essential to the success of many pricing decisions regardless of whether the consumer base is favorably disposed to green products. The strategy forces the firm to determine its costs, and green technologies that lower the cost of operations are implemented. For example, propane is a variable cost that poultry farmers face in the operation of their facilities. These farmers are switching to biofuels to lower their costs of operation and to reap the ecological benefits of renewable fuel.[41]

Cost-based pricing. A cost-based pricing program adds a markup to the cost of the product to establish the price. This strategy is used by many firms to establish pricing structures. For example, utility companies use their cost structures as bases for determining the cost of water within the municipalities they serve.[42] The marketer of green technology can influence purchasing by illustrating how the investment in green technology can lower their overall cost of operations. Because price is directly linked to cost, lower costs translate to lower prices for consumers. For example, Staples is committed to lowering its energy to 7% below 2001 levels. It is retrofitting lighting systems and using biogas, wind, solar, and biomass for more than 14% of its energy needs. Its integrated strategy for energy conservation has enabled it to reduce its net greenhouse gas emissions by nearly 5% as compared with 2001. These cost reductions help Staples to remain competitive in a volatile retail market.[43]

Value-based pricing. This pricing strategy uses the consumers' perceived value of a good to establish price. In contrast to the preceding strategies that focus on cost to determine price, this strategy addresses the relative value of the product to the consumer. The firm begins by identifying the desired benefits and relative costs of a product; then the value assessment can be determined. Thus, the various facets of benefits and the multiple facets of cost are used to determine the price. Products that feature the Energy Star label offer one example of value-based pricing. *Energy Star*-qualified refrigerators, for instance, are 20% more efficient than other products, but the *initial* cost of the Energy Star product is typically higher than the cost of other models.[44] Consumers evaluating Energy Star products weigh initial cost and value in use over the productive life of the appliance versus the alternative, non-Energy Star appliances.

Status quo price. The *status quo price* refers to charging a price that is consistent with the competition. Firms can effectively use this strategy to offer a product that is superior in terms of green marketing, yet the product sells at the same price point as the alternative. For example, Starbucks has made a corporate commitment to sustainability throughout its supply chain. The company has also employed a status quo pricing strategy in which it charges $1 for an 8-ounce cup of coffee.[45] This pricing strategy enables the firm to remain price competitive while still pursuing the company's sustainability objectives.

Skimming pricing. This pricing strategy refers to setting a price to reach consumers willing to pay a higher price for a product prior to marketing the product to more price-sensitive consumers.[46] For example, Seventh Generation is committed to becoming the world's most trusted brand of authentic, environmentally responsible products for the home.[47] The household cleaners offered for sale by this company tend to be higher priced than the products sold by competitors such as Procter and Gamble.[48] The skimming strategy would seem to work best when there is a sizeable group of consumers in the true blue market segment. In contrast to the skimming strategy, P&G has adopted a status quo pricing strategy for Bounty Select. These paper towel sheets are 45% smaller than regular towels and enable the consumer to use a smaller amount of paper with every cleaning task. The innovations in product design and logistics enable P&G to market a relatively eco-friendly product at a competitive price.

Penetration pricing. A penetration pricing policy sets a low initial price in an attempt to increase market share rapidly.[49] This policy is effective if demand is perceived to be fairly elastic. For example, the three largest utilities in California were instructed in 2007 to reduce the amount of energy consumed or face strong financial penalties. Pacific Gas and Electric and other utilities elected to pour millions of dollars into subsidizing the cost of compact fluorescent light (CFL) bulbs. As a result, bulbs that were sold for $5 to $10 in 1999 could be purchased for 25 cents to 50 cents.[50] This strategy resulted in sales of more than 7.6 million CFL bulbs in 2007 in California alone.

Product Line Pricing

In some cases, the specific strategies the firm will use are not based on the firm's position in the market, but they primarily focus on relationships among products in the product line. Consider how these product line strategies have been used to market products with ecological benefits:

Price lining. This strategy refers to the offering of merchandise at a number of specific predetermined prices. By offering ecological benefits at several price points, the marketer grants the consumer the flexibility to engage in green consumption action that is consistent with the consumer's budget. For example, the carbon offset programs offered by Sustainable Travel enable consumers to select from among several plans. These plans vary in price based on the level and location of the offset carbon activity.

Bundling. *Bundling* is the practice of offering two or more products or services for sale at one price. Bundling can be used across contexts to lower consumers' overall costs and enhance sustainability. For example, retailers that market personal electronic devices such as cameras can market product bundles that include rechargeable batteries. By bundling the batteries to the electronics, consumer satisfaction is raised and the product yields a lower carbon footprint due to the rechargeable devices. This strategy is also used in the construction industry to bundle sustainable products within a new building. Construction certified by the U.S. Green Building Council receives leadership in energy and environmental design (LEED) certification.[51] The certification ensures that all the products (e.g., lighting, windows, heating/air conditioning) are sustainable.

Summary

A. Introduction

The purpose of this chapter has been to outline the relationship between pricing strategies and green marketing. Because the pursuit of green marketing may not be paramount to the consumer, the green pricing strategy must be incorporated into the overall strategy and planning process. We therefore outlined the influences of internal constraints, customer demand, legal constraints, and competitive action on the price planning process. We then outlined the relationship between corporate strategy and pricing objectives. The internal and external constraints and the corporate strategy provided a basis for development of the pricing objectives and the pricing strategy. We finished our treatment of pricing by outlining specific carbon offset, competitive, and product line pricing tactics.

B. Internal Pricing Constraints

The constraints within the firm reflect the costs incurred to produce, sell, and deliver a product. *Fixed costs* refer to cost factors that do not change in the short run, whereas *variable costs* refer to costs that fluctuate with the amount of product sold. It is also relevant to consider how costs are allocated among the products manufactured at a specific location. Firms that invest in technology and infrastructure to enhance sustainability should recognize that this cost burden is carried by all products leaving a facility or location.

C. Customer Demand

In order to understand the role of consumers, it is essential to frame value as the relationship between desired benefits in relation to the relative cost. *Desired benefits* refer to things that consumers are willing to pay for and that they genuinely want. These benefits must weighed against the acquisition, possession, usage, and opportunity cost associated with a product. The value offered by a product offering must also be superior to the value of competitive products, and the marketer must ensure that the value proposition generates a profit.

D. Legal Constraints

Legal constraints refer to regulatory requirements associated with the marketing of products. Industries face regulations concerning sourcing of component parts, promotions, and postconsumption product disposal. The need to adhere to these regulations can result in higher costs of sourcing, production, distribution, promotion, and disposal. These constraints are established and regulated at the international, federal/regional, state, and local levels.

E. Competitive Action

The role of competition should be considered in conjunction with the consumer's attitude toward green products. The organization must examine the differentiability based on greenness. Companies have resources that enable them to compete favorably based on the ecological sensitivity of the strategy. The competition to the firm also has resources that could be (or are already) committed to achieving sustainability. By understanding the needs of the consumer base and the influence of competition, firms can successfully develop strategies that lead to increased market share.

F. Corporate Mission and Pricing Objectives

The pricing strategy should be consistent with the overall objectives of the firm. The specific pricing strategy may focus on multiple objectives and varying levels of these potentially inconsistent objectives. Firms that have objectives that emphasize market share or a level of profitability will price their products with these goals in mind. Similarly, firms that seek to raise perceptions of sustainability will similarly adjust price to achieve these objectives.

G. Pricing Strategies

Three types of pricing strategies include carbon offset pricing, competitive pricing, and product line pricing. Carbon offset pricing refers to situations under which the marketer of a product enables the purchaser to compensate for the greenhouse gas emissions associated with consumption. Competitive pricing is a pricing strategy based on the firm's position in the market. These strategies include break-even pricing, cost-based pricing, value-based pricing, status quo pricing, skimming, and penetration pricing. Product line pricing includes price lining and bundling techniques that use the relationships among products in the product line to establish prices.

Keywords

Questions

1. How does Sustainable Travel International enable consumers to reduce the environmental cost of air travel? What does such action do to the overall cost to the consumer?

2. Why is it necessary for companies to incorporate product, promotion, and distribution considerations into pricing decisions?

3. How can a company determine the desired benefits and costs inherent to a pricing decision?

4. Distinguish among four costs that factor into value decisions.

5. Name and describe an international, national, and local sustainability based regulation that influences a firm's pricing strategy.

6. How does the level and form of competition influence pricing decisions?

7. How do the objectives and mission of the firm influence the pricing strategy?

8. Describe the two parameters associated with determining the offset prices, and explain why different firms come up with different estimates for these parameters.

9. Describe a skimming strategy and a penetration strategy used by a company to help it increase sales of sustainable products.

10. How do firms use price lining and price bundling to increase the market share of sustainable products?

Endnotes

[1] Joy Murray and Christopher Dey, "The Carbon Neutral Free For All," *International Journal of Greenhouse Gas Control* 3, no. 2 (2009): 237–248.

[2] Rebecca Knight, "Green Entrepreneurs with the Drive to Transform Travel," *Financial Times*, September 26, 2008, 16.

[3] Sustainable Travel International, "Our Programs: Carbon Offsets," https://sustainabletravelinternational.org/documents/op_carboncalcs.html (accessed May 10, 2010).

[4] Michael H. Morris and George A. Siragusa, "Strategic Pricing," in *The Dartnell's Marketing Manager's Handbook*, ed. Sidney J. Levy, George R. Frerichs, and Howard L. Gordon (Chicago, IL: The Dartnell Corporation, 1994), 835–854.

[5] William McDonough and Michael Braungart, "Design for the Triple Top Line: New Tools for Sustainable Commerce," *Corporate Environmental Strategy* 9, no. 3 (2002): 251–258.

[6] "Joint Investment in Diesel," *Automotive Engineer* 30, no. 10 (2005): 4–5.

[7] Stephen J. Hoch and Shumeet Banerji, "When Do Private Labels Succeed?" *Sloan Management Review* 34, no. 4 (1993): 57–67.

[8] Daniel C. Esty and Andrew S. Winston, *Green to Gold* (New Haven, CT: Yale University Press, 2006), 366.

[9] J. Nicholas DeBonis, Eric Balinski, and Phil Allen, *Value-Based Marketing for Bottom-Line Success* (New York, NY: McGraw-Hill, 2002), 266.

[10] See Note 5 above.

[11] See Note 9 above.

[12] Kevin Lane Keller, *Strategic Brand Management* (Englewood Cliffs, NJ: Prentice Hall, 2008), 635.

[13] John B. Stephenson, "Electronic Waste: EPA Needs to Better Control Harmful U.S. Exports Through Stronger Enforcement and More Comprehensive Regulation," *GAO Reports GAO-01-1044*, (2008): 1–62.

[14] Jonathan Linton, "Electronic Products at Their End-of-Life: Options and Obstacles," *Journal of Electronics Manufacturing* 9, no. 1 (1999): 29–40.

[15] Product Stewardship Institute, "PSI Homepage," http://www.productstewardship.us/ (accessed May 10, 2010).

[16] Joe Truini, "Recycling Burden Shifting Toward Manufacturers," *Waste & Recycling News* 14, no. 18 (2009): 13.

[17] See Note 9 above.

[18] Jacqueline A. Ottman, "Know Thy Target," in *Business*, (September–October, 2003): 30–31; Jill M. Ginsberg and Paul N. Bloom, "Choosing the Right Green Marketing Strategy," *MIT Sloan Management Review* (Fall, 2004): 79–84.

[19] United Nations Framework Convention on Climate Change, *Kyoto Protocol to the United Nations Framework Convention on Climate Change* (Kyoto, Japan: United Nations, 1998), 21. http://unfccc.int/resource/docs/convkp/kpeng.pdf (accessed May 10, 2010).

[20] Nicholle Winters, "Carbon Dioxide: A Pollutant in the Air, But is the EPA Correct That It is Not an 'Air Pollutant'?" *Columbia Law Review* 104, no. 7 (2004): 1996–2031.

[21] Alan D. Hecht, "Exploring How Today's Development Affects Future Generations Around the Globe," *Sustainable Development Law & Policy* 8 (Fall, 2007), 19–26.

[22] U.S. Environmental Protection Agency, "Clean Water Act Enforcement," http://www.epa.gov/compliance/civil/cwa/index.html (accessed May 10, 2010).

[23] 2006 California.gov, "Assembly Bill No. 32," http://www.climatechange.ca.gov/publications/legislation/ab_32_bill_20060927_chaptered.pdf (accessed May 10, 2010).

24 The California Energy Commission, "Welcome to the Website of the California Energy Commission!" http://www.energy.ca.gov/commission/index.html (accessed May 10, 2010).

25 Catherine A. Cardno, "California Energy Commission Approves San Francisco 'Green' Ordinance," *Civil Engineering* 79, no. 2 (2009): 19–22.

26 Jill M. Ginsberg and Paul N. Bloom, "Choosing the Right Green Marketing Strategy," *MIT Sloan Management Review,* (Fall, 2004): 79–84.

27 Joel Makower, *Strategies for the Green Economy* (New York, NY: McGraw Hill, 2009), 290.

28 Reena Jana, "Nike Goes Green, Very Quietly," *BusinessWeek,* 4136, June 22, 2009, 56.

29 David Phillips, "Yogurt Still the Bright Spot," *Dairy Foods* 109, no. 11 (2008): 66–73.

30 Michael E. Porter, *Competitive Advantage* (New York, NY: Free Press, 1985), 592.

31 "How green is your wardrobe?" *Economist* 381, no. 8506 (2006): 67–68.

32 Ramon Casadesus-Masanell and others, "Households' Willingness to Pay for 'Green' Goods: Evidence from Patagonia's Introduction of Organic Cotton Sportswear," *Journal of Economics & Management Strategy* 18, no. 1 (2009): 203–233.

33 Patagonia, "Environmentalism: What We Do," http://www.patagonia.com/web/us/patagonia.go?slc=en_US&sct=US&assetid=2329 (accessed May 10, 2010).

34 P&G, "2009 Annual Report Designed to Lead," http://www.annualreport.pg.com/ (accessed May 10, 2010).

35 Robert F. Lanzillotti, "Pricing Objectives in Large Companies," *American Economic Review* 48, no. 5 (1958): 921–940.

36 Dominic Wilson, "Pricing Objectives," *Blackwell Encyclopedic Dictionary of Marketing* (2005), 163.

37 Timberland, "Focus on Energy: Become carbon neutral by 2010 and beyond," http://www.timberlandonline.co.uk/csr-strategy-energy/csr_strategy_energy,default,pg.html (accessed May 10, 2010).

38 Gerard J. Tellis, "Beyond the Many Faces of Price: An Integration of Pricing Strategies," *Journal of Marketing* 50, no. 4 (1986): 146–160.

39 Pallavi Gogoi, "Carbon Offsets Take Flight," *BusinessWeek,* March 24, 2008, 26.

40 Sustainable Travel, "Carbon Offset Pricing," http://www.sustainabletravelinternational.org/documents/op_carbonoffsets_price.html (March 11, 2009).

41 Donna Uptagraff, "Co-op Development Action: Poultry Industry Explores Ecological Options to Save Energy," *Rural Cooperatives* 75, no. 6 (2008): 14–15.

42 John C. Moorhouse, "Competitive Markets for Electricity Generation," *CATO Journal* 14, no.3 (1995): 412–423.

43 Marianne Wilson, "Staples Aims for a Greener Planet," *Chain Store Age* 82, 13 (2006): 60–66.

44 U.S. Department of Energy, "Energy Department Announces More Stringent Criteria for Energy Star Refrigerators," http://www.energy.gov/news/archives/5290.htm (accessed May 10, 2010).

45 Janet Adamy, "Starbucks Tests $1 Cup, Free Refills in Seattle," *Wall Street Journal,* January 23, 2008, B4.

46 American Marketing Association, "Dictionary," http://www.marketingpower.com/_layouts/Dictionary.aspx (accessed May 10, 2010).

47 Seventh Generation "Seventh Generation Mission," http://www.seventhgeneration.com (accessed May 10, 2010).

48 Todd Wasserman, "Will Green Product Sales Wither?" *Adweek* 49, no. 36 (2008): 5.

49 See Note 46 above.

50 Rebecca Smith, "Utilities Amp Up Push to Slash Energy Use," *Wall Street Journal* 251, no. 7 (2008): A1–A12.

51 U.S. Green Building Council, "Welcome to USGBC," http://www.usgbc.org/Default.aspx (accessed May 10, 2010).

Macroeconomic Energy Consumption

The Role of Household Consumption

A. Identify Influences of Households on Energy Consumption

A January 2008 fashion show in New York City featured styles from several well-known designers including Calvin Klein, Narciso Rodriguez, and Versace. When the lights went down, models strutted across the runway wearing fabrics quite different from the designers' standard fare. Traditional fabrics such as silk and cashmere were replaced with sustainable materials that included hemp, peace silk (a process that enables silkworms to live out their life cycle), and sasawashi (a Japanese fabric made from herbs and paper).[1]

FIG. 11-1 *ecoStyle* Fashion Show in Kuala Lumpur, Malaysia 2007

Source: © *Rob Loud/Getty Images*

This *FutureFashion* show and other similar events in Kuala Lumpur, Malaysia, and Seattle, Washington, were sponsored by Earth Pledge, a nongovernment organization (NGO) established in 1991 to foster development that meets the needs of the present without compromising the ability of future generations to meet their own needs.[2] The *FutureFashion* program is one of the NGO's six sustainability initiatives. Fashion was selected because it uses more water than any other industry except agriculture. Furthermore, more than 8,000 chemicals are used to turn raw materials into textiles, and 25% of the world's pesticides are used to grow nonorganic cotton. Chemical use yields irreversible damage to people and the environment, yet two thirds of a garment's carbon footprint occurs after it is purchased.[3]

Since 2005, Earth Pledge has worked with environmentally conscious mills and textile manufacturers to identify, promote, and collect renewable, reusable, and nonpolluting materials and production methods. The runway shows illustrate the possibilities for sustainable fabrics in the industry and connect the world's fashion designers with leading materials producers.[4] Barneys, a specialty retailer in New York, participated in 2008 by commissioning environmentally friendly lines from Theory, 3.1 Phillip Lim, and Stella McCartney. It also dedicated its Christmas windows and catalog to green fashion. Not surprisingly, more recognizable brands such as Banana Republic, Guess, and Target followed this trend and rolled out green lines designed to promote sustainability to larger audiences.[5]

The fashion industry illustrates how consumer purchases influence climate change and sustainability. In this chapter, we look closely at the relationship between household consumption and sustainability. We begin by describing household consumption patterns and their influences on energy consumption. We then present a framework for consumer decision making and describe processes designed to influence prepurchase decisions and purchasing. We close the chapter by examining consumption and postconsumption decisions.

If we are to influence energy consumption in the home, then it is necessary to examine the amount and manner of this consumption. Home energy consumption represents 29% of total energy consumption. Figure 11-2 provides an overview of how households consume this energy and how their consumption of energy has changed over time. Households consume energy through space heating, appliances, water heating, lighting, and cooking. In addition, households are involved in indirect energy use associated with food purchases.

Figure 11-3 contrasts per capita energy consumption across the globe. Per capita consumption in the United States and Canada is twice the rate of all other OECD (Organization for Economic Co-operation and Development) countries. Moreover, the rate of consumption in these two countries is more than seven times the rate of consumption for most other markets. Individuals in these two markets and in other parts of the world are making efforts to enhance fuel efficiency, and consumers in North America have the greatest opportunity to have an influence on energy conservation in the household. Consider first energy consumption associated with space heating.

Space Heating

At 53%, space heating represents the largest portion of energy consumption in the household. Since the oil crisis of the 1970s, many OECD countries have established mandatory energy efficiency codes that focus on improving energy consumption

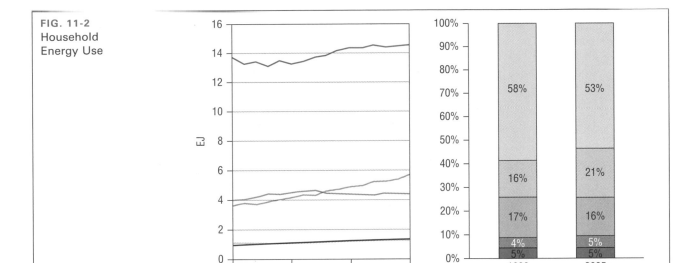

FIG. 11-2
Household
Energy Use

Source: *International Energy Agency,* Worldwide Trends in Energy Use and Efficiency: Key Insights from the IEA Indicator Analysis *(Paris, France: © OECD/IEA, 2008), figure 4.3, page 46.*

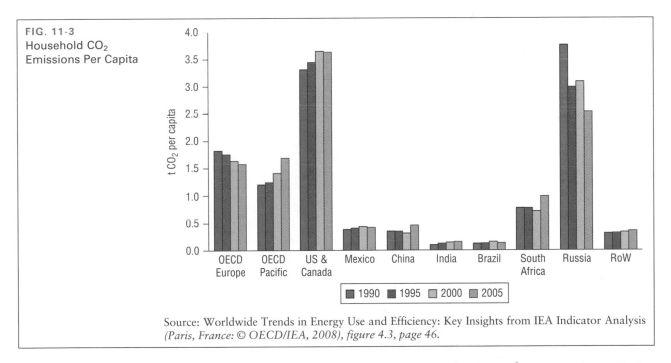

FIG. 11-3
Household CO$_2$
Emissions Per Capita

Source: Worldwide Trends in Energy Use and Efficiency: Key Insights from IEA Indicator Analysis *(Paris, France: © OECD/IEA, 2008), figure 4.3, page 46.*

related to heating equipment, building design, and insulation.[6] Importantly, analysis of space heating must examine the productivity of the entire system rather than a single facet of space heating. The **whole-building concept** encompasses consideration of the location, infrastructure, utilities, and ancillary devices within the home.[7] Ancillary devices include appliances and lighting addressed in a subsequent section.

Consumers that seek to limit their space heating costs should consider all facets of the whole-building concept. The first consideration is the location. Location

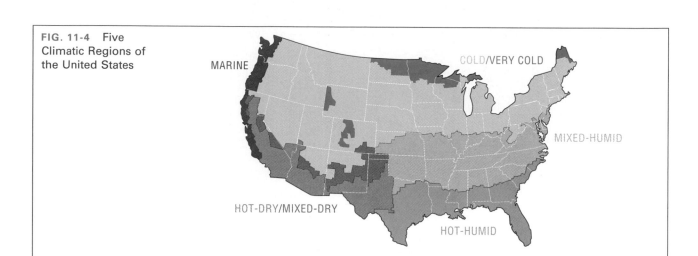

FIG. 11-4 Five Climatic Regions of the United States

MARINE

COLD/VERY COLD

MIXED-HUMID

HOT-DRY/MIXED-DRY

HOT-HUMID

Source: *U.S. Department of Energy*

consideration includes the climate and the specific housing location. The U.S. Department of Energy, for example, classifies the climates in the contiguous 48 states into five climatic regions as outlined in Figure 11-4. Climate dictates the need for heating and cooling as well as the efficiency of alternative forms of these home utilities and components of the infrastructure of the house. For example, windows that offer optimal insulation in cold climates are less than effective in southern regions because they tend to localize overheating and sun glare.

Another important location consideration is the actual site of the home. Management of energy and light from the sun should be considered in location decisions. Proper orientation of a house can result in substantial savings of heating and cooling costs, and the orientation is dependent on specific site conditions and house designs. For most designs, homes that favor exposure to the north or south generally encounter less sunlight and are therefore preferred to homes with pronounced exposure to the east and west.[8] Planting of shade trees limits a home's exposure to sun, whereas site grading and landscaping assist in maintaining the integrity of the building.[9]

The second aspect of the home-related heating cost is the infrastructure. The infrastructure includes the walls, roof, foundation, windows and doors, natural lighting, and duct system in the home. The energy efficiency of most components of the infrastructure varies based on environmental factors, design needs, and climate zone. Windows and doors that use multiple panes of glass and incorporate argon or krypton gases offer substantial energy savings that result in needing smaller heating and ventilation systems.[10] Nevertheless, the value to the consumer of these doors and windows varies by climatic zone. *U-factor* is the measure that indicates how well a product prevents heat from escaping a home or building, and the solar heat gain coefficient (SHGC) measures how well a product blocks heat from the sun. While northern climates prefer products that prevent heat loss, southern climates prefer products that provide shade.[11]

Examination of the infrastructure must also consider areas where air is transferred between the inside and outside of the home. Figure 11-5 illustrates potential sources of heat and energy transfer in a single-family dwelling. The U.S. Environmental Protection Agency (EPA) estimates that a homeowner can save 10% of a home's total energy costs (equivalent to 20% of heating and cooling costs) by air

FIG. 11-5 Potential Sources of Air Transfer

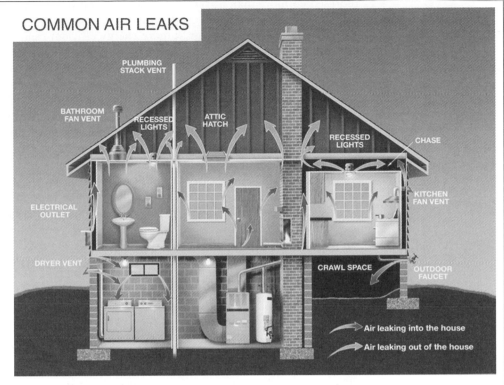

COMMON AIR LEAKS

Source: © AP Images/PRNewsFoto/US GreenFiber LLC

sealing the home and providing proper insulation materials in the attic, over the crawlspace, and in the basement.[12]

The utilities in the home are the heating and air-conditioning systems. Since the oil crisis of the mid 1970s, governments have been establishing standards for these home utilities. As technology has advanced, the productivity of these systems has increased along with increases in efficiency standards. For example, gas steam boilers sold in the United States that were required to have a minimum of 75 % efficiency in 1987 must now be at least 84% efficient.[13]

Although space heating capabilities and insulation have improved, these gains have been offset by a higher number of dwellings occupied by fewer people. Although fewer people may live in a dwelling, the heating costs may not be reduced.[14] In some markets, the space heating needs are further increased by increases in home size. For example, in the United States, houses built in the 1990s heat 33% more floor space than homes built before 1950.[15]

The Energy Star branding discussed in Chapter 4 has also been expanded to include the housing sector. Through the EPA Web site[16], consumers can gain access to builders of on-site and modular homes that offer Energy Star homes. In addition, consumers can also gain access to lenders that offer special rates for energy-efficient housing.

Appliances Energy consumption analysis for appliances distinguishes between large and other appliances. Large appliances include refrigerators, freezers, washing machines, dishwashers, and televisions. Figure 11-7 illustrates how the usage of energy among these products has changed over time. Although large appliances once represented more than 60% of fuel consumption (Figure 11-6a), all large appliances except televisions have reduced their average energy consumption with time (Figure 11-6b). Television technology is more energy efficient than it was 20 years ago, but the average screen is substantially larger than the previous era.

The proliferation of small appliances represents an increasingly important part of household energy consumption. These devices include mobile phones, personal computers, personal audio equipment, and other home electronics. Many of these products continue to draw energy even though their batteries are recharged and the products are not currently in use. Consequently, product developers have strived to achieve minimal levels of energy absorption during inactive modes. Another aspect of productivity for these devices is the level of efficiency during operational mode. There are nearly 2.5 billion devices in use that rely on power supplies in the United States alone.[17] These supplies may be located inside or outside of devices such as cordless phones, answering machines, video games, computer speakers, and cordless tools. Research indicates that enhanced efficiency of power supplies could yield savings equivalent to 1% of the total United States electricity use. This energy savings of 32 billion kilowatts per year is equivalent to the power output of seven large nuclear or coal-fired power plants.[18]

Water Heating

The third largest percentage of home energy consumption is water heating. Multiple means for heating water are employed in various countries, but in many cases data outlining the extent to which sustainable sources of energy are used are unavailable.[19] In the United States, most traditional storage units are either gas or electric. Of the 9.8 million water heater shipments in 2006, 4.8 million were conventional

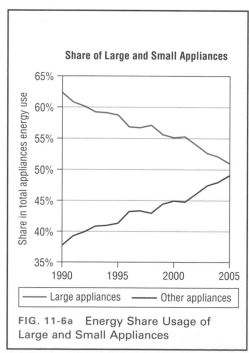

FIG. 11-6a   Energy Share Usage of Large and Small Appliances

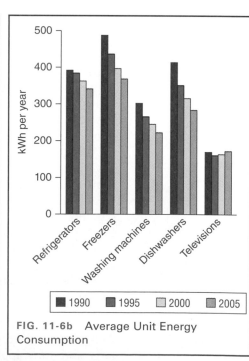

FIG. 11-6b   Average Unit Energy Consumption

Source: International Energy Agency, Worldwide Trends in Energy Use and Efficiency: Key Insights from the IEA Indicator Analysis *(Paris, France: © OECD/IEA, 2008).*

electric resistance and 4.7 million were conventional gas storage.[20] Advanced water heating technologies constitute a small portion of the market. Of the advanced technologies, gas tankless water heaters represent 2.6% of the market (254,600 units in 2006). Tankless water heaters do not contain a storage tank and operate when there is a demand for hot water. The elimination of standby losses from the tank reduces energy consumption by 10 to 15%. Solar water heater shipments were estimated at 2,430 units in the same year.

The use of solar energy for heating water varies markedly by country. The current volume of solar energy usage for water heating amounts to an annual avoidance of 34.1 million tons of carbon dioxide emissions and the equivalent to 12.1 billion liters of oil.[21] At the end of 2005, worldwide operation of solar thermal energy was 111.0 gigawatts (GW). Of those, 86.3 GW were associated with flat-plate and evacuated-tube collectors primarily used for home water heating, and the remaining 23.9 GW were associated with unglazed plastic collectors used for heating swimming pools. China, the largest market for the flat-plate technology, represents 48% of the world market. Turkey, Japan, Germany, Israel, and Greece are also leading countries in terms of the total demand for flat-plate and evacuated-tube technology. The United States is the primary market for the unglazed plastic collectors technology.

Lighting and Cooking

Lighting and cooking together represent about 10% of energy consumption in the home. In many regions of the world, marketers of lighting and cooking appliances have developed mandatory efficiency standards. Standards such as Energy Star have been effective in eliminating the most inefficient models from the market. In addition, countries have implemented labeling that identifies the energy consumption of products and endorsement labels (e.g., Energy Star) that promote the most energy-efficient products.[22] The Efficient Lighting Initiative (ELI) is an international branding system for high-quality, energy-efficient lighting products. In 2005, the China Standard Certification Center (CSC) was commissioned to develop the ELI certification and branding system globally. The expanded ELI program is operated by the ELI Quality Certification Institute. This institute is led by CSC with assistance from a team of international experts from Asia, North America, and Latin America. The ELI Quality Certification Institute is currently promoting voluntary technical specifications for energy-efficient fluorescent lighting. It is focusing on the developing countries of Asia/Asia Pacific, Latin America, and Africa and seeks to harmonize its test methods and performance specifications with other voluntary labeling programs internationally.[23]

Food

The energy use associated with food consumption includes the direct energy consumption associated with shopping trips as well as the storing and cooking of food. The indirect costs are those associated with agricultural production, food processing, and distribution. The indirect costs are substantially greater than the direct costs.[24] In addition to fossil fuel usage, food production is also a source of methane and nitrous oxide. Methane is associated with animal production, and nitrous oxide is derived from fertilizer. Although these gases are powerful greenhouse gases, they do not represent the primary sources of energy use in food consumption.

The primary food energy use occurs during the processing and distribution of food. In the United States, approximately 10% of the total primary energy supply is associated with food production. Only 20% of this energy is attributed to farm production. Thirty-four percent of farm production energy use is for farm vehicles, 28% is in fertilizer use, and the remainder is used for irrigation, crop drying, pesticides, and other farm operations. By contrast, the remaining 80% of energy is used for food processing, storage, packaging, and retail distribution. Processed foods make up three fourths of total world food sales, and the costs to process food are substantial. For instance, processing breakfast cereals requires more than five times as much energy as is contained in the cereal itself. These processed foods are often individually wrapped, bagged, and boxed. This packaging requires large amounts of energy and raw materials to produce, yet most of it ends up in landfills.[25]

The recognition that food processing is a central issue in food energy costs has prompted speculation about reduction measures. The use of organic food has been touted as a way to eliminate fertilizer and pesticide costs while enhancing food quality. Because organic farms have lower yields per acre, however, more fuel is required for clearing land, cultivating, and harvesting.[26] A second consideration is the degree to which the consumer diet relies on meat products versus grains, vegetables, and fruits. Meat tends to require more energy for production than vegetables, and reductions in this area should influence carbon emissions. Nevertheless, a recent Swedish study suggested that transitioning to a nutritionally and environmentally sustainable diet would result in a negligible change in energy use and greenhouse gas emission.[27] These findings suggest that there is a need to develop a keener understanding of consumption and its ramifications for energy use and other essential areas, including nutrition.

B. Understand the Consumer Decision-making Process

The **consumer decision-making process** is the series of steps that buyers take before, during, and after consumption. Marketers have the opportunity to influence consumption at each stage of the buying process. Figure 11-7 provides an overview of the various stages of the process from prepurchase evaluation to postpurchase product disposal. The process that a consumer goes through when deciding to trade in a currently owned car for a new automobile provides the opportunity to examine all phases of this decision-making process.

The first stage of the decision-making process is the **prepurchase stage**. The first phase of this stage is **need recognition**, or the point at which a consumer senses a difference between an ideal state of affairs and the current state.[28] For example, the driver of a 1996 Camry may realize that the cost of recurring repairs for this car puts her in a less-than-desirable situation.

Once consumers realize a gap between current and ideal conditions, they begin to **search** for alternatives. Thus, *search* refers to efforts to acquire information and solutions that satisfy unmet needs. Consumers engage in search behavior to bridge the gap between current conditions and an ideal state of affairs. For example, the owner of the Camry may search for new cars that have warranties that suggest consumers will not have to invest time or money in auto repairs.

The third phase in the prepurchase stage is the **prepurchase evaluation** of alternatives. In this phase, consumers evaluate options identified during the search

FIG. 11-7 Consumer Decision-making Process	Stage of the Process	Phase of the Decision-making Process	Example
	Prepurchase	*Need recognition:* point at which a consumer senses a difference between an ideal state of affairs and the current state	The driver of a 1996 Camry realizes that the cost of recurring car repairs puts her in a less-than-desirable situation.
		Search: efforts to acquire information and solutions that satisfy unmet needs. Consumers engage in search behavior to bridge the gap between current conditions and an ideal state of affairs.	The Camry owner searches for new cars that have warranties that suggest consumers will not have to invest time or money in auto repairs.
		Prepurchase evaluation: Consumers evaluate options identified during the search process.	The Camry owner evaluates current Toyota and General Motors cars based on price, fuel efficiency, and other attributes
	Purchase Stage	*Purchase decision:* Consumer decides whether and the conditions under which to buy the product.	The Camry owner buys a new Prius at the local Toyota dealership.
	Consumption	*Product usage:* the manner in which the consumer uses the product	The owner of a new Prius may decide to use the automobile in a variety of ways that have repercussions for the environment if the tires on the car are not properly inflated.
	Postconsumption	*Postconsumption evaluation:* evaluation of a product after consumption has occurred	The former Camry owner is no longer satisfied with the car. The Camry's value is exceeded by that of the Prius.
		Divestment: disposal of products after they no longer offer utility to the consumer	The Camry is traded in to the dealer in purchase of the Prius.

process. Thus, the owner of the Camry may evaluate current Toyota and General Motors cars based on price, fuel efficiency, and other attributes.

Once consumers have engaged in the prepurchase evaluations, they enter the second stage. The **purchase stage** refers to the point at which the consumer decides whether and the conditions under which to buy the product. The owner of the Camry may elect to go to the local Toyota dealer to purchase a new Prius automobile.

The third stage of the consumer decision-making process refers to the **consumption** of a product offering. This stage refers to the manner in which the product is used by the consumer. The owner of a new Prius, for example, may decide to use the automobile in a variety of ways that have repercussions for the environment. For example, if the tires on the car are not properly inflated, the fuel efficiency of the car will suffer dramatically.

The fourth and final stage of the consumer decision-making process is the **postconsumption stage**. After consumption begins, the consumer makes periodic evaluations of product performance in light of expectations before the purchase. **Postconsumption evaluation** refers to the evaluation of a product after consumption has occurred. At some point, the consumer recognizes that the value of a currently owned product is not substantially lower than alternatives. The former Camry owner has evaluated that the car's value is exceeded by the Prius. **Divestment** refers to the disposal of products after they no longer offer utility to the consumer.

If green marketers are to have an influence on the entire consumption process, it is essential that they understand the nature of decision making throughout the consumer decision-making process. Therefore, we dedicate the remainder of this chapter to understanding and influencing consumer decision making. Consider first the prepurchase stage.

C. Identify Sustainable Marketing Action Designed to Influence Prepurchase Decisions

Consumers may pass through three phases before they are ready to make a purchase, and green marketing initiatives can play an important role throughout the prepurchase stage. The first phase, need recognition, occurs when the consumer recognizes a discrepancy between current and desired conditions. Several inherent conditions can influence consumer perceptions of the current state of affairs. For example, someone buying groceries for a home knows that the passage of time influences food quality. Although the consumer may realize a discrepancy between current conditions and desired states, the marketer can have a strong influence on both facets of need recognition. Marketers often stimulate demand by altering consumer perceptions of currently owned products. For example, the GE Silicone III ad depicted in Figure 11-8a informs consumers that up to 40% of the energy used to heat and cool a home may be lost due to leakage associated with tiny cracks and holes in the home's exterior. The current state, the porous exterior, is less desirable than the desired state, the silicone-sealed home exterior.

The second way in which to influence need recognition is to increase the perceived value of alternative products. For example, the ad depicted in Figure 11-8b informs consumers that Osram fluorescent bulbs last several years at normal usage.

When a firm elects to stimulate need recognition, it has two essential means by which to do so. First, the organization may employ a **generic need recognition strategy** to stimulate demand by drawing attention to the entire product class.[29] The two ads depicted in Figure 11-8 exemplify promotions designed to stimulate demand for compact fluorescent bulbs rather than for the offerings of a single manufacturer such as Osram/Sylvania. Since many environmentally based product offerings are in their infancy, it is not uncommon for advertisers to promote the product class rather than a specific product. Advertisers promoting green marketing and sustainability projects may be sellers of the product, but they may also represent some other interest group. These groups may include industry-wide advocacy groups, nongovernment organizations, governmental agencies, utilities, industry foundations, or other parties. For example, utility companies and NGO's (nongovernment organizations) may share the cost of campaigns that promote the use of compact fluorescent light bulbs. Each of these groups has motivations to limit the amount of energy consumed, and fluorescent lighting helps them achieve this objective.

Brand-specific need recognition refers to efforts to stimulate demand for a specific branded product rather than for the industry or technology. For example, the Burt's Bees ad in Figure 11-9 emphasizes purchases of the brand rather than the

FIG. 11-8a Stimulate Need Recognition by Altering Consumer Perceptions of Currently Owned Products

Source: © *AP Images/PRNewsFoto/GE Sealants and Adhesive*

FIG. 11-8b Stimulate Need Recognition by Altering Consumer Perceived Value of Alternative Products

Source: © *Image courtesy of The Advertising Archives*

product class. In some industries, the need to draw awareness of a product category is essential prior to marketing the merits of a single purveyor. For example, Figure 11-9 draws attention to the merits of beeswax while at the same time calling attention to the Burt's Bees brand.

Once consumers identify unmet needs, they begin to engage in search activities to satisfy the need. The search activities can be internal or external to the consumer. **Internal search** refers to retrieving knowledge from memory, whereas **external search** refers to collecting information from outside sources.[30] In many cases, consumers rely solely upon previous experiences in their search efforts. Consumer psychology indicates that reliance on prior experiences is dependent on the degree of confidence in the decision making, satisfaction with prior decisions, and the ability to retrieve knowledge.[31]

The strategic implication of the internal search lies in recognizing the extent to which a consumer relies on personal experiences to frame judgments. Consumers that express high levels of confidence in brands that offer high levels of satisfaction will be reluctant to consider new information in their purchasing decisions. If the marketer has the luxury of this consumer as a client, then the marketing effort should emphasize how new product offerings retain attributes that yield high satisfaction yet provide new environmental benefits that exceed prior product offerings. When this consumer is not currently a firm's client, the task of promotion is much more challenging because it may be necessary to persuade the consumer to seek additional information.

External search efforts draw information from the environment so that evaluations can be made about product offerings. Family, friends, the media, and opinion leaders are sources of information not controlled by marketers of a product. This information may come via word of mouth or, increasingly, by *word of mouse* computer-based interaction. Word-of-mouth communication has been shown to be the most important source of influence in the purchase of household goods.[32]

FIG. 11-9 Brand-specific Need Recognition

Source: © AP Images/PRNewsFoto/Burt's Bees

In addition, research indicates that advice from other consumers about a service exerts more influence than all marketer-generated information combined.[33] Word-of-mouse communication using Facebook, Twitter and other services enables consumers to nurture relationships, refine evaluations of brands, develop an understanding of marketer efforts to influence decisions, and reflect upon the consumption experience.[34]

External search efforts provide an opportunity for nonmarketing entities to influence consumer decision-making processes. Nongovernment organizations can be informative to consumers engaged in search activities. Greenpeace, for example, annually publishes a *Guide to Greener Electronics* that evaluates electronics companies based on chemical usage, e-waste, and energy consumption. Similarly, *Consumer Reports* has published evaluations of the degree to which companies have achieved product claims such as being environmentally friendly, biodegradable, and gentle on the earth.[35]

Marketers must make several considerations based on these external sources of information. First, they must examine the degree to which the consumer is involved in the purchase because involved consumers are inclined to spend more time evaluating alternatives and collecting information.[36] Consumers are more likely to collect more information about an auto purchase, for example, than the purchase of paper towel. Second, the marketer should consider the degree to which the consumer is likely to rely on the information provided by the third party. Given the amount of information available today, there are likely to be many credible sources of information that are not incorporated into search activities. Underwriters Laboratories and the United Nations, for example, publish substantial amounts of product information, but it is questionable whether consumers use this information during their external search efforts. While it would be reckless for the marketer to ignore these sources of information, the sources are not frequently incorporated into decision making.

The third consideration for green marketing strategy concerns the nature of the evaluations by the external source. When positive evaluations are provided by third parties, they can become effective parts of a marketing campaign. For example, the Honda Motor Company uses data from the U.S. Environmental Protection Agency to support its claim of being the most fuel-efficient car company in North America. When evaluations of company products are not favorable, the firm should investigate the evaluation process. To the extent that the evaluation is flawed, marketers should be explicit in expressing concerns for the basis for evaluation. Furthermore, evaluations that indicate limitations in current product offerings provide impetus for new product designs. For example, the Chevrolet announcement of the Volt electric car was motivated in part by the less-than-favorable evaluations of older models of General Motors cars.[37]

After consumers engage in search activities, they make their initial prepurchase evaluations.[38] Consumers often use evaluative criteria that are standards and specifications used in the comparison of different brands and products. Consumer psychology distinguishes between *salient product attributes* that are important to the decision and *determinant product attributes* that influence which brand or product will be chosen.

Although the merits of green marketing initiatives may be known to the consumer, these product benefits are rarely the primary motivation for purchase decisions. The green marketer must necessarily assess the value of a product offering in its entirety rather than solely on the environmental value. In their book examining sustainability strategies, Daniel Esty and Andrew S. Winston emphasize that green benefits of a product are typically at least the third benefit offered by a product.[39] Thus, hybrid automobiles provide a family of benefits beyond fuel efficiency that must be considered by marketing strategy. Japanese researchers, for instance, report that drivers understand the deleterious influences of greenhouse gases, but recognition of the problem does not lead to purchases of fuel-efficient cars.[40] In the Japanese market, researchers discovered that price constraints made purchases of some hybrid or fuel-efficient cars infeasible. The marketer that wants to influence green consumption must have a product offering with comparable value to the consumer that also provides environmental benefits. When consumers realize the total value offered by products developed through sustainability efforts, the likelihood of purchase should also increase.

D. Identify Sustainable Marketing Action Designed to Influence Purchases

The second stage of the decision-making process is the point at which the consumer decides to make a purchase. This decision has many components that can be influenced by green marketing strategy. The essence of this stage is the actual purchase of the product. A central issue in the decision process is the level of involvement consumers have with the purchase. When consumers are heavily involved in the purchase, they perceive differences among brands, express interest in gathering information about the product category, and make comparisons about product attributes among brands.[41] Appeals to heavily involved consumers can be designed to illustrate the long-term returns from purchases of environmentally friendly products. Marketers should identify the sources of information for these purchases and monitor evaluations of their products at the information sources. For example, the automobile owner that is heavily interested in buying a fuel-efficient and environmentally friendly auto may rely on reviews in *Car and Driver* and *Consumer Reports*. It is clearly important for strategists and public relations managers at auto companies to keep pace with news articles in these periodicals.

Most consumer decisions do not rely on heavy involvement of the consumer. Indeed, most mundane purchases are performed without much cognitive effort. Under low-involvement conditions, there is a greater likelihood that conditions surrounding the purchase influence the selection decision. Therefore, in-store promotions and point-of-sale displays can have an influence on these consumers when they make purchases.[42]

There are a couple of notable means marketers employ in packaging and paper usage that influence the emissions associated with purchasing. In general, purchasing that limits the amount of paper yields lower emission costs. Note that this cost is substantial given that $1 of every $11 spent in the grocery store goes to packaging.[43] Simpler packaging limits waste and is therefore preferred. Paper can be virtually eliminated, for example, when the consumer downloads software rather than purchasing it in a store.

The nature of the good also influences the carbon emission associated with selling products. Marketers in multiple industries offer products that either economize on product usage or employ recyclable materials. Both economical design and recycling limit energy consumption. For example, if every United States consumer replaced one roll of 1,000 sheet virgin fiber bathroom tissues with recycled paper, 373,000 trees, 1.48 million cubic feet of landfill space, and 155 million gallons of water would be saved.[44] Substitution of recycled materials is not limited to paper; marketers of athletic apparel and bedding also offer many products with recycled components. An alternative to recycling is to offer products that can be reused. For instance, refillable razors enable the consumer to reuse the product and only discard the cutting mechanism. These efforts to recycle or reuse product should influence some consumers as they make purchase decisions.

A second consideration endemic to the purchase is the timing of the purchase. The timing of purchases influences not only the costs of delivery but also the environmental costs associated with the product. Consider, for example, that the U.S. Post Office handles more than 10 million packages per day.[45] Transportation consumes 75% of their $2.35 billion annual budget. When the consumer elects to send a letter via traditional mail courier, the price of a 1-ounce letter is $0.42. If the letter needs to be sent overnight, however, the cost is $16.50. Unfortunately, postal services do not currently provide consumers with information concerning the carbon-related costs of sending the letter. Since expedited services are related to the use of faster transportation services that generate more carbon dioxide, it is likely that the expedited services come with heftier carbon costs. It seems reasonable to suspect that consumers informed about greenhouse gases will find situations in which the environmental cost of overnight delivery exceeds the returns from the service.

The decision about where to buy a product is related to the timing decision. In today's Internet economy, the consumer has a variety of ways to shop. Some firms, for example, espouse online shopping because the person buying in the home is not burning fossil fuel to get to the store. Of course, the environmental cost of two alternative locations is driven by the transportation costs for the product and the consumer. The consumer buying books online may have lower personal transport costs, but the carbon-based costs of delivering multiple books (from multiple locations) will likely be greater than the costs incurred by a local bookstore. Clearly, consideration of where to purchase needs to examine the entire carbon-related costs of purchasing. Note that services such as Apple's iTunes yield minimal product delivery costs and consumer transportation costs.

Timing of the purchase decision for hot water heaters contributes to the continuing small percentage of solar heating. In the United States, for example, two thirds of consumers replace their water heaters due to sudden failure of their existing model. Of those replacements, 60% are emergency replacements.[46] When a water heater fails suddenly, consumers typically have their water heater replaced with the cheapest, most readily available and easily installed model from their plumber or contractor. The timing of the purchase and the need for quick replacement do not encourage consumers to make the extra effort to consider advanced technologies or lifetime cost savings.[47]

E. Identify Sustainable Marketing Action Designed to Influence Consumption

The consumption process continues as the consumer makes the transition from purchase to usage. The consumer that buys the product must decide the time, place, and manner by which to consume.[48] Socially responsible marketing can direct each of these facets of consumption in a manner that promotes sustainability. First, consider the timing of consumption.

Timing

The timing of consumption is related to the timing of purchasing, but these temporal concerns often occur at different times. Consumers ordinarily have some flexibility regarding the time at which they buy products. In the food sector, for example, consumers buying produce and groceries often monitor the expiration dates when making purchases. In one study, consumer psychologists found evidence that up to 12% of products bought for the pantry are never consumed.[49] Among food products that are stored in a consumer's pantry before consumption, this same research indicates that 57% of these stockpiled purchases are thrown away. Consequently, the environmental cost to manufacture and distribute the product is realized, but there is no consumer benefit from the purchase. Purchase without consumption therefore raises the carbon footprint of the consumer without added value. One marketing implication is to market specific-use products close to the usage date for the product. For example, sale of canned pumpkin should be promoted very close to the Canadian and United States Thanksgiving holidays. In addition, marketing communications about product usage should be timely and frequent.[50] For example, the Campbell's Soup Web page and advertisements provide reminders and helpful usage ideas that decrease the likelihood that the product will be stockpiled.

Despite the merits of promotional activities that emphasize proper use of products, advertising emphasizes the immediate purchase of products rather than usage. Since consumer education regarding proper use of a product reduces the consumer's carbon footprint and enhances customer satisfaction, marketers should consider dedicating some portion of advertising to product usage. In addition, many of these food products that will never be consumed can be recycled as donations to community action groups. Public service announcements that promote this form of recycling aid the underprivileged and lower the carbon footprint of the community.

Location (Place)

The place chosen to consume products can have a marked influence on the sustainability of the product. In the restaurant industry, for example, consumers have purchased more takeout food than on-premise meals since 1988.[51] Restaurants like these off-premise meals because they increase revenue without raising costs associated with dining facilities. Nevertheless, the amount and form of materials used for carry-out items typically exceed the costs for on-premises meals.

This trend toward carry-out sales has typically been associated with the quick-service portion of the business, but increasingly, casual-dining restaurants are offering takeout food in the form of home meal replacement. In 2007, 47% of casual dining restaurateurs forecasted increases in the amount of carry-out business. Meals taken away from the casual dining restaurants often are designed to be reheated in a microwave. In many cases, the restaurateur has to weigh the additional cost of sustainably developed packaging versus the lower costs of alternative packaging (e.g., Styrofoam).

Manner of Consumption

The manner of consumption refers to how and how much of a product consumers use. Consistent with the reduce–reuse–recycle perspective, this action should ensure reductions in the amount of product used. Consumption of many energy-consuming products can be enhanced via green marketing efforts. Although there is a wealth of information available regarding energy consumption, consumers in many cases are either unaware that this information exists or they do not act based on this information. Consider first how consumption of energy to heat homes could be done more efficiently.

Efforts to enhance space heating must address both the amount of energy consumed and the related factor of how the energy is consumed. Although there have been strides in the fuel efficiency of heaters, the average American home wastes 30 to 50% of the energy it uses. The consumer's energy bill and carbon footprint are lowest when the home is properly sealed and insulated.[52] Duct systems should be periodically inspected for leakage because porous duct systems waste substantial amounts of energy. Similarly, ducts located in unheated parts of the home (e.g., attic) should be insulated to reduce heat loss in the system. Air filters should be changed in accordance with manufacturer requirements because the clean filters remove debris that reduces the efficiency of heating systems. Where possible, consumers should also use ceiling fans rather than air conditioners. Ceiling fans are substantially less expensive to operate than room and central air units.[53] The homeowner should also recognize that older heating systems are less efficient than systems of today. If the central heating unit is 15 years old, then it is likely that a new system will lower the consumer's energy cost. Consumers should also consider adjusting thermostats to relatively low temperatures in the winter and high temperatures in the summer. Home energy managers that use digital controls provide the ability to control multiple appliances, maintain the utility of the appliances, and conserve energy[54]

The manner of consumption also influences the fuel efficiency of water heaters and therefore their carbon emissions. First, consumers should recognize that every minute saved in the shower can conserve more than four gallons of water. Shorter showers use less water and require less energy to heat warm water. Similarly, low-flow plumbing devices reduce consumption of energy and water. Showers account for about 20% of total indoor water use. By replacing standard 4.5-gallon-per-minute showerheads with 2.5-gallon-per-minute heads, a family of four can save approximately 20,000 gallons of water per year. These low-flow devices cost less than $5 each.[55] Energy use can also be curtailed by insulating the water heater and hot water pipes. Water heater insulation jackets can save 4 to 9% of water heating bills, and insulation of pipes also reduces energy costs. In addition, maintaining the water heater at lower temperatures saves energy; a 10°F reduction in water temperature generally saves 3 to 5% on water heating costs.[56]

The cost and carbon emissions associated with appliances and lighting can also be enhanced by effective consumption. Many appliances use batteries that account for a disproportionate amount of the toxic heavy metals contained in municipal solid waste, yet they make up less than 1% of that waste[57]. Single-use alkaline batteries contain fewer toxic chemicals than rechargeable batteries, but there are many more of them in the waste stream. Nickel-cadmium and lead-acid batteries have been targeted for elimination under an anticipated European Union directive, and they are banned from solid-waste disposal facilities in several states. A single rechargeable nickel-metal hydride or nickel-cadmium battery can replace up to 1,000 single-use alkaline batteries over its lifetime.[58] Although the toxins in rechargeable batteries warrant their recycling, all rechargeable batteries except alkalines can be recycled. Fuel consumption for appliances and lighting can also be reduced by turning off these electronic devices when they are not in use. Ten percent of the energy consumed in the home is burned by communications devices and appliances that are turned off. If U.S. citizens turned off their computers and cell phone chargers when they were not being used, the country would save more than $100 million.[59]

The manner in which food is consumed influences the environmental costs of consumption. Consumers can generate fewer emissions by efforts to reuse and reduce food-related products. Thus, consumers that reuse drinking receptacles limit the amount of solid waste. The water bottles that are sold in stores can be used over and over again to limit solid waste. The water that comes from the tap is more highly regulated than bottled water and is less expensive. Similarly, consumers that repeatedly use ceramic coffee mugs rather than Styrofoam cups limit environmental costs for product preparation and disposal. In addition, consumers can reduce consumption by using fewer napkins in restaurants and at home.

Another area of consumption that benefits from conservation is the use of paper. Conservation efforts that use less paper mean that less energy is consumed for production and less waste is generated after consumption. A simple way to reduce costs is to use both sides of paper when writing or making copies. In addition, one can save paper costs by printing multiple pages on each side of a page. Moreover, consumers should now question whether it is necessary to use paper when they communicate. Many messages can now be delivered via e-mail without loss of content to message equality. Consumers should also consider whether they need paper copies of financial data such as pay stubs, ATM receipts, and bank statements. Every time the consumer opts exclusively for the digital version of these items, carbon emissions are lowered.

F. Identify Sustainable Marketing Action Designed to Influence Postpurchase Decisions

The final stage of the consumer decision process occurs after some consumption of the product has begun. Postconsumption evaluation refers evaluation of a product after consumption has occurred. The buyer evaluates whether the level of satisfaction with the product meets or exceeds preperchase performance expectations. When the performance of the product meets or exceeds expectations, the level of satisfaction reported by the consumer is greater than when the product does not perform as expected.[60] Higher levels of satisfaction increase the likelihood of repeat purchases, mollify price sensitivities, and influence word-of-mouth communication about a product.[61] In addition, as the level of satisfaction decreases, the consumer is more likely to sense a difference between ideal conditions and current conditions. Low levels of satisfaction increase the likelihood of need recognition occurring that prompts the consumer to engage in the decision-making process. When this process leads to the purchase of new products, the consumer no longer has a need for the older products.

The recognition that a product no longer offers sufficient utility should prompt consideration about what to do with the product. Divestment refers to the disposal of products after consumers deem that the products no longer offer utility. The decision about how to deal with products that no longer offer utility is an important issue. Figure 11-10 and Table 11-1 indicate the amount of solid waste produced in the United States in 2005. Note that the percentage of reclamation varies markedly across products and ranges from 2.4% for food to 72% for nonferrous metals. Lead-acid batteries are recovered at a rate of 98.8%, whereas high levels of newspapers (88.9%), corrugated boxes (71.5%), major appliances (67.0%), steel packaging (63.3%), and aluminum cans (44.8 %) are also recovered.

Before disposal occurs, the consumer must evaluate whether the product offers value to the owner or some other consumer. Thus, the consumer should decide whether the product can be *reused* in some way. For example, packaging and shopping bags are often reused for storage purposes. Consumers have always engaged in

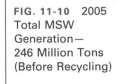

FIG. 11-10 2005 Total MSW Generation— 246 Million Tons (Before Recycling)

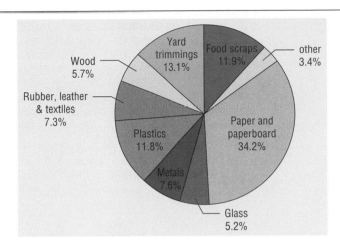

Source: *U.S. Environmental Protection Agency "Municipal Solid Waste", http://www.epa.gov/osw/ nonhaz/municipal/pubs/mswchar05.pdf (accessed March 16, 2010).*

some forms of this activity, but increasingly they recognize value in the reuse of products in novel ways. For example, yard and food waste account for about 25% of consumer waste in the United States. The disposal of these items in landfills is not the most environmentally effective means of divestment. Yard waste breaks down slowly in landfills and produces methane gas and acidic leachate as it decays.[62] Composting of this waste has the potential to reduce municipal solid waste by almost one fourth, and it also contributes to improved soil structure, texture, aeration, and water retention. Another means for facilitating reuse is to donate products. Computers, cell phones, and other equipment may no longer have value to a user, but these products can offer utility to other consumers.

When the product is no longer useful or capable of being reused by the consumer, then one must consider whether the product offers utility to other consumers. A number of classes of products offer examples of ways to make products available to other consumers. In the auto industry, for instance, consumers often sell used cars or trade cars in when making a new purchase. One of the motivations to establish franchised channels in the auto industry was to facilitate resale of cars when they no longer offered utility to the consumer.[63] In conjunction with government, bottlers of soft drinks and malt beverages also work in some markets to enable reuse. In Norway, for example, more than 95% of all soft drink and beer containers are returned, reused, or recycled.[64]

The most prominent means for making products available to other consumers for use is the Internet. For example, eBay facilitated more than $60 billion in transactions in 2007, and the vast majority of these transactions involved making existing products available to other consumers.[65] eBay and other Internet merchants provide online markets for the resale of virtually every type of product.

When reuse or resale is infeasible, the consumer must find some other means to discard the product. *Recycling* of products can take many forms depending on the product class and consumer needs. Unwanted Appliances, for example, specializes in the removal of household appliances, exercise equipment, electronics, air conditioners, and water heaters. Most of the products that they buy are sold for scrap, but some products are resold to other consumers. Some industries that operate in

TABLE 11-1 GENERATION AND RECOVERY OF MATERI-ALS IN MUNICIPAL SOLID WASTE, 2005 (IN MILLIONS OF TONS AND PERCENT OF GENERATION OF EACH MATERIAL)

MATERIAL	WEIGHT GENERATED	WEIGHT RECOVERED	RECOVERY AS A PERCENTAGE OF GENERATION
Paper and paperboard	84.0	42.0	50.0
Glass	12.8	2.76	21.6
Metals			
Steel	13.8	4.93	35.8
Aluminum	3.21	0.69	21.5
Other nonferrous metals*	1.74	1.26	72.4
Total metals	18.7	6.88	36.8
Plastics	28.9	1.65	5.7
Rubber and leather	6.70	0.96	14.3
Textiles	11.1	1.70	15.3
Wood	13.9	1.31	9.4
Other materials	4.57	1.17	25.6
Total Materials in Products	180.7	58.4	32.3
Other wastes			
Food, other**	29.2	0.69	2.4
Yard trimmings	32.1	19.9	61.9
Miscellaneous inorganic wastes	3.69	Neg.	Neg.
Total Other Wastes	65.0	20.6	31.6
TOTAL MUNICIPAL SOLID WASTE	245.7	79.0	32.1

Source: *U.S. Environmental Protection Agency "Municipal Solid Waste," http://www.epa.gov/osw/ nonhaz/municipal/pubs/mswchar05.pdf (accessed March 16, 2010)*

conjunction have a remarkable job of recycling used products. The EU and U.S. auto industries, for instance, recycle more than 95% of auto batteries sold.[66]

In the consumer electronics industry, consumers have combined interests in recycling and in wanting to ensure that sensitive data are not compromised or accessed after recycling. Dell provides free recycling of old computers and peripherals when a new computer is purchased from the company. The company evaluates whether a product can be resold, and proceeds from this resale are returned to the customer. If the product cannot be resold, Dell recycles it in a manner consistent with local, state, and federal requirements.[67] Importantly, such services enable the consumer to recoup some part of the investment in the computer, securely dispose of the computer, and contribute positively to the environment.

Increasingly, there are community and corporate efforts that encourage the recycling of products that pose threats to persons exposed to products after consumption. Americans, for example, generate 1.6 million tons of household hazardous waste per year, and the average home can accumulate as much as 100 pounds of this waste stored in closets, basements, and garages.[68] Community action plans enable consumers to dispose of paints, cleaners, oils, batteries, and pesticides that require special care during disposal.

Although our treatment of recycling has focused on postconsumption, it is also meaningful to recognize that recycling today begins in the new-product development process. Savvy marketers are designing products in such a way that much of the product can be recouped after consumption. In the auto industry, approximately 15 million cars and trucks reach the end of their useful lives each year, and more than 75% of the materials from end-of-life vehicles are profitably recovered and recycled.[69] Planning for postconsumption enhances the value of products to consumers and limits the influence of the products on the environment.

Summary

A. Identify Influences of Households on Energy Consumption

Households consume energy through space heating, appliances, water heating, lighting, and cooking. The rate of consumption varies considerably throughout the world, with the United States and Canada markedly outstripping levels in other countries.

B. Understand the Consumer Decision-making Process

The *consumer decision-making process* is the series of steps that buyers take before, during, and after consumption. The first stage of the decision-making process is the prepurchase stage. The first phase of this stage is need recognition, or the point at which a consumer senses a difference between an ideal state of affairs and the current state. Once consumers realize a gap between current and ideal conditions, they begin to search for alternatives (the second phase). The third phase in the prepurchase stage is the prepurchase evaluation of alternatives. The purchase stage refers to the point at which the consumer decides whether and the conditions under which to buy the product. The third stage of the consumer decision process refers to the consumption of a product offering. The final stage of the consumer decision-making process is the postconsumption stage.

C. Identify Sustainable Marketing Action Designed to Influence Prepurchase Decisions

Need recognition occurs when the consumer recognizes a discrepancy between current and desired conditions. Marketers often stimulate demand by altering consumer perceptions of currently owned products. They also may influence need recognition to increase the perceived value of alternative products. When a firm elects to stimulate need recognition, it may employ a generic need recognition strategy or employ a brand-specific need recognition designed to stimulate demand for a specific branded product.

D. Identify Sustainable Marketing Action Designed to Influence Purchases

The second stage of the decision-making process is the point at which the consumer decides to make a purchase. This decision has many components that can be influenced by green marketing strategy. A central issue in the decision process is the level of involvement consumers have with the purchase. When consumers are heavily involved in the purchase, they perceive differences among brands, express interest in gathering information about the product category, and make comparisons about product attributes among brands. Under low-involvement conditions, there is a greater likelihood that conditions surrounding the purchase will influence the selection decision. Therefore, in-store promotions and point-of-sale displays can have an influence on these consumers when they make purchases.

E. Identify Sustainable Marketing Action Designed to Influence Consumption

The consumption process continues as the consumer makes the transition from purchase to usage. The consumer that buys the product must decide the time, place, and manner by which to consume.

F. Identify Sustainable Marketing Action Designed to Influence Postpurchase Decisions

The final stage of the consumer decision-making process occurs after some consumption of the product has begun. The buyer evaluates whether the level of satisfaction with the product meets or exceeds performance expectations before the purchase. When the performance of the product meets or exceeds expectations, the level of satisfaction reported by the consumer is greater than when the product does not perform as expected. Higher levels of satisfaction increase the likelihood of repeat purchases, mollify price sensitivities, and influence word-of-mouth communication about a product. As the level of satisfaction decreases, the consumer is more likely to sense a difference between ideal conditions and current conditions. Low levels of satisfaction increase the likelihood of need recognition occurring that prompts the consumer to engage in the decision-making process. When this process leads to the purchase of new products, the consumer no longer has a need for the older products.

Keywords

brand-specific need recognition, 224
consumer decision-making process, 222
consumption, 223
divestment, 224

external search, 225
generic need recognition strategy, 224
internal search, 225
need recognition, 222
postconsumption evaluation, 223

postconsumption stage, 223
prepurchase evaluation, 222
prepurchase stage, 222
purchase stage, 223
search, 222
whole-building concept, 217

Questions

1. Why would designers such as Calvin Klein be interested in participating in a green fashion show?
2. How do companies benefit from examining the decision-making processes for sustainable products?
3. What are the trends for energy use for small and large appliances, and what ramifications do these trends have for marketing these products?
4. How can companies influence the need recognition process for consumers?
5. Why do companies adopt a generic need recognition strategy when they are trying to sell their specific brands?
6. How does the level of involvement influence consumer decision making, and how does this level influence the form of promotion used by a company marketing a sustainable product?
7. Why should a green marketer be concerned about consumption when revenue is generated when the product is sold?
8. Describe three factors that influence how a product is consumed.
9. To what extent do consumers engage in divestment, and how does this vary by product type?
10. What factors increase the likelihood that consumers will divest themselves of a product in a sustainable manner?

Endnotes

[1] Anna Kuchment, "Sense and Sensibility: Clothes That Are Stylish and Sustainable Are Hitting the Fashion Shows. Will They Get to Your Closet?" *Newsweek*, April 14, 2008, 68.

[2] Earhtpledge, "Earthpledge.org," http://www.earthpledge.org/ (accessed May 13, 2010).

[3] Earhtpledge, "About FutureFashion," http://www.earthpledge.org/ff (accessed May 13, 2010).

[4] Earhtpledge, "FutureFashion: Projects and Programs," http://www.earthpledge.org/ff/projects-andprograms (accessed May 13, 2010).

[5] See Note 1 above.

[6] United Nations Department of Social and Economic Affairs, "Sustainable Consumption and Production," April 30, 2007, 35, http://www.un.org/esa/sustdev/publications/household_consumption.pdf (accessed May 13, 2010).

[7] U.S. Department of Energy, "Residential Buildings: Energy Efficient Building Practices," http://www1.eere.energy.gov/buildings/residential/ (accessed May 13, 2010).

[8] Robin K. Vieira, Kenneth G. Sheinkopf, and Jeffrey K. Sonne, *Energy-Efficient Florida Home Building* (Cocoa, FL: Florida Solar Energy Center/University of Central Florida, Publication Number FSEC-GP-33-88), 7. http://www.fsec.ucf.edu/en/

consumer/buildings/homes/priorities.htm (accessed May 13, 2010).

[9] See Note 7 above.

[10] See Note 8 above.

[11] NFRC, "Questions About Doors and Energy? NFRC Has the Answers," http://www.nfrc.org/documents/Doors.pdf (accessed May 13, 2010).

[12] U.S. Environmental Protection Agency and the U.S. Department of Energy, "Air Seal and Insulate with Energy Star," http://www.energystar.gov/index.cfm?c=home_sealing.hm_improvement_sealing (accessed May 13, 2010).

[13] U.S. Department of Energy, "Residential Buildings: Energy Efficient Building Practices," http://www1.eere.energy.gov/buildings/appliance_standards/residential/pdfs/fb_fr_tsd/chapter_1.pdf (accessed May 13, 2010).

[14] International Energy Agency, *Worldwide Trends in Energy Use and Efficiency* (Paris, France: International Energy Agency, 2008), 94.

[15] Energy Information Association, "Table CE2-2c. Space-Heating Energy Consumption in U.S. Households by Year of Construction," in *2001 Residential Energy Consumption Survey*, http://www.eia.doe.gov/emeu/recs/recs2001/ce_pdf/spaceheat/ce2-2c_construction2001.pdf (accessed May 13, 2010).

[16] United States Environmental Protection Agency, http://www.epa.gov/ (accessed May 13, 2010).

[17] Electric Power Research Institute, "Energy Savings Opportunity by Increasing Power Supply Efficiency" http://www.efficientpowersupplies.org/efficiency_opportunities.html (accessed May 13, 2010).

[18] Chris Calwell and Travis Reeder "Power Supplies: A Hidden Opportunity for Energy Savings," Natural Resources Defense Council, http://www.efficientpowersupplies.org/pages/NRDC_power_supply_report.pdf (accessed May 13, 2010).

[19] See Note 6 above.

[20] Energy Star, "Energy Star® Residential Water Heaters: Draft Criteria Analysis," http://www.energystar.gov/ia/partners/prod_development/new_specs/downloads/water_heaters/WaterHeaterDraftCriteriaAnalysis.pdf (accessed May 13, 2010).

[21] Werner Weiss, Irene Bergmann, and Gerhard Faninger, *Solar Heat Worldwide* (Gleisdorf, Austria: International Energy Agency, 2008), 47.

[22] See Note 6 above.

[23] Efficient Lighting Initiative, "Learn About ELI," http://www.efficientlighting.net/index.php?option=com_content&task=view&id=18&Itemid=41 (accessed May 13, 2010).

[24] See Note 6 above.

[25] Danielle Murray, "Oil and Food: A New Security Challenge," *Asia Times* on-line, June 3, 2005, http://atimes01.atimes.com/atimes/Global_Economy/GF03Dj01.html (accessed May 13, 2010).

[26] See Note 6 above.

[27] Anna Wallén, Nils Brandt, and Ronald Wennersten, "Does the Swedish Consumer's Choice of Food Influence Greenhouse Gas Emissions?" *Environmental Science and Policy* 7, no. 6 (2004): 525–535.

[28] Roger D. Blackwell, Paul W. Miniard, and James F. Engel, *Consumer Behavior* (Mason, OH: Thomson Higher Education, 2005), 832.

[29] Amitav Chakravarti and Chris Janiszewski, "The Influence of Generic Advertising on Brand Preferences," *Journal of Consumer Research* 30, no. 4 (2004): 487–502.

[30] See Note 28 above.

[31] John T. Caioppo and Richard E. Petty, "The Elaboration Likelihood Model of Persuasion," *Advances in Consumer Research* 11, no. 1 (1984): 673–675; Geoffrey C. Kiel and Roger A. Lyon, "Dimensions of Consumer Information Seeking Behavior," *Journal of Marketing Research* 18, no. 2 (1981): 233–239.

[32] Elihu Katz, and Paul F. Lazarsfeld, *Personal Influence: The Part Played by People in the Flow of Mass Communications* (Glencoe, IL: The Free Press, 1955), 434.

[33] P. L. Alreck and R. B. Settle, "The Importance of Word-of-Mouth Communication to Service Buyers," *AMA Winter Educators' Proceedings*, ed. D. W. Stewart and N. J. VLlcassim (Chicago, IL: American Marketing Association, 1995), 188–193.

[34] H. M. Kineta Hung and Li Yiyan, "The Influence of eWOM on Virtual Consumer Communities: Social Capital, Consumer Learning, and Behavioral Outcomes," *Journal of Advertising Research* 47, no. 4 (2007): 485–495.

[35] "It's Not Easy Buying Green," *Consumer Reports* 72, no. 9 (2007): 9.

[36] Richard L. Celsi and Jerry C. Olson, "The Role of Involvement in Attention and Comprehension Processes," *Journal of Consumer Research* 15, no. 2 (1988): 210–224.

[37] Don Sherman, "G.M. at 100: Is Its Future Electric?" *New York Times*, September 14, 2008, AU1.

[38] See Note 28 above.

[39] Daniel C. Esty and Andrew S. Winston, *Green to Gold* (New Haven, CT: Yale University Press, 2006), 384.

[40] Kunihiro Kishi and Keiichi Satoh, "Evaluation of Willingness to Buy a Low-Pollution Car in Japan," *Journal of the Eastern Asia Society for Transportation Studies* 6, (2005): 3121–3134.

[41] Judith Lynne Zaichkowsky, "Measuring the Involvement Construct," *Journal of Consumer Research* 1, no. 3 (1985): 341–352.

[42] Hugh Philips and Roy Bradshaw, "How Customers Actually Shop: Customer Interaction with the Point of Sale," *Journal of the Market Research Society* 35, no. 1 (1993): 51–62.

[43] Elizabeth Rogers and Thomas M. Kostigen, *The Little Green Book* (New York, NY: Three Rivers Press, 2007), 201.

[44] eco.cycle, "Tidbits and Facts," http://www.ecocycle.org/tidbits/ (accessed May 13, 2010).

[45] U.S. Post Office Service, "Enhance Sustainability," http://www.usps.com/strategicplanning/stp2007/enhance_001.htm?from=greeninnovation&page=stp (accessed May 13, 2010).

[46] KEMA Inc., *Assessment of the Residential Water Heater Market in the Northwest* (Portland, OR: Northwest Energy Efficiency Alliance, 2005), 49.

[47] See Note 20 above.

[48] See Note 28 above.

[49] Brian, S. Wansink, Adam Brasel, and Steven Amjad, "The Mystery of the Cabinet Castaway: Why We Buy Products We Never Use," *Journal of Family and Consumer Sciences* 92, no. 1 (2000): 104–107.

[50] Brian Wansink and Rohit Deshpandé, "'Out of Sight, Out of Mind': Pantry Stockpiling and Brand Usage Frequency," *Marketing Letters* 5, no. 1 (1994): 91–100.

[51] Derek Gale "The Ten-Minute Manager's Guide to Improving Carryout Sales," Nation's Restaurant News, July 15, 2007, 20–21.

[52] University of Tennessee Agricultural Extension Service, "Tennessee Home-A-Syst," http://economics.ag.utk.edu/extension/pubs/sp508h.pdf (accessed May 13, 2010).

[53] See Note 43 above.

[54] Masahiro Inoue and others, "Network Architecture for Home Energy Management System," *IEEE Transactions on Consumer Electronics* 49, no. 3 (2003): 606–613.

[55] U.S. Environmental Protection Agency, "How to Conserve Water and Use It Effectively," http://www.epa.gov/owow/nps/nps-conserve.html (accessed May 13, 2010).

[56] American Council for an Energy-Efficient Economy, "Consumer Guide to Home Energy Savings: Condensed Online Version," http://www.aceee.org/consumerguide/waterheating.htm (accessed May 13, 2010).

[57] U.S. Environmental Protection Agency, "Wastes - Partnerships - Product Stewardship" http://www.epa.gov/epr/products/batteries.html (accessed May 13, 2010).

[58] Inform, "Fact Sheets," http://www.informinc.org/fact_CWP battery.php#note4 (accessed May 13, 2010).

[59] See Note 54 above.

[60] Richard L. Oliver, "A Cognitive Model of the Antecedents and Consequences of Satisfaction Decisions," *Journal of Marketing Research* 17, no. 4 (1980): 460–469.

[61] See Note 28 above.

[62] HowToCompost.org, "Composting: The Basics," http://www.howtocompost.org/info/info_composting.asp (accessed May 13, 2010).

[63] Charles L. Vaughn, *Franchising: Its Nature, Scope, Advantages and Development*, 2nd ed. (Lexington, MA.: Lexington Books, 1979), 281.

[64] Ole Jørgen Hanssen and others, "The Environmental Effectiveness of the Beverage Sector in Norway in a Factor 10 Perspective," *The International Journal of Life Cycle Assessment* 12, no. 4 (2007): 257–265.

[65] eBay, *Annual Report* (San Jose, CA: eBay, 2007), 213.

[66] Jason Gerrard and Milind Kandlika, "Is European End-of-life Vehicle Legislation Living up to Expectations? Assessing the Impact of the ELV Directive on 'Green' Innovation and Vehicle Recovery," *Journal of Cleaner Production* 15, no. 1 (2007): 17–27.

[67] Dell, "Environmental Responsibility," http://www.dell.com/content/topics/global.aspx/about_dell/values/sustainability/environment/env_resp?c=us&cs=19&l=en&s=dhs (accessed May 13, 2010).

[68] U.S. Environmental Protection Agency, "Household Hazardous Waste," http://www.epa.gov/osw/conserve/materials/hhw.htm (accessed May 13, 2010).

[69] Edward J. Daniels and others, "Sustainable End-of-life Vehicle Recycling: R&D Collaboration Between Industry and the U.S. DOE," *Journal of the Minerals, Metals and Materials Society* 56, no. 8 (2004): 28–32.

Energy Consumption in the Services Sector

A. Introduction: Service Sector Contributors to Carbon Emissions

KIMPTON HOTELS

A woman walks into a hotel bar in San Francisco and asks whether any of the featured wines are organic. At the same time, a vacationer checking into a room in New York asks whether the hotel uses recycled paper and nontoxic cleaning supplies. In both cases, the hotel and restaurant staff at Kimpton Hotels are able to provide a satisfying answer to the patrons. Founded in 1981, the Kimpton Hotel chain now includes more than 50 properties in the United States. Kimpton hotels boast the highest customer satisfaction and emotional attachment scores of any hotel company operating in America.[1]

Although many things contribute to the customer evaluations of a hotel, Kimpton has made a notable investment in sustainability for several years, and it has actively promoted this investment with its customers, vendors, and other stakeholders. One of the more noticeable features of these hotels is the practice of remodeling and refurbishing existing buildings in urban settings.[2] For example, Kimpton has transformed a Seattle building constructed in 1901 into the Alexis Hotel. These preservation activities nurture urban traditions while fostering increased sustainability.

In 2005, Kimpton initiated a campaign called EarthCare that examined more than 40 eco-friendly practices performed daily at each hotel.[3] The program involved such practices as placing recycling bins in guest rooms for the disposal of organic mini-bar items.[4] This program was developed with a particular interest in guest experience and financial performance. Kimpton recognized early on that this sustainability initiative would only be successful if it did not compromise the quality of the hotel experience or detract from the bottom line for shareholders.

As a complement to the EarthCare program, Kimpton also developed EarthCare Champions in every restaurant and hotel. Any associate can be a champion—from general managers to housekeepers. These champions meet twice a month to ensure compliance with standards, develop tools to train new employees, and keep the sustainability focus on the minds of all employees. These champions have also generated many of the new ideas for products and services that enable Kimpton to remain at the forefront of sustainability in the hotel industry. For example, an employee suggestion to recycle wire coat hangers for guest laundry saved approximately to two tons of steel per year.[5]

The sustainability efforts of the firm are also incorporated into the product offerings in the restaurants. One of the means for pursuing sustainability in the food service industry is to buy food products grown locally. This practice increases food freshness while decreasing the restaurant's carbon footprint. In addition, this practice provides the opportunity for chefs to offer unique menu options not available in other parts of the country. Implementation of this strategy enables Kimpton chefs to serve unique menu choices made from fresh and organic ingredients.[6] Where healthy local alternatives are not available, the firm emphasizes sourcing of eco-friendly products produced in a sustainable, organic, or biodynamic fashion. For example, currently 30% of all wines sold in Kimpton restaurants bear an eco-friendly label. This criterion is enforced regardless of the size of the cellar (from 50 to 1,400 selections) or the price of the wine (ranging from $5 to $500).[7]

Kimpton has been able to incorporate sustainability into operations while simultaneously achieving milestones in financial, relational, and environmental performance. In the first year of EarthCare, Kimpton attributed more than $500,000 in new revenue to the program. It also saved considerably from EarthCare directives to upgrade lighting—San Francisco's Galleria Park Hotel alone saved $4,000 from changing exit lighting to LEDs. The company has fostered closer relationships with employees via the EarthCare Champions program, and the eco-friendly requirement for food service products has nurtured relationships with local producers. Among the environmental benefits are reduced water usage and reduced use of toxins. In the first year of EarthCare operations, the company saved more than 103,000 gallons of water at the Hotel Allegro in Chicago.[8]

The Kimpton Hotels example underscores the work being done in the services sector to enhance sustainability. In order to contribute to these efforts, it is meaningful to take stock of current sustainability programs in this sector of the economy. Therefore, the purpose of this chapter is to provide an overview of the role of the services economy in energy consumption. We begin by providing an overview of this sector and its use of energy. We subsequently describe the use of energy in retailing, administration, education, health care, and lodging.

Despite the fact that services account for more than 50% of the GDP in most mature economies, few countries collect detailed information concerning energy consumption in this sector.[9] Japan, the United States, and Canada provide the greatest level of information concerning services and energy consumption. Given the lack of global information and the size of the American economy, our development of energy use focuses on this country. Consider first the overall influence of this sector.

Services are product offerings that possess several traits that distinguish them from goods and other product offerings. The delivery of most services is contingent of the action of people, and the personnel-based facet distinguishes these products from goods. Services are products that are essentially intangible and vary based on the provider. Because services are associated with the time the services provider has available to render the service, the amount of available service is perishable.[10]

The service sector includes service businesses (e.g., retail stores, hotels), educational institutions, correctional facilities, religious groups, and fraternal organizations. The service sector of an economy is an important source of employment and GDP. In the United States, for example, the services sector accounts for more than 80% of the jobs in the economy as well as 80% of the GDP.[11]

On a global level, the service sector accounts for 9% of total final energy consumption and 12% of carbon emissions.[12] In 2003, total *on-site* energy consumption in the U.S. services sector surpassed 6.5 quadrillion British Thermal Units (BTUs).[13] This estimate of U.S. energy consumption refers to energy deployed at a location and does not include energy consumed in generating and transmitting electricity. The costs incurred to generate and transport electricity are nearly equivalent to the on-site costs. Because the reporting facilitates efforts to raise efficiency at the point of service, our discussion addresses *on-site* energy consumption.

The three primary sources of energy for services are electricity, natural gas, and fuel oil. Electricity usage represents more than 50% of all energy use, and the largest uses of electricity are in air cooling, lighting, office equipment operations, refrigeration, and ventilation. Natural gas represents nearly 40% of energy use, and it is the primary source of energy for space heating, water heating, and cooking. Electricity is also used for these purposes, but gas is generally a more efficient and more popular energy source for these applications. Fuel oil is predominantly used for space heating.[14]

Figure 12-1 illustrates the primary uses of energy in the service sector. Space heating (36%) and lighting (20%) account for the majority of energy consumption within the services sector. Water heating, cooling, ventilation, and refrigeration each represent 6 to 8% of energy usage. Cooking and office equipment each account for 3% of energy consumption in this sector.

It is noteworthy that the number of commercial buildings and the amount of floor space has steadily increased, yet total energy consumption in this sector has not risen at comparable levels. In virtually every application—from computers to space heating—there have been significant enhancements to energy efficiency. Space heating is primarily achieved via boilers and furnaces. Furnaces heat air and distribute it through ducts; boilers heat water, providing either hot water or steam for heating. Steam is distributed via pipes to steam radiators, and hot water can be distributed through baseboard radiators or radiant floor systems.[15] Boilers are more likely in larger buildings, whereas furnaces are more prevalent in smaller facilities.

FIG. 12-1 Major Fuel Consumption by End Use—2003

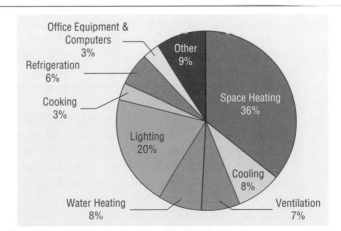

Source: *U.S. Department of Energy*

The energy efficiency of a furnace or boiler is measured by **annual fuel utilization efficiency** (AFUE). The U.S. Federal Trade Commission requires new furnaces or boilers to display each unit's AFUE for consumer comparison purposes. AFUE is the ratio of heat output of the furnace or boiler compared to the total energy consumed by a furnace or boiler. For example, a furnace with an AFUE of 95% uses 95% of the energy as heat whereas the remaining 5% escapes through the chimney or elsewhere. The U.S. Department of Energy has established federal minimums of 80% efficiency for gas-fired furnaces, 82% for oil-fired furnaces, 84% gas fired–boilers, and 83% for oil fired–boilers. These minimums are below Energy Star requirements that are currently set at 90% for furnaces and 85% for boilers.[16]

The fuel efficiency of furnaces and boilers has improved markedly over the years. As a result of this enhanced efficiency, there are substantial savings and, simultaneously, reduced carbon emissions realized from upgrading space heating systems. For example, many furnaces installed in the 1970s had AFUEs of 60%.[17] The replacement of one of these systems with a highly fuel-efficient system with an AFUE of 95% lowers fuel consumption costs by $37.80 for every $100 spent on energy.[18] Consequently, carbon emissions and fuel cost are both reduced via the upgrade to more efficient space-heating technology.

One area of energy consumption that has changed markedly over the past 10 years is in the form of lighting used within this sector. In contrast to the household sector, the services sector has substantially more locations that rely on fluorescent lighting rather than incandescent lighting. Although there are some energy savings to be realized from replacing the incandescent lighting, the energy savings from upgrading fluorescent lighting are more appreciable.[19] The enhancements to commercial lighting include electronic ballasts and lighting control systems. Ballasts are devices designed to stabilize the flow of electricity in an electric circuit. The ballasts used in fluorescent lighting before the 1980s were magnetic, but increasingly these devices are being replaced with electronic ones. These newer devices increase the efficiency of fluorescent lighting by 25%.[20] For example, a study of a 440,000-square-foot office building in Washington, DC, revealed a potential for annual savings of about $27,000 (290,000 kWh) per year to the building owner. These savings are realized when fluorescent lamps and magnetic ballasts are replaced with smaller-diameter lamps and electronic ballasts. Together, these lighting changes reduced power per fixture by 20% from 110 watts to 88 watts.[21] Estimates from the U.S. National Academy of Sciences study suggest that electronic ballasts sold through 2005 provide $15 billion in energy savings. Moreover, the heightened efficiency results in electronic ballasts currently accounting for more than 80% of the ballast market.

Improvements in electronic control technology complement advances in the efficiency of lighting and space heating equipment. The development of digital thermostats enables one to control the temperature in a home by the day, week, and hour. Thus, facilities operated in climates that demand air-conditioning and heating in the same day can be managed effectively. Moreover, the electronic programming of the heaters enables one to raise or lower the temperature in a location. For example, the U.S. Department of Energy claims that one realizes a savings of as much as 1% for each degree change in temperature if the setback period is eight hours long.[22] Digital thermometers that are properly programmed to reduce the temperature by 10° to 15° for 8 hours yield about 5% to 15% a year on heating costs and limit the amount of carbon emissions associated with the location. Similarly, digital control devices for lighting also lower fuel costs and emissions. The lighting control devices include dimmers, sensors, and timers. Dimmers used with fluorescent lighting are dedicated fixtures and bulbs that provide even greater energy savings than a regular fluorescent lamp. By contrast, dimmers used with incandescent lighting do not increase energy efficiency. Sensors are devices that sense motion, light (photo sensors), and occupancy. These devices enhance fuel efficiency by reducing the use of power when conditions do not warrant energy consumption. For example, photo sensors are used in outdoor applications to turn appliances off during daylight hours.[23] Similarly, timers attempt to limit energy use via programs that allow energy to flow to lighting appliances on predetermined schedules.

Figure 12-2 illustrates the various facets of the services sector, as elsewhere as well as their respective energy consumption in the United States. At 20% of total energy consumption, the mercantile section represents the largest user of energy in the services sector of the economy. Mercantile services include the malls and strip centers that house nonfood, nonlodging components of retailing. At 17% of total energy usage, offices are the second largest consumers in the services sector. Education facilities account for 13% of energy consumption, whereas food service, health care, and lodging are each associated with at least 8% of total energy consumption. Consider first the role of the mercantile sector.

B. Nonfood Retailing

The mercantile component of the services sector includes all buildings used for the sale and display of goods other than food. This category includes enclosed malls, strip shopping centers, car dealerships, liquor stores, video rental stores, and every type of retail building other than food retailing.[24] In order to assess the potential to enhance sustainability in the nonfood retail sector, it is valuable to look at the *inputs, processes,* and *outputs.* Two inputs associated with carbon emissions are packaging and energy sourcing. Manufacturers and distributors are increasingly examining ways to enhance sustainability while simultaneously shoring up logistics costs associated with marketing to retailers. For example, Georgia-Pacific worked in conjunction with A. O. Smith Water Products to reconfigure the packaging of the company's water heaters.[25] The new package

FIG. 12-2
Commercial
Buildings'
Consumption by
Energy Source, 2003
(6,523 Trillion BTUs)
* "Other" includes
public assembly,
public order and
safety, religious
worship, warehouse
and storage, and
vacant properties.

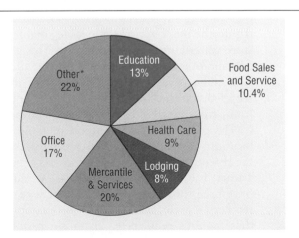

Source: *U.S. Department of Energy*

design reduced material usage by one third, decreased storage and logistical costs, and simultaneously resulted in a 1,423-ton decrease in greenhouse emissions. This example underscores the merits of the green marketing strategy to participants throughout the value chain. The manufacturing and transportation efficiencies result in lower costs to the retailers and consumers while the overall carbon emissions are reduced.

The efforts by Georgia-Pacific represent action taken by manufacturers to limit the packaging and floor space associated with products. Retailers also are initiating procedures to limit the emissions associated with products sold in their establishments. For example, Target has eliminated harmful perfluorooctanoic (PFOA) chemicals from products used in fabric and garment processing. Target also actively looks to reduce polyvinyl chloride (PVC) plastic in products and packaging.[26] Approximately 66% of the paper used at Target's in-house printing facility is recycled.[27] The company further uses 100% recycled-content paper bags, 80% recycled shoe boxes, and plastic bags with 5 to 25% recycled content.[28]

A second input that is being aggressively modified is the form of energy employed at the retail location. For example, Walmart has a long-term goal to use 100% renewable forms of energy in its retail stores. Walmart has entered into a four-year power purchase agreement with Duke Energy whereby it will purchase wind power at competitive rates from Duke's Notrees, Texas, facility. By purchasing clean, renewable energy, Walmart will avoid producing more than 139,000 metric tons of carbon dioxide (CO_2) emissions per year. The energy purchase is equivalent to taking approximately 25,000 cars off the road.[29]

The process component of nonfood retailing concerns the management of energy usage at a retail location. Walmart and Target have implemented programs designed to reduce energy consumption without affecting the consumer shopping experience. At Walmart, the average savings per store from daylight harvesting is approximately 800,000 kWh per year, enough energy to power 73 homes. The company also uses dimmable fluorescent lighting systems and LED technologies that are more efficient than older fluorescent lights. Since about 80% of the energy consumed in a retail location is associated with heating and cooling, Target has made substantial strides to enhance the energy efficiency of these systems. Heating and air-conditioning systems within Walmart stores are well above retailing requirements, and humidification systems are energy-efficient systems that make the trip to the market more enjoyable. Walmart has also implemented a plan to reduce store water consumption by 17%. This goal is achieved by installation of new faucets and other plumbing that limits the flow of water. In addition, Walmart is replacing some percentage of cement with fly ash and slag. The company also uses recycled materials in its cabinetry and counters, and it uses 100% recycled plastics (most from unused diaper scraps) in its baseboards.

The third aspect of nonfood retailing concerns the waste derived from a retail location. Retailers have collected paper waste for recycling for many decades, but the attention to waste reduction has increased dramatically in the last few years. Target, for instance, now recycles or reuses more than 70% of waste that would have been thrown into landfills a few years ago. Municipalities are mandating that retailers recycle plastic bags. For example, New York City passed a law in 2008 that requires retailers to establish in-store recycling programs for plastic bags.[30] In response to the increasing criticism of plastic bags, retailers are actively switching to other bags. Walmart has set a goal to reduce its shopping bag waste by 33%

by 2013.[31] It will achieve this goal by training associates to bag products more efficiently, introducing reusable bags, and accepting worn-out bags for recycling. In October 2008, Walmart U.S. introduced a reusable bag that cost consumers 50 cents. Similar initiatives have already yielded plastic reductions for the company in Canada, Europe, Argentina, and Brazil. In Japan, 46% of Walmart customers now use their own bags.[32]

C. Food Retailing

Food retailing represents 10.4% of consumption in the services sector.[33] The **food service** component refers to buildings used for preparation and sale of food and beverages. These buildings include restaurants, cafeterias, and fast food restaurants. **Food sales** refers to buildings used to sell food at the retail or wholesale level and includes grocery stores, food markets, and convenience stores. Food service accounts for 6.8% of total energy consumption, whereas food sales represent 3.8% of total energy consumption.

Although food retailing represents slightly more than 10% of consumption in the services sector, the energy intensity for food marketing is more than twice the average among all commercial buildings. In the food service subsector, electricity represents slightly more than 50% of energy usage with the remainder primarily associated with natural gas. Companies operating in this market are addressing ways to reduce fuel input costs, operating costs, and waste removal. Food retailers of varying size have taken measures to conserve energy and use sustainable sources of fuel. McDonald's, for instance, has implemented TEEM (The Energy-Efficient McDonald's) strategies that save each restaurant more than $2,000 annually. The design elements include skylights that allow fluorescent lights to be dimmed during the day, as well as windows with specially treated glass that filter out the sun's infrared and ultraviolet light. Infrared rays raise the temperature in dining areas, whereas ultraviolet light fades colorful fabrics inside restaurants.[34]

Many other restaurateurs are recognizing financial and brand advantages. The Austin Grill, for example, made the switch to wind power in 2003 and was the first multiunit restaurant in the United States powered exclusively via wind power. The switch to wind power cost the restaurant chain about 2% more per kilowatt hour versus fuels generated from traditional sources.[35] Similarly, Holland Inc. began using wind power for all of its electrical needs at Burgerville and Noodlin' restaurants in 2005. By converting 40 restaurants to wind power, Holland Inc. avoids adding 17.4 million pounds of carbon dioxide to the air each year.[36]

A second facet of sustainability associated with inputs to the restaurant and food service industry concerns food sourcing. Restaurateurs can lower their carbon footprints by purchasing sustainably grown products and products sourced locally. Sustainably grown products are generally associated with lower carbon emissions, but they currently cost more than their counterparts.[37] Local purchasing offers many benefits to the restaurateur and the community. The purchase of locally produced products lowers the carbon emissions costs associated with delivery and results in generally lower shipping costs. In addition, the firm can support its claims associated with freshness by buying locally grown products. The purchase of these products also supports the local community that is vital to the success of the restaurants.[38]

Retailers are also recognizing the multiple benefits associated with limiting fuel consumption. Since heating/air conditioning, lighting, cooking, and refrigeration account for about 75% of fuel costs in the sector, companies are looking for efficiencies realized through equipment purchases and operations. Commercial restaurant equipment that bears the Energy Star label offers significant fuel savings and carbon reductions. Energy Star fryers are more than 50% more efficient than other fryers. Similarly, Energy Star steamers are 25 to 60% more efficient, and food warming/heating equipment is up to 137% more efficient than products that do not carry the Energy Star label.[39] In addition, restaurateurs can invest in tankless water heaters that reduce water consumption and are up to 70% more efficient than conventional water heaters.

Energy management for refrigeration equipment requires retailers to examine ozone depletion and global warming.[40] Retailers can reduce energy expenses by investing in refrigeration equipment that offers the highest possible evaporation temperature and the lowest possible condensing temperature while maintaining optimal storage temperature.[41] Newer-model commercial refrigerators meet these specifications and are 30% more efficient than older models. In addition, these units may use coolants that are more environmentally friendly than CFC- or HFC-based refrigerators. For example, Danish producer Vestfrost has developed refrigerators that use R-134A as the refrigerant.[42] The need to maintain adequate temperature, however, must also include consideration of the humidity conditions. Since moisture removal is more energy intensive than lowering air temperature, it is essential to regulate humidity.[43] Proper dehumidification makes the shopping experience more enjoyable and can make supermarket refrigeration cases up to 20% more efficient. Furthermore, moisture elimination is a main factor in the control of biological contamination, particularly for meat and poultry. Retailers must simultaneously consider the energy efficient rating (EER) and the moisture removal efficiency (MRE). Whereas the former measures the kilowatt cost per hour to maintain temperature, the latter addresses the amount of condensate per kilowatt hour.[44]

Importantly, refrigerators and cooking equipment only realize energy savings when installations are maintained properly. Store-level operations must, for example, regularly clean evaporator coils and condensers to ensure fuel efficiencies and avoid wear on compressors. Refrigerators should also be maintained and properly loaded to ensure quick access to products without affecting the flow of air throughout the units. When proper maintenance is part of the energy assessment, the life cycle savings of commercial products can be realized.[45]

The final aspect of energy conservation for food retailing concerns the amount of waste produced. In the United States alone, the Environmental Protection Agency (EPA) estimates that the processing of wasted food costs the country more than $1 billion annually. These costs are curtailed by recycling, reusing, donating, and composting materials.[46] Recycling centers, for example, will pay retailers for non-contaminated paper, glass, and aluminum. By contrast, retailers lower their costs by reusing cardboard, paper, and plastic. They can also lower overall costs by donating food, used uniforms, furniture, and appliances to the needy. Finally, retailers recognize the financial rewards associated with composting. Since 1997, San Francisco restaurateurs have been composting more than 300 tons of materials every day. The compost ferments for 60 days before it is sold to local vineyards.[47]

D. Offices and Administrative Buildings

Office buildings include locations used for general office space, professional offices, and administrative offices.[48] Twenty-nine percent of the energy used in these locations is associated with electricity for lighting, and another 16% is associated with office equipment. They also rely on natural gas and electricity for space heating; together, space heating fuels account for 25% of energy use in office buildings.

Efforts to control energy expenditures for commercial offices include **green design** and office equipment operations. *Green design* refers to the development and maintenance of buildings that are sensitive to the environment, resource and energy consumption, the quality of the work setting, cost effectiveness, and the world at large.[49] In the United States, the nonprofit Green Building Council (USGBC) has established the **Leadership in Energy and Environmental Design (LEED)** rating system. LEED includes 34 performance criteria associated with sustainable sites, water efficiency, energy and atmosphere, materials and resources, indoor environmental quality, and innovation and design processes. Four levels of certification (certified, silver, gold, and platinum) correspond to increasingly higher levels of sustainability of a building.

The decision whether to incorporate LEED criteria into buildings is contingent on the cost effectiveness of the sustainability-based enhancements. Regrettably, there is limited research on the costs incurred with green design. The **green premium** refers to the additional expenditures associated with green design. Green design decisions are often not priced out in comparison to nongreen ones, and the relative newness of green technologies results in conservative cost estimates by designers, architects, and their clients. The benefits of green design include cost savings from reduced energy, water, and waste as well as lower operating and maintenance costs. In addition, green design yields enhanced occupant productivity and health. Furthermore, green buildings are 25 to 30% more energy efficient and lower peak energy consumption. They are also more likely to generate renewable power on site and purchase power from renewable energy sources.[50]

Although survey and census data are not available to characterize the trade-offs associated with using a green design, available evidence suggests strong financial benefits over a 20-year horizon. In a 2003 study of 33 LEED projects, the state of California used net present value calculations to estimate the benefits and costs of using a sustainable design. The green premium was estimated at $4 per square foot, but the net present value of energy (NPV) savings was estimated at $5.79. When the benefits of lowered emissions, enhanced water quality, and occupant productivity are added to the energy savings, the net present value of a certified or silver location was estimated at $52.47 per square foot. Consequently, the benefit of a green building was approximately $48.87 per square foot. These figures should not be used to assume that green building is necessarily more cost effective. These preliminary data underscore the need to consider the inherent costs and benefits of employing a sustainable design. When the costs are assessed over the life of the property, the merits of green building strategies are likely to be pronounced.

The second facet of energy savings most associated with office buildings is office equipment. This equipment includes personal computers, facsimile (fax) machines, photocopiers, telephones, and other instruments designed to facilitate office operations. In 2006, the International Sustainable Development Foundation established the Green Electronics Council (GEC) to support the effective design, manufacture, use, and recovery of electronic products. GEC works in conjunction with the electronics industry to recognize and reward environmentally sensitive products. GEC has established the Electronics Products Environmental Assessment Tool (EPEAT) to identify electronics that are environmentally preferable. The EPEAT sourcing criteria call for the reduction or elimination of environmentally sensitive materials (e.g., cadmium and mercury), the use of recycled content, and the implementation of design features that enable recycling at the end of a product's life. Operational criteria include energy conservation concerns (e.g., Energy Star), packaging, and upgradeability of products. Products are also evaluated based on corporate environmental performance and whether the corporation has implemented a return policy for obsolete products.[51]

Products that meet EPEAT standards use less energy and use more recycled materials while producing less greenhouse gas, air and water pollution, and solid and hazardous waste. In 2006, less than 10% of desktop, laptop, and computer monitors met the EPEAT standards. These products saved 13.7 billion kWh of electricity and 24.4 million metric tons of materials. In addition, these EPEAT-certified products prevented 56.5 million metric tons of air pollution, 1.07 million metric tons of global warming gases, 118,000 metric tons of water pollution, and avoided disposal of 41,100 metric tons of hazardous waste.[52] Given the benefits of these products, however, it is not surprising to see manufacturers such as Apple and Dell marketing EPEAT products. Apple markets the 13-inch MacBook as the greenest MacBook ever. This computer is arsenic, mercury, and PVC free and is enclosed in recyclable aluminum and glass.[53] Dell is also striving to achieve higher levels of sustainability and currently offers 28 products that are EPEAT registered.[54]

E. Educational Institutions

Educational institutions are buildings used for academic or classroom instruction. These buildings include elementary, middle, or high schools and classrooms on college or university campuses.[55] Educational institutions account for 13% of energy consumption in the services sector. Space heating (41%), water heating (22%), and lighting (20%) represent more than 80% of the power expenditures in education. Most educational facilities are part of multibuilding campuses, and schools in the Northeast and Midwest are generally larger than schools in the South and West. Almost two-thirds of the schools are government owned, and three-fourths of the government-owned buildings are owned by local government.

Although there are notable efforts to raise the sustainability of operations at the elementary and high school levels, the action undertaken at the collegiate level provides the opportunity to compare green marketing action across campuses. In 2005, the Rockefeller Philanthropy Advisors established the **Sustainable Endowments Institute (SEI)**. SEI is a nonprofit organization engaged in research and education to advance sustainability in campus operations and endowment practices. Since 2007, SEI has been publishing the **College Sustainability Report Card**. This assessment of sustainability evaluates the policies and programs of 100 leading colleges and universities. These schools hold more than $258 billion in endowments and represent about 75% of all higher education endowment investments. Collegiate institutions are evaluated on the following criteria:[56]

Administration. This category addresses action regarding sustainability by colleges and universities at the administrative or trustee level. This action includes commitments to sustainability in the institution's mission statement or master plan and commitments to local, national, or international sustainability agreements.

Climate change and energy. Climate change initiatives seek to improve energy efficiency and to obtain energy from renewable resources. Conservation campaigns may encourage college community members to monitor their energy consumption, retrofit appliances or power plants with energy-efficient technology, conduct a carbon emissions inventory, and commit to emissions reductions.

Food and recycling. This category examines the sustainability practices of dining services. Schools earn higher evaluations based on the quantity and availability of locally grown food, as well as organic and sustainably produced food. The use of reusable dishware and eco-friendly to-go containers is also taken into consideration. In addition, this category also examines campus-wide and dining-specific programs for recycling and composting food and landscape waste.

Green building. The green building category assesses the degree to which schools adopt high-performance green building design. This category includes the adoption of campus-wide green building policies and the integration of green building practices into new and existing buildings, construction projects, and the incorporation of green building design features into retrofits of existing buildings. Colleges earn better evaluations when they use the LEED rating system.

Student Involvement. This category considers the degree to which students participate in sustainability initiatives as well as the support for these activities by school administrators.

Transportation. The transportation category examines the extent to which a school promotes alternative transportation choices through the policies and practices of facilities management and the administration.

Endowment transparency. This factor addresses the control information about endowment investment holdings and shareholder proxy voting records. Access to endowment information fosters constructive dialogue about opportunities for clean-energy investments and shareholder voting priorities.

Investment priorities. Investment priorities focus on prioritizing return on investment, investing in renewable energy funds, and investing in community-development loan funds.

Shareholder engagement. Colleges illustrate shareholder engagement by establishing committees of students, faculty, and alumni to advise the trustees regarding sustainability.

The College Sustainability Report Card offers a number of benefits to institutions of higher education. The specific criteria in the report card provide opportunities to make significant advances in aspects of a university's sustainability evaluation that fall below desired levels. By charting this activity over time, universities can illustrate to stakeholders the amount of progress achieved over time. For example, Table 12-1 identifies the best-performing institutions in 2009. The relative rankings indicate how the efforts of one college fare in comparison to all other higher educational institutions.

The scorecard provides insight to colleges, but it also provides insight to marketers that seek to make product offerings available to institutions of higher learning. By analyzing these criteria, firms can develop campaigns that illustrate how their product offerings help schools achieve sustainability goals. For example, Leviton markets a line of dimmer switches that accommodate fluorescent lighting.[58] Sales representatives marketing these products to colleges and universities can illustrate how retrofitting of these devices to existing fixtures can enable the institution to achieve sustainability goals while simultaneously lowering operating costs.

F. Health Care

Health care buildings are those used as diagnostic and treatment facilities for both inpatient and outpatient care.[59] Doctors' and dentists' offices are considered health care buildings if they use any type of diagnostic medical equipment and offices if they do not. Skilled nursing or other residential care buildings are categorized as lodging.

TABLE 12-1   **BEST SUSTAINABILITY PERFORMERS AMONG COLLEGES AND UNIVERSITIES—2009**[57]

	Overall Grade	Administration	Climate Change and Energy	Food and Recycling	Green Building	Student Involvement	Transportation	Endowment Transparency	Investment Priorities	Shareholder Engagement
Oberlin College	A-	A	A	A	A	A	B	B	A	A
University of New Hampshire	A-	A	A	A	B	A	A	A	B	–
University of British Columbia	A-	A	B	A	A	A	A	A	B	B
Columbia University	A-	A	B	A	A	A	B	B	A	A
Dickinson College	A-	A	A	A	B	B	A	B	A	A
Harvard University	A-	A	A	A	A	A	B	C	A	A
Middlebury College	A-	A	A	A	A	A	A	D	A	A
University of Washington	A-	A	A	A	A	B	A	B	A	B
Brown University	A-	B	B	A	A	A	A	C	A	A
Carleton College	A-	A	B	A	B	A	B	B	A	A
University of Colorado	A-	A	A	A	A	A	A	A	A	F
Dartmouth College	A-	C	B	A	A	A	B	A	A	A
University of Pennsylvania	A-	A	A	A	A	B	B	C	A	A
Stanford University	A-	A	B	A	A	A	B	C	A	A
University of Vermont	A-	A	A	A	A	B	B	B	B	A

Source: *www.GreenReportCard.org*

Health care accounts for 9% of the energy consumption in the services sector. The health care sector has a set of unique conditions that influence the measures taken to conserve energy. Similar to food retailing, health care buildings have energy intensities that are more than twice the average of all buildings in the sector. Health care facilities must cope with 24/7 operations accompanied by chemical use, infectious disease control requirements, and substantial regulatory requirements that challenge efforts to achieve higher levels of sustainability.

The health care industry has been working toward developing sustainability standards since the 2002 release of the Green Healthcare Construction Guidance statement by the American Society for Healthcare Engineering. In the following year, the Green Guide for Health Care initiative began when a team of geographically and professionally diverse industry leaders established a steering committee to guide development of the document. Importantly, the members of this committee include a wide range of stakeholders who do not have direct financial interests in certification processes or products addressed in the document. The guide has evolved from a pilot project to become a full-fledged registration and certification program. In its current form, the **Green Guide for Health Care** (version 2.2) is intended to serve as a reference for best practices in the industry. The Guide provides the health care sector with a voluntary, self-certifying metric toolkit that designers, owners, and operators can use to guide and evaluate their progress toward high-performance healing environments. The detailed guide provides insight into the manner by which health care facilities can enhance the extent of sustainability in building construction and operations.

The guidelines for health care sustainability examine issues associated with new construction and current operations. When a hospital elects to add new construction or analyzes current operations, it is increasingly basing decisions on the Green Guide for Health Care. The construction and operations-related issues for health care facilities include:[60]

Integrated design. The health care facility must implement a collaborative multi-stakeholder goal-setting and design process and establish human health as a criterion for design, construction, and operations.

Sustainable sites. Site development must limit the environmental impact from the location of a building on a site. Developments in urban areas should protect greenfields and preserve natural resources, and developments in rural areas should focus on previously developed sites. Facilities should also rehabilitate sites where development is complicated by environmental contamination. Sites should be regulated to limit pollution from automobiles as well as pollution from storm water runoff.

Water efficiency. Health care facilities must eliminate the use of potable water for cooling of medical equipment or for landscape irrigation. At the same time, the health care facility should maximize drinkable water efficiency within facilities and monitor water consumption practices over time.

Energy and atmosphere. The health care facility should establish minimum energy efficiency standards, encourage performance above these standards, and monitor this performance over time. The facility should also encourage use of renewable and self-supplied energy while simultaneously reducing energy consumption. In addition, the facility should be in compliance with the Montreal Protocol for ozone depletion.

Materials and resources. Eliminate the use of mercury-containing building products and reduce the release of bio-accumulative toxic chemicals associated with building materials. Redirect recyclable resources into manufacturing, redirect reusable materials to appropriate sites, and direct hazardous waste in compliance with governmental regulations.

Environmental quality. Provide natural ventilation to enhance occupant comfort and minimize indoor air contaminants that are potentially harmful. Minimize the use of furnishings that release air contaminants and limit the amount of disruptive sound near the facility.

Innovation and design process. Establish programs that reward design teams and projects that achieve performance above the goals established by the Green Guide for Health Care.

Chemical management. Minimize airborne effluents and hazardous spills while also reducing the potential for building occupant exposure to PCBs and PCB combustion by-products. Limit the amount of pharmaceutical waste in sanitary sewer discharge.

Waste management. Establish minimum reduction and recycling programs. Reduce solid waste in landfills and incinerators through reuse, reduction, recycling, and composting. Reduce medical waste through improved segregation and modified work practices.

Environmental services. Develop grounds management practices that enhance the ecological integrity of the property. Reduce exposure to physical and chemical hazards. Limit land development and pollution effects by limiting the amount of vehicle transportation.

The merits of the Green Guide for Health Care are similar to those enjoyed by universities that use the College Sustainability Report Card. The guidelines provide clear objectives for the hospitals, and they enable health care institutions to track their level of progress over time. Moreover, the Green Guide provides significant help to marketers seeking to make their product offerings available to hospitals. Marketers that can illustrate how their products augment construction and operations guidelines are well positioned to increase market shares in the health care industry.

G. Hotels and Lodging

The hotel and lodging industry accounts for 8% of energy consumption in the services sector. The hotel industry is one of the world's largest employers and represents more than 195 million jobs and 10.2% of the world's GDP. In addition, the industry reports annual capital investments of $685 billion.[61]

The tourism industry is forecast to reach more than 1.56 billion people by the year 2020, and the hotel industry will need to accommodate the demand by providing more properties. Industry participants recognize that new hotel construction must occur in a manner that incorporates sustainability issues.[62] The industry recognizes the need to enhance sustainability, but many of the efforts in operations have occurred independently by various hoteliers.[63] The International Business Leaders Forum (IBLF) and Green Globe certification represent two attempts to draw consensus about sustainability efforts. In 2005, the IBLF and Conservation International developed a plan for implementing sustainability into hotel planning and development to help guide planners, investors, hotel owners, and developers.[64] This plan was developed in conjunction with nine of the world's leading hotel companies: Accor, Carlson, Four Seasons, Hilton, InterContinental, Marriott, Rezidor SAS, Starwood Hotels & Resorts Worldwide Inc., and Taj Hotels Resorts and Palace. This plan focuses on site selection, building design, and construction. Key facets of the plan include:[65]

Sustainable building site and design. Design concerns examine architectural features such as site location, passive solar design, day lighting, renewable energy, water conservation, and landscaping. In addition, the plan examines environmental considerations associated with windows, insulation, and other building materials. The design also calls for resource-efficient technologies and appliances.

Reuse of existing buildings. The plan recognizes that, when feasible, retrofitting and repairing of existing properties is preferred to new construction. When buildings must be leveled, existing materials should be evaluated for reuse.

Sustainable construction. Sustainability in construction involves ensuring that modifications to initial plans do not impair the sustainability features of the design, nor do they reduce energy efficiency. The environmental integrity of the site is to be preserved at all costs. Additionally, the site must be a clean and safe workplace.

Although the IBLF plan provides guidelines for property development, it does not represent a form of accreditation that hotel properties can obtain. Green Hotel Certification, however, is a third-party certification that integrates IBLF logic and other industry documentation. The Green Globe seal is an independent recognition of sustainability efforts that benchmarks properties against the highest worldwide principles. Its object is to introduce and strengthen sustainability and social practices at all levels of management in the hospitality industry. Green Globe certification reviews energy efficiency, greenhouse gas emissions, water conservation, indoor and outdoor air quality, waste management, facility management, policy and governance, purchasing, community, destination protection, conservation and management, and cultural and social issues.

Summary

A. Introduction: Service Sector Contributors to Carbon Emissions

This chapter provides an overview of energy consumption in the services sector. This economic sector includes service businesses (e.g., retail stores, hotels), educational institutions, correctional facilities, religious groups, and fraternal organizations. On a global level, the service sector accounts for 9% of total final energy consumption and 12% of carbon emissions. The three primary sources of energy for services are electricity, natural gas, and fuel oil.

B. Nonfood Retailing

The mercantile component of the services sector includes enclosed malls, strip shopping centers, car dealerships, liquor stores, video rental stores, and every type of retail building other than food retailing. Manufacturers and distributors that provide inputs are increasingly examining ways to enhance sustainability while simultaneously shoring up logistics costs associated with marketing to retailers. The process component of nonfood retailing concerns the management of energy usage at a retail location. Large and small retailers have implemented programs designed to reduce energy consumption without affecting the consumer shopping experience.

C. Food Retailing

The food service component refers to buildings used for preparation and sale of food and beverages. These buildings include restaurants, cafeterias, and fast food restaurants. Given that the energy intensity for food marketing is substantial, companies operating in this market are addressing ways to reduce fuel input costs, operating costs, and waste removal.

Food sales refers to buildings used to sell food at the retail or wholesale level and include grocery stores, food markets, and convenience stores. Firms in this industry can lower their carbon footprints by purchasing sustainably grown products and products sourced locally. They further can lower their energy emissions by upgrading to fuel-efficient equipment.

D. Offices and Administrative Buildings

Efforts to control energy expenditures for commercial offices include green design and office equipment operations. *Green design* refers to the development and maintenance of buildings that are sensitive to the environment, resource and energy consumption, the quality of the work setting, cost effectiveness, and the world at large. The second facet of energy savings most associated with office buildings is office equipment. The International Sustainable Development Foundation established the Green Electronics Council to support the effective design, manufacture, use, and recovery of electronic products.

E. Educational Institutions

Educational institutions are buildings used for academic or classroom instruction. Sustainable Endowments Institute publishes the College Sustainability Report Card that evaluates universities' and colleges' efforts to attain sustainability in administration, climate change and energy, food and recycling, buildings and construction, endowment transparency, investment priorities, and shareholder engagement.

F. Health Care

The Green Guide for Health Care provides health care facilities with guidelines about construction issues that include integrated design, sustainable sites, water efficiency, energy and atmosphere, materials, environmental quality, innovation, and design. The ongoing operations of the facility are also addressed with respect to energy efficiency, water conservation, chemical management, waste management, and environmental services.

G. Hotels and Lodging

Firms operating in the lodging industry can increase the level of sustainability via proper building site and design, refurbishing and reusing existing buildings, and sustainable construction.

Key Terms

annual fuel utilization efficiency, 242

College Sustainability Report Card, 248

food sales, 245

food service, 245

green design, 247

Green Guide for Health Care, 250

green premium, 247

Leadership in Energy and Environmental Design (LEED), 247

Sustainable Endowments Institute (SEI), 248

Questions

1. What is the merit of examining the state of progress on sustainability issues for each sector of the services economy?
2. What is the relative influence of the services economy on energy consumption, and what are the primary sources of energy used in the sector?
3. Describe the primary energy-intensive inputs, processes, and outputs in nonfood retailing, and describe recent efforts to use energy more efficiently.
4. How does local food sourcing enhance sustainability?
5. Why would an organization seek to have LEED certification for its new facility?

6. Is the green premium increasing or decreasing? What evidence supports your answer?
7. What are the components of the College Sustainability Report Card?
8. How does your college or institution rate on the Collegiate Sustainability Report Card, and what can it do to enhance its performance?
9. What can your college or institution do to enhance the sustainability of the classroom in which your class is held?
10. What types of firms marketing to hospitals would benefit from knowing that the health care facility is using GGHC logic to direct its purchasing?
11. To what extent is the hotel and lodging industry engaging in sustainability efforts?

Endnotes

[1] Kimpton Hotels and Restaurants, "About Us," http://www.kimptonhotels.com/about-us/about-us.aspx (accessed May 14, 2010).

[2] Kimpton Hotels and Restaurants, "Earthcare History," http://www.kimptonhotels.com/programs/earthcare-history.aspx (accessed May 14, 2010).

[3] Lisa Hurley, "The Green Room," *Association Meetings*, August, 2009, 35.

[4] Lisa Jenning, "Eco-friendly Ways Bring in Green," *Nation's Restaurant News*, October 1, 2007, 90, 92.

[5] See Note 1 above.

[6] Kimpton Hotels and Restaurants, "Restaurants," http://www.kimptonhotels.com/restaurants/restaurants.aspx (accessed May 14, 2010).

[7] Elissa Elan, "Wines Leads Kimpton's Eco-Friendly Efforts with Wines," *Nation's Restaurant News*, August 10, 2009, 20, 65.

[8] Jeff Slye, "The Greening of Kimpton Hotels: Five Valuable Lessons" *Hotel Business Review*, http://www.businessevolutionconsulting.com/Greening_of_Kimpton.pdf (accessed May 14, 2010).

[9] International Energy Agency, *Tracking Industrial Energy Efficiency and CO_2 Emissions* (Paris, France: OECD/IEA, 2008), 94.

[10] A. Parasuraman, Valarie A. Zeithaml, and Leonard L. Berry, "A Conceptual Model of Service Quality and Its Implications for Future Research," *Journal of Marketing* 49, no. 4 (1985): 41–50.

[11] Daniel Berg, "Analysis of the Service Sector," *International Journal of Information Technology & Decision Making* 5, no. 4 (2006): 699–701.

[12] See Note 9 above.

[13] U.S. Energy Information Administration, "Major Fuel Consumption (Btu) by End Use for All Buildings, 2003," http://www.eia.doe.gov/emeu/cbecs/cbecs2003/detailed_tables_2003/2003set19/2003html/e01a.html (accessed May 14, 2010).

[14] U.S. Energy Information Administration, "Preliminary End-Use Consumption Estimate," http://www.eia.doe.gov/emeu/cbecs/enduse_consumption/intro.html (accessed May 14, 2010).

[15] U.S. Department of Energy, "Energy Savers: Your Home" http://apps1.eere.energy.gov/consumer/your_home/space_heating_cooling/index.cfm/mytopic=12530 (accessed May 14, 2010).

[16] "DOE Updates Furnace Efficiency Standards," *Energy Design Update* 26, no. 12 (2006): 2–4.

[17] "Furnaces: Upgrades and Replacements," *Consumer Reports* 10, (1993): 660–661.

[18] See Note 15 above.

[19] See Note 14 above.

[20] U.S. Energy Information Administration, "At Home and At Work: What Types of Lights Are We Using?" http://www.cia.doe.gov/emeu/cbecs/lit-type.html (accessed May 14, 2010).

[21] Avis Brad, Gustafson Woods and Jeff Harris, "Monitored Savings from Energy-Efficient Lighting in DC Office," *Center for Building Science News* 4, no. 1 (1997), http://eetdnews.lbl.gov/cbs_nl/nl16/dcoffice.html (accessed May 14, 2010).

[22] See Note 15 above.

[23] U.S. Department of Energy, "Energy Savers: Your Home," http://apps1.eere.energy.gov/consumer/your_home/lighting_day lighting/index.cfm/mytopic=12200 (accessed May 14, 2010).

[24] U.S. Energy Information Administration, "Commercial Buildings Energy Consumption Survey," http://www.eia.doe.gov/emeu/cbecs/pba99/mercantile/mercantile.html (accessed May 14, 2010).

[25] "Georgia-Pacific Program Drives Sustainability," *Paper Film & Foil Converter* 82, no. 10 (2008): 30.

[26] Target.com, "Eco-Friendly Products and Packaging," http://sites.target.com/site/en/company/page.jsp?contentId=WCMP04-031817 (accessed May 14, 2010).

[27] Target.com, "The Importance of the three R's," http://sites.target.com/site/en/company/page.jsp?contentId=WCMP04-031813 (accessed May 14, 2010).

[28] Joe Truini, "Wal-Mart, Target Explore Enviro Retailing," *Waste News* 9, no. 13 (2003): 19.

[29] Walmart, "Sustainability," http://walmartstores.com/press room/FeaturedTopics/?id=6 (accessed May 14, 2010).

[30] "NYC Mandates Plastic Bag Recycling," *Paper, Film & Foil Converter* 82, no. 6 (2008): 17.

[31] Walmart, "Sustainability Fact Sheet," http://walmartstores.com/ViewResource.aspx?id=2392 (accessed May 14, 2010).

[32] Walmart, "Reusable Bags," http://walmartstores.com/Sustainability/7990.aspx (accessed May 14, 2010).

[33] U.S. Energy Information Administration "Annual Energy Review," http://www.eia.doe.gov/emeu/aer/pdf/pages/sec2_25.pdf (accessed May 14, 2010).

[34] Amy Zuber, "Go, T.E.E.M.! New McDonald's Units Conserve Energy, Save Money," *Nation's Restaurant News* 34, no. 11 (2000): 30.

[35] Jim Johnson, "Restaurant Chain Converts to Wind," *Waste News* 9, no. 6 (2003): 1–5.

[36] Jim Johnson, "Restaurant Chain to Devour Wind," *Waste News* 11, no. 9 (2005): 16.

[37] Carolyn Walkup, "Chicago's Epic Burger Serves Up 'More Mindful' Menu in Quest to Minimize its Carbon Footprint," *Nation's Restaurant News* 40, no. 24 (2008): 1–4.

[38] Pamela Parseghian, "Restaurants Get Help Finding Produce," *Nation's Restaurant News* 40, no. 39 (2006): 30.

[39] Brian Stys, "Green Restaurants: Commercial Kitchens Face Unique Challenges as Well as Opportunities for Saving Energy and Materials," *Environmental Design & Construction* 11, no. 5 (2008): 64.

[40] Marianne Wilson, "Energy Management: Changes in Refrigerants and Energy Procurement are Major Concerns," *Chain Store Age* 83, no. 5 (2007): 164–166.

[41] "Electric End Use Cools Off," *Nation's Restaurant News*, 2 (2 suppl., 2003): 18.

[42] Energysmart Library Room, "Refrigerators," http://www.energyguide.com/library/EnergyLibraryTopic.asp?bid=austin&prd=10&TID=17257&SubjectID=8371 (accessed May 14, 2010).

[43] See Note 40 above.

[44] Dusty Jackson, "Upping Energy Efficiency Through Dehumidification," *Chain Store Age* 82, no. 11 (2007): 92.

[45] See Note 39 above.

[46] National Restaurant Association, "Recycling/Waste Reduction/Composting," http://conserve.restaurant.org/issues/recycling_detail.cfm (accessed May 14, 2010).

[47] Nancy Mullane, "San Francisco Compost a Hit with Local Vineyards," *National Public Radio*, http://www.npr.org/templates/story/story.php?storyId=6619306 (accessed May 14, 2010).

[48] U.S. Energy Information Administration, "Characteristics by Activity: Office," http://www.eia.doe.gov/emeu/cbecs/pba99/office/office.html (accessed May 14, 2010).

[49] Greg Kats and others, "The Costs and Financial Benefits of Green Buildings," California Sustainable Building Task Force (2003), 134.

[50] See Note 49 above.

[51] "Environmental Benefits of Buying Green Computers," *Air Pollution Consultant* 17, no. 6 (2007): 1.1–1.4.

[52] International Sustainable Development Foundation, "What We Do," http://isdf.org/what_we_do (accessed May 14, 2010).

[53] Apple, "MacBook and the Environment," http://www.apple.com/macbook/environment.html (accessed May 14, 2010).

54 Dell, "Dell Products recognized for Environmental Achievement on EPEAT," http://www.dell.com/content/topics/global.aspx/corp/environment/en/epeat?c=us&l=en&s=gen (accessed May 14, 2010).

55 U.S. Energy Information Administration, "Characteristics by Activity: Education," http://www.eia.doe.gov/emeu/cbecs/pba99/education/education.html (accessed May 14, 2010).

56 The College Sustainability Report Card, "Sustainability Categories," http://www.greenreportcard.org/reportcard-2009/categories (accessed May 14, 2010).

57 The College Sustainability Report Card, "Report Card 2009," http://www.greenreportcard.org/report-card-2009/schools/search/34 (accessed May 14, 2010).

58 Levitonproducts.com, "Leviton Monet Mark X 277V MarkXFluorescent Ballast (Narrow Fin)," http://www.levitonproducts.com/catalog/model_MNX20-7L.htm (accessed May 14, 2010).

59 U.S. Energy Information Administration, "Characteristics by Activity: Health Care," http://www.eia.doe.gov/emeu/cbecs/pba99/healthcare/healthcare.html (accessed May 14, 2010).

60 Green Guide for Health Care, "Green Guide," http://www.gghc.org/PilotDocsPub//2008%20GGHC%20Ops%20Revision/GGHC-Ops-08Rev-clean.pdf (accessed May 14, 2010).

61 William F. Theobald, *Global Tourism* (Burlington, MA: Elsevier Science, 2005), 406.

62 Conservation, "World's first publication on sustainable hotel siting, design and construction guiding principles released," http://www.conservation.org/sites/celb/news/Pages/091405_worlds_first_publication_on_hotel_siting_design_construction.aspx (accessed May 14, 2010).

63 Hervé Houdré, "Sustainable Development in the Hotel Industry," *Cornell Industry Perspectives*, no. 2, August, 2008, 1–77

64 "Environmental Development" *International Business Leaders Forum*, http://www.iblf.org/what_we_do/Environmental_Development.jsp (accessed May 14, 2010).

65 "The sustainable siting, design and construction of tourism facilities," *International Hotel and Restaurant Association*, 57, http://www.ih-ra.com/marketplace/docs/3environmental_teaching.pdf (accessed May 14, 2010).

Energy Consumption in the Transportation Sector

A. Introduction: Transportation Sector Contributors to Carbon Emissions

SIEMENS

St. Petersburg, the one-time capitol of Russia, is 396 miles (637 km) from Moscow. Because they are the two largest cities in Russia, the route between them is well traveled. In December 2009, a new opportunity for transportation began to take shape as the Russians implemented high-speed trains purchased from Siemens. The Russian state railway spent $485 million upgrading the track and $926 million for eight Siemens Sapsan trains and a 30-year service agreement. German-based Siemens is a multinational firm with more than 430,000 employees working in the industry, energy, and health care sectors. In 2008, Siemens had revenue of €77.3 billion and income from continuing operations of €1.859 billion.[1]

FIG. 13-1 Siemens Sapsan Train Arriving in St. Petersburg, Russia

Source: © AFP PHOTO/INTERPRESS/NEWSCOM

The Siemens Sapsan (Russian for *peregrine falcon*) train uses a breakthrough technology that stands in contrast to earlier trains. Instead of a locomotive, the Sapsan uses electric motors attached to wheels all along the train cars. The train's top speed is 217 miles (349 km) per hour, but it has reached 255 miles (410 km) per hour in some tests.

The Siemens high-speed trains will compete with airlines. The trip from downtown Moscow to downtown St. Petersburg is estimated to be 3 hours and 45 minutes. Although the actual flying time is shorter, the average travel time including the trips to and from the airport, check-in, and security clearance is five hours[2]. The service will be offered four times per day and will cut 45 minutes from the fastest train service available operating before 2009.

The Russian example is consistent with other markets in which high-speed trains have roundly beaten planes on price, overall travel time, and convenience at ranges up to 600 miles (965 km) between major cities. In addition, using electricity provides the opportunity to use replenishable sources of energy. Due to the benefits of this form of travel, the construction of a high-speed rail route between Paris and Lyons eliminated most commercial flights between the cities. Similarly, the Madrid-to-Barcelona high-speed link cut the air travel market for this route about 50% in a single year.[3]

Global spending on trains, tracks, and equipment is expected to reach €122 billion ($182 billion) in 2009—a figure that is up 18% since 2004. Moreover, projections suggest that this figure will rise to €150 billion by 2016, propelled by environmental concerns and stimulus projects.[4] Currently, Japan, France, Germany, Spain, Britain, Italy, Taiwan, Korea, and China have high-speed trains in operation. Spain plans to surpass Japan with the world's largest network of high-speed routes in 2010, but China and India should surpass Spain before long. France hopes to double its high-speed track to about 2,500 miles by 2020, and Denmark is shifting transportation funding from roads to rail-based public transportation. Four of the largest providers to this market are Siemens, Hitachi, Alstom, and Bombardier. General Electric is a developer of locomotive freight trains, but this company is also committed to serving the high-speed passenger train market.

It is interesting to note that Siemens hopes that the Sapsan will be stopping at platforms in the United States in the near future. President Barack Obama has vowed to spend $13 billion over five years to build high-speed rail links between major cities. Eight billion dollars are included in the economic-stimulus plan. The United States Department of Transportation has identified 11 corridors where high-speed trains could compete with air and intercity car travel. For example, Siemens Sapsan is a candidate for the Los Angeles-to-San Francisco route slated to be opened in 2020.[5]

The evolving market for high-speed rail travel illustrates how energy consumption is changing in the transportation sector. In order to gain a better understanding of this energy usage, this chapter offers an overview of the role of transportation in global energy consumption. We initially describe the use of energy associated with transportation, and we subsequently outline the use of energy for passenger and freight transportation. In the process, we discuss efforts to enhance the fuel efficiency of alternative modes of transportation. We begin with a description of personal modes of transportation that dominate fuel consumption in this macroeconomic sector. We subsequently describe current and planned levels of mass transit. We also outline energy consumption associated with freight transportation.

The transportation sector accounts for 26% of worldwide energy consumption and 25% of direct and indirect carbon emissions.[6] Over the past 15 years, transportation has been the fastest growing macroeconomic sector as energy consumption has risen by 37% and now exceeds 75 exajoules (one exajoule = 10^{18} joules) annually. The increase in carbon emissions correlates with the increase in energy consumption and now stands at more than 5.3 gigatons per year. At 89%, road travel—for freight and passengers—is the largest user of energy, and it is the main contributor to increased transportation energy use. Since 1990, energy consumption via other modes of transportation has increased by 13%, yet the increase in energy use for road travel over the same period is 41%.

Geographic location is significantly associated with the increase in demand for energy. Among Organization for Economic Cooperation and Development (OECD) nations, the increase in demand for energy use since 1990 has been 30%, whereas the increase outside of the OECD has been more than 55%. The rapid growth of the economy in several nations has resulted in increased personal income that is associated with higher vehicle ownership. In addition, the rise in income increases the need for freight transportation. The Chinese economy illustrates some of these trends. Although 15 years ago there were virtually no private cars in China, by the end of 2007, the number of privately owned cars had risen to more than 15 million.[7] The Chinese began aggressively promoting consumption as a way to balance their export-driven economy in 2000, and the purchase of automobiles was strongly encouraged.

Interestingly, the Chinese consumer has purchased many types of vehicles including cars, sport utility vehicles, and pickup trucks. Both government incentives and consumer preferences prompt ownership of larger vehicles. Many cities ban cars with engines smaller than one liter from entering their downtowns because such cars are typically old and dirty. Some municipalities ban smaller cars from expressways because they claim these cars endanger their owners when traveling at high speed. Consumer preferences also are associated with bigger vehicles. Because many car owners want to appear wealthy enough to have a chauffeur, Chinese autos tend to be slightly longer than their American counterparts. Consequently, Volkswagen, Audi, Honda, and General Motors have been successful in marketing larger cars, passenger vans, and sport utility vehicles. China is Buick's biggest market, where the company had sales of 332,115 vehicles in 2007, compared with 185,791 in the United States.[8]

Although efforts to economize on the use of energy require consideration of energy use and carbon emissions across the globe, complete data for the transportation sector are not currently available. As the Chinese example illustrates, there is a strong rate of change in consumption habits in emerging economies. Estimates suggest that sometime after 2010, greenhouse gas emissions from the developing world will exceed those in the industrialized world.[9] Nevertheless, comprehensive data addressing all modes of transportation (other than international air travel) are only available for the 18 countries affiliated with the International Energy Agency (IEA). These countries include Australia, Austria, Canada, Denmark, Finland, France, Germany, Greece, Ireland, Italy, Japan, the Netherlands, New Zealand, Norway, Sweden, Switzerland, the United Kingdom, and the United States.

The transportation sector includes energy associated with *passenger* travel and *freight* travel. Although similar technologies are associated with both transportation needs, the opportunities to realize energy savings vary across transportation sectors.

B. Personal Modes of Transportation

In 2005, passenger travel energy use was 30 exajoules, which represents an increase of 24% since 1990. More than 2.1 gigatons of carbon emissions are generated through passenger travel. As Figure 13-2 indicates, automobile transportation accounts for 87% of energy use. Buses, rail, and passenger ships together represent 3% of final energy use, and domestic air travel accounts for the remaining 10%.

Figure 13-3 indicates that the high percentage of auto travel is consistent across these mature economies. With the exception of Japan, auto travel accounts for at least 75% of passenger travel among countries analyzed by the International Energy Agency. Across countries in the analysis, auto travel accounted for 82% of passenger kilometers in 1990 as well as in 2005. Since 1990, per capita increases in car passenger travel have increased on average 1.1% per year, and air travel has increased by 2.7% per year. Although there have been increases in the amounts of auto travel, these improvements have occurred simultaneously with increases in auto efficiency. Nevertheless, higher passenger transport energy use is associated with a 23% increase in auto-related carbon emissions since 1990. Carbon emissions are greatest in Australia, the United States, and Canada, where vehicles are larger and heavier and travel distances are longer. In contrast, countries such as the Netherlands and Japan have higher population densities and lower levels of travel per capita.

Political aspirations and gas economy have at times been at odds since the 1973–74 oil embargo. This embargo sent a message that countries need to be conservative

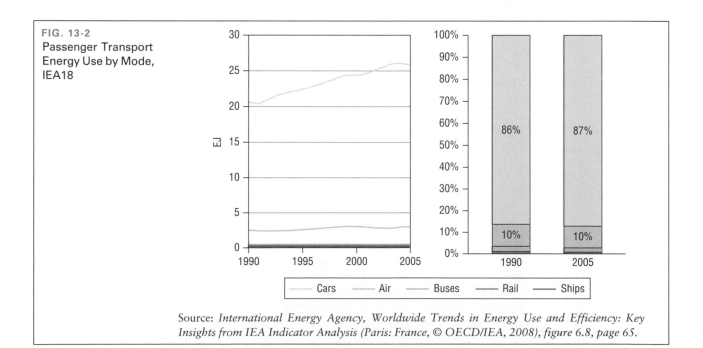

FIG. 13-2
Passenger Transport Energy Use by Mode, IEA18

Source: *International Energy Agency, Worldwide Trends in Energy Use and Efficiency: Key Insights from IEA Indicator Analysis (Paris: France,* © *OECD/IEA, 2008), figure 6.8, page 65.*

FIG. 13-3 Share of Total Passenger Travel by Mode

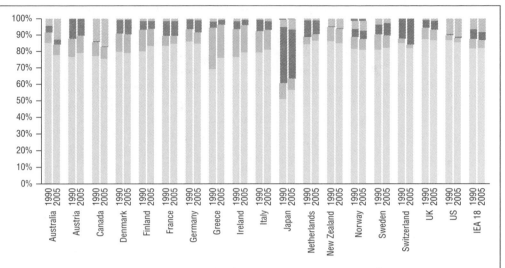

Source: *International Energy Agency*, Worldwide Trends in Energy Use and Efficiency: Key Insights from IEA Indicator Analysis *(Paris: France, © OECD/IEA, 2008), figure 6.4, page 61 (2008)*

in their use of oil and seek alternative sources of energy. In the United States, Congress passed the 1975 Energy Policy and Conservation Act that required the doubling of fuel efficiency to 27.5 miles per gallon by 1985.[10] These fuel efficiency ratings are referred to **corporate average fuel economy** (CAFE) standards. The ratings for automobiles are higher than those for light trucks and SUVs for automobiles.

Although energy efficiency increased, President Reagan rolled efficiency back to 26 miles per gallon. Over the next two decades, the United States witnessed very few modifications to these fuel requirements. Congress deliberated on occasion about the most efficient manner by which to induce conservation efforts. Enhancements to the corporate average fuel economy have been discussed as alternatives to higher gasoline taxes, but the U.S. government has done little to intervene via either mechanism during this era.[11] In 2003, fuel economy standards in China moved ahead of U.S. standards[12]. It was not until 2007 that Congress moved U.S. standards back to 35 miles per gallon, but this standard is not enforceable until 2020. The United States' 35-mile-per-gallon standard is in the proximity of the standards already in place in Japan and Europe.[13]

The amount of energy used has been increasing, yet the energy use per passenger kilometer is declining. People are traveling more, but technology has enabled individual modes of transportation to run more fuel efficiently. *Car ownership* similarly influences energy consumption. In most IEA countries, the percentage of ownership has increased over the past 15 years, and this increased car ownership generally is associated with higher per capita car energy consumption. *Car usage* refers to the distance traveled by each car. Car usage has fallen as more households increasingly own more than one car. When homes own multiple cars, journeys are shared between cars and travel per car declines. Car ownership and usage provide the total distance traveled per capita. In most IEA countries, reductions in the fuel intensity of cars were not sufficient to offset the increases in car ownership and car use. Thus, car energy use per capita increased in most IEA countries. The exceptions to this were Canada, Finland, Germany, Norway, and the United Kingdom.[14]

Efforts to reduce emissions in the transportation sector must recognize that changing transportation energy use takes time.[15] For example, autos and light trucks ordinarily last about 15 years, whereas new aircraft are typically in use for 20 to 35 years. Passenger cars are completely redesigned approximately every eight years, but the essential technologies are in place three years prior to bringing the car to market. New technologies, therefore, often take up to 10 years to be implemented fully into production. In addition, retail marketing must make new fuel technology (e.g., low-sulfur diesel fuel) available across a market.

Given that auto-related usage continues to dominate the transportation sector, one must consider ways to reduce consumption. These ways include changes in personal transportation devices and increased use of mass transit. Personal, motorized modes include diesels, hybrids, and enhanced gasoline technologies. Other technologies (e.g., electric vehicles, natural gas, hydrogen fuel cells) have been proposed as alternatives to gasoline, but these concepts are not currently available at a price level that would capture appreciable market share. The percentage of each diesel, gasoline, and hybrid technology varies markedly from market to market. Although the North American market remains a gasoline market, diesel engines have the dominant market share in Europe.[16] Consider first the use of diesel engines.

Diesel

The **diesel engine** was invented by Rudolph Diesel in the 1880s as an alternative to steam and gasoline engines.[17] The gasoline engine and diesel developed over time, but for many years the choice between diesel and gasoline technology was a simple decision. While the diesel engines of 20 years ago had better fuel efficiency than gasoline engines, they produced significant amounts of soot. In addition, they were noisy and offered lower pickup relative to gasoline engines.

In order to appreciate the advantages of diesel over gasoline, it is valuable to examine the basic operation of each motor. Both gasoline and diesel engines are internal combustion devices, and both engines use the standard piston-based cylinder engine block. The combustion process is different for the two engines. In a gasoline version, the engine intakes a mixture of gas and air, compresses it, and then ignites the mixture via a sparkplug. In diesel motors, no sparkplug is required because the fuel is ignited by the high temperature generated during compression. Diesel fuel is a heavier and less volatile mixture of hydrocarbons than gasoline and therefore offers more energy per gallon than gasoline. Diesel engines have higher compression ratios, more rapid combustion, and leaner operations. Consequently, diesel engines offer greater thermodynamic efficiency and lower fuel consumption than gasoline engines.[18]

Diesel technology has changed dramatically over the past 15 years, and the changes make these new vehicles viable alternatives to gasoline engines. The first issue with diesel has been the high level of sulfur produced by the engines. The U.S. Environmental Protection Agency (EPA) mandates of 2006 required oil refiners to produce a clean diesel fuel with sulfur concentrations no greater than 15 parts per billion. This mandate reflects a 98% improvement over 1970s-era diesel output. The result is substantially lower levels of sulfur dioxide pollutants, and lower sulfur in the air means less acid rain and better engine performance.[19] The exhaust systems also eliminate sulfur and other harmful nitrogen oxide compounds.

A second concern with diesel has been the soot produced by these engines. Diesel soot is **particulate matter,** a mixture of solid and liquid material made up of carbon particles, hydrocarbons, and inorganic material. The American Lung Association

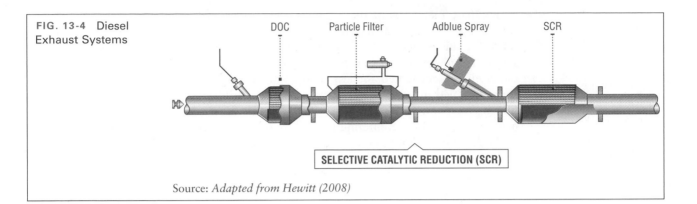

FIG. 13-4 Diesel Exhaust Systems

DOC   Particle Filter   Adblue Spray   SCR

SELECTIVE CATALYTIC REDUCTION (SCR)

Source: *Adapted from Hewitt (2008)*

reports that short-term increases in exposure to particulate matter have been linked to death from respiratory and cardiovascular causes, including strokes, increased numbers of heart attacks, inflammation of lung tissue, and aggravated asthma attacks. Long-term exposure has been associated with increased hospitalization for asthma, stunted lung function growth in children and teenagers, damage to the small airways of the lungs, increased risk of heart attacks and strokes, increased risk of dying from lung cancer, and greater risk of death from cardiovascular disease.[20] The U.S. EPA estimates that more than 4,700 premature deaths occur each year in just nine cities analyzed (Detroit, Los Angeles, Philadelphia, Pittsburgh, St. Louis, Boston, Phoenix, Seattle, and San Jose).[21] The exhaust systems on new diesel motors ensure that the limited levels of soot enter the atmosphere. The selective catalytic reduction (SCR) exhaust system outlined in Figure 13-4 illustrates these enhancements. Initially, the exhaust runs through a diesel oxidation catalyst that minimizes hydrocarbons and carbon monoxide. In the next phase, a urea-based solution is sprayed onto the exhaust flow. The hot exhaust air transforms the urea into ammonia and mixes with nitrogen oxides in the SCR, where the mixture converts to water vapor and harmless nitrogen gas.

These enhancements complement other inherent advantages to diesel power. One of the advantages offered by diesel is the potential to refine the fuel from a variety of sources. The fuel can be derived from crude oil, but it can also be processed from bio waste. Biodiesel is made through a chemical process in which fat or vegetable oil is separated into methyl esters (biodiesel) and glycerin (a by-product used in soaps and other products). In North America, most biodiesel is made from soybean oil, but in Europe rapeseed (canola) oil is the most common source. Biodiesel is biodegradable, nontoxic, and essentially free of sulfur and aromatics.[22]

The performance advantages of diesel engines are also noteworthy. The higher compression ratios of these motors mean more energy is derived from the air/fuel combination, and the car also enjoys relatively better power than one powered by a gasoline engine. Although the higher compression ratio means that engines require heavier crankshafts and connecting rods, the stronger design and the low coefficient of friction result in engines that last longer. It is not uncommon to see these engines operating for well over 200,000 miles. Mercedes-Benz, for example, has High Mileage Awards for cars that achieve the 250,000, 500,000, 750,000, one million-kilometer and one million-mile marks. Gregorios Sachinidis, a Greek taxi driver who has driven his 1976 Mercedes-Benz 240 diesel more than 2.8 million miles, is the reigning high mileage champion.

The new fuel systems, the enhanced exhaust mechanisms, the enhanced fuel injection operations, and the inherent physical advantages have resulted in a renaissance for this engine. The initial market for the diesel has been Western Europe. In 2006, diesel engines outsold gasoline engines for the first time in this region. The diesel engine accounted for less than 25% of auto sales in 1998, but this market share doubled in less than a decade. Consequently, most European, Japanese, and North American auto producers offer multiple diesel options in Europe, and these new diesel designs are entering into many other markets.

At the start of 2009, new diesel engine technology was being reintroduced to the United States market. In the United States, the standards established by the state of California are the most stringent, and 16 other states have adopted or have announced their intention adopt the California tailpipe standards.[23] The new diesel technologies offered by Mercedes-Benz, BMW, Honda, and other manufacturers now meet California standards and can be sold throughout the American market. Nevertheless, the market share for these cars is less than 3%.

The Volkswagen VW Jetta TDI exemplifies the challenges associated with marketing these new vehicles. Relative to its gasoline counterpart, the TDI (diesel) offers 30% more fuel economy, 25% less greenhouse gas emissions, and about 50% more power (torque). To the extent that the firm can inform consumers about the environmental and economic advantages of the cars, it has the potential to capture market share in the midsize sedan product class.

VW must contend with price, fuel availability, and quality perceptions. The price of diesel vehicles is due in part to their heavier, more expensive parts. Although the list price of the Jetta TDI is higher than the SE model, the diesel is eligible for a tax credit.[24] While some options on diesel vehicles are more expensive than on gas counterparts, the purchase price of this car is not appreciably different. In addition, the resale price of a diesel is expected to be high, but there is no basis for comparison yet in North America.

The other salient price issue concerns the availability and cost of diesel fuel. Of the 175,000 gas stations in the United States, only 45% carry diesel fuel. Moreover, the price of diesel fuel is higher than that of gasoline, and the demand for diesel has been increasing at a more rapid rate. In December 2008, the average price for gasoline in the United States was $1.69, whereas the per-gallon price for diesel fuel was $2.45. Thus, the diesel owner pays a higher price for fuel, but the car offers better fuel efficiency and performance. Furthermore, the tank of fuel will take the driver a longer distance in the diesel engine.

While consumers undoubtedly weigh the initial and fuel costs of operations, there remains a substantial portion of the population with strong negative perceptions of diesel cars. These consumers may be previous owners of VW Golfs or Mercedes 240 from an earlier era of diesel technology. The challenge will be to change consumer perceptions of this technology. Manufacturers such as BMW are touting the ecological (low carbon emissions) value of their products as well as the fuel efficiency.

Hybrids

Hybrid technology has drawn substantial attention in North America despite modest sales levels. In 2007, hybrids accounted for 2.6% of the market—a level exceeded by diesel engines.[25] Toyota boasts that 10% of its sales are associated with hybrids, but most other manufacturers do not report significant levels of hybrid sales. Estimates indicate, however, that hybrid sales will account for 14% of the worldwide market for automobiles by 2020.[26]

In order to understand the advantages of hybrid vehicles, it is valuable to examine the manner by which these engines convert and store energy. Hybrid technology includes the standard **hybrid engine** and the plug-in hybrid. Figure 13-5 illustrates the four phases of engine operations for a standard hybrid engine. The hybrid system adds two pieces of equipment—an electric motor and fuel cells. At the point of ignition, the engine sends energy to the electric motor and drive train. The electric motor sends this energy to the fuel cells. During acceleration, energy is provided to the drive train via the electric motor and **gas engine**. When the vehicle is cruising, the gasoline engine is not in operation, and energy is provided by the fuel cells. Finally, the hybrid engine has the ability to capture the energy from the operation of the brakes and store this energy in the fuel cells.[27]

The standard hybrid offers some advantages and disadvantages relative to gasoline engines. First, the hybrid uses a much smaller engine than the typical gasoline engine. Larger engines require more fuel to carry them, limit acceleration, and use more energy while idling. The lighter engine is complemented with lighter materials throughout the car, and these lighter materials also reduce energy needs. In addition, the plug-ins take advantage of advanced aerodynamics and low-rolling-resistance tires that contribute to fuel efficiency.[28]

The hybrid engine outperforms the gasoline engine, but for many consumers, the performance advantages do not motivate consumption. Analysts in the auto industry recognize three niche markets for hybrids.[29] Environmentalists are those motivated based on the ecological benefits of the product. A second group of

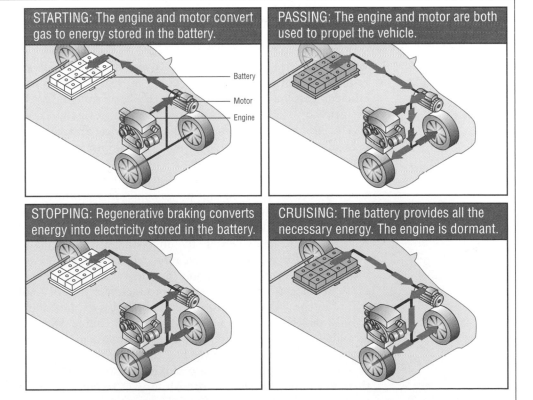

FIG. 13-5 Hybrid Engine Operations

STARTING: The engine and motor convert gas to energy stored in the battery.

Battery
Motor
Engine

PASSING: The engine and motor are both used to propel the vehicle.

STOPPING: Regenerative braking converts energy into electricity stored in the battery.

CRUISING: The battery provides all the necessary energy. The engine is dormant.

Source: *Adapted from http://www.hybridcars.com/2010 Hybridcars.com, (accessed January 29, 2009)*

consumers is motivated to buy them primarily as a fashion statement. The third market is people who budget for gas and do the calculations to determine whether the purchase is economical as well as ecological.

The plug-in hybrid has the advantages of the hybrid but also enables the owner to obtain electricity from a power outlet rather than from the gasoline engine. The use of the power outlet enables the *charged* hybrid to run for some period of time without using gasoline. For example, the 2009 Ford Escape plug-in uses high-voltage lithium-ion batteries that enable the vehicle to travel up to 30 miles on battery power alone.[30] Plug-in technology is in its infancy, but the fuel efficiency advantages of this technology are noteworthy. The Toyota Prius averages 42 miles to the gallon, but the plug-in averages 67 miles per gallon.[31] When the cost to refuel batteries is included, the plug-in averages 53 miles per gallon.

There are notable limitations on this technology in its current form. First, the increased battery usage results in a smaller weight capacity in which four or five adults may overload the vehicle. Second, the current cost to modify a hybrid for plug-in use can exceed $10,000. At $4 per gallon for gas, the cost to operate the standard Prius is about 10 cents per mile, but the plug-in cost is about 8 cents per mile. At this 2-cent differential, the break-even point for the plug-in is 500,000 miles. Without rebates or tax incentive, hybrids will not be economical for many consumers.

Enhanced Gasoline

Consumers interested in enhancing fuel efficiency do not necessarily need to move away from gasoline engines. Fuel efficiency can economically be enhanced by buying smaller-engine vehicles, using ethanol, and purchasing cars with new fuel injection systems.

It may seem obvious that one way to enhance fuel efficiency is to buy a smaller vehicle that has much better fuel economy. Given that government average fuel economy requirements are increasing, most manufacturers are bringing new fuel-efficient gasoline-based cars to market. For example, BMW's Mini Cooper has a list price of $19,200 and averages 32 miles per gallon in the city. The entry-level BMW 328i series (automatic) has a list price of $33,600 and averages 19 miles per gallon. Thus, one way to lower one's footprint and cut costs is by moving to smaller vehicles.

A related option is to consider the form of gasoline used by new vehicles. Flex fuel cars are designed to run on gasoline or a mixture of gasoline and ethanol.[32] Ethanol is a renewable fuel that comes from agricultural feedstocks. Using ethanol results in less pollution and reduces smog-forming emissions by as much as 50% relative to gasoline.[33] Despite the limits on emissions, ethanol has a few limitations. Using corn for fuel rather than food reduces the supply of food without complementary increases in the supply of energy. For example, the United States used 20% of its 2007 corn harvest to produce less than 4% of the demand for auto fuel.[34] In some markets, the price of ethanol is greater than that of gasoline, and it is only widely available in the Midwestern United States. Finally, the mixture of gasoline and ethanol contains less energy than a gallon of gas. Consequently, these engines have 20 to 30% lower fuel efficiency when operated using ethanol.

Auto manufacturers are also making improvements in gasoline engines to make them more fuel efficient.[35] Ford Motor Co. recently introduced an EcoBoost direct-injection technology that offers greater performance and a 20% increase in fuel economy over comparable traditional engines. By 2012, Ford expects to produce

750,000 EcoBoost vehicles annually worldwide. Ford claims that the premium for EcoBoost—a price Ford has not disclosed—is a better value than a hybrid or diesel. General Motors is also using new direct-injection engines in about 10% of its global production.

Of course, there are multiple technologies in development designed to enhance auto fuel efficiency. Mercedes-Benz, GM, and other makers are developing gas engines that use a homogenous-charge compression-ignition (HCCI) technology. HCCI provides substantial boosts in fuel economy by burning gas faster at lower temperatures and by reducing some of the energy lost during the combustion process. This technology and other digital components will increase the viability of gasoline engines that will be around for the foreseeable future.[36]

One of the simplest and most cost-efficient means by which to save energy in the auto sector is the education of drivers. Although many U.S. state programs instruct new drivers about fuel efficiency, there is substantial degradation of fuel efficiency apparently due to lost enthusiasm and learning loss by drivers.[37] Table 13-1 outlines a number of strategies that drivers can implement to reduce the amount of gasoline used by their vehicles.

TABLE 13-1 EFFICIENT AUTOMOBILE OPERATIONS[38]

Vehicle Operations

a. Observe the speed limit and maintain a steady pace. Excessive speed is inefficient and requires more energy for stopping.

b. Extend one's vision 10 to 12 seconds down the road and anticipate stops as far ahead as possible.

c. Avoid tailgating; it reduces chances for planning economic modes of driving.

d. Adjust driving habits to changing road conditions.

e. Use air conditioning at higher speeds and keep the windows closed. Avoid air conditioner use at lower speeds.

f. Instead of heavy braking, take advantage of rolling resistance to help slow down. This technique saves a lot of fuel.

g. Before turning off ignition, turn off all power-consuming accessories (e.g., air conditioning). This action minimizes engine load during startup.

h. Avoid revving the engine just before turning off the ignition; it costs extra fuel and can cause engine damage.

i. Limit idling time to 30 seconds, but restarting the engine within 8 to 10 minutes causes little engine wear.

j. Avoid unnecessary steering wheel movement; sideward movements cause fuel-consuming drag.

k. Slowly accelerate on slippery pavement and gravel roads.

l. Avoid quick starts and unnecessary braking.

Vehicle Maintenance

a. Change oil regularly; dirty oil increases friction and engine wear.

b. When possible, use multiviscosity motor oil.

c. Regularly check points and plugs.

d. Upon fill-up, check the engine oil, coolant, transmission fluid, and battery levels.

e. Maintain proper wheel alignment.

f. Maintain tires at maximum pressure, and check pressure when tires are cold.

g. Reduce the engine's idling speed.

h. Regularly replace air and fuel filters.

i. Adjust the automatic choke for proper operation.

j. Monitor the positive crankcase ventilation (PCV) valve regularly.

k. Assess carburetor, fuel pump, gas line, and gas tank fuel leaks.

l. Regularly lubricate the axle and wheel bearings.

Trip Planning

a. Make sure your vehicle is safe and economically road ready for long trips.
b. Consolidate short trips to avoid as many cold starts as possible.
c. Record and monitor gas mileage.
d. Avoid idling by starting the engine when actually ready to go.
e. Whenever possible, use the telephone rather than making a trip.
f. Plan routes to avoid traffic congestion.
g. Carpool. Multiple parties in the car mean fewer auto trips.
h. Carry as little extra weight as possible in auto's trunk.
i. Park in the first reasonable parking place available.

Vehicle Choice

a. Select a car with a high rear axle ratio and overdrive transmission.
b. Avoid permanent roof racks and wide-tread tires.
c. Consider radial tires.
d. If more than one car is available, use the most economical one as much as possible.
e. Avoid power-consuming accessories.
f. Consider a diesel-powered or electric hybrid car.
g. Choose a streamlined car with a small frontal area.
h. Use automatic speed control.

Driver Attitude

a. Always consider fuel economy when driving and drive for fuel economy.
b. Avoid driving when angry or upset.
c. Use public transportation whenever possible.
d. Use a bike or walk for short distances.

Source: *Government of the District of Columbia.*

Importantly, the marketing efforts of auto manufacturers and auto dealers and the efforts of government can be focused on the continuous education of drivers regarding fuel efficiency. Estimates developed in the 1980s indicate that a 10% savings in fuel efficiency can be realized through proper vehicle operations, selection, and maintenance.[39] Despite recognition of the merits of conservation, large-scale efforts at continuing driver education have been absent in many markets.

Another means that drivers can use to enhance fuel efficiency is geographic positioning systems (GPS). Drivers equipped with GPS input an address and let the GPS sketch the route. Although these systems can draw the most efficient route, there is tremendous variability in their operations and routing procedures.[40] Nevertheless, GPS saves energy by indicating wrong turns and highlighting points of interest to consumers.

Another means for saving energy in the auto industry is ride share and carpool programs. Although there have been appreciable efforts to raise the number of shared rides, more than 10 trillion seats remain empty in car trips, and the average number of passengers per car trip marginally exceeds one passenger.[41] One program that increases auto occupancy is **high-occupancy vehicle** (HOV) lanes. Several states have implemented these HOV on freeways to reduce people-hours of travel without significantly increasing vehicle-hours of travel.[42]

C. Mass Transit

There is a growing consensus that between one fourth and one half of the recoverable resources in conventional oil have been consumed, and the halfway point will be reached in the next 5 to 25 years.[43] The use of oil for transportation can be reduced not only through personal modes, but also via mass transportation systems.

Among the International Energy Agency's 18 countries, nonauto transportation currently accounts for 13% of energy consumption. Ten percent of this transportation is associated with domestic air travel.[44] Together, buses, passenger rail, and passenger ships account for about 3% of energy consumption.

Improvements to mass transit systems are rarely due to progress in one mode of transportation, but often involve consideration of the connecting points among alternative transportation modes. Progress, therefore, is not solely due to the advent of new technology. The effectiveness and performance of these systems is measured in passengers carried, ridership growth, travel speeds, and land development effects.[45] It can take appreciable amounts of time to integrate new technologies into transportation grids. In the following section, underscore trends in air, bus, and rail technology that have potential to reduce carbon emissions in the transportation sector. Consider first air transportation.

Air Travel

A recent study from the Intergovernmental Panel on Climate Change (IPCC) estimates that the aviation contribution to global warming is 3.5% of the sum of all anthropogenic effects and projects that this contribution will grow.[46] In the United States, air travel has increased at an average annual rate of more than 5% per year since 1970. Passenger miles per gallon for commercial air travel, however, have increased by 150% since 1975. This increase is primarily due to energy efficiency improvements, but is also associated with increased occupancy rates. Although local, federal, and international entities pressure the aviation industry to enhance fuel efficiency, most efficiency enhancements have been driven by profit motives rather than by regulation.[47]

Peculiarities of air travel contribute to the emissions. More than 90% of the exhaust emitted from aircraft is in the form of oxygen or nitrogen. About 7% of the exhaust is composed of CO_2 and H_2O, and another 0.5% is composed of NOx, HC, CO, SOx, other trace chemical species, and carbon-based soot particulates. The combination of these gases is estimated to be a factor of more than 1.5 times that of carbon dioxide alone. The majority of aircraft emissions are injected into the upper troposphere and lower stratosphere at altitudes ranging from 5 to 8 miles above Earth. Consequently, the influence of burning fossil fuels at these altitudes is approximately double that due to burning the same fuels at ground level.

Reductions in climate effects require consideration of the *technological performance* of aircraft as well as the *operational activities*. New technologies from manufacturers have reduced emissions and achieved the largest reductions in energy intensity of any transportation system. These include enhanced engine designs, aerodynamic efficiencies, and structural efficiencies.[48] For example, Boeing is committed to improving the fuel efficiency of each new generation of commercial airplanes by at least 15%.[49] Boeing's 787 Dreamliner incorporates new engines, increased use of lightweight composite materials, and modern aerodynamics that yield improvements in fuel use and reductions in carbon dioxide emissions.

Operational activities also contribute to an aircraft's carbon emissions. Airlines have increased the number of seats on each plane by more than 35% since 1950, and they have increased the load factor, or percentage of occupancy, by 15%[50]. When more people are on a flight, the relative cost of travel is lowered.

Airlines and airports can enhance efficiency by reducing the amount of time that planes are idling on the ground or in holding patterns in the air. The International Air Transport Association (IATA) estimates that air traffic management enhancements

FIG. 13-6 Boeing
787 Dreamliner

Source: © *AFP PHOTO/THE BOEING COMPANY/Newscom*

could improve fuel efficiency and reduce carbon emissions substantially.[51] Boeing has developed a Tailored Arrival concept that increases airplane arrival efficiency via continuous (versus step-down) descent that lowers fuel usage, noise, and emissions.[52] Boeing's initial trials suggest that advanced arrival techniques can save up to 800 gallons of fuel per flight and save airlines up to $100,000 annually in fuel costs per aircraft flying into major airports.[53] Airlines and airports also benefit from quick turnaround at the gate. Southwest Airlines, for example, uses quick turnaround at the airport terminal as a strategic competitive advantage. Quick turnaround lowers operational costs and raises customer satisfaction.[54]

Enhancements in technology and operations are essential to the future of air travel. Historically, air transportation growth (5.5% per year) has outpaced reductions in energy consumption (3.5% per year), and research suggests that this trend will continue into the foreseeable future.[55]

High-Speed Trains

Since the introduction of the Shinkansen high-speed train service between Tokyo and Osaka, Japan, in 1964, the **high-speed train** (HST) has increasingly become a vibrant part of transportation in many parts of the globe.[56] *High-speed trains* are a family of technologies that provide high-capacity, frequent railway services achieving an average speed of more than 200 kilometers per hour (124 miles per hour).[57]

HSTs have been widely used in Asia and Europe and have also been proposed or implemented in the Middle East as well as South and North America. The advent of HST has brought to consideration trade-offs between compatibility and speed. The original Shinkansen HST achieved a speed in excess of 200 kilometers per hour, but it required special tracks due to the narrow design of the light rail system. Other systems developed since the Shinkansen have utilized existing track to varying degrees. The ability to use existing track results in lowered costs of implementation but limits the returns from the HST operations.

As we discussed earlier in this section, cost-benefit analysis of a mode of transportation is context specific and requires consideration of the interface between modes of transportation. Nevertheless, there are some notable benefits associated with HST. Since introduction, these systems have been designed to increase capacity. In the short term, the introduction of another mode of transportation increases the opportunities to travel. The costs of alternative reasonable travel modes and travel conditions influence long-term term capacity and acceptance of HST.

A second notable advantage is the reduced travel time relative to other rail systems. The Shinkansen line reduced rail travel between Osaka and Japan to 2½ hours from 7 hours.[58] HST draws travelers from trains, but it also gains travelers from air and car travel. For example, an analysis of the potential of the HST to free runway capacity at London Heathrow indicates that the HST could lead to travel time savings on 10 routes currently served from the airport.[59] If the airport became a rail station, the substitution of HST for air travel would eliminate about 20% of its Heathrow's runway capacity.

The third important benefit of HST is the safety record of these train systems. In most markets, these trains offer substantially greater safety records than any alternative mode of transportation. Japan's Shinkansen HST, for example, has not has had a fatality over the 45 years of operation.[60] Although Japan is noted for the high incidence of earthquakes, these catastrophes have infrequently lead to derailments and never resulted in fatalities.

Although there are substantial benefits to HST, there are some notable environmental outcomes.[61] Because HSTs are predominantly electric powered, emissions are related to sources used to generate the electricity. HST operations increase local air pollution, climate change, noise, and land conversion. The most harmful pollutants related are sulfur dioxide (SO_2) and nitrogen oxides (NOx). Although evidence suggests that HST operations have a smaller influence on environment than the aircraft and the car, because the environmental influence of HST and other modes depends on infrastructure and interface to other transportation modes and services, the environmental trade-offs between HST and other modes remain unclear. The merits of HST depend on balance between the amount of travelers that substitute HST for air or auto travel versus the amount of new traffic generated by HST.

Rapid Transit

Since 1995, public transit use has increased by 20%, yet it still only accounts for about 1% of total passenger miles. One technology that has drawn substantial recent attention is **bus rapid transit** (BRT). BRT is a rubber-tired rapid transit mode that combines stations, vehicles, services, running ways, and intelligent transportation system (ITS) elements into an integrated system.[62] BRT systems and features have been implemented in South America, Europe, and Australia, and BRT systems are integrated into urban planning programs in more than 20 cities in the United States and Canada.[63]

BRT offers a number of benefits. First, these bus-based systems can be flexibly integrated into existing transportation routes. In congested areas, rapid bus lines can be integrated at relatively lower cost than alternative transit systems such as light rail. Second, digital operating systems used in BRT systems provide increased service quality in terms of on-time performance and speed. For example, the BRT line on Wilshire Boulevard in Los Angeles operates at speeds that are 75% faster than local service.[64] The introduction of BRT systems also has been associated with increased patronage. In Brisbane, Australia, for instance, bus ridership was up 40% in the six months after the introduction of a BRT system.[65]

Rapid transit system designers have also benefitted by using some of the attractive components of light rail systems throughout bus routes. Thus, BRT systems emphasize simple and direct routes. In addition, they emphasize the permanency of routing and ease of use. Not surprisingly, these features, along with speed of transportation, increase the attractiveness of BRT to consumers.[66]

Together, these benefits yield lower carbon footprints for communities. The carbon footprint per capita for the bus is substantially lower than the footprint for auto travel. Each time someone elects to ride rather than drive, the footprint is lowered.

Due to the popularity of BRT, a number of applications with varying benefits have adopted this term.[67] The Orange Line in Los Angeles is a full-scale BRT because it incorporates all facets of BRT systems—including dedicated bus lanes with intelligent transportation systems, full-scale stations, low floor/level boarding, branded vehicles, and off-vehicle ticket vending. In contrast, partial BRT systems run part of their routes in city streets and part of their routes in dedicated transit lanes. They offer most of the other amenities and efficiencies of full BRT systems. For example, the Euclid Busway in Cleveland combines in-traffic operations with single bidirectional dedicated lanes. Other rapid bus systems do not employ most BRT benefits but are primarily express buses. Although they may employ intelligent transportation systems, they do not operate via dedicated traffic lanes.

FIG. 13-7 Los Angeles MTA Valley College Stop

Source: © *Jeremy Oberstein*

FIG. 13-8 Orlando's Lymmo Bus Rapid Transit

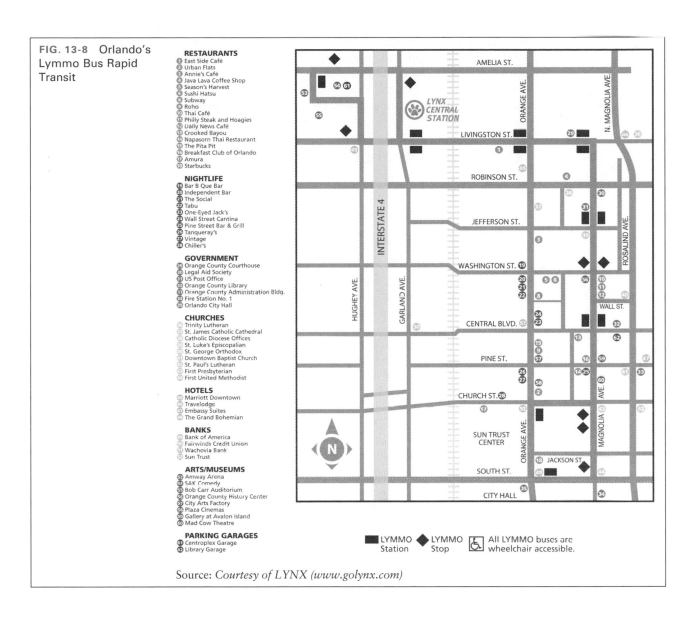

RESTAURANTS
1. East Side Café
2. Urban Flats
3. Annie's Café
4. Java Lava Coffee Shop
5. Season's Harvest
6. Sushi Hatsu
8. Subway
9. Roho
10. Thai Café
11. Philly Steak and Hoagies
12. Daily News Café
13. Crooked Bayou
14. Napasorn Thai Restaurant
15. The Pita Pit
16. Breakfast Club of Orlando
17. Amura
18. Starbucks

NIGHTLIFE
19. Bar B Que Bar
20. Independent Bar
21. The Social
22. Tabu
23. One-Eyed Jack's
24. Wall Street Cantina
25. Pine Street Bar & Grill
26. Tanqueray's
27. Vintage
28. Chiller's

GOVERNMENT
29. Orange County Courthouse
30. Legal Aid Society
31. US Post Office
32. Orange County Library
33. Orange County Administration Bldg.
34. Fire Station No. 1
35. Orlando City Hall

CHURCHES
36. Trinity Lutheran
37. St. James Catholic Cathedral
38. Catholic Diocese Offices
39. St. Luke's Episcopalian
40. St. George Orthodox
41. Downtown Baptist Church
42. St. Paul's Lutheran
43. First Presbyterian
44. First United Methodist

HOTELS
45. Marriott Downtown
46. Travelodge
47. Embassy Suites
48. The Grand Bohemian

BANKS
49. Bank of America
50. Fairwinds Credit Union
51. Wachovia Bank
52. Sun Trust

ARTS/MUSEUMS
53. Amway Arena
54. SAK Comedy
55. Bob Carr Auditorium
56. Orange County History Center
57. City Arts Factory
58. Plaza Cinemas
59. Gallery at Avalon Island
60. Mad Cow Theatre

PARKING GARAGES
61. Centroplex Garage
62. Library Garage

■ LYMMO Station ◆ LYMMO Stop ♿ All LYMMO buses are wheelchair accessible.

Source: *Courtesy of LYNX (www.golynx.com)*

The introduction of BRT must be accompanied by appropriate marketing efforts to ensure patronage.[68] These BRT systems should have a unique and consistent brand image. For example, the Lymmo system operated in downtown Orlando is a BRT system that operates within the city's Linx transit program. The Lymmo signs use attractive and distinct lettering that distinguish the Lymmo system from the rest of transit operations. BRT systems should also promote rider awareness and usage via logos, color combinations, and graphics that are applied consistently to vehicles, stations, and printed materials. Thus, the Orlando Lymmo buses use distinctive colors and the Lymmo logo consistently throughout their routes. Promotional programs also should include public information, service innovation, and pricing incentives. As Figure 13-7 illustrates, Orlando's Lymmo provides information that links the BRT system to points of interest as well as to other modes of transportation. In addition, the free cost of this system to consumers is emphasized throughout promotional materials.

The introduction of BRT to Orlando has reaped many benefits. The city enjoys reduced congestion and reduced parking demand in the downtown area. Lymmo has also encouraged more transit use and increased mobility and accessibility to major downtown destinations. Moreover, BRT has enhanced public perceptions of downtown Orlando and allowed for additional downtown development capacity.[69]

D. Freight Transportation

Within the transportation sector, freight accounts for 30% of energy consumption among the International Energy Agency's 18 countries. Freight transport energy use was 18 exajoules, and this consumption level was 27% greater than the level in 1990.[70] Freight includes the transport of products by highway, air, rail, sea, and pipeline. At 99% of total final energy consumption, oil is far and away the fuel of choice for moving freight. Most of this fuel is some form of diesel. Diesel fuel represents 87% of trucking and 88% of rail transport. Ships use fuel oil (59%) and diesel fuel (41%) to move products across waterways. Because the movement of freight via rail, water, and pipeline is relatively energy efficient, our analysis focuses on the highway sector.[71]

Movement of freight via highways occurs via light, medium, and heavy-duty trucks.[72] Light trucks include utility vans and step vans, whereas medium-sizes trucks include walk-in trucks, city delivery trucks, school buses, and beverage delivery vehicles. Between 1990 and 2000, light truck energy use grew at a faster rate than for any other mode.[73] Together, light and medium-sized trucks use about 26.8 billion gallons of fuel per year. Heavy-duty vehicles include refuse trucks, dump trucks, cement trucks, and conventional semi-trailers. These trucks use about 10.6 billion gallons of fuel per year.

Since 1975, the amount of energy required to move a ton of freight has been cut in half.[74] Enhancements in the efficiency of freight transportation are associated with engine systems, heavy-duty hybrids, parasitic losses, idle reductions, and safety considerations.[75] Consider first technological enhancements to engine systems.

Engine systems are inextricably related to pollution, emissions, oil dependency, and safety. Twin goals of engine systems are to lower emissions and improve thermal efficiency of engine operations. Over the past two decades, NOx and particulate matter have been decreased 85% and 95%, respectively. Today's state-of-the-art highway trucks achieve 42% thermal efficiency—thus 58% of the energy is not converted to mechanical work. In the United States, the goal is to achieve another 83% reduction in NOx and particulate matter while simultaneously increasing thermal efficiency another 20% (resulting in thermal efficiency of 50%) by 2010.

A second initiative associated with engine operations is **hybrid electric vehicles** (HEV). In heavy-duty hybrid trucks, two power sources are combined to obtain the required power to propel the vehicle. HEVs combine advantages of the electric motor drive and an internal combustion engine to propel the vehicle. The electric traction motor is powered from a battery pack that serves as a secondary energy storage device. The HEV also has the ability to absorb energy from the operation of the brakes and store this energy in the fuel cells. In a conventional vehicle, only 10 to 15% of the energy contained in gasoline is converted to traction, but the hybrid can potentially be improved to 30 to 40%. This increase in efficiency reduces emissions and increases fuel economy.[76] Regrettably, the development of heavy hybrid technology has not kept pace with advancements in passenger vehicles (e.g., Prius) and demands more research before commercialization.

The operations activities associated with a truck influence the potential to reduce energy consumption. Large trucks are not only the means of transportation for drivers, but they are also the homes for drivers on the road. **Parasitic energy losses** are energy losses incurred due to a number of factors that include aerodynamics, auxiliary operations, and other operations. Together, these constraints account for 40% of the energy used by heavy trucks. Improved technologies that limit energy use contribute to reductions in parasitic energy loss. The aerodynamics and rolling resistance of trucks can be enhanced somewhat, but the rectangular shape of the cargo area is a significant constraint. Auxiliary operations include heating, lighting, and on-board amenities (e.g., computers, entertainment systems, appliances). These ancillary activities also contribute to efforts to minimize idling. In many cases, the long-haul trucks stand in the idle position for more than six hours per day. This inactive time produces particulate matter, raises the level of noise, and consumes fuel. The energy cost of auxiliary functions can be reduced via technologies that reduce the power requirements associated with these operations. In addition, the time spent idling can be reduced by enhanced freight scheduling, new idling technologies, and turning trucks off.

In order to attract and retain competent drivers, it is essential that safety improvements accompany other efforts to enhance energy efficiency. Crash avoidance and survival are enhanced via advanced braking technologies, stability controls, lane-tracking systems, and video-based visibility systems. The introduction of these technologies can be incompatible with other efficiency goals given that many safety features increase the weight and reduce the aerodynamics of trucks. Therefore, strong coordination between safety and energy efficiency is critical to long-term sustainability concerns.

Summary

A. Introduction: Transportation Sector Contributors to Carbon Emissions

The purpose of this chapter has been to provide an overview of the role of transportation in energy consumption. Given that the transportation sector accounts for 26% of worldwide energy consumption, no review of energy is complete without analysis of transportation. We provided a summary of the energy use associated with passenger and freight transportation. In the process, we discussed efforts to enhance the fuel efficiency of alternative modes of transportation. Importantly, we highlighted opportunities to engage in green marketing action that contributes to energy conservation in transportation.

B. Personal Modes of Transportation

Passenger travel energy use has increased by 24% since 1990, and this increase has prompted substantial effort to reduce energy consumption associated with personal transportation devices. Personal, motorized modes include diesels, hybrids, and enhanced gasoline technologies. Each of these innovations has benefits and limitations. Furthermore, the market share of each technology varies considerably across national and international market regions. The fuel efficiency of auto transportation can also be enhanced via increased educational efforts for drivers, new traffic plans (e.g., HOV), and improved energy utilization technologies.

C. Mass Transit

Mass transit includes travel via air, bus, and rail. The net result of burning fossil fuels in the air is double that of burning the same fuels at ground level. Reductions in climate effects for air travel require consideration of the technological performance of aircraft as well as the operational activities. New technologies from manufacturers have reduced emissions and achieved the largest reductions in energy intensity of any transportation system. High-speed trains reduce travel time relative to other rail systems, are extremely safe, and use electricity that can be derived from replenishable sources. Bus rapid transit is a rubber-tired rapid transit mode that combines stations, vehicles, services, running ways, and intelligent transportation system elements into an integrated system. These buses can be flexibly integrated into existing transportation routes and provide increased service quality in terms of on-time performance and speed. Rapid transit system designers have also benefitted by using some of the attractive components of light rail systems throughout bus routes.

D. Freight Transportation

Enhancements in the efficiency of freight transportation are associated with engine systems, heavy-duty hybrids, parasitic losses, idle reductions, and safety considerations. Engine system enhancements seek to lower emissions and improve thermal efficiency of motor operations. Hybrid electric vehicles combine the advantages of the electric motor drive and an internal combustion engine to propel the vehicle. *Parasitic energy losses* are inefficiencies due to aerodynamics, auxiliary operations, and other operations. Idling can occur for many hours a day, and efforts are being made to reduce the particulate matter, noise, and fuel use created while idling. Safety considerations include crash avoidance technologies such as advanced braking and stability controls.

Keywords

bus rapid transit (BRT), 271
corporate average fuel economy (CAFE), 261
diesel engine, 262

gas engine, 265
high-occupancy vehicle (HOV), 268
high-Speed Trains (HSTs), 270
hybrid electric vehicle (HEV), 274

hybrid engine, 265
parasitic energy losses, 275
particulate matter, 262

Questions

1. The Siemens Sapsan example illustrates how new technologies can be applied to reduce carbon emissions. What is the influence of low oil prices on such efforts?
2. The Siemens example mentions 11 corridors that could use high-speed rail. Name three routes between major cities that would be candidates, and name one route that would not be a candidate. Explain your answers.
3. How have diesel technologies changed over the past few years?
4. What factors account for the poor acceptance of hybrid automobiles for personal travel?
5. What are the limitations associated with using corn as a fuel for automobiles?
6. Table 13–1 outlines a number of mechanisms designed to increase fuel efficiency of personal vehicles. How can these ideas be communicated to the public more effectively?
7. From a carbon footprint standpoint, what are the merits of jet travel versus high-speed train travel between Los Angeles and San Francisco?
8. Why is it necessary to examine the links between transportation systems to gain an understanding of usage and fuel efficiency?
9. To what extent has your community promoted use of mass transit systems? What could be done to enhance this effort?
10. About 40% of the energy consumed by a semi-tractor trailer is consumed when the vehicle is not moving. What contributes to this overhead cost, and what can be done to reduce this cost?

Endnotes

[1] Siemens, "Siemens Global Website," http://w1.siemens.com/entry/cc/en/ (accessed May 15, 2010).

[2] Andrew E. Kramer, "Siemens Fills Russia's Need for High-Speed Train," *New York Times,* September 24, 2009, B1.

[3] Paul Glader, "High-Speed Rail Keeps Train Makers on Track," *Wall Street Journal*, October 21, 2009, B1.

[4] See Note 3 above.

[5] See Note 2 above.

[6] International Energy Agency, *Tracking Industrial Energy Efficiency and CO_2 Emissions* (Paris, France: OECD/IEA, 2008), 324.

[7] Ariana Eunjung Cha, "China's Cars, Accelerating a Global Demand for Fuel," *Washington Post Foreign Service*, July 28, 2008, A01.

[8] Greg Kable, "Auto China 2008," *AutoWeek*, May 5, 2008, 11–12.

[9] Daniel Sperling and Deborah Salon, *Transportation in Developing Countries: An Overview of Greenhouse Gas Reduction Strategies,* (Arlington, VA: Pew Center on Climate Change, May, 2002), 1–49. http://www.pewclimate.org/docUploads/transportation_overview.pdf (accessed May 15, 2010).

[10] Robert P. Rogers, "The Effect of Energy Policy and Conservation Act Regulation on Petroleum Prices, 1976–1981," *Energy Policy* 24, no. 2 (1985): 63–94.

[11] U.S. Congressional Budget Office, "The Economic Costs of Fuel Economy Standards Versus a Gasoline Tax," (December, 2003), 37 http://www.cbo.gov/ftpdocs/49xx/doc4917/12-24-03_CAFE.pdf (accessed May 15, 2010).

[12] Feng An and Amanda Sauer, *Comparison of Passenger Vehicle Fuel Economy and Greenhouse Gas Emission Standards Around the World* (Arlington, VA: Pew Center for Climate Change, December, 2004). 1–36. http://www.pewclimate.org/docUploads/Fuel%20Economy%20and%20GHG%20Standards_010605_110719.pdf (March 16, 2010).

[13] Thomas Friedman, *Hot, Flat, and Crowded* (New York, NY: Farrar, Straus and Giroux, 2008), 448.

[14] See Note 6 above.

[15] David L. Greene, and Andreas Schafer, "Reducing Green Gas Emissions for U.S. Transportation," *Pew Center on Global Climate Change*, May, 2003, 1–80, http://www.pewclimate.org/docUploads/ustransp.pdf (accessed May 15, 2010).

[16] "Hybrids Higher, Diesels Dip," *Automotive News* 82, no. 6290 (2008): 19.

[17] Tom Nash "Get on the diesel wagon," *Motor*, May 2004, 30–38. http://www.motor.com/magazine/pdfs/052004_07.pdf.

[18] J. L. Sullivan and others, "CO_2 Emission Benefit of Diesel (versus Gasoline) Powered Vehicles," *Environmental Science and Technology* 38, no. 14 (2004): 3217–3223.

[19] Ben Hewitt "The Case for Diesel: Clean, Efficient, Fast Cars (Hybrids Beware!)" *Popular Mechanics* 185, no. 1 (2008), 70–75.

[20] American Lung Association, "Facts about Particle Pollution," April, 2008, 1–4, http://www.lungusa2.org/sota/SOTA08__PMFacts.pdf.

[21] Ellen Post and others, *Particulate Matter Health Risk Assessment for Selected Urban Areas* (Washington, DC: U.S. Environmental Protection Agency, 1–180. http://www.epa.gov/ttnnaaqs/standards/pm/data/pm_risk_tsd_finalreport_2005_mainbody.pdf

[22] Biodiesel, "Biodiesel basics," http://www.biodiesel.org/resources/biodiesel_basics/ (accessed May 15, 2010).

[23] Pew Center for Climate Change, "Vehicle Greenhouse Gas Emissions Standards," http://www.pewclimate.org/what_s_being_done/in_the_states/vehicle_ghg_standard.cfm (accessed May 15, 2010)

[24] Lawrence Ulrich, "Green-Fuel Guide," *Popular Science* 270, no. 5 (2007), 76–81.

[25] See Note 16 above.

[26] Matthew Dolan, "Gas Engines Get Upgrade in Challenge to Hybrids," *Wall Street Journal*, January 14, 2009, B1.

[27] Sherri Koucky "Designs to Be Proud of—Hybrid-Electric Vehicles Hit the Streets," *Machine Design* 72, no. 10 (2000), 42–5.

[28] Karim Nice and Julia Layton. "How Hybrid Cars Work," 20 July, 2000, *HowStuffWorks.com*, http://auto.howstuffworks.com/hybrid-car.htm (accessed May 15, 2010).

[29] David Kiley, "Are Hybrid Sales Running Out of Gas?" *Business Week*, March 20, 2006, 20.

[30] Ford, "2010 Ford Escape Hybrid," http://www.fordvehicles.com/suvs/escapehybrid/ (accessed May 15, 2010).

[31] "Our Prius Hybrid Gets Plugged In," *Consumer Reports* (February, 2009), 49–50.

[32] U.S. Environmental Protection Agency, "Flex-fuel vehicles," www.fueleconomy.gov (accessed May 15, 2010).

[33] HybridCARS, "Guide to Ethanol Cars & Vehicles," http://www.hybridcars.com/ethanol-car (accessed May 15, 2010).

[34] Lester P. Brown, *Plan B 3.0: Mobilizing to Save Civilization* (New York, NY: W.W. Norton and Company, 2008), 398.

[35] See Note 26 above.

[36] Bob Brooks, "Mercedes Gasoline Engine Cuts Fuel Use 29% Below Diesel," *Automotive Industries* 187, no. 9 (2007): 20.

[37] David L. Greene, *Driver Energy Conservation Awareness Training: Review and Recommendations for a National Program*, Report # ORNL/TM-9897, (Oak Ridge, TN: U.S. Department of Energy, 1986), 84.

[38] District Department of the Environment, "Fuel-Saving Tips for Drivers," http://ddoe.dc.gov/ddoe/cwp/view,a,1210,q,492495.asp (accessed May 15, 2010).

[39] See Note 37 above.

[40] "GPS Navigators," *Consumer Reports* 73, no. 6 (2008): 18–21.

[41] See Note 37 above.

[42] Michael J. Cassidy and others, *Empirical Reassessment of Traffic Operations: Freeway Bottlenecks and the Case for HOV Lanes*, Research Report UCB-ITS-RR-2006-6 (2006) (University of California, Berkeley: Institute of Transportation Studies), 24.

[43] See Note 37 above.

[44] See Note 6 above

[45] Samuel Zimmerman and Herbert Levinson, "The Facts About BRT," *Planning* 72, no. 5 (2006): 34–35.

[46] J. E. Penner and others, eds., *Aviation and the Global Atmosphere: A Special Report of the Intergovernmental Panel on Climate Change* (Cambridge, UK: Cambridge University Press, 1999), 23.

[47] J. J. Lee and others, "Historical and Future Trends in Aircraft Performance, Cost and Emissions," *Annual Review of Energy and the Environment* 26 (2001): 167–200.

[48] See Note 47 above.

[49] Boeing, "2008 Environment Report," http://www.boeing.com/aboutus/environment/environmental_report/environmentally-progressive-products.html (accessed May 15, 2010).

[50] Jim Corridore, "Cleared for Take-off," *BusinessWeek*, June 13, 2006, 5.

[51] International Air Transport Association, "IATA's Industry Priorities for 2010," http://www.iata.org/about/priorities.htm (accessed May 15, 2010).

[52] Richard A. Coppenbarger, Rob W. Mead, and Douglas N. Sweet, "Field Evaluation of the Tailored Arrivals Concept for Datalink-Enabled Continuous Descent Approach," *Journal of Aircraft* 46, no. 4 (2009): 11.

[53] David Hughes "Saving Fuel With '4D'; San Francisco Tests Build on Flight Trials in Australia and Holland," *Air Transport* 165, no. 14 (2006): 54.

[54] Jody Hoffer Gittell, *The Southwest Airlines Way: The Power of Relationships for Superior Performance* (New York: McGraw-Hill Professional, 2005), 320.

[55] See Note 47 above.

[56] Shigeru Miura and others, "The Mechanism of Railway Tracks," *Japan Railway and Transport Review* 15, (March, 1998): 38–45.

[57] Moshe Givoni, "Development and Impact of the Modern High-speed Train: A Review," *Transport Reviews* 26, no. 5 (2006): 593–611.

[58] M. Matsuda, "Shinkansen: The Japanese Dream," in *High Speed Trains: Fast Tracks to the Future*, eds. J. Whitelegg, S. Hultén, and F. Torbjörn, (Hawes, North Yorkshire: Leading Edge, 1993), 111–120.

[59] Moshe Givoni, "Aircraft and High Speed Train Substitution: The Case for Airline and Railway Integration" (PhD thesis, University College London, 2005).

[60] Kaho Shimizu, "Derailment Mars Shinkansen Safety Myth," *The Japan Times Online*, November 19, 2004, http://search.japantimes.co.jp/cgi-bin/nn20041119f1.html (accessed May 15, 2010).

[61] See Note 59 above.

[62] D. Hess, B. Taylor, and A. Yoh, "Light-Rail Lite or Cost-Effective Improvements to Bus Service? Evaluating the Costs of Implementing Bus Rapid Transit," *Journal of the Transportation Research Board* no. 1927 (2005): 22–30.

[63] Herbert S. Levinson and others, "Bus Rapid Transit: An Overview," *Journal of Public Transportation* 5, no. 2 (2002): 1–30.

[64] See Note 62 above.

[65] Sean Rathwell and Stephen Schijns, "Ottawa and Brisbane: Comparing a Mature Busway System with Its State-of-the-Art Progeny," *Journal of Public Transportation* 5, no. 2 (2002): 163–182.

[66] Graham N. Carey, "Applicability of Bus Rapid Transit to Corridors with Intermediate Levels of Transit Demand," *Journal of Public Transportation* 5, no. 2 (2002): 97–114.

[67] See Note 62 above.

[68] See Note 45 above.

[69] Michael Baltes and Joel Rey, *Bus Rapid Transit Evaluation*, Summary of Final Report, BC137-17 2003, 1–2, http://www.dot.state.fl.us/research-center/Completed_Proj/Summary_PTO/FDOT_BC137_17.pdf (accessed May 15, 2010).

[70] See Note 6 above.

[71] See Note 15 above.

[72] U.S. Department of Energy, *Roadmap and Technical White Paper*, 21CTP-0003, 2006, 1–78. http://www1.eere.energy.gov/vehiclesandfuels/pdfs/program/21ctp_roadmap_2007.pdf (accessed May 15, 2010).

[73] Stacy C. Davis and Susan W. Diegel, *Transportation Energy Data Book*, 22nd ed. (Oak Ridge, TN: U.S. Department of Energy, Report # ORNL-6967, 2002), 382.

[74] See Note 72 above.

[75] See Note 72 above.

[76] Ali Emadi and others, "Topological Overview of Hybrid Electric and Fuel Cell Vehicular Power System Architectures and Configurations," *IEEE Transactions on Vehicular Technology* 54, no. 3 (2005): 763–770.

The Role of Industrial Consumption

A. Primary Industrial Contributors to Carbon Emissions

AMERICAN INSTITUTE OF STEEL CONSTRUCTION—STEEL DAY

On September 18, 2009, Hillsdale Fabricators of St Louis, Missouri, held an open house to inform members of the community about its sustainable operations. Hillsdale Fabricators is a full-service steel fabricator that specializes in complex fabrication, and it is the only St. Louis-area fabricator certified in major steel bridges. The recently opened Lucas Oil Stadium that serves as the home of the Indianapolis Colts is one of this company's celebrated accomplishments.[1]

The open house at the Hillsdale facility was one of 173 events hosted by the American Institute of Steel Construction (AISC). Engineers, architects, university faculty and students, and the general public visited steel mills, fabricators, service centers, galvanizers, and other steel facilities to network and witness advanced technologies in action. Moreover, Steel Day enabled visitors to see how the structural steel industry is building high-performance and sustainable projects. More than 7,000 people throughout the United States participated in the Steel Day activities.[2]

Steel Day drew attention to the critical role of structural steel in the country's infrastructure, economy, and employment. In addition, the day enabled the U.S. steel industry to illustrate some of the tremendous strides it has made toward sustainability. Steel is the world's most recycled material, and greenhouse gas, air, and water emissions have markedly dropped in this industry over the past 20 years.

The Steel Day project underscores some of the significant changes taking place in the industrial sector. In this chapter, we provide an overview of green marketing efforts associated with this part of the economy. Given that this sector accounts for one third of all energy consumption, there are important dividends that can be realized from effective management of energy usage and carbon emissions. We therefore begin by outlining several industries in this sector that reflect the largest usage of energy as well as the highest potential to reduce carbon emissions. We subsequently describe international efforts to enhance the sustainability of industry. Consider first the leading contributors to climate change in industry.

In a recent review of energy consumption in the industrial sector, the International Energy Agency (IEA) recognized marked potential to reduce emissions.[3]

FIG. 14-1 Lucas Oil Stadium in Indianapolis, Indiana

Source: © *Jeremy A. Williams*

On a worldwide basis, industry accounts for 33% of energy consumption and 36% of carbon emissions. There have been tremendous strides in the improvement of industrial efficiency, yet IEA estimates suggest that the equivalent of 600 to 900 million tons of oil equivalence could be reduced in the industrial sector. Moreover, the equivalent reduction in carbon emissions is 7 to 12% of global emissions or 1.9 to 3.2 gigatons of carbon dioxide.

The use of energy and the amount of carbon emissions varies considerably from one industry to the next. Figure 14-2 indicates that more energy is used in the chemical and petrochemical industries than in any other sector. Although chemicals are associated with the highest amount of energy use, a substantial portion of the energy is feedstock that is incorporated into chemical products. For example, much of the oil used in refining automobile fuel is incorporated into gasoline. In addition, the chemical sector, the iron and steel and the nonmetallic minerals industries are also large users of energy.

Figure 14-3 illustrates that 70% of carbon emissions for the sector are associated with iron and steel (27%), nonmetallic minerals (27%), and chemical/petrochemical industries (16%). In addition to these industries, there are substantial opportunities to reduce the amount of carbon emissions associated with the paper industry and nonferrous metal sectors. Unlike the household sector, there is not a single indicator associated with emissions across industries. Each industry has different factors that must be considered in efforts to reduce emissions. Therefore, we highlight factors associated with enhanced energy efficiency and carbon emissions in each of these industries.

FIG. 14-2 Final Energy Consumption by Industry, 2004

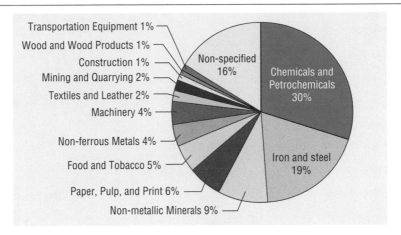

Source: *Based on International Energy Agency data, Tracking Industrial Energy Efficiency and CO₂ Emissions, (Paris, France:* © *OECD/IEA, 2007).*

FIG. 14-3 Carbon Emissions by Industry, 2004

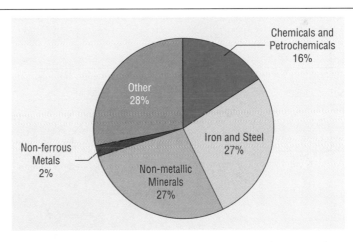

Source: *International Energy Agency, Tracking Industrial Energy Efficiency and CO₂ Emissions (Paris: France,* © *OECD/IEA, 2007), figure 2.3, page 44.*

B. Carbon Emissions Associated with Steel Production

In 2007, more than 1.3 billion tons of steel were produced in the world. Steel is a seemingly ubiquitous commodity that is incorporated into many final products.[4] Figure 14-4 indicates that construction is the largest user of steel, followed by machinery, metal products, and the automotive sector.

The steel industry and the nonmetallic minerals industry are the largest producers of carbon emissions in this economic sector. Figure 14-5 indicates that more than 90% of worldwide production of steel is concentrated in 10 markets. The industry has realized important efficiency gains over the past 20 years, but the worldwide average has not increased. Over this two-decade era, most growth has been in China, and the steel production in this country is relatively inefficient. In addition,

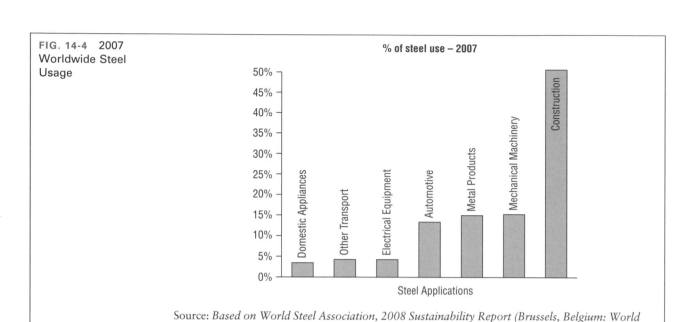

FIG. 14-4 2007 Worldwide Steel Usage

Source: *Based on World Steel Association, 2008 Sustainability Report (Brussels, Belgium: World Steel Association, 2008), p. 7.*

FIG. 14-5 Worldwide Steel Production, 2007

Source: *Based on World Steel Association, 2008 Sustainability Report (Brussels, Belgium: World Steel Association, 2008), p. 7.*

the Chinese market does not have substantial amounts of scrap available for steel recycling. China, Russia, India, and Ukraine account for almost half of all steel production and more than half of all carbon dioxide emissions associated with iron and steel.[5]

The production of iron and steel is complex and varies from one country to the next, yet there are similarities in the processes employed across geographic regions. In order to gain an understanding of energy consumption, it is necessary to outline the processes endemic to steel production. Figure 14-6 provides an overview of the

FIG. 14-6 Steel Production Processes[a]

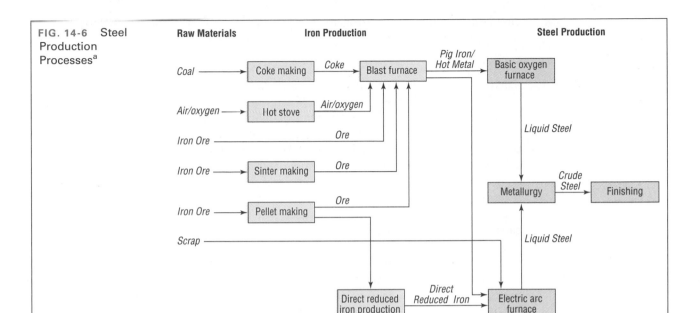

[a]Processes are shaded; Inputs and outputs are in italicized text.
Source: *Based on International Energy Agency, Tracking Industrial Energy Efficiency and CO$_2$ Emissions, (Paris, France: © OECD/IEA, 2008).*

essential processes associated with most steel production. Two methods, **basic oxygen** and **electric arc furnaces**, account for approximately 97% of all steel production. Basic oxygen is ordinarily used for high-tonnage production of carbon steels, and electric arc furnaces are to produce low-tonnage specialty steels.[6] More than 66% of production occurs through basic oxygen processes, and 31% occurs via electric arc procedures. After one of these processing methods has been employed, the metal is ready for metallurgy and finishing.

Basic Oxygen Furnaces

The production process for steel involves converting raw materials (i.e., iron ore, coal) into iron followed by converting iron into steel. Steel is then transformed via metallurgy and finishing that make the product useful to the construction, automotive, and other industries.

The *basic oxygen furnace* process produces products such as automotive fenders, encasements of refrigerators, and packaging.[7] The production of iron via basic oxygen furnaces involves the introduction of coke, iron ore, and oxygen into a furnace. In order to make coke, bituminous coal is fed into a series of ovens in which it is heated at high temperature for 14 to 36 hours in the absence of oxygen.[8] During this process, compounds are driven off and collected. Ammonia liquor is a by-product taken to wastewater facilities, and tar removed during this process is also stored. Light oil taken from the coke ovens becomes benzene, toluene, and xylene that are useful in chemical production (see petrochemicals below). Naphthalene is also derived as a by-product, and the remaining carbon is coke. The coke is then transferred to a quenching tower, where it is cooled either by a water spray or circulating an inert gas (nitrogen) in a process referred to as **dry quenching**. Coke making requires 0.75 to 2.0 GJ per ton of crude steel and sintering requires 2 to 3 GJ per ton.

The production of coke results in several forms of waste. Coke ovens produce air emission in the forms of particulate matter, volatile organic compounds, methane, sulfur oxides, and other pollutants. Wastewater is generated from the cooling of the coke oven gas and the processing of by-products (e.g., ammonia, tar). Coke production generates coke breeze during the quenching process. This compound is used to make sinter or is sold as a by-product. In addition to breeze, coke produces solid waste containing hazardous components such as benzene.[9]

Iron is produced when coke is combined with oxygen, flux, and iron ore in a blast furnace. In hot stoves, compressed air is blended with additional oxygen and heated to 1100°C. Oxygen is then injected at the bottom of the blast furnace. Because hot stoves account for 10 to 20% of the total energy requirement in an integrated steel mill, efficient hot stoves can yield substantial energy savings.[10]

Iron ore is ordinarily introduced into the blast furnace in the form of sinter or pellets. Sintering is the more efficient process for making direct feed for blast furnaces, and more than 50% of all iron ore is converted into sinter. Sintering involves heating fine ore and causing it to agglomerate into larger granules.[11] The heat consumed for the sintering reaction is about 33% of the total heat input into a steel plant. Since almost half of this energy is released into the atmosphere, waste heat recovery is a key strategy for improved efficiency. Although sintering is more efficient than pellet production, it results in greater amounts of dust levels per ton of steel produced.

Iron is produced in the blast furnace from coke, oxygen, iron ore, and flux. Limestone in the form of flux is added to remove sulfur and other impurities.[12] Impurities in the furnace produce blast furnace slag that rises to the top of the furnace.[13]

Iron that is produced in blast furnaces is then introduced into the basic oxygen furnace. The oxygen steelmaking process converts the molten iron from the blast furnace and steel scrap into steel. High-purity oxygen is introduced that lowers carbon, silicon, manganese, and phosphorous content of the iron, and flux is added to reduce sulfur and phosphorous levels.[14] These impurities are carried off in the slag that floats on the surface of the hot metal. The basic oxygen furnace production of steel requires approximately 1 to 13 GJ per ton of crude steel, including the hot stove, blast furnace, and oxygen furnace.

Electric Arc Furnaces

The *electric arc furnace* (EAF) produces products whose primary requirement is strength. For example, structural beams, steel plates, and reinforcement bars are made via electric arc furnaces.[15] Processing of steel from ore occurs in this manner via direct reduced iron production and electric arc furnace operations. In direct reduced iron production, oxygen is removed from lump iron oxide pellets to produce direct reduced iron (DRI).[16] The electric arc furnace employs this direct reduced iron and scrap to produce steel. Scrap is the most important element because about 80% of the inputs are of this nature.[17] Consequently, it is difficult to control the purity and quality of the steel produced. Mills that focus on EAF steel production normally concentrate on market segments where steel quality is not as critical.[18] During melting and refining operations, some of the undesirable materials within the bath are oxidized and become electric arc slag.[19] The production of direct reduced iron using natural gas requires about 12 GJ per ton of crude steel. Electric arc furnaces use 1 to 1.5 GJ of electricity per ton of crude steel.

Metallurgy and Finishing

The use of a basic oxygen or electric arc furnace yields crude steel, but refinement does not end. The liquid steel output from the furnaces is further refined via a series of processes referred to as **metallurgy**. The objectives of these processes are the removal of oxygen, hydrogen, sulfur, and other impurities. After removal of these impurities, the steel is cast into either ingots or semifinished shapes (e.g., slabs). Continuous casting into semifinished shapes requires less time, labor, energy, and capital than ingot casting.[20] Additional finishing such as galvanization is also incorporated into steel during this final phase.

Sustainability

The steel industry is attempting to enhance environmental sustainability via initiatives associated with *climate change*, *environmental protection*, and *management of natural resources*.[21] One aspect of climate change efforts focuses on reductions in the amount of carbon dioxide produced for each ton of steel produced. Part of this effort includes investments in technologies that raise the eco-efficiency of production. The International Energy Agency indicates that more than 3% of total sector energy use (2.9 EJ) and 3% of CO_2 emissions can be realized through improved efficiency of production processes and better reclamation of by-products of these processes.[22] Improved production processes include application of dry coke quenching in coke making, blast furnace and electric arc furnace enhancements, and steel finishing improvements.[23] The reductions associated with changes in these processes are realized when companies upgrade to the best available technologies.

The steel industry's concerns with environmental protection focus on monitoring of production and life cycle inventory management. Because the monitoring of operations is essential to this industry, most steel producers operate facilities that are ISO 14001 certified. *ISO 14000* refers to a family of management standards established by the International Standards Organization. The ISO 14001 standard enables firms to assess the environmental impact of their activities, improve environmental performance, and implement a systematic approach to achieving environmental objectives.[24] More than 85% of all employees and contractors in the steel industry operate at ISO-registered facilities.[25]

The third facet of environmental sustainability in the steel industry concerns the management of natural resources. *Material efficiency* refers to the amount of material that is not sent to permanent disposal in a landfill or incineration. This efficiency is realized by the familiar reduce, reuse, and recycle perspective. Material *reductions* are realized by using cokeless steel production technologies that do not rely on coke production. Marketing the blast furnaces' and electric arc furnaces' slag to the road construction and cement industries reduces energy costs and overall carbon emissions for the industrial sector.

The *reuse* of material is exemplified by an industry that boasts a 97% material efficiency level. This 100% efficiency goal is approached by working together with other industries. Efforts to use by-products of steel production more efficiently include coke oven and basic oxygen furnace gas recovery, blast furnace gas use, and slag/steel usage in cement making. Notably, slag marketed to the cement industry has the potential to reduce cement-related CO_2 by 50%.

The steel industry is also very active in *recycling*. Virtually all steel is recyclable, and as one of the few magnetic metals, it can easily be separated from waste and other metals. Steel is the most widely recycled material in the world. In 2006, for example, the industry recycled 459 metric megatons (mmt), equivalent to 37% of the crude steel produced in the year.[26] This recycling reduced carbon emissions by 827 mmt and saved the equivalent of 868 mmt of iron ore.[27]

C. Carbon Emissions in the Nonmetallic Minerals Industry

Nonmetallic minerals account for 9% of industrial energy use but represent 27% of carbon emissions.[28] The largest contributor to energy usage in the nonmetallic minerals sector is concrete production, and a central process to this production is the production of **cement**. After water, concrete is the second most consumed product in the world.[29] In 2000, worldwide concrete sales exceeded $97 billion.[30] The production of cement represents about 80% of energy use for nonmetallic metals and is an important source of CO_2 emissions. There have been substantial improvements in energy use in this industry over the past 15 years, yet there is potential for additional reduction associated with adoption of best available technologies.

Concrete is a global industry operating in 150 countries with more than 850,000 employees. At 46% of global cement production in 2005, China is the largest producer of cement. The top 10 producers (China, India, United States, Japan, Korea, Spain, Russia, Thailand, Brazil, and Italy) account for more than 71% of global production. Transportation costs for cement are extensive, and concrete is rarely transported more than 300 kilometers. The United States exports concrete to Mexico and Canada, and most of the country's imports come from China, Thailand, Canada, Thailand, and Greece.[31]

Concrete production is a relatively simple four-stage process.[32] The first stage is acquisition of raw materials. These materials include limestone, sand, and clay that typically come from quarries located near the cement manufacturing plant. These components provide the four main ingredients for cement: lime, silica, alumina, and iron.[33] In the second stage, these materials are analyzed, blended, and ground for further processing. In the third stage, materials are heated in a very large kiln that is more than 200 meters long with a diameter of 3 to 7.5 meters. The kiln reaches temperatures of 1,450°C, which turn the material into a marble-sized substance called **clinker**. When the limestone is heated, it undergoes a reaction in which carbon dioxide is released and calcium oxide is formed. Importantly, about half of the carbon emissions for concrete are associated with this process, and these emissions are unaffected by fuel switching or other efforts to enhance efficiency. In the fourth stage, gypsum is added, and the mixture is ground to a fine powder called **Portland cement**. Although there are other forms of cement, Portland cement is the most common and represents over 98% of cement sales in the United States.[34] Portland cement is marketed in eight different compounds that vary based on physical and chemical requirements such as durability and strength.[35]

Cement production can occur via wet or dry processes. The wet process facilitates easier control of chemical activity, but it has higher energy requirements due to the need to evaporate water prior to making calcium dioxide. Because the dry process does not require evaporation, the energy costs associated with cement production are lower. Consequently, dry processes are replacing wet processes on a worldwide basis.

Sustainability

Due to the amount of carbon emissions associated with the industry, concrete has been implicated as an industry that contributes to global warming.[36] Most of the carbon emissions in concrete production, however, are associated with the production of calcium oxide (a product essential to cement), and most sustainability efforts cannot address this primary source of emissions in the industry. Nevertheless, several strategies have been employed to limit the industry's impact on climate change.

Substantial efforts have been dedicated to *reducing* the amount of energy employed in the manufacturing process. The size of the kiln used to make cement influences energy costs. In China, the world's largest producer at nearly 50% of production, small kilns are being replaced by more efficient larger kilns. Concrete producers are also working with alternative fuels in order to reduce production costs, dispose of waste, reduce carbon emissions, and limit fossil fuel usage. These fuels may include tires, wood, plastics, chemicals, animal carcasses, sewage sludge, and construction waste. The use of alternative fuels varies by country. At one extreme, Germany relies on alternative fuels for about 37% of clinker production, yet South Korea, at the other extreme, incorporates less than 5% alternative fuels.

The process of grinding materials represents the largest electricity demand in the cement industry. Grinding associated with processing of raw materials and grinding of cement account for almost 100 kilowatt hours per metric ton of cement produced. Best industry practice indicates, however, that there is potential to reduce electricity usage by another 20%. Despite this potential, more than 90% of the energy associated with grinding is converted to heat that is not used in the production of cement. Clearly, there are opportunities to develop new processes that facilitate cement production at efficiency levels greater than 10%.

The concrete industry relies on *reuse* to limit carbon emissions. In many production processes, some Portland cement is replaced or supplemented with industrial by-products referred to as supplementary cementitious materials (SCMs).[37] Slag procured from the steel industry can be used as a substitute for limestone. Steel slag requires little additional fuel to convert it to cement clinker. As a result, carbon emissions are reduced due to lower energy needs. Fly ash, a by-product of coal burning, and silica fume, a by-product of silicon manufacturing, are also reused in as slag in the production of cement. The recovery of industrial by-products avoids the use of virgin materials in cement manufacturing and limits the amount of material disposed of in landfills. Moreover, greenhouse gas reductions are achievable by using SCMs to replace some Portland cement. The manufacture of Portland cement requires significant energy use, and replacement with SCMs reduces this energy burden. In addition, reuse of SCMs can improve workability of the concrete mixture, decrease concrete permeability, improve durability, and enhance strength.

Concrete is also one of the most *recycled* materials on the planet.[38] Recycling of concrete pavement involves breaking, removing, and crushing concrete from an existing pavement. Crushed concrete is then used as an aggregate in new Portland cement or other concrete processes.[39] In recent years, there have been advancements in concrete crushing technologies and methods to remove steel from concrete. This recycled concrete meets most specifications and is currently being used with other concrete and asphalt products and yielding better performance over comparable virgin concrete. The material is lighter than other concrete, which lowers the cost of material handling and transportation. Furthermore, recycling limits the amount of concrete discarded in landfills.

Analyses of the sustainability of concrete need to augment consideration of reduce–reuse–recycle logic with consideration for the long-term benefits of using concrete as a construction material.[40] The predominant raw material for the cement in concrete is limestone, the most abundant mineral on earth. Because the materials for concrete are readily available, concrete can be made from local resources and processed near a jobsite. Local shipping minimizes fuel requirements for handling and transportation. Concrete also yields durable, long-lasting structures whose life spans can be double or triple those of other common building materials. Finally, homes built with concrete (walls, foundations, and floors) are energy efficient because they take advantage of concrete's inherent ability to absorb and retain heat. Consequently, homeowners can significantly cut their heating and cooling bills and install smaller-capacity HVAC equipment.

D. Carbon Emissions Endemic to Chemical Production

The chemical industry produces plastics, synthetics, resins, detergents, fertilizers, and many other products on which we rely daily. The industry accounts for 30% of industrial energy usage, and this usage rate is growing at 2.2% annually.[41] The chemical industry also represents 16% of carbon emissions in the industrial sector.

Three types of intermediary products span raw materials (crude oil, natural gas, coal, and other minerals) and consumer goods. These intermediary products include **olefins, aromatics,** and **other intermediates.** Olefins include ethylene, propylene, and xylene. These chemicals are used to make a variety of products such as bottles and trash bags. Aromatics include benzene, toluene, and xylene used to make products such as footwear and car tires. The other intermediaries include synthetic gas used in ammonia and methanol production. The primary feedstock for olefins and aromatics is crude oil, whereas the primary feedstock for synthetic gas production is natural gas. Within the industry, 75% of feedstock is crude oil.

Nine chemical processes account for more than 65% of global energy use in the industry. These processes are associated with petrochemicals, inorganic chemicals, and fertilizers.

Petrochemicals

Steam cracking. Steam cracking is a process in which saturated hydrocarbons are broken down into smaller hydrocarbons. Steam cracking occurs in ovens in which feedstocks are broken down in the presence of steam.[42] This process also results in the removal of by-products such as hydrocarbons, water, and acid gas. Steam cracking accounts for more than 39% of final energy use in the chemical industry. It is the principal method for producing olefins (ethylene, propylene, and butadiene). This procedure has incurred a 50% reduction in energy consumption since the 1970s, yet implementation of improved technologies for the removal of by-products yields greater energy efficiency.

Aromatic extraction. Aromatic extraction includes the production of benzene, toluene, and xylene used to make products ranging from medicine to DVDs. Because the majority of energy employed in this process is feedstock, there is limited potential to reduce energy consumption.

Methanol. **Methanol** is a chemical that occurs as a result of biological processes conducted by vegetation, microorganisms, and other living species. It is produced synthetically through the catalytic steam process that typically uses natural gas as the feedstock. Methanol can be produced from natural gas, coal, municipal wastes, landfill gas, wood wastes, and seaweed, and it is used to make a variety of products such as plastics, paints, construction materials, and windshield washer fluid.[43] In 2006, 40% of methanol use was for formaldehyde and another 19% was used as a fuel additive. Seventeen countries account for more than 90% of methanol production. China is the largest producer and the only one that uses coal as a feedstock. The carbon emission cost associated with natural gas plants is lower than the emissions in coal-based facilities.[44]

Olefin and aromatic processing. Olefins are used to make plastics and synthetic rubber. The Unipol reactor process marketed by Union Carbide in 1977 was developed to manufacture polyethylene while the process for the manufacture of polypropylene was announced in 1983.[45] Polypropylene is the world's most widely used plastic, and Unipol is the most widely used process for making this plastic.[46] The Innovene process developed by BP is also widely used.[47] The rights to market Innovene are now owned by Ineos.

Inorganic Chemicals

Chlorine and sodium hydroxide. Chlorine is procured when salt is electrochemically decomposed into chlorine and sodium hydroxide. Chlorine is further processed to make polyvinyl chloride (PVC), used in plumbing, whereas sodium chloride is used by the paper, textile, and other industries. At more than 25% of total output, the United States is the world leader in production. Chlorine and sodium hydroxide are produced through three processes that vary in their sodium hydroxide concentration. These methods include the mercury, diaphragm, and membrane processes. The greatest potential for energy savings lies in the conversion of mercury and diaphragm process plants to membrane technology.

Carbon black. **Carbon black** is a form of carbon that is primarily used as reinforcement in vulcanized rubber products. The tire industry uses approximately 85% of the output of this inorganic compound. In the past decade, there have been efforts to replace some portion of carbon black with silica. Silica tires wear better, offer greater fuel efficiency, and provide better traction. Nevertheless, the material costs of silica are twice the cost for carbon black.

Soda ash. **Soda ash** or sodium carbonate is primarily used to make glass, but it is also used in water softeners, detergents, brick manufacturing, and photographic processes. In the United States, the world's largest producer (31% share), soda ash is drawn from natural deposits and soda recovery from lakes. In contrast, soda ash is produced via synthetic process in every other country. This synthetic process is more costly and energy intensive than natural soda.

Industrial gases. Industrial gases are commonly found in the air and other gases. Nitrogen, the largest-selling gas, is used in the food and beverage industry and in multiple manufacturing processes. Oxygen, the second largest-selling gas, is used in manufacturing and health care. Carbon dioxide is used in the food industry but is also used in the refrigeration and health care industries. Acetylene, the fourth largest-selling gas, is used in welding.

Fertilizers

Ammonia is an essential element in fertilizer that is produced by combining hydrogen and oxygen. The nitrogen is procured from the air, whereas the hydrogen is obtained from fossil fuel. Throughout most of the world, natural gas is used to produce hydrogen. Natural gas represents 77% of ammonia production. Coal gasification is a different process for hydrogen procurement and represents 14% of the world market. Coal is primarily used to produce ammonia in China. The remaining 9% of the market relies on partial oxidation of oil to produce hydrogen. This form of production is employed in China and India, the number one and two producers, respectively, of ammonia.

Sustainability

There have been marked enhancements in technology that enable the chemical industry to *reduce* energy consumption. The specific energy consumption associated with steam cracking, for example, has been reduced by 50% since 1970.[48] These improvements have occurred via introduction of enhanced technologies such as process-to-process heat recovery systems. Similarly, application of best practice technologies in the production of olefins and aromatics has potential to improve energy efficiency by more than 30%. Best practice technologies include use of improved reactors and enhanced polymerization processes.

Among the three processes used to make chlorine, the membrane process requires the least energy. The total energy requirements include electricity used in the decomposition of salt and steam consumption. The membrane process is at least 16% more efficient than either of the other processes.[49] Conversion of chemical plants to this procedure results in reductions in the amount of energy consumed in the industrial sector.

Although many chemicals cannot be reused, there are substantial efforts to recycle by-products through the manufacturing of chemicals. In steam cracking, substantial amounts of by-products are recycled, and the form of the by-products varies with the feedstock. For example, for every metric ton of ethane that undergoes steam cracking, 803 kilograms of ethylene are produced. Ethylene is processed into a wealth of products that range from packaging to antifreeze to detergents. The by-products include propylene and butadiene used to produce plastics as well as hydrogen and methane used to fuel the steam cracking furnace.[50]

E. Carbon Emissions Associated with the Paper and Pulp Industries

At 5.7% of total industry energy consumption, the paper and pulp industry is the fourth largest user of energy in the industrial sector. The United States is the largest producer at 24% of worldwide output. The top 10 producers (United States, China, Japan, Canada, Germany, Finland, Sweden, Korea, France, and Italy) account for almost 75% of output. Since 1990, Chinese production of paper and paperboard has more than tripled.

Approximately one half of industry production is in the form of packaging, wrapping, and paperboard, and one third of production is printing and writing paper. Since 1960, the annual growth rate for printing and writing paper has exceeded increases in demand in other sectors of this industry, and the rise in computer and photocopier use is associated with this increase. The remaining output is newsprint, sanitary paper, and household paper.[51] As the popularity of the Internet and electronic media has increased, the demand for newspapers and periodicals has decreased. The demand for various forms of production is related to Organisation for Economic Cooperation and Development (OECD) membership. Within the OECD, there is a greater demand for paper used for printing and writing. By contrast, paper and paperboard used in packaging fuels demand outside of the OECD.

There are several characteristics that influence the ability to make generalizations about paper production. First, the various producers differ in their access to virgin timber and recycled materials. In addition, the energy requirements technologies and plant sizes differ considerably across markets.[52] The paper and pulp industry also differs from other industries because it is a large producer and user of biomass. Across the industry, more than one third of the energy consumed is biomass. Much of this biomass is black liquor that is produced in the making of pulp. This biomass and other forms of energy are primarily used to generate heat in the production process. Two-thirds of the energy consumed is used to produce heat, while another third is used to make electricity. The biomass use results in relatively low levels of carbon emissions in this industry and suggests that there are modest opportunities to enhance energy efficiency. Estimates from the International Energy Agency, however, indicate significant opportunities to enhance energy efficiency.

In order to understand the potential for savings, it is important to understand the flow of resources in the production process. Raw materials such as logs are cut into wood pulp, and this pulp is processed to separate wood fibers from the **lignin** that binds fibers into solid wood.[53] The processing of pulp occurs through either mechanical pulping or chemical pulping. Mechanical pulping is used for lower-grade papers and offers high yields. Chemical pulping is a thermochemical process in which a combination of solvents and heat is applied to separate lignin from wood fibers.[54] The two most common processes are sulfite and sulfate pulping. Sulfate pulping employs the Kraft process whereby sodium sulfate is used to produce a pulp of high physical strength and bulk, but relatively poor sheet formation. Sulfite pulping uses sulfurous acid and an alkali to produce pulps of lower physical strength and bulk that offer better sheet formation. These pulps are used in newsprint, printing, bond papers, and tissue.

Approximately 18% of energy use is associated with pulping, and most of this consumption (15%) is due to mechanical pulping. Chemical pulping produces large amounts of black liquor that is used to generate electricity. Thus, this pulping process produces about one third of the energy used in the industry.

Once the pulping procedure and energy recovery have occurred, the pulp is bleached and dried to prepare for papermaking. The making of paper includes the blending of pulps and additives, sheet formation, and finishing. The process of papermaking represents 47% of total energy use in the industry.

Sustainability

There have been tremendous strides toward sustainability in the industry, yet there are additional measures that would reduce the amount of energy consumption and carbon emissions. These additional measures include advanced pulp drying technologies, enhanced black liquor recovery technologies, and improved heat recovery systems. The International Energy Agency indicates that implementation of best available technologies has the potential to limit final energy consumption by 14%.

The reuse of materials in the production process has already posted strong dividends for the paper industry. The reuse of black liquor as a fuel limits reliance on fossil fuel. Moreover, use of this technology has the potential to enable chemical pulp plants to serve as net providers to the electricity grid.

Figure 14-7 outlines the value chain for the recycling of paper products. Because archival documents, construction materials, and other products cannot be recycled, the theoretical maximum for recycling of paper is 81%. At 60% recycling, Japan is the largest recycler, followed by the European Union at 52%.[55] The average global

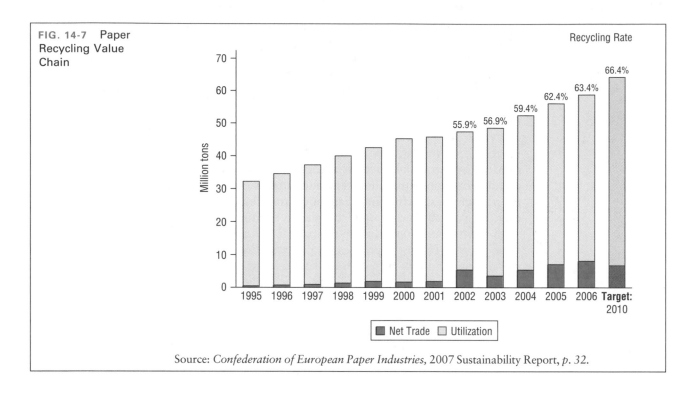

FIG. 14-7 Paper Recycling Value Chain

Source: *Confederation of European Paper Industries*, 2007 Sustainability Report, *p. 32.*

rate of recycling is 45%, which suggests marked opportunity to recycle. The Confederation of European Paper Industries is a colloquium of EU members, Norway, and Switzerland that has set a target of 66% by 2010.[56]

The effort to promote recycling in the paper industry underscores one of the intriguing challenges of green marketing. There are situations under which one must choose among environmental goals that are somewhat incompatible. For example, the reclamation of recycled paper now accounts for 45% of inputs to global production. Note that although recycling results in use of fewer natural resources, the effort to gather and process recycled materials yields carbon emissions. By contrast, chemical pulping plants that use virgin timber may be carbon neutral. The effort to yield lower carbon emissions must be viewed simultaneously with the desire to manage natural resources such as timber.

F. Industrial Standards that Seek to Limit Carbon Emissions

The preceding review of industrial users of energy and producers of carbon dioxide illustrates the challenges associated with attempting to act in an environmentally responsible manner. The criteria for achieving sustainability vary by industry, but due to differences in environments and technologies, it is often difficult to compare levels of sustainability within or across industries. Efforts to identify standards for comparison enable firms to examine sustainability relative to produces in an industry and across industries. One organization that facilities this activity is the **International Organization for Standardization** (ISO).

ISO is a Geneva, Switzerland-based network of the national standards institutes of 157 countries. The organization was formed in 1946 to promote international standards.[57] ISO has more than 17,000 international standards focused on a broad range of industries that include agriculture, construction, mechanical engineering, manufacturing, distribution, transportation, medical devices, information and communication technologies. For example, ISO established a standard format for ATM cards that enables these cards to be used worldwide.[58] ISO has also developed standards for good management practice and for services.[59] The vast majority of standards are specific to an industry, but ISO has developed two families of generic strategies applicable to any industry.[60] In contrast to most other ISO standards, both of these families of standards focus on process rather than specific industrial measures. ISO 9000 is a generic set of requirements for implementing a quality management system. These standards codify efforts to improve quality on an ongoing basis while simultaneously managing quality requirements, regulatory requirements, and customer satisfaction.[61]

ISO 14000 is a second generic managerial system that supports organizational action designed to minimize harmful effects on the environment and achieve continual improvement of environmental performance.[62] Implementation of ISO 14000 offers many benefits to an organization.[63] First, the organization realizes cost savings due to a focus on resource consumption and waste management. Energy and material use are lowered and the overall costs to distribute products are also held in check.[64] A second benefit is associated with risk management. The organizations that establish ISO 14000 standards have fewer legal and financial liabilities because these systems help identify current and forthcoming legislation and requirements. Adherence to ISO 14000 standards lowers the risk of noncompliance.

A third facet of ISO accreditation is the marketing opportunities that it offers to the organization. Because virtually every industry today faces sustainability issues, achieving certification provides the opportunity to promote the environmental aspects of product offerings. Environmental opportunities accrue in the production process as well as the distribution and logistics functions. The development of an environmental management system that incorporates ISO 14000 certification increases the opportunities to identify customer requirements and establish ecologically based systems for projects developed with customers and suppliers.[65] Thus, the corporate image for environmental sensitivity is heightened through ISO accreditation.

Another benefit of ISO accreditation is the influence that it has on interested parties within and outside the organization. Internal stakeholders such as employees can nurture sensitivities to environmental issues that bolster their loyalty to the organization. Accreditation also assures external stakeholders such as customers, regulatory agencies, and communities that the organization is managing its relation with the environment. It supports the organization's claims about its own environmental policies, and it provides a framework for demonstrating conformity to environmental policies.[66]

Within the ISO 14000 family, ISO 14001:2004 provides the generic requirements for an environmental management system (EMS). EMS is a systematic way of managing an organization's environmental affairs that addresses the immediate and long-term influences of its products and processes on the environment.[67] It provides order for organizations to address environmental concerns through the allocation of resources, assignment of responsibilities, and ongoing evaluation of practices.

ISO 14001:2004 facilitates the establishment of an appropriate environmental policy. In addition, it incorporates a planning phase that covers the identification of the environmental aspects of the organization's activities, identification and access to legal requirements, establishment and documentation of objectives and targets consistent with the policy, and establishment of a program for achieving targets and objectives.[68] It further outlines a strategy for implementation of EMS including documentation and communication of roles and responsibilities for ecologically related activity. ISO 14001:2004 also provides procedures for monitoring key characteristics of the operations and activities, and it outlines a strategy for periodic reviews of the EMS. ISO 14001:2004 provides assurance to management and employees that they are controlling organizational processes and activities related to the environment. ISO 14001:2004 is the standard that indicates the firm's commitment to maintaining an environmental management system. This system will be established either through self-compliance efforts or via third-party registration.[69]

In contrast to ISO 14001:2004, which outlines requirements for an EMS, ISO 14004:2004 gives general EMS guidelines. ISO 14004:2004 provides guidance on the establishment, implementation, and maintenance of an EMS. ISO14004:2004 provides an overall picture of the commitment and policy of EMS, and it further provides for the creation of a plan to fulfill the policy. This standard also outlines the process for putting the plan into action by providing human, financial, and physical resources. ISO 14004:2004 also provides procedures for monitoring and improving the EMS.[70]

ISO 14000 also incorporates a number of other directives associated with environmental management.[71] The auditing systems (ISO 14010–14012) provide guidelines and procedures for auditing and outline the qualifications for auditors. The *environmental aspects of product standards* are a related set of guides for the inclusion of environmental aspects in product standards. Conformance to this standard increases the likelihood that product designers are familiar with the environmental consequences of their designs. Similarly, ISO 14062 enables organizations to identify the likely effects on the environment of their future products and make effective decisions during the design and development stages to improve their environmental performance. ISO 14064 directly addresses greenhouse gas (GHG) emissions. Implementation of ISO 14064 promotes transparency in GHG quantification and enables organizations to identify and manage GHG-related liabilities, assets, and risks. It also facilitates the trade of GHG credits and supports the development of systems to limit emissions.[72]

Another set of standards in the 14000 family is the set that enables a company to claim that its products are designed with consideration for the environment.[73] ISO 14020-24 seeks to achieve consistency in labeling methods and procedures by outlining criteria for self-declaration, green reporting, and labeling. Adherence to these standards provides credibility to claims about production and distribution methods employed by a firm.

The overall influence of ISO 14000 standards is the assurance that a company is attempting to address ecological concerns throughout its operations. Consumers are increasingly focused on whether a firm is environmentally responsible, and implementation of these standards enables firms to demonstrate their commitments to the environment.

Summary

A. Primary Industrial Contributors to Carbon Emissions

The purpose of this chapter has been to outline the major influences of industry on the environment. We offer evidence that the iron and steel, petrochemical and chemical, nonmetallic metals, and paper and pulp industries are the largest users of energy and largest producers of carbon dioxide.

B. Carbon Emissions Associated with Steel Production

The steel industry and the nonmetallic minerals industry are the largest producers of carbon emissions in this economic sector. The production of iron and steel is complex and varies from one country to the next, yet two methods account for nearly all steel production. Basic oxygen is ordinarily used for high-tonnage production of carbon steels, and electric arc furnaces are to produce low-tonnage specialty steels.

C. Carbon Emissions in the Nonmetallic Minerals Industry

The largest contributor to energy usage in the nonmetallic minerals sector is concrete production, and a central process to this production is the production of cement. Concrete production is a relatively simple four-stage process. The first stage is acquisition of raw materials. In the second stage, these materials are analyzed, blended, and ground for further processing. In the third stage, materials are heated in a very large kiln. In the fourth stage, gypsum is added, and the mixture is ground to a fine powder called Portland cement.

D. Carbon Emissions Endemic to Chemical Production

The chemical industry also represents 16% of carbon emissions in the industrial sector. Three types of intermediary products (olefins, aromatics, and other intermediates) span between raw materials that include crude oil, natural gas, coal, and other minerals. Nine chemical processes associated with petrochemicals, inorganic chemicals, and fertilizers account for more than 65% of global energy use in the industry.

E. Carbon Emissions Associated with the Paper and Pulp Industries

The paper and pulp industry is the fourth largest user of energy in the industrial sector. Approximately one half of industry production is in the form of packaging, wrapping, and paperboard, and one third of production is printing and writing paper. Since 1960, the annual growth rate for printing and writing paper has exceeded increases in demand in other sectors of this industry, and the rise in computer and photocopier use is associated with this increase. The demand for various forms of production is related to OECD membership.

F. Industrial Standards that Seek to Limit Carbon Emissions

ISO 14000 is a managerial system that supports organizational action designed to minimize harmful effects on the environment and achieve continual improvement of environmental performance. Implementation of ISO 14000 enables organizations to realize cost savings due to a focus on resource consumption and waste management. Adherence to ISO 14000 standards lowers the risk of noncompliance, and accreditation offers marketing opportunities to firms that pursue these standards.

Keywords

aromatics, 288
basic oxygen furnace, 283
carbon black, 289
cement, 286
clinker, 286
dry quenching, 284

electric arc furnace, 283
International Organization for
  Standardization (ISO), 292
ISO 14000, 285
lignin, 291
metallurgy, 285

methanol, 288
olefins, 288
other intermediates, 288
Portland cement, 286
soda ash, 289

Questions

1. What is the value that a marketing student derives from gaining an understanding of energy usage and sustainability in the industrial sector?

2. What three industries account for the most energy usage in the industrial sector, and what is their contribution to energy consumption?

3. What are the two primary forms of steel production?
4. What efforts are being made to enhance the sustainability of the steel industry? To what extent have they already been successful in enhancing sustainability?
5. What is the difference between concrete and cement?
6. To what extent have concrete producers attempted to achieve sustainability in their production processes?

7. What three products span between raw materials and consumer products, and what consumer products do they become?
8. How has the paper industry attempted to achieve sustainability? What is the role of the consumer in their efforts?
9. Contrast the influence of ISO 9000 and ISO 14000 regarding each standard's ability to help organizations achieve sustainability.
10. How does ISO 14000 accreditation enable an organization to market its products more effectively?

Endnotes

[1] American Institute of Steel Construction, "SteelDay 2009," http://www.aisc.org/WorkArea/showcontent.aspx?id=21730 (accessed May 15, 2010).

[2] American Institute of Steel Construction, "SteelDay Events Draw More than 7,000 Attendees," http://www.aisc.org/news detail.aspx?id=22246 (accessed May 15, 2010).

[3] International Energy Agency, *Tracking Industrial Energy Efficiency and CO_2 Emissions* (Paris, France: OECD/IEA, 2008), 324.

[4] World Steel Association, *2008 Sustainability Report* (Brussels, Belgium: World Steel Association, 2008), 1–35, http://www.worldsteel.org/pictures/publicationfiles/Sustainability%20Report%202008_English.pdf (accessed May 15, 2010).

[5] See Note 3 above.

[6] The World Bank Group, *Pollution and Prevention Abatement Handbook 1998: Toward Cleaner Production* (Washington, D.C.: World Bank Group, 1998) 1–472, http://www.ifc.org/ifcext/sustainability.nsf/AttachmentsByTitle/p_ppah/$FILE/PPAH.pdf (accessed May 15, 2010).

[7] Steel Recycling Institute, "2006 The Inherent Recycled Content of Today's Steel," http://www.recycle-steel.org/PDFs/Inherent2006.pdf (accessed May 15, 2010).

[8] See Note 6 above.

[9] See Note 6 above

[10] See Note 3 above.

[11] See Note 3 above.

[12] American Iron and Steel Institute, "How a Blast Furnace Works," http://www.steel.org/AM/Template.cfm?Section=Articles3&CONTENTID=25317&TEMPLATE=/CM/ContentDisplay.cfm (accessed May 15, 2010).

[13] Energy Solution Center "Blast Furnace: Process Description," Metals Processing Advisor, http://www.energysolutionscenter.org/heattreat/MetalsAdvisor/iron_and_steel/process_descriptions/raw_metals_preparation/ironmaking/blast_furnace/ironmaking_blastfurnace_processdescription.htm (accessed May 15, 2010).

[14] See Note 7 above.

[15] See Note 7 above.

[16] Energy Solution Center, "Direct Reduction: Process Description," Metals Processing Advisor, http://www.energysolutionscenter.org/heattreat/MetalsAdvisor/iron_and_steel/process_descriptions/raw_metals_preparation/ironmaking/direct_reduction/ (accessed May 15, 2010).

[17] See Note 4 above.

[18] Energy Solution Center, "Electric Arc Furnace: Process Description" Metals Processing Advisor, http://www.energysolutionscenter.org/HeatTreat/MetalsAdvisor/iron_and_steel/process_descriptions/raw_metals_preparation/steelmaking/electric_arc_furnace/electric_arc_furnace_process_description.htm (accessed May 15, 2010).

[19] Jeremy A. T. Jones, "Electric Arc Furnace Steelmaking," *American Iron and Steel Institute*, http://www.steel.org/AM/Template.cfm?Section=Home&template=/CM/HTMLDisplay.cfm&ContentID=21169 (accessed May 15, 2010).

[20] Energy Solution Center, "Continuous Casting: Process Description," Metals Processing Advisor, http://www.energysolutionscenter.org/heattreat/MetalsAdvisor/iron_and_steel/process_descriptions/raw_metals_preparation/steelmaking/primary_finishing/continuous%20casting/continuous_casting_process_description.htm (accessed May 15, 2010).

[21] See Note 4 above.

[22] See Note 3 above.

[23] See Note 6 above.

[24] International Organization for Standardization, "ISO 14000 Essentials," http://www.iso.org/iso/iso_14000_essentials.htm (accessed May 15, 2010).

[25] See Note 4 above.

[26] See Note 4 above.

[27] See Note 4 above

[28] See Note 3 above.

[29] World Business Council for Sustainable Development, *The Cement Sustainability Initiative, 2007* (Conches-Geneva: World Business Council for Sustainable Development), http://www.wbcsd.org/DocRoot/nlYHAK4ECDi7EEcarBSH/csi-brochure.pdf (accessed May 15, 2010).

[30] World Business Council for Sustainable Development, *The Cement Sustainability Initiative, 2002* (Conches-Geneva: World Business Council for Sustainable Development), http://www.wbcsdcement.org/pdf/agenda.pdf (accessed May 15, 2010).

[31] Portland Cement Association, "Overview of the Cement Industry," http://www.cement.org/basics/cementindustry.asp (accessed May 15, 2010).

[32] Portland Cement Association, "Four Steps to Produce Cement," http://www.cement.org/smreport08/sec_page1_3_A.htm (accessed May 15, 2010).

[33] See Note 3 above.

[34] Buckley Rumford Fireplaces, "A History of Cement," http://www.rumford.com/articlemortar.html (accessed May 15, 2010).

[35] U.S. Department of Transportation Federal Highway Administration, "Portland Cement," http://www.fhwa.dot.gov/infrastructure/materialsgrp/cement.html (accessed May 15, 2010).

[36] Elisabeth Rosenthal, "Cement Industry is at Center of Climate Change Debate," *New York Times*, October 27, 2007, 1.

[37] ConcreteNetwork.com, "Recycling Concrete," http://www.concretenetwork.com/concrete/demolition/recycling_concrete.htm (accessed May 15, 2010).

[38] American Concrete Pavement Association, "Natural Advantage," http://www.pavements4life.com/QDs/Environment_2Recycle.asp (accessed May 15, 2010).

[39] See Note 37 above.

[40] Environmental Council of Concrete Organizations, "Homepage," http://www.ccco.org/ (accessed May 15, 2010).

[41] See Note 3 above.

[42] Amos A. Avidan, Michael Edwards, and Hartley Owen, "Innovative Improvements Highlight FCC's Past and Future," *Oil & Gas Journal* 88, no. 2 (1990): 33–58.

[43] Methanol Institute, http://www.methanol.org/pdfFrame.cfm?pdf=faqs.pdf (accessed May 15, 2010).

[44] See Note 3 above.

[45] Union Carbide Corporation, "History," http://www.unioncarbide.com/history/index.htm (accessed May 15, 2010).

[46] See Note 3 above.

[47] INEOS, "Business Overview," http://www.ineos.com/abo_cha.html (accessed May 15, 2010).

[48] See Note 3 above.

[49] See Note 3 above.

[50] See Note 3 above.

[51] See Note 3 above.

[52] RISI, "World Pulp Annual Historical Data – Excerpt," http://www.risiinfo.com/Marketing/ahd/Excerpts/world_pulp.pdf (accessed May 15, 2010).

[53] University of Helsinki, "Environmental Biotechnology and Biotechnology of Renewable Natural Resources: The 'lignin group'" http://www.biocenter.helsinki.fi/groups/HATAKKA/english/background.html (accessed May 15, 2010).

[54] Oy Keskuslaboratorio - Centrallaboratorium Ab KCL Science and Consulting, "Chemical Pulping," http://www.kcl.fi/page.php?page_id=90 (accessed May 15, 2010).

[55] See Note 3 above.

[56] Confederation of European Paper Industries, "Sustainability Report 2007," http://www.twosides.info/Content/rsPDF_8.pdf (accessed May 15, 2010).

[57] Amir M. Hormozi, "ISO 14000: The Next Focus in Standardization," *SAM Advanced Management Journal* (Summer, 1997): 32–41.

[58] Jennifer Nash and John Ehrenfeld, "Code Green," *Environment* 38, no. 1 (1996): 16–30.

[59] International Organization for Standardization, "Discover ISO," http://www.iso.org/iso/about/discover-iso_the-scope-of-isos-work.htm (accessed May 15, 2010).

[60] International Organization for Standardization, "What's Different About ISO 9001 and ISO 14001," http://www.iso.org/iso/about/discover-iso_whats-different-about-iso-9001-and-iso-14001.htm (accessed May 15, 2010).

[61] International Organization for Standardization, "ISO 9000 and ISO 14000," http://www.iso.org/iso/iso_catalogue/management_standards/iso_9000_iso_14000.htm (accessed May 15, 2010).

[62] See Note 24 above.

[63] Martin Baxter, "Taking the First Steps in Environmental Management," *ISO Management Systems* (July–August, 2004): 13–18.

[64] International Organization for Standardization, "Business benefits of ISO 14000," http://www.iso.org/iso/iso_catalogue/management_standards/iso_9000_iso_14000/business_benefits_of_iso_14001.htm (accessed May 15, 2010).

[65] See Note 57 above.

[66] See Note 24 above.

[67] N.C. Division of Pollution Prevention and Environmental Assistance, "EMS & ISO 14000 FAQ," http://www.p2pays.org/iso/emsisofaq.asp#faq1 (accessed May 15, 2010).

[68] See Note 24 above.

[69] See Note 57 above.

[70] Robert Anthony Reiley, "The New Paradigm: ISO 14000 and Its Place in Regulatory Reform," *Journal of Corporation Law* 22, (1997): 535–569.

[71] See Note 57 above.

[72] International Organization for Standardization, "New ISO 14064 standards provide tools for assessing and supporting greenhouse gas reduction and emissions trading," http://www.iso.org/iso/pressrelease.htm?refid=Ref994 (accessed May 15, 2010).

[73] See Note 57 above.

Green Marketing and Sustainability Reporting

Chapter 15
Reporting Value to Stakeholders

Reporting Value to Stakeholders

A. Introduction

APPLE, INC.

On November 24, 2008, the environmental activist group Greenpeace released the 10th iteration of its *Guide to Greener Electronics*.[1] This guide urges producers of electronics to eliminate hazardous substances, responsibly recycle obsolete products, and reduce the climate impact of their products and operations. This guide also ranks the various producers of computers and electronics based on their environmental influences throughout the life cycles of their products. The guide notably ranked Apple below most of its competition due to Apple's use of brominated fire retardants (BFRs). These chemicals are coated on printed circuit boards to prevent fires inside computers. The company also uses a polyvinyl chloride (PVC) coating on cables.[2] BFRs have been implicated as deterrents to neurological development and hormone system functionality, whereas the incineration of PVCs produces chemicals that are toxic at low concentrations.[3]

Over the past 20 years, continued assessment of the environmental impact of the firm's products has enabled Apple to illustrate sustainability efforts and quantify progress in environmental concerns.[4] The recent negative evaluation by Greenpeace called public attention to the need for Apple to reestablish its commitment to the environment. Since the publication of this greener electronics guide, Apple has developed a number of initiatives to improve its environmental performance. Importantly, the company no longer uses PVC or BFR in its personal computers or in its iPhones and iPods.[5] These improvements have been praised by Greenpeace and have led the NGO to call on competitors such as HP, Dell, Lenovo, Acer, and Toshiba to follow suit.[6] Soon after the publication of the Greenpeace guide, Apple began a television campaign that proclaimed Apple's MacBook line of laptops to be the world's greenest family of notebooks. The ads emphasized MacBook's low power consumption, the ability to recycle the enclosure, and the lack of hazardous materials.[7] These ads are not greenwashing because they are supported by environmental action within the firm and an increasing commitment to the environment that Apple initially publicized in 1990.

Apple's efforts toward enhanced sustainability are made available to the public via a series of analyses of the supply chain for the company and each of its products. The company's environmental Web site outlines the influence

FIG. 15-1 Life Cycle
Impact of Apple
Products

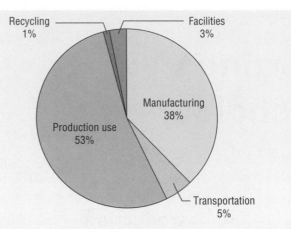

Source: *Adapted from "The Environment," Apple.com, http://www.apple.com/environment/ (accessed October 16, 2009).*

of each step in the product life cycle (see Figure 15-1). The manufacture of products accounts for 38% of emissions; and transportation (5%), facilities (3%), and recycling (1%) are also factored into the emissions costs. Interestingly, product use accounts for 53% of all emissions associated with Apple products. Each product report provides analyses of climate change, energy efficiency, material efficiency, and restricted substances. Moreover, Apple provides sustainability reports that address its recycling efforts, facilities management, and suppliers. These reports are developed to reflect the Global Reporting Initiative (GRI) Sustainability Reporting Guidelines.[8] GRI is a nonprofit organization established in 1997 that developed the world's most widely used sustainability reporting framework. GRI provides guidelines on the development and use of sustainability reports and maintains a database of reports developed throughout the world. For example, Apple's 2008 report is one of more than 1,000 sustainability reports collected by GRI in the year.

The Apple example illustrates how companies are following closed-loop systems in which they plan, implement, and report on their sustainability efforts. Cradle-to-cradle logic is employed in efforts to minimize energy use throughout a product's life. Firms that report on this activity are more inclined to yield sustainable results relative to their competition. In this chapter, we will look closely at the sustainability reporting practices of firms. We begin by examining the purposes and benefits of sustainability reporting. We proceed by outlining the components of sustainability reports, and we subsequently examine the reporting of financial, environmental, and social performance.

B. Purposes of Sustainability Reporting

The magnitude and urgency of the sustainability risks faced by organizations demand that firms provide complete information regarding their financial, environmental, and social performance. This information enables stakeholders of all types to make decisions about their relationships and commitments to the firm. If the firm offers complete disclosure of its actions as they relate to sustainability, stakeholders can make better decisions.

The ability of stakeholders to make evaluations about the firm is contingent on their ability to view the firm's operations. **Transparency** refers to the degree to which an entity provides complete disclosure of all activity related to economic, environmental, and relational performance.[9] Firms that provide complete disclosure concerning all interaction with stakeholders that is relevant to triple bottom line performance offer evidence of the transparency of their operations. In order to assess the level of transparency, it is germane to determine the sustainability topics and indicators that a firm employs. Although firms are not required to report on all facets of triple bottom line performance, they are increasingly providing financial and social performance indicators as well as environmental outcomes. In addition, it is essential for the firm to ensure the quality of the information provided in the report.

Transparent disclosure enables sustainability reports to be used for three purposes:[10]

Demonstrating. Firms demonstrate their commitment to sustainability by illustrating how the firm influences and is influenced by sustainable development.[11] For example, the Best Buy 2009 sustainability report acknowledges the critical importance of electronics recycling, and it illustrates the measures undertaken by the firm in Canada and the United States to increase recycling rates.[12]

Benchmarking. Benchmarking refers to comparison of a firm's performance relative to laws, codes, norms, and voluntary initiatives. For example, Bayer Corporation's 2008 sustainability report indicates that approximately one third of its production sites have been certified in accordance with ISO 14001 or the European environmental management regulation EMAS (Eco-Management and Audit Scheme) standards.[13]

Comparing. Comparing enables a firm to illustrate changes in performance over time. These comparisons illustrate improvements in sustainability efforts by a company and illustrate its longitudinal performance relative to the competition. The Ford 2008 sustainability report indicates, for instance, the performance of current auto models relative to previously sold products.[14] Firms that view themselves as industry leaders that engage in best practices can confirm these perceptions via comparison. For example, Apple's report that it no longer uses PVC or BFR in its products makes its stand out relative to the competition.[15]

Because sustainability reports provide insight to stakeholders, it is relevant to consider what should and should not be incorporated into these documents. The Global Reporting Initiative uses the following four criteria to guide the development of sustainability reports:[16]

Materiality. Because firms face a wide range of topics that could be the subject of these reports, it is relevant to establish what *material* is relevant. The firm must determine which facets of the economic, environmental, and social context substantially influence the evaluations made by stakeholders. Firms use internal and external factors to determine whether information is material. These factors include the firm's mission and competitive strategy as well as the concerns expressed by stakeholders.

Stakeholder inclusiveness. The insight offered by the report is contingent on the interaction with all entities that are significantly affected by the firm's action.[17] These groups include employees, suppliers, customers, NGOs, governments, and other groups with a vested interest in the firm's sustainability efforts. Stakeholder inclusiveness requires the firm to identify all these interest groups and to report on how they have responded to the groups' expectations and interests. For example, the Sun Microsystems 2008 sustainability report emphasizes the need to gain input from customers, employees, partners, NGOs, CSR experts, and investors.[18]

Sustainability context. The sustainability context criterion ensures that the organization explains how it is meeting the demands of achieving sustainability.[19] The action of the firm must be viewed not in isolation, but in the context in which the firm operates. Consequently, the firm should not only provide a summary of its sustainability efforts, but it also should indicate how these efforts contribute to improvements to environmental, economic, and social conditions at the local, regional, and global levels.[20]

Completeness. Due to the breadth of issues associated with triple bottom line performance, the firm faces a daunting task in determining the amount of information to present. *Completeness* refers to the provision of sufficient information about economic, environmental, and social performance to enable stakeholders to make informed decisions.[21] Completeness encompasses the dimensions of *time*, *scope*, and *boundary*. In order to track progress, it is essential to specify the time period associated with the report. The scope of the report should be broad enough to cover significant influences on triple bottom line performance. The boundary of the report concerns the range of groups represented by the study. Firms need to consider their broad supply chains in this regard and examine the influences of upstream suppliers, employees, and downstream customers. For example, Apple recognizes that 53% of the energy impact of its products is associated with downstream product usage. The boundary of the report is a difficult consideration because different firms in the same industry may make different evaluations of the boundaries of their consumption. While sustainability reporting guidelines suggest that firms should report on any entity over which they have control or influence,[22] different companies may interpret their level of influence via contrasting decision logics.

C. Benefits of Sustainability Reporting

Sustainability reporting is a relatively new phenomenon that is increasingly employed by firms in many sectors of the economy. It is difficult to state the origins of this type of reporting. Some annual reports, for instance, have addressed corporate interaction with the environment for decades. The first separate environmental reports were developed in 1989, and the number of these types of reports has risen substantially since that time.[23] This genre of reporting takes on a variety of names that bear *social*, *environmental*, and *sustainability* monikers. Sustainability reports that address the role of the firm with respect to the triple bottom line of financial, relational, and environmental performance provide insight into the broadest spectrum of sustainability and its importance to the firm. Nevertheless, there are many forms of reporting that focus on environmental or social facets of sustainability without regard for other facets of triple bottom line performance.

More than 10 years ago, the United Nations began analyzing motivations for developing sustainability.[24] Their research indicated a number of reasons why some firms do not develop sustainability reports. Some firms are skeptical of the advantage that is derived from this type of reporting, whereas other companies believe there are other ways to communicate a message about the environment to consumers. The motivation to develop a sustainability report also varies by market. Although most firms participating in the chemical or computer industries publish these reports, firms operating in the retail and banking sectors develop substantially fewer sustainability studies.[25]

Some companies continue to refrain from developing sustainability reports, yet the number of these studies is increasing in most sectors of the economy.[26] The benefits that accrue from sustainability reporting include:[27]

Increased discipline about environmental performance. The Kyoto Protocol and other international activity designed to control greenhouse gas emissions have prompted many firms to recognize that carbon rationing and trading affect an organization's business strategy and financial performance. Firms that report on efforts to control carbon emissions are simultaneously confronted with efforts to control the firm's interaction with the environment. Strategic cost management systems, for instance, provide the ability to evaluate the carbon emissions costs of products and services over their product life cycles. Firms that develop this information provide insight into human resource management, marketing, supply chain operations, and financial performance.[28] The organization that develops sustainability reports develops a broader awareness of environmental issues throughout the organization, and this awareness should yield a smaller carbon footprint for the firm.

Conveys an environmental message to all stakeholders. One of the primary benefits of sustainability reporting lies in the ability to promote dialogue with stakeholders. Recall from Chapter 2 that the stakeholders for the firm include consumers, suppliers, employees, competitors, the legal system, financial institutions, government, media, stockholders/owners, the scientific community, nongovernment organizations, and the general public. Companies recognize that they can enhance credibility with each of these groups via transparency. For example, Apple Computer Company became vocal about its sustainability policies in 2007. At the time, CEO Steve Jobs noted Apple ordinarily does not proclaim its plans for the future, but the current policies had left important stakeholders (customers, shareholders, employees) in the dark.[29] By taking a proactive stance toward sustainability reporting, Apple and other firms can have a strong influence on the way they are perceived in the markets in which they compete. Thus, sustainability reporting provides a context that enables the firm to model changes in employees' values, beliefs, and core assumptions about the organization.[30]

Track progress versus targets. When sustainability reporting is completed on an annual or regular basis, it enables the organization to chart its progress against objectives over time. For example, Electrolux has been developing sustainability reports since 1998. In its 2008 report, the company identifies its objectives over the past several years and also identifies the extent to which its has achieved these objectives. The report not only identifies past progress, it lists specific targets for the future.[31] The charting over time of performance indicates progress to all stakeholders and further emphasizes the gravity of the firm's sustainability interests.

Reduce environmental risk. Sustainability poses a series of risks that are distinct from other forms of risk. Firms must address risks associated with climate change, boycotts, ecosystem services, social justice, and harmful substances; and these risks can pose specific liabilities for directors and officers of the firm.[32]

Firms that examine the risks encountered in the procurement, processing, consumption, and disposition of products can reduce their liabilities due to environmental factors.

Identify savings and efficiencies. Organizations that begin to monitor the use of energy subsequently begin to recognize the magnitude of energy expenses and the distribution among alternative needs. Firms that annually provide sustainability reports quantify their energy use and begin to find ways to reduce these expenditures. For example, by charting energy use over successive years, IBM was able to reduce consumption throughout the company by more 3.5% in 2008.[33]

Identify new business opportunities. In order to develop a sustainability report, a firm must necessarily review all of its business operations. In this review, firms on occasion find resources within the firm that have not been marketed. For example, Shell Oil pumps carbon dioxide from Dutch refineries to greenhouses. Before Shell assessed the sustainability of the refinery, this carbon dioxide was released into the atmosphere.[34]

D. Overview of Sustainability Reporting

Many firms adopt contrasting styles and formats to present their efforts to achieve some level of sustainability. Despite these alternative styles, several essential elements should be addressed if the firm is to offer a meaningful discussion of its sustainability efforts and performance. The firm initially outlines its strategy with respect to sustainability, and it then provides specific economic, environmental, and social indicators of its efforts. Although the firm may use a variety of styles to present this information, many companies illustrate how their sustainability analyses dovetail with the GRI Sustainability Reporting Guidelines.[35] For example, General Electric indexes its 2008 sustainability report with the point-by-point criteria outlined by GRI. Figure 15-2 provides an overview of the elements of a sustainability report.

Strategy and analysis. The initial component of a sustainability report provides a summary of the corporate strategy and the managerial approach to sustainability. The discussion of corporate strategy should focus on the relationship between the

FIG. 15-2 Elements of a Sustainability Report	I. Summary of Corporate Sustainability Strategy
	Strategy and Analysis
	Organizational Profile
	Report Parameters
	Governance, Commitments, and Engagement
	II. Performance Indicators
	Economic Indicators
	Environmental Indicators
	Social Indicators
	III. Third-party Validation

firm and its stakeholders with respect to economic, environmental, and social conditions. Importantly, the strategic overview should include a letter from the senior decision maker of the organization about the relevance of sustainability to the organization and its strategy.[36] In addition, this initial discussion should provide a review of the key influences of the firm as well as a treatment of its risks and opportunities in the markets it serves. For example, the General Electric 2008 sustainability report provides a letter from Chairman Jeff Immelt about the company's commitment to sustainability. The report also provides a review of the commitments and progress made by the firm over the last year's report and the progress made toward achieving those objectives in 2008, as well as expectations for 2009.[37]

Organizational profile. The organizational profile identifies the name of the company, the nature of its ownership, and its headquarters. In addition, the company describes the countries and markets served as well as its primary products, brands, and services. The company also indicates its level of involvement in the production and the amount of outsourcing employed during production.

Report parameters. The report parameters concern the period represented by the study and the frequency of reporting by the company. The firm also identifies the scope and boundary of the study at this point, and it recognizes known limitations with respect to these parameters. The firm also provides a review of its measurement techniques, and it describes the policies and practices associated with gaining external assurance about the report.

Governance, commitments, and engagement. The governance system provides an overview of how the firm seeks to attain its objectives. Governance includes the structure of the organization and the committees responsible for the firm's strategy and organizational oversight. The firm also outlines its mission and values with respect to economic, environmental, and social performance. The incentive structures of the senior officers are also outlined, and the firm indicates procedures for employees and other stakeholders to provide recommendations.

The firm also outlines its external commitments. One vital part of a firm's commitment lies in its participation in the development of industry standards. Companies supply lists of industrial groups and affiliates. In addition, they report on externally developed triple bottom line principles that they endorse. For example, the United States Climate Action Partnership is a nonpartisan coalition of 26 corporations along with the Environmental Defense Fund, the Pew Center, Natural Resources Defense Council, World Resources Institute, and the Nature Conservancy.[38] GE's 2008 sustainability report recognizes the company's support for this group and its efforts to develop legislation creating a nationwide cap-and-trade system.[39]

The final component of the strategic overview is the engagement of stakeholders. Since all of the information in the report derives from these groups, it is essential to identify their level of involvement. The firm provides its rationales for the selection and identification of stakeholders and describes the frequency of engagement with each type of stakeholder. The company also provides a review of the topics addressed in meetings with stakeholders.[40]

Third-party validation. When the firm has completed its summary of the corporate sustainability strategy, it then reports on the economic, environmental, and social performance as outlined in the following sections. After these performance indicators have been provided, firms increasingly provide some evidence of assurance via a third party.[41] Although many firms have established procedures for determining sustainable action, assurance is significantly enhanced via evaluation by some entity external to the organization. In reporting on third-party evaluations, firms indicate that the evaluation is performed by an external party that uses individuals who are not limited by their relationship with the firm. The third-party report should be completed by persons competent in the subject matter and related practices. In addition, the report should be developed in a systematic, documented approach, and it should result in the development of a publicly available opinion of the firm's sustainability performance.[42]

E. Reporting Economic Value

The economic value provided by an organization is not a substitute or replacement for accounting and financial reporting. On the contrary, this part of the sustainability report is designed to illustrate the flow of capital among stakeholders and illustrate the economic influence of the firm throughout society.[43] Economic reporting includes reviews of *financial performance*, *local market presence*, and *indirect economic influences* of the firm (see Figure 15-3).

Financial performance. **Financial performance** refers to the presentation of the firm's value in terms of accounting and financial standards. The **value added statement** identifies the direct economic value generated and distributed to capital providers and government. This section of the report summarizes revenues, employee compensation, operating costs, donations and other community investments, retained earnings, and payments. For example, Henkel is one of the world's leading suppliers of laundry and home care products (e.g., Purex), cosmetics and toiletries (e.g., Schwarkopf Professional hair care), and adhesives (Loctite glue). Table 15-1 illustrates the value added to the company in financial terms.

TABLE 15-1   HENKEL VALUE ADDED STATEMENT 2008

	€ MILLIONS	RELATIVE VALUE, %
Source of funds		
Total sales	14,131	90.6
Other income	1,458	9.4
Distribution of funds		
Cost of materials	6,508	42.3
Depreciation and amortization	540	3.5
Other expenses	3,973	25.5
Value added	4,472	28.7
Employees	2,436	54.4
Central and local government	437	9.8
Interest expense	366	8.2
Shareholders	227	5.1
Minority shareholders	12	0.3
Reinvested in the company	994	22.2

Source: *Based on "Sustainability/CSR at Henkel", Henkel AG & Co. KGaA, http://www.henkel.de/ SID-0AC83309-45A7D75E/nachhaltigkeit.htm (accessed October 14, 2009).*

A second financial consideration is the disclosure of the financial implications of climate change for the firm. As the level of regulation associated with climate change increases, firms face regulatory risk due to increased costs. These regulations also provide opportunities via new markets and technologies. Firms report on these considerations to illustrate their planning efforts and control risks. For example, Timberland reports on its efforts to attain carbon neutrality by 2010. This strategy notably involves reductions in its demand for energy, procurement of renewable energy, and investing in renewable energy through carbon offset purchases.[44]

The firm supplies two additional pieces of information that are pertinent to employees, investors, and other stakeholders. Firms disclose the financial obligations associated with benefit plans.[45] In addition, they indicate whether they receive significant financial assistance from government.[46]

Local market presence. The second set of economic indicators addresses the role of the firm in the local markets in which it has a significant presence. The firm reports on the relative wage rate by illustrating the relationship between company wages and local minimum wages.[47] It also reports on the policies and practices associated with hiring personnel from the local community. Similarly, firms report on the procedures associated with securing locally based suppliers. For example, Unilever's 2008 sustainability report outlines the efforts of the company in the areas of leadership development and corporate diversity. It further outlines the business partner code that specifies sourcing requirements for business ethics, health and safety, labor standards, and the environment.[48]

Indirect economic influences. Indirect economic influences are the firm's efforts to enhance public welfare. The organization reports on the development of infrastructure and services. For example, Unilever reports that it invested more than $136 million (€91 million) in communities in 2008, enabling them to support around 16,500 community organizations.[49] In addition to investments in infrastructure, firms also report on other economic activity derived from their sustainability efforts. The Unilever 2008 report, for example, reports on the company's ongoing efforts to address political unrest in Kenya.[50]

F. Reporting Environmental Value

The reporting of environmental performance addresses the extent to which the action of the firm is associated with *material usage, energy, water, biodiversity, by-products and waste, products and services,* and *transportation.*[51] Consider first the firm's material use.

Materials. Material usage directly addresses the overall cost of operations, and the tracking of this factor enables the firm to monitor material efficiency and costs associated with the flow of material. Companies report on raw material, processed material, semimanufactured goods, and packaging materials. They also report on the extent to which they use recycled materials as inputs. For instance, the 2008/9 Ford Motor Company sustainability report indicates that recycled materials account for more than 20% of the content of cars sold in North America.[52] The report also indicates that Ford employs a life-cycle design strategy.

Energy. The monitoring of energy usage is instrumental to achieving fuel efficiency. Firms monitor direct and indirect energy consumption. **Direct energy** refers to consumption of energy without conversion, whereas **indirect energy** refers to use of energy that has been transformed via some process. For example, an electrical plant has a direct use of coal to produce its output—electricity. The use of this electricity by an auto plant is a form of indirect energy use. In the direct energy category, firms provide reports of the use of nonrenewable forms of energy that include coal, natural gas, gasoline, and others. Direct energy also includes renewable sources of energy such as biofuels, ethanol, and hydrogen. Similarly, reporting on indirect energy use distinguishes nonrenewable energy purchases of electricity, heating/cooling, steam, and nuclear energy from renewable sources such as solar, geothermal, wind energy.

Reporting on energy utilization over time enables companies to illustrate results of their efforts to limit the amount of energy consumed. For example, the Merck 2008 Sustainability Report tracks purchases of coal, fuel oil, and electricity over five years.[53] Firms offer evidence of the degree to which conservation activities increase energy efficiency leading to reductions in direct and indirect energy consumption. They also indicate the extent to which they provide products that rely on energy-efficient technologies or that employ renewable sources of energy. For example, the Ford 2008/9 sustainability report outlines the firm's efforts to reduce its direct and indirect energy consumption. The report also highlights Ford's development of products that strive to achieve efficiency via alternative fuels, electrification, and new drive train technologies.[54]

Water. Because access to clean freshwater is declining, the firm's reporting on its use of water provides insight into the financial and social risks faced by the organization.[55] Firms report on the amount of water withdrawn from surface sources (*rivers, lakes, oceans, and wetlands*), ground water, rainwater, municipal sources, and waste water. They further identify sources of water significantly influenced by water removal. They also indicate the total volume of water reused or recycled. The Abbott Laboratories 2008 sustainability report, for example, outlines the firm's efforts to reduce water consumption by 40% relative to 2004 standards.

Biodiversity. Given the imminent risks to flora and fauna, it is essential that environmental reviews take stock of the firm's efforts associated with enhancing habitat. Firms report on their strategies, operations, and influences on wildlife in areas of high biodiversity value and in protected areas. The reporting further indicates the number of endangered species affected by operations and the habitats restored or protected by the firm. For example, Shell Oil indicates how it uses its partnerships with Wetlands International and the International Union for the Conservation of Nature to conserve tundra ecosystems in the Arctic. This partnership also enables them to protect wetlands along the flight paths of migratory birds.[56]

By-products and waste. By-products and waste are the gaseous, liquid, and solid outputs discarded in the supply chain. Gaseous by-products include **greenhouse gas emissions** as well as **ozone-depleting substances**. Firms report on the process used to determine the level of these outputs as well as their initiatives to lower emissions. For instance, Vodaphone's energy performance report indicates its total direct and indirect greenhouse gas emissions.[57] Liquid by-product reporting indicates total water discharges and discusses spills of oil, chemicals, and other materials. Shell, for instance, reports that it carried more than 40 million tons of cargo in 2008 without a single spill. It further reports, however, that a single-hull ship on short-term hire dropped about 300 tons of diesel fuel into the Elbe River in Germany. Shell's sustainability report indicates that it is phasing in double-hull ships to reduce the likelihood of spills.[58]

Firms also report on the total waste and the methods of disposal for waste. This material includes liquid, solid, hazardous, and nonhazardous waste. Abbot

Laboratories, for example, indicates that in 2008 it achieved a 21% reduction in the relative amount of hazardous waste over 2007.[59] Firms indicate the degree to which they use composting, reuse, recycling, recovery, deep well injection, on-site storage, incineration, or landfills to dispose of by-products.

Products and services. Conservation efforts associated with products address the inputs into development and production. Firms provide summaries of the material, water, emissions, and other factors associated with their products. Apple's annual sustainability report, for example, provides an account of the life cycle costs associated with each of its products.[60] Product reporting also considers the degree to which the firm engages in efforts to reclaim products. Since many products (e.g., computers) have historically been made with hazardous materials such as brominated flame retardants, it is pertinent to develop programs to reclaim these products and dispose of them properly. The Lexmark sustainability program, for instance, reports on the company's efforts to reclaim inkjet cartridges, laser toner cartridges, printers, and other products.[61]

Compliance. This facet of reporting concerns the extent to which a company complies or fails to comply with environmental regulations. Compliant firms generally face less financial risk and are better positioned to gain permits or otherwise expand operations.[62] In some sustainability reports, firms provide a review of their environmental policy and provide evidence of their compliance with acceptable industry standards. For example, Merck's 2008 sustainability report outlines its commitment to safety and environmental performance and indicates its compliance with prevailing environmental law concerning spills. Firms also explain conditions under which they have failed to comply with prevailing standards by reporting monetary fines and nonmonetary sanctions associated with environmental regulations. The Merck 2008 report, for example, indicates that the company faced 178 environmental inspections in 2008 and paid more than $1 million in fines due to violations.[63]

Transportation. Since the distribution and supply chains for products are primary sources of value for many firms, it is important for companies to report on the influence of transportation. Firms identify their strategies to mitigate transportation costs. Importantly, they report on the energy used in transportation, the emissions associated with transportation, and the waste, noise, and spills associated with transportation. The United Parcel Service (UPS) environmental stewardship report, for example, provides summary statistics on energy use for shipping by road, rail, and air. The report indicates that shifts from ground to rail and air to ground prevented absolute emissions of 3 million metric tons of carbon dioxide.

G. Reporting Social Value

Reporting on social value provides the third component of sustainability reporting. This section includes reporting on human rights, labor practices, product responsibility, and society.

Human rights. In the human rights sector, the firm indicates how it maintains and respects the basic rights of human beings.[64] The firm indicates the extent to which investment agreements and trading partners have been reviewed for human rights considerations. For example, Ford Motor Company's 2008 sustainability report discusses collaboration on human rights issues with its partners in the supply chain.[65] Firms report on the extent to which they have invested in training employees about human rights issues, and they report on the number of incidents of discrimination.

The human rights section also outlines some policies that concern working conditions. Firms report on operations that have significant potential to limit **freedom of association** and **collective bargaining**. They also report on operations with potential to engage in child labor or compulsory labor. For example, Starbucks' 2009 sustainability report outlines the firm's effort to achieve a goal of 100% responsibly grown, ethically grown coffees.[66] Coffee grown under these criteria is unlikely to violate working condition standards.

Labor practices. The analysis of labor practices centers on the concept of decent work.[67] The firm discloses the scope and diversity of its workforce and emphasizes aspects of gender and age distribution. The firm also provides an account of its employee benefits and discloses the extent to which it uses collective bargaining agreements. In addition, it provides demographic and financial reports of employee data to provide evidence of diversity and equal opportunity. For example, Shell's 2008 sustainability report outlines its progress toward the goal of increasing the proportion of women in senior management to a minimum of 20%.[68]

The well-being and physical protection of employees is covered by occupational **health and safety standards** and the ongoing training provided by the firm. These safety and occupational health indicators chart statistical performance and enable firms to communicate their health and safety programs to employees. Companies report on the amount of training and counseling dedicated to informing community members about serious illness and disease. For example, Coca-Cola reports on the company's prevention and treatment programs to limit the spread of HIV/AIDS.[69]

Product responsibility. Product responsibility reporting addresses the effects of products and services on customers and users. Organizations are expected to exercise diligence to ensure that products are fit for intended use and do not pose any unintended hazards to health and safety. Companies report on the health and safety impacts of their products and report on the incidents of noncompliance with regulations. For example, IBM reports on the assessment of product health and safety in concept development, R&D, product certification, production, marketing distribution, use, and disposal.[70] Firms also indicate the type of product labeling.

Product responsibility reporting also includes consideration of marketing communications and security of customer information. Companies must outline programs for adherence to standards and laws concerning advertising, promotion, sponsorship, and other marketing communiqués.[71] For example, the Ford 2008 sustainability report indicates the company's adherence to the Federal Trade Commission Act and its amendments.[72] Reporting firms must also reveal the number of incidents of noncompliance with regulations and report any fines incurred due to noncompliance. Customer privacy is also a concern addressed within product responsibility reporting. The organization indicates the number of substantiated complaints regarding breaches of privacy and losses of consumer data.

Society. Whereas human rights, labor, and product considerations focus on a specific stakeholder group, the society performance indicators reflect interaction with the community at large.[73] The firm provides an overview of its programs designed to manage and assess the influence of its operations on the community. For example, Shell Oil reports on its efforts to reduce the influence of operations on local communities. Shell partners with the Living Earth Foundation to promote dialogue between the firm and communities in Alaska concerned about oil and gas procurement, refinement, and distribution. The reporting company also provides a discussion of its participation in public policy development and lobbying and offers an account of its contributions to political parties, politicians, and related institutions in all the markets it serves.

The firm also reports on its compliance with laws and regulations and reports judgments associated with corruption or anticompetitive behavior. Shell, for instance, outlines a code of conduct that specifically outlines policies associated with bribery and corruption, conflicts of interest, gifts and hospitality, insider dealing, and political action.[74] The reporting firm also identifies the number of business units analyzed for risk of corruption, and it describes the extent to which employees have been trained in the firm's anticorruption practices.

Summary

A. Introduction

The goal of this chapter has been to outline the logic, merits, and processes associated with sustainability reporting. Firms that report on this activity are more likely to yield sustainable results relative to their competition. We examine the purposes and benefits of sustainability reporting, and we outline the components of sustainability reports. We also examine the reporting of financial, environmental, and social performance.

B. Purposes of Sustainability Reporting

Sustainability reporting serves three primary purposes for the firm. First, these reports enable firms to demonstrate their commitment to sustainability. Second, sustainability reporting enables companies to compare their performance to laws, codes, norms, and voluntary initiatives. Third, these reports enable companies to illustrate their longitudinal performance relative to the competition.

C. Benefits of Sustainability Reporting

Companies can realize multiple benefits from sustainability reporting. Firms can become more disciplined about environmental performance, and they can convey environmental messages to all stakeholders. They can also track progress relative to targets and reduce their overall risk due to sustainability reporting. Furthermore, this reporting enables companies to identify savings and efficiencies, and it enables them to identify new business opportunities.

D. Overview of Sustainability Reporting

Sustainability reports provide an overview of the firm's sustainability strategy by reviewing corporate strategy and governance and by profiling the organization's approach to the markets it pursues. The company also provides detailed reviews of its economic, environmental, and social performance. Third-party verification of these reports provides assurance of their level of quality.

E. Reporting Economic Value

Economic performance includes analyses of financial performance, market presence, and indirect market influences. Financial performance addresses the flow of capital between the firm and its stakeholders, and market presence concerns the local market performance of the firm relative to alternative employers. Indirect influences refer to contributions in the forms of services and infrastructure.

F. Reporting Environmental Value

Environmental performance concerns the extent to which the action of the firm is associated with material usage, energy, water, biodiversity, by-products and waste, products and services, and transportation. Material usage directly addresses the overall cost of operations, and the tracking of this factor enables the firm to monitor material efficiency and costs. The monitoring of energy usage addresses direct and indirect energy consumption. Firms also report on the amount of water withdrawn from multiple sources, and they identify water sources significantly influenced by water removal. Biodiversity reporting concerns the influence of the firm on flora and fauna, whereas by-product reporting outlines the firm's procedures for treating waste and other nonproduct outputs of production. Product reporting summarizes material, water, emissions, and other factors associated with products, and transportation reporting identifies strategies employed to control transportation-related costs.

G. Reporting Social Value

Reporting on social value includes discussions of human rights, labor practices, product responsibility, and society. The firm reports on its basic human rights policies, and it reports on the use of collective bargaining. Labor reporting discloses the scope and diversity of the workforce as well as the firm's occupational health and safety standards. Product responsibility reporting addresses the effects of products and services on customers, and societal reporting addresses the firm's interaction with the community at large.

Keywords

collective bargaining, 312
direct energy, 309
financial performance, 308
freedom of association, 312

greenhouse gas emissions, 310
health and safety standards, 312
indirect energy, 309
ozone-depleting substances, 310

transparency, 303
value added statement, 308

Questions

1. If sustainability reporting is not required by law, why do firms bother to develop these reports?
2. How is sustainability reporting related to triple bottom line performance?
3. How do firms illustrate transparency, and how does this effort help stakeholders?
4. What stakeholders are relevant to sustainability reporting? Why might the number of stakeholder groups vary for different types of organizations?
5. What is the role of stakeholders in developing sustainability reports?
6. Why is it essential for companies to describe their corporate strategy governance in sustainability reports?

7. How does third-party verification influence evaluations of sustainability reports by stakeholders?
8. To what extent is the economic part of the sustainability report redundant with the firm's annual report? Why do firms include indirect economic consequences in the economic section of sustainability reports?
9. What are the elements of the environmental section of the sustainability report? How does reporting of each facet of the environment contribute to ecological performance?
10. Who benefits from reporting on social performance, and how do they benefit from this practice?

Endnotes

[1] Greenpeace.org, "Guide to Greener Electronics," March 2009, http://www.greenpeace.org/raw/content/usa/press-center/reports4/guide-to-greener-electronics-11.pdf (accessed May 15, 2010).

[2] Arik Hesseldahl, "Apple is Greener than Greenpeace Says," *BusinessWeek Online*, December 12, 2008, 1.

[3] Greenpeace.org, "Toxic Tech: The Dangerous Chemicals in Electronic Products," http://www.greenpeace.org/international/

PageFiles/24478/toxic-tech-chemicals-in-elec.pdf (accessed May 15, 2010).

[4] Apple.com, "The Environment," http://www.apple.com/environment/ (accessed May 15, 2010).

[5] Peter Burrows and Arik Hesseldahl, "Finally, a Big Green Apple?" *BusinessWeek*, October 5, 2009, 68–69.

[6] Dan Moren, "Greenpeace Shows a Little Apple Love," *Macworld*, 26, 2009, 28.

[7] See Note 2 above.

[8] See Note 4 above.

[9] "Accountability, Completeness, Credibility and the Audit Expectations Cap," *Journal of Corporate Citizenship*, 14 (Summer, 2004): 97–115.

[10] Global Reporting Initiative, "Sustainability Report Guidelines," (Amsterdam, NL: Global Reporting Initiative, 2000–2006), 45, http://www.globalreporting.org/NR/rdonlyres/ED9E9B36-AB54-4DE1-BFF2-5F735235CA44/0/G3_Guidelines ENU.pdf (accessed May 15, 2010).

[11] See Note 10 above.

[12] Best Buy Co., Inc., "Corporate Responsibility 2009," 1–51, http://www.bby.com/cmn/files/BBY_CSR_2009.pdf (accessed May 15, 2010).

[13] Bayer.com, "Bayer Sustainable Development Report 2008," 1–120, http://www.sustainability2008.bayer.com/en/Sustainable-Development-Report-2008.pdfx (accessed May 15, 2010).

[14] Ford.com, "2008/9 Blueprint for Sustainability Our Future Works," 1–8, http://www.ford.com/doc/sr08-blueprint-summary.pdf (accessed May 15, 2010).

[15] See Note 5 above.

[16] See Note 10 above.

[17] David Hess, "The Three Pillars of Corporate Social Reporting as New Governance Regulation: Disclosure, Dialogue, and Development," *Business Ethics Quarterly* 18, no. 4 (2008): 447–482.

[18] Sun.com, "Sun's Corporate Social Responsibility Report," 1–103, http://www.sun.com/aboutsun/csr/report2008/sun_2008_csr_plain_text.pdf (accessed November 6, 2009).

[19] See Note 17 above.

[20] See Note 10 above.

[21] See Note 17 above.

[22] See Note 10 above.

[23] Ans Kolk, "A Decade of Sustainability Reporting: Developments and Significance," *International Journal of Environment and Sustainable Development* 3, no. 1 (2004): 51–64.

[24] See Note 23 above.

[25] Ans Kolk, "Trends in Sustainability Reporting by the Fortune Global 250," *Business Strategy and the Environment* 12, no. 5 (2003): 279–291.

[26] Ans Kolk, "Sustainability, Accountability and Corporate Governance: Exploring Multinationals' Reporting," *Business Strategy and the Environment* 17, no. 1 (2008): 1–15.

[27] Ans Kolk, "Green Reporting," *Harvard Business Review*, 78 no. 1 (2000): 15–16.

[28] Janek T. D. Ratnatunga and Kashi R. Balachandran, "Carbon Business Accounting: The Impact of Global Warming on the Cost and Management Accounting Profession," *Journal of Accounting, Auditing and Finance* 24, no. 2 (2009): 333–355.

[29] Joe Truini, "Jobs Finally Unveils 'Greening of Apple' Plan," *Waste News*, 13, 2007, 22.

[30] Martina K. Linnenluecke and Andrew Griffiths, "Corporate Sustainability and Organizational Culture," *Journal of World Business* (2009, in press).

[31] Electrolux.com, "GRI summary report 2008," 1–23, http://www.electrolux.com/Files/Sustainability/PDFs/2009_PDF/Elux_ENG_Sustainability08_20090810_Low.pdf (accessed May 15, 2010).

[32] Dan R. Anderson, "Sustainability Risk Management," *CPCU eJournal* (May, 2006): 1–17.

[33] IBM.com, "Section Three Environment: Minimizing IBM's Impact on the Planet," 1–18, http://www.ibm.com/ibm/responsibility/ibm_crr_downloads/pdf/section3_environment_ibm_crr.pdf (accessed May 15, 2010).

[34] H. Deliser, "Gas for the Greenhouse," *Nature* 442 (2006): 499.

[35] See Note 10 above.

[36] See Note 10 above.

[37] GE.com, "GE Citizenship: GRI," http://www.ge.com/citizenship/reporting/gri.jsp (accessed May 15, 2010).

[38] GE.com, "GE Citizenship," http://www.ge.com/citizenship/priorities_engagement/energy_and_climate_change.jsp (accessed May 15, 2010).

[39] See Note 10 above.

[40] See Note 26 above.

[41] See Note 10 above.

[42] See Note 10 above.

[43] Timberland, "Timberlands Climate Strategy 2009 Report," 1–23, http://www.earthkeeper.com/Resource_/PageResource/Timberlands-Climate-Strategy_2009-Report.pdf (accessed May 15, 2010).

[44] Fay Hansen, "A Home for HR Metrics," *Workforce Management*, 86, 2007, 10–11.

[45] See Note 10 above.

[46] See Note 44 above.

[47] Unilever.com, "Sustainability People and Partners," http://www.unilever.com/sustainability/people/ (accessed May 15, 2010).

[48] See Note 47 above.

[49] See Note 47 above.

[50] Global Reporting Initiative, "Environmental Performance Indicators," (Amsterdam, NL: Global Reporting Initiative, 2000–2006).

[51] See Note 14 above.

[52] Merck and Company Inc., "Advancing the Dialogue Toward a Healthier Future," 1–71, http://merck-ut.merck.com/corporate-responsibility/docs/cr2008.pdf (accessed May 15, 2010).

[53] See Note 14 above.

[54] See Note 50 above.

[55] Shell.com, "Working with biodiversity experts," http://www.shell.com/home/content/environment_society/environment/biodiversity/biodiversity_experts/ (accessed May 15, 2010).

[56] Vodafone.com, "Vodafone Group CR Report 2007/08: Index of conformance with the GRI G3 Guidelines," 1–19, http://www.vodafone.com/etc/medialib/attachments/cr_downloads.Par.49655.File.dat/Vodafone%202007-08%20CR%20Report%20GRI%20Index3.pdf (accessed November 11, 2009).

[57] Royal Dutch Shell PLC, "Responsible Energy: Sustainability Report," http://sustainabilityreport.shell.com/2008/servicepages/

downloads/files/entire_shell_ssr_08.pdf (accessed May 15, 2010).

[58] Abbott Laboratories, "Business & Citizenship," http://www .abbott.com/global/url/content/en_US/40.10:10/general_content/ General_Content_00036.htm (accessed May 15, 2010).

[59] See Note 4 above.

[60] Lexmark International, Inc., "Collection and Recycling Program," http://www1.lexmark.com/content/en_us/about_us/ collecting-recycling_program/collectingrecycling_program_ overview.shtml (accessed March 19, 2010).

[61] See Note 50 above.

[62] See Note 52 above.

[63] Global Reporting Initiative, "Human Rights Performance Indicators," (Amsterdam, NL: Global Reporting Initiative, 2000–2006).

[64] See Note 14 above.

[65] Starbucks.com, "Ethical Sourcing," http://www.starbucks. com/sharedplanet/ethicalSourcing.aspx (accessed May 15, 2010).

[66] Global Reporting Initiative, "Labor Practices and Decent Work Performance Indicators," (Amsterdam, NL: Global Reporting Initiative, 2000–2006).

[67] Shell.com, "Diversity and inclusion," http://www.shell.com/ home/content/responsible_energy/performance/social/kpi_ diversity_inclusion/ (accessed November 11, 2009).

[68] The Coca-Cola Company, "Sustainability: HIV/AIDS," http:// www.thecoca-colacompany.com/citizenship/hiv_aids.html (accessed May 15, 2010).

[69] IBM.com, "Global Reporting Initiative (GRI) report" http:// www.ibm.com/ibm/responsibility/gri.shtml (accessed May 15, 2010).

[70] See Note 67 above.

[71] Ford.com, "Sustainability Report 2008/9: Governance," http://www.ford.com/doc/sr08-section-governance.pdf (accessed May 15, 2010).

[72] Global Reporting Initiative, "Society Performance Indicators," (Amsterdam, NL: Global Reporting Initiative, 2000–2006).

[73] Royal Dutch Shell PLC, "Business integrity," http://www .shell.com/home/content/responsible_energy/society/using_ influence_responsibly/business_integrity/business_integrity.html (accessed May 15, 2010).

[74] See Note 73 above.

Glossary

A

acquisition costs   the energy expended to make the purchase as well as to the purchase price; include the time dedicated to learning about the salient criteria associated with a purchase as well as the time dedicated to evaluating alternatives

advertising   one-way impersonal mass communication about a product or organization that is paid for by a marketing organization

annual fuel utilization efficiency   a measurement of the energy efficiency of a furnace or boiler used by the U.S. Federal Trade Commission to determine the ratio of heat output compared to the total energy consumed

apathetics   a psychographic marketing segment made up of consumers who do not concern themselves with sustainability or green marketing practices

aromatics   intermediate products used in transforming raw materials (crude oil, natural gas, etc.) into consumer goods that include the chemicals benzene, toluene, and xylene; used to make things like footwear and car tires

asset considerations   conditions under which a firm invests in specific technologies that have limited use outside of their intended purpose

B

basic oxygen furnace   a furnace ordinarily used for high-tonnage production of carbon steels; accounts for 66% of steel production worldwide

benefit positioning   a strategy for market positioning that emphasizes a functional, emotional, or self-expressive return realized from product consumption

benefit segmentation   the delineation of marketing segments based on the benefits that buyers hope to derive from a purchase

biodegradable   refers to materials that will break down and return to nature within a reasonably short time after the usual disposal

biodiesel   a type of biofuel produced from oilseed crops, like soy, or from other vegetable sources, like waste cooking oil

biodynamics   a specific form of organic farming that augments organic processes with consideration of the time of year, location, soil type, existing flora and fauna, and other factors

biofuels   a family of fuel products that use at least some percentage of agricultural products, like corn or sugar cane

brand   a name, term, design, or symbol that identifies a seller's products and differentiates them from competitors' products

brand imagery   imagery that influences how consumers think about a brand rather than their objective assessment of product attributes

brand recall   the ability to retrieve the brand when given the product category, the needs fulfilled by the category, or some other type of clue

brand recognition   the consumers' ability to confirm exposure to the brand when given the brand as a cue

brand-specific need recognition   a method of stimulating need recognition in which organizations draw attention to a specific branded product (see *need recognition*)

break-even pricing   a pricing strategy in which the organization attempts to establish a price that covers all costs of operations

bundling the practice of offering two or more products or services for sale at one price

bus rapid transit (BRT) a rubber-tired rapid transit mode that combines stations, vehicles, services, running ways, and intelligent transportation system (ITS) elements into an integrated system

buygrid framework an organizational buying process based on the type of purchase and the stage of the buying process

C

carbon the most common element found on Earth, the primary building block of most fuel sources and common component of greenhouse gases

carbon black a form of carbon that is primarily used as reinforcement in vulcanized rubber products

carbon offset pricing situations under which the marketer of a product enables the purchaser to compensate for the greenhouse gas emissions associated with consumption; places the cost of sustainability directly in the hands of the consumer

carbon offsets part of the Kyoto Protocol's emissions trading program, by which companies that surpass their regulated emissions levels may invest in emission-reducing strategies in emerging markets to "offset" their own carbon output

cement a key ingredient in the manufacture of concrete

certified emission reduction (CER) part of the Kyoto Protocol's clean development mechanism, by which industrialized countries that finance investment projects for greenhouse gas emission abatements in developing countries generate credits used to meet their own commitments

channel a set of organizations involved in the process of making a product available for consumption

chlorine a disinfectant in the water purification process that in excess reacts naturally with organic matter to produce unwanted by-products like chloroform

climate change change in climate attributed directly or indirectly to human activity that alters the composition of the global atmosphere and that is in addition to natural climate variability over comparable periods of time

clinker the marble-like product of the second stage of concrete production, created when the raw materials for cement are heated in a large kiln

close-looped systems systems in which manufacturers work with downstream channel partners to ensure the reclamation of products (e.g., Ford Motor Company's partnering with Alcan to ensure recycling of auto aluminum)

coagulants substances like aluminum or iron salts used in the water purification process that act as important barriers to microbiological contaminants

collective bargaining negotiations between an employer and a group of employees in order to establish the conditions of employment, e.g., wages, hours, benefits, etc.

College Sustainability Report Card an assessment of sustainability that evaluates the policies and programs of 100 leading colleges and universities

competitive positioning a strategy for market positioning that uses a direct reference to the competition in order to illuminate the benefits of the firm's own brand

component restriction limits placed on the ingredients (e.g., asbestos) that can be incorporated into a product

compostable items refers to materials that break down organically into humus-like material and return nutrients to the earth

consumption the third stage of the consumer decision-making process that refers to the manner in which the product is used by the consumer

contradiction anything that limits the performance of a system relative to its goal

contradiction matrix a problem-solving tool in which a series of 39 factors represent the potentially favorable or harmful outcomes associated with a process

conventionals a marketing segment made up of consumers who are practical and enjoy seeing the results of their action and are therefore likely to recycle and conserve energy

conveyors the pipes and fittings used to transport water

corporate average fuel economy (CAFE) standards for rating the fuel efficiency of consumer vehicles

corporate credibility the degree to which consumers believe that a company is willing and able to provide products and services that satisfy the needs and wants of consumers

cost-based pricing a pricing strategy in which the organization establishes the price of a product by adding a markup to the cost of producing it

cradle-to-cradle a form of reclamation that emphasizes recovery, recycling, and reuse of products; as opposed to the cradle-to-grave approach that focuses more on disposal at products' end-of-life

criteria pollutants six pollutants regulators measure in order to establish air quality levels: sulfur dioxide, nitrogen dioxide, carbon monoxide, ozone oxygen, lead, and particulate matter (PM)

cultural services the factor of biodiversity pertaining to the spiritual, recreational, and aesthetic benefits of an ecosystem

D

defensive green a marketing situation in which the market for green products is large but the ability to differentiate based on the ecological merits of the product is low

demarketing action undertaken by marketers to discourage consumption

demographics segmentation a marketing segmentation strategy in which an organization separates and identifies consumers based on age, gender, income, or occupation

diesel engine an internal combustion engine in which the fuel is ignited by the high temperature created during compression; tends to be noisy and to produce soot

diffuse point sources water contaminant conditions under which there are many small point sources (see *point sources*)

direct energy consumption of energy without conversion; for example, a utility company that

burns coal to produce electricity uses *direct energy*; also includes the use of renewable resources (see *indirect energy*)

direct marketing direct efforts to target an audience via the Internet, direct mail, telemarketing, direct-action advertising, and catalog selling

divestment the disposal of products after they no longer offer utility to the customer

drifters a marketing segment made up of consumers who are not highly concerned about the environment and believe that environmental problems will eventually be resolved

dry quenching a process used in basic oxygen furnaces wherein the fuel, coke (derived from charcoal) is cooled by circulating it with an inert gas (usually nitrogen)

E

eco-labels labels that reflect adherence to some standard associated with food safety and environmental performance

efficient usage the extent to which organizations and individuals engage in efforts to reduce, reuse, or recycle resources (see *reduce*, *reuse*, and/or *recycle*)

electric arc furnace a furnace ordinarily used for low-tonnage specialty steels; accounts for 31% of steel production worldwide

emission reduction units (ERUs) part of the Kyoto Protocol's joint implementation program, by which industrialized countries can participate jointly in emissions abatement projects, thereby earning credits toward protocol targets

End-of-Life Directive a European Union (EU) directive that requires automotive manufacturers and component suppliers to reclaim auto products

Energy Star a label for consumer products indicating that the products possessing it are among the most energy efficient products in their class

enhanced greenhouse effect an increase in Earth's surface temperature brought about by an increase in the amount of greenhouse gases being emitted into the atmosphere.

enteric fermentation   intestinal processing of methane associated with the digestion process for cattle

environmental management systems (EMS)   a set of regulations established to achieve environmental goals

external search   a form of the search stage of the consumer decision-making process in which the consumer collects information from outside sources (see *search, internal search*)

extreme green   a very competitive marketing situation in which the demand for green products is large and the ability to differentiate based on product greenness is substantial

F

F gases   synthetic fluorinated gases resulting from industrial activity that have a direct influence on climate change; includes hydrofluorocarbons (HFCs), perfluorocarbons (PFCs), and sulfur hexafluoride (SF6)

feel good   one of the goals of promotion that instill brand preference in consumers

financial performance   the presentation of an organization's value in terms of accounting and financial standards

fixed costs   cost factors that do not change in the short run

food sales   buildings used to sell food at the retail or wholesale level and includes grocery stores, food markets, and convenience stores

food service   buildings used for preparation and sale of food and beverages

freedom of association   the freedom of individuals to associate as an end to itself or with a view to engaging constitutionally protected activities; in this context, to form trade unions or other para-business organizations

freight travel   the transportation of goods via truck, rail, ship, or airplane

G

gas engine   an internal combustion engine in which the engine intakes a mixture of gas and air, compresses it, and then ignites the mixture using a sparkplug

gates   the points in the development process at which the firm evaluates the potential for a product

general demarketing   a marketing situation in which companies try to shrink the level of total demand

generic need recognition strategy   a method of stimulating need recognition in which organizations draw attention to the entire product class (see *need recognition*)

geography segmentation   a market segmentation strategy in which an organization separates and identifies consumers based on where they live

global positioning systems   American radio-navigation systems that provide free positioning, navigation, and timing services on a continuous worldwide basis using satellite transmissions

green brand identity   a specific set of brand attributes and benefits associated with reduced environmental influence of a brand and the perception of being environmentally sound

green design   the development and maintenance of buildings that are sensitive to the environment, resource and energy consumption, the quality of the work setting, cost effectiveness, and the world at large

Green Guide for Health Care   a registration and certification program that is intended to serve as a reference for best practices in the healthcare construction industry

green marketing   the study of all efforts to consume, produce, distribute, promote, package, and reclaim products in a manner that is sensitive or responsive to ecological concerns

green marketing management   the process of planning and executing the marketing mix to facilitate consumption, production, distribution, promotion, packaging, and product reclamation in a manner that is sensitive or responsive to ecological concerns

green marketing planning   the process of creating and maintaining a fit between the environment and objectives and resources of the firm

green premium the additional expenditures associated with green design (see *green design*)

greenback greens a psychographic marketing segment made up of consumers who are interested in environmental sustainability but not inclined to be politically active

greenfield development construction on previously unused property; a type of development associated with increases in air pollution, energy use, greenhouse gas production, and traffic congestion

greenhouse gas emissions gaseous byproducts of the supply-chain process that enter the atmosphere and contribute to the *enhanced greenhouse effect*

greenwashing a term describing situations in which there is a significant disparity between an organizations expressed intentions and its genuine commitments to sustainability

grid-connected photovoltaic (PV) cells a form of solar power in which photovoltaic solar cells are connected to an area's electrical grid and can sell unused energy back into the system

grousers a psychographic marketing segment made up of consumers who tend to be cynical about their ability to bring about change and who are relatively uneducated about ecological concerns

H

health and safety standards standards employed by organizations to ensure that the working environment is healthy and safe for its employees; includes everything from safe food handling to the promotion of ergonomically designed cubicle workstations

high-occupancy vehicle (HOV) a consumer vehicle transporting three or more persons; many states have HOV lanes meant to reward carpoolers by being less crowded

high-speed trains (HST) a family of technologies that provide high-capacity, frequent railway services achieving an average speed of more than 200 kilometers per hour (124 miles per hour)

hybrid electric vehicle (HEV) vehicles in which two power sources, an electric motor drive and an internal combustion engine, are combined to obtain the required power to propel the vehicle

hybrid engine an engine which uses an internal combustion engine combined with electric fuel cells

I

indirect energy consumption of energy that has been created or transformed by some process; for example, an automaker that buys electricity from a utility company uses *indirect energy*, because the electricity they use has been created elsewhere

innovation the effort to create purposeful, focused change in an enterprise's economic, social, and ecological potential.

inputs resources that an organization puts into their processes for manufacturing or retailing their product or service (e.g., packaging or energy sources)

integrated brand promotion the use of the promotional mix to build brand awareness, identity, and preference

integrated marketing communication coordination among the elements of the promotional mix to ensure the consistency of the message delivered at every contact point between the consumer and the company

internal search a form of the search stage of the consumer decision-making process in which the consumer retrieves knowledge from memory (see *search, external search*)

International Organization for Standardization (ISO) a Geneva, Switzerland-based network of the national standards institutes of 157 countries; has established standards focused on a broad range of industries that include agriculture, construction, mechanical engineering, manufacturing, distribution, transportation, medical devices, information and communication technologies

inventory management software technology that incorporates mathematical models that enable managers to plan product manufacture and distribution around complex market scenarios, thereby optimizing inventory throughout the supply chain

ISO 14000 a generic managerial system that supports organizational action designed to minimize harmful effects on the environment and achieve continual improvement of environmental performance

K

Kyoto Protocol international agreement adopted in 1997 designed to limit emissions of greenhouse gases by industrialized nations

L

lead users consumers that expect attractive innovation-related benefits from a solution and experience needs for an innovation earlier than most participants in a target market

Leadership in Energy and Environmental Design (LEED) a rating system for the construction industry that includes 34 criteria associated with sustainable sites, water efficiency, energy and atmosphere, materials and resources, indoor environmental quality, and innovation and design processes

lean green a marketing situation in which the size of the green market is modest and the firm has limited ability to differentiate itself based on the greenness of its products

life cycle assessment accounting for production and processing as well as resource energy usage, emissions, and waste

life cycle inventory assessment an assessment that identifies the sum amount of resources and emissions associated with a product or service over its life

lignin the naturally occurring substance in wood that binds the wood fibers into a solid; removed during the pulping process

logistics the process of planning, allocating, and controlling human and financial resources dedicated to physical distribution, manufacturing support, and purchasing operations

LOHAS (Lifestyles Of Health And Sustainability) refers to a marketing segment made up of consumers who are focused on health, the environment, social justice, personal development, sustainable living, and the future of society

M

macroenvironmental issues the overall level of risk encountered in the social, economic, and natural environments

market all organizations or people with a need or want and the ability and willingness to make purchases to address those needs and wants

market segmentation the process of dividing a market into distinct subsets of customers that have similar needs, similar resources, and/or similar behaviors

marketing the activity, set of institutions, and processes for creating, communicating, delivery, and exchanging offerings that have value for customers, clients, partners, and society at large

marketing action any exchange between two or more parties that is associated with the procurement, purchasing, sales, consumption, and post-consumption of product offerings

marketing plan a blueprint that outlines how the organization will achieve its objectives by providing an analysis of the current marketing situation, opportunities and threats analysis, marketing objectives, marketing strategy, action programs, and projected income statements

message strategy the objectives established by the promotional manager and the methods employed to achieve these objectives

metallurgy a series of processes used to refine and strengthen steel by removing oxygen, hydrogen, sulfur, and other impurities

methanol a chemical that occurs as a result of biological processes conducted by vegetation, microorganisms, and other living species; also manufactured synthetically through a catalytic steam process from natural gas

mission statement a statement that describes an organization's fundamental, unique purpose, indicating what the firm intends to accomplish, the markets in which it operates, and the philosophical premises that guides its action

Montreal Protocol   an international agreement originally signed in 1987 that stipulated that all ozone-depleting substances (ODS) be phased out of production by 2000

N

natural   a problematic label often given to products to make them seem environmentally sound

natural greenhouse effect   a natural process through which greenhouse gases trap thermal radiation released by Earth and prevent it from leaving the atmosphere, thereby keeping the planet warm enough to sustain life

naturalites   a marketing segment made up of consumers who are primarily concerned about personal health and wellness

need recognition   a phase of the prepurchase stage of the consumer decision-making process in which a consumer senses a difference between an ideal state of affairs and the current state

new construction   in an environmental context, represents an opportunity to use technology to develop, install, and maintain component parts that conserve energy and use renewable energy resources

niche marketing strategies   marketing strategies often employed by small businesses, in which they serve a selected market better than their competition

nonpoint sources   widely spread water contaminant sources that may be difficult to identify as origins of pollutants; may include fuel storage locations, chlorinated solvents, and pesticides

North American Industry Classification System (NAICS)   the standard used by federal statistical agencies to classify business establishments for the purpose of collecting, analyzing, and publishing statistical data related to the American business economy

O

off-grid solar systems   a form of solar power in which solar cells are employed outside of regional or national electricity grids, including "minigrids" designed for rural or island areas

old construction   in an environmental context, represents an opportunity to use technology to make old buildings more energy efficient and sustainable

olefins   intermediate products used in transforming raw materials (crude oil, natural gas, etc.) into consumer goods that include the chemicals ethylene, propylene, and xylene; used to make things like bottles and trash bags

operational activities   (of aircraft) a means of evaluating and improving the climate effects of aircraft by analyzing cost and pricing structures and working with technology to create solutions (see *technological performance*)

opportunity cost   cost factors forfeited by the consumer when incurring a cost (e.g., the consumer who purchases an oil-burning water heater forfeits the chance to invest in solar water heaters)

ostensible demarketing   a marketing situation that involves limiting consumption for the purpose of increasing demand for a product, thereby increasing sales

other intermediates   intermediate products used in transforming raw materials (crude oil, natural gas, etc.) into consumer goods that include gases used in ammonia and methanol

outputs   the waste products generated by the production and distribution of an organization's product or service

ozone-depleting substances   gaseous byproducts of the supply-chain process that enter the atmosphere and contribute to the depletion of the *ozone layer*

ozone layer   a large amount of ozone found in the layer of Earth's atmosphere known as the stratosphere; it absorbs some of the sun's biologically harmful ultraviolet radiation

P

parasitic energy losses   energy losses incurred due to a number of factors that include aerodynamics, auxiliary operations, and other operations

particulate matter   material made up of carbon particles, hydrocarbons, and inorganic material; a component of both soot and smog

passenger travel   the transportation of people via privately-owned vehicles or public or semi-public means including buses, trains, ships, and airplanes

penetration pricing   a pricing policy in which organizations set a low initial price in an attempt to increase market share rapidly

personal selling   personal, face-to-face interaction with a potential consumer

point sources   water contaminant sources in which pollution is discharged from a specific location; includes on-site sanitation waste disposal locations

Portland cement   the product of the fourth stage of concrete production, in which the clinker is mixed with gypsum and ground to a fine powder

positioning   the development of the marketing mix to yield a distinctive appeal to the target segment; should reflect the values sought by consumers in the target market

possession costs   all expenditures associated with gaining possession of the product after the purchase decision has been made; include taxes, insurance, and transportation

postconsumption evaluation   a phase of the postconsumption stage of the consumer decision-making process during which the consumer evaluates the product after consumption has occurred

postconsumption stage   the fourth and final stage of the consumer decision-making process, during which the consumer makes periodic evaluations of the product or service in light of expectations prior to purchase (see *postconsumption evaluation*)

postretail packaging   the form of packaging used by the consumer to transport product away from a retail establishment

power   a source or means of supplying energy

prepurchase evaluation   a phase of the prepurchase stage of the consumer decision-making process in which consumers evaluate options identified during the search phase

prepurchase stage   the first stage of the consumer decision-making process, during which the consumer identifies a need, searches for products or services that will meet that need, and evaluates those products or services prior to purchase

price lining   a pricing strategy in which merchandise is offered at a number of specific predetermined prices

private label   a product in which the brand is owned by the retailer or wholesaler rather than by the producer

process innovation   novel techniques for producing goods and services

process management standards   standards that provide the opportunity to assess how well processes are managed

process performance evaluation   an evaluation based on a comparison to set of standards, which are usually reached by industry consensus and codified by the industry's trade organization

processes   the methods by which an organization manufactures, distributes, or provides their product or service

product innovation   new goods and services that offer improvements in technical abilities, functional characteristics, ease of use, and other dimensions

product placement   efforts on the part of brand owners to feature their products in films, movies, plays, or other performances

Product Stewardship Institute (PSI)   a United States-based NGO that seeks to reduce the health and environmental impacts of consumer products by focusing on waste management and reclamation

production blocking   a possible part of the group idea generation process characterized by group members' inability to offer opinions simultaneously

promotion   all communication from the marketer designed to persuade, inform, or remind potential buyers of a product in order to elicit a response or influence an opinion

promotional mix   the tools used in promotion, which include advertising, personal selling, public relations, sales promotion, and direct marketing

promotional strategy   a plan for the optimal use of advertising, sales promotion, public relations, direct marketing, and personal selling

provisional services   the factors of biodiversity pertaining to the supply of food, fuel, or fiber made available for consumption in an ecosystem

psychographic segmentation a market segmentation strategy in which an organization separates and identifies consumers based on their apparent attitudes, opinions, motives, values, lifestyles, interests, or personality

public relations the use of publicity and other nonpaid forms of promotion and information to influence attitudes about a company, its products, or the values of its organization

purchase stage the second stage of the consumer decision-making process, in which the decides whether, and the conditions under which, to buy the product

R

radio frequency identification (RFID) a technology consisting of a radio frequency tag with a printed antenna and a radio frequency emitter/reader, which can be read to ensure that all items associated with an assembly are present, confirm accurate plant deliveries, and enable management to determine the appropriate placement of products in storage, among other uses

reclamation the responsible collection of products once they no longer offer value to consumers

recycle part of the effort to use energy more efficiently; involves converting waste products into new materials

reduce part of the effort to use energy more efficiently; involves strategies for lowering the amounts of energy consumed

Registration, Evaluation, Authorization and Restriction of Chemical Substances (REACH) a European Union (EU) regulation requiring businesses to register the substances in their products and make public any potential risks from the use of these chemicals

regulatory services the factors of biodiversity that control interaction between the various participants in an ecosystem

Restriction of Hazardous Substances (RoHS) a European Union (EU) directive that severely restricts the use of lead, hexavalent chromium, mercury, cadmium, and some flame retardants

reuse part of the effort to use energy more efficiently; involves reusing materials in order to avoid costs associated with producing new ones

reverse logistics the process of planning, allocating, and controlling human and financial resources dedicated to tracing products back from the point of consumption through returned goods, disposal of products at end-of-life, production planning and inventory management, and supply chain management

reverse marketing the proactive efforts within a firm or organization to identify potential product providers or vendors

routing and tracking computer system a method of electronic information management that can improve a company's efficiency and price competitiveness while simultaneously offering improved information handling and customer service

S

sales promotion all marketing communication action other than advertising, personal selling, public relations, and direct marketing designed to influence consumer purchases and relationships with intermediaries in distribution channels

search a phase of the prepurchase stage of the consumer decision-making process in which the consumer searches for alternatives to the current state by acquiring information and solutions that satisfy unmet needs (see *internal search*, *external search*)

selective demarketing a marketing situation in which an organization discourages demand from certain classes of consumers

shaded green a marketing situation in which the demand for ecologically sensitive products is low, but there is substantial opportunity to differentiate based on ecological viability of the product

skimming pricing setting a price to reach consumers willing to pay a higher price for a product prior to marketing the product to more price-sensitive consumers

slice of life a way of situating a brand so that it appears in an ideal "real-life" usage setting

Smart Growth Network an organization funded by the U.S. EPA that is focused on enhancing the quality of living conditions in cities

social labels labels that reflect adherence to some standard associated with human rights and labor standards

soda ash a compound used in the manufacture of glass, water softeners, detergents, bricks, and in photographic processes; in the U.S., it is drawn from natural deposits and in soda recovery from lakes, while in the rest of the world it is primarily created from synthetic processes

solar water heaters heaters that use solar energy to heat water; active heaters use pumps and controls to heat water and passive heaters do not use any other mechanism than solar power

sprouts a psychographic marketing segment made up of consumers who appreciate the merits of environmental causes but do not take that appreciation with them into the marketplace

stakeholders the individuals, organizations, and groups that have an interest in the action of an organization and the ability to influence it

status quo price a price that is consistent with the competition

STP marketing a form of marketing characterized by efforts to segment, target, and position (see *market segmentation*, *target marketing*, and *positioning*)

supply cycles the set of entities associated with yielding environmental, social, and economic value from resource procurement through resource processing, consumption, and postconsumption

supporting services the factors of biodiversity that maintain the conditions for life on Earth, including soil formation and protection, and nutrient and water cycling

sustainability development that meets the needs of the present without compromising the ability of future generations to meet their own needs

sustainability scorecard a document developed by Wal-Mart that identifies 14 categories of products or processes with the greatest environmental impact

Sustainable Endowments Institute (SEI) a non-profit organization engaged in research and education to advance sustainability in campus operations and endowment practices, which publishes the College Sustainability Report Card (see *College Sustainability Report Card*)

T

target market a subgroup of the total market selected as the focal point for the marketing mix

target marketing an organization's efforts to serve a selected subset or segment of the market

technological performance (of aircraft) a means of evaluating and improving the climate effects of aircraft by analyzing data and creating innovative solutions to problems (see *operational activities*)

transparency the degree to which an entity provides complete disclosure of all activity related to economic, environmental, and relational performance

triple bottom line the focus of companies pursuing sustainable development, compromised of balanced performance in three areas: economic growth; social interaction with customers, suppliers, consumers, and other interest groups; and environmentally aware production and marketing processes

true blues a psychographic marketing segment made up of consumers with strong environmental values who seek to bring about positive change, often through political activism

U

unconcerned a marketing segment made up of consumers whose priorities are focused on things other than the environment and society, and who buy based on convenience, price, quality, and value with little regard for the actions of companies marketing the products

universal product code (UPC) a code placed on retail items (informally known as a bar code) that provides retailers with access to market information on product movement, consumer purchasing behavior, and the use of marketing mix variables by manufacturers and retailers

urban sprawl the widespread movement of households and private firms from city centers and inner suburbs to very low-density suburbs

usage cost the cost of operations as well as the disposal cost

user positioning a strategy for market positioning in which the marketer develops a profile of a specific target user

V

value the central factor in the pursuit of sustainability; can be expressed in terms of economic, social, and environmental outcomes. It may also be expressed by the equation
Value = Desired benefits/relative costs

value-added statement a statement identifying the direct economic value generated and distributed to capital providers and government

value-based pricing a pricing strategy that uses the consumers' perceived value of a good to establish price

value proposition a statement of the emotional, functional, and self-expressive benefits delivered by a brand that provide value to consumers in a target market

variable costs costs that fluctuate with the amount of product sold

W

Waste Electrical and Electronic Equipment Directive (WEEE) a European Union (EU) directive designed to reduce the amount of electronic waste in landfills

whole-building concept a concept of space heating that encompasses consideration of the location, infrastructure, utilities, and ancillary devices within the home

World Health Organization (WHO) the directing and coordinating authority for health within the United Nations system; responsibilities include leadership on global health matters, shaping the health research agenda, setting norms and standards, etc.

Index